My Life In the Old Army

The Reminiscences of Abner Doubleday

Abner Doubleday

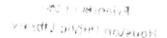

My Life in the Old Army

The Reminiscences of Abner Doubleday
from the Collections of the New-York
Historical Society

Edited and Annotated by Joseph E. Chance

Illustrations by Wil Martin

Texas Christian University Press
Fort Worth

The Abner Doubleday Papers from which these pages were transcribed are the property of the New-York Historical Society (New York, New York). Rights for publication in this edition have been arranged between the New-York Historical Society and Texas Christian University Press.

Introduction, Endnotes, Bibliography copyright © 1998, Joseph E. Chance

Illustrations copyright © 1998, Wil Martin

Library of Congress Cataloging-in-Publication Data

Doubleday, Abner, 1819-1893.
    My life in the old Army: the reminiscences of Abner Doubleday from the collections of the New-York Historical Society / edited by Joseph E. Chance; with illustrations by Wil Martin.
       p cm.
    Includes bibliographical references and index.
    ISBN 0-87565-185-2 (alk. paper)
    1. Doubleday, Abner, 1819-1893. 2. United States, Army—Officers—Biography. 3. Mexican War, 1846-1848—Personal narratives. 4. Indians of North America—Wars—Texas. 5. Seminole Indians—Wars—Florida. 6. United States. Army—Military life History 19th century. I. Chance, Joseph E., 1940-
II. Title.
E411.D75A3 1998
972'.05—dc21
                                                             97-34316
                                                               CIP

Design by Shadetree Studio

*Dedicated to my wife Carolyn
whose patience with me during my
labors on this volume made this
work possible, and to my friend
Bruce Aiken.*

CONTENTS

ACKNOWLEDGMENTS

I am indebted to many persons and organizations for the completion of this book. First and foremost, I wish to express my gratitude to the New-York Historical Society for allowing me to reproduce the memoirs of Abner Doubleday and to perform the necessary editing to put this manuscript in shape for publication.

A manuscript of this scope which covers a span of almost forty years in the life of Abner Doubleday necessarily required the use of many rare sources and volumes not owned by the library of my university. The Inter-Library Loan Department of the University of Texas—Pan American were most helpful in finding materials that I needed in a prompt and courteous manner. Thanks are offered to Virgie Waller, Alice Patino, and Ruben Coronado.

Anyone who does serious research knows how difficult it is to keep library due dates and other library administrative dictates in good order. My special thanks are extended to Edna Luna of the Pan Am library who helped me on many occasions to cut red tape and to retain a great many books often for a great length of time. She is a rare and radiant treasure.

For matters and materials pertaining to the Rio Grande border between south Texas and northern Mexico at the time of mid-nineteenth century, I am appreciative to the following: George Gause, curator of the Rio Grande Historical Collection housed at University of Texas—Pan American; Tom Fort, assistant director of the Hidalgo County Historical Museum; Laurier McDonald of Edinburg, Texas; Bruce Aiken, director of the Historical Brownsville Museum; Don Clifford, curator of the Charles Stillman House in Brownsville, Texas; Dr. Anthony Knopp, department of history, University of Texas at Brownsville; Bill Young of Brownsville, Texas; and Dr. Linda Vance of Austin, Texas.

For the able assistance of my daughter, Rachel Chance, who would often take her lunch hour to find materials for me at the Center for American History at the University of Texas in Austin, I am yet indebted. She became so enthusiastic about this project that she would label return addresses on correspondence to me with the name, "Zenas Bliss."

Abner Doubleday spoke and wrote the Spanish language and several of his comments required the use of a person fluent in that language. Mr. Al Ramirez of Edinburg, Texas, and Dr. Jose Castrillon of University of Texas—Pan American were kind enough to come to the aid of the editor and unsnarl his twisted syntax.

Questions on Corpus Christi, Texas, at the time of Zachary Taylor's encampment there in 1845 and 1846 were very ably answered by Margaret Rose of the Corpus Christi Library. My thanks to her and her staff.

Unpublished letters from William W. and Helen Chapman that shed light on Abner Doubleday's disastrous tour of duty at Fort Brown under the command of the tyrannical Thomas West "Battery" Sherman in 1848 were generously provided by the Chapmans' descendent, Mr. Caleb Coker, of Jacksonville, Florida.

Useful comments on the voluminous thousand-page reminiscences of Zenas Bliss were supplied by Dr. Richard Sommers of the

United States Army Military History Institute at Carlisle Barracks, Pennsylvania. Permission to reproduce portions of the Bliss manuscript was graciously granted by Mr. Ben Pingenot of Brackettville, Texas.

Biographies on the lives of the famous North Carolinians, Duncan McRae and Hamilton Jones, were furnished by Mr. Tom Belton, of the North Carolina State Museum of History, and excerpts from the journal of Henry Edwards were supplied by Paul Brockman of the Indiana Historical Society.

The Naval Historical Center of Washington, D.C., furnished the Confederate service record for Captain William Hunter, who accompanied Abner Doubleday to Mexico to investigate the Gardiner Mine Claim.

Mr. Wil Martin, associate professor of art at University of Texas—Pan American, supplied the excellent illustrations that appear between these covers. The models that posed for Mr. Martin's illustrations were neither the most handsome nor talented that he could find, but were simply the most readily available. My thanks to these hardy individuals, whose visages have now achieved immortality on the printed page.

Finally, a debt is owed the Texas Christian University Press for publishing this manuscript and my special thanks to Tracy Row for his outstanding skills in putting together this book which I venture to say would have made Abner Doubleday proud to claim authorship.

INTRODUCTION

A bner Doubleday was born on June 26, 1819, in Ballston Spa, New York, the son of a newspaper editor and grandson of a Revolutionary War veteran.[1] Doubleday's father was editor of the *Cayuga Patriot* from 1819 until 1828, then co-editor of *The Gospel Advocate* for the next three years, and finally editor of *The Primitive Christian*. As these last two titles suggest, the Doubleday family was serious about its religion, and a reader of Doubleday's reminiscences will no doubt be impressed by the solid moral values that were inculcated into the writer by his mother and father. Even in his later years, Doubleday never abandoned the virtues of modesty, self control, and abstinence. His staff officers remembered General Doubleday as a man who neither used a profane word nor partook of liquor or tobacco.

Young Abner showed an early interest in Spanish and French literature, art, history, mathematics, and military history while attending the Auburn Academy near his home in Cooperstown, New York. His special interest, however, was browsing through his father's newspaper library and reading the exchange copies from other newspapers. He later confessed that, "he was brought up at his father's Auburn newspaper."[2] Abner delighted in hearing the stories retold of his grandfather's experiences in the American Revolutionary War serving under "Mad" Anthony Wayne, and expressed such an interest in military matters that his father enrolled him, upon graduation from Auburn Academy, in the Military Academy at Cooperstown, New York. Abner Doubleday was admitted to the United States Military Academy and became a cadet there on September 1, 1838. The records at West Point indicate that

> Abner Doubleday was correct in his deportment, social and communicative, with his companions, unobtrusive in conversation, yet freely taking part therein, and quite entertaining. He enjoyed a good anecdote and had some of his own to tell. He was rather averse to outdoor sports and retiring in his manner. He was a diligent and thoughtful student, something of a critic, and fond of questions in moral philosophy. He was free from the use of tobacco, from profane words, or any vicious habits.[3]

On July 1, 1842, he graduated from the Point, twenty-fourth in a class of fifty-six cadets. Included in this class were such notables as William S. Rosecrans, John Pope, Daniel Harvey Hill, Lafayette McLaws, Earl Van Dorn, and James Longstreet.

Thus commences the first chapter of this book: Doubleday's reminiscences of his graduation and first assignment as a brevet second lieutenant in the 3rd Regiment of Artillery, stationed in garrison duty at Fort Johnson, North Carolina. Doubleday titled this portion of his reminiscences "Chapter Two," suggesting that another chapter recounting his childhood must have been originally included. This chapter cannot now be located, but surely might have been useful in shedding some light on the origins of the game of baseball.

He remained at Fort Johnson until 1844, when he was sent to Fort McHenry, Maryland, then to Fort Moultrie, South Carolina, ending up in early 1845 assigned to the garrison of Fort Preble, Maine.

His first opportunity for battlefield action came in 1845, when he was sent to Corpus Christi, Texas, as a part of General Zachary Taylor's Army of Occupation. After facing the cold blue south Texas northers that blew in across Nueces Bay in the winter of 1845-1846, he advanced with Taylor's Army to the Rio Grande. Doubleday was stationed at Point Isabel to man the earthen walls of Fort Polk on May

8, 1846, and from there could hear the boom of Major Ringgold's field batteries at Palo Alto. The opening guns of the Mexican War were being fired, but even during the peril of that time, Doubleday paused to record an amusing anecdote. He remembered with glee the chaos that resulted when the officers of the United States Navy attempted to drill their salt water tars in the unfamiliar field maneuvers of infantry troops. The Home Fleet, anchored offshore, had sent their marines and most of their sailors to reinforce the garrison at Point Isabel against a possible Mexican attack that never materialized.

Doubleday quickly developed the nickname "Forty-Eight Hours" from his fellow officers for his methodical and deliberate way of doing things; they also noted, however, that he was quiet and cool in times of danger and could not be rattled. This latter assessment of the man was clearly evident in his narration of the attack and capture of Monterrey, Mexico, from September 21 to 25, 1846. As part of General William J. Worth's forces, he participated in the daring attack on the western side of the city. Doubleday's reminiscences of his own participation in these actions is the veritable model of modesty and understatement.

Doubleday's narration of the campaign in northern Mexico could be dramatic, however; his account of the fear and tension in Monterrey just prior to the battle of Buena Vista, when word was received in that city of a large Mexican Army bearing down on Taylor's forces in Saltillo, is gripping.

Doubleday, escorting Taylor's heavy artillery from Monterrey, was ordered to remain at Rinconada Pass and hold that narrow stricture in the mountains as a possible avenue of retreat for the American Army. Thus, Doubleday missed the battle, but was ordered up to the field the next day, just in time to see the retreat of the Mexican forces.

During the remainder of the war with Mexico, Doubleday was stationed at Saltillo, Mexico, and favors the reader with his accounts of the misdeeds of a mid-nineteenth century Mexican city under the pressing yoke of an American military government. His account documents the unrest among American occupation forces along the northern line. Taylor's forces were anxious to regain the offensive, and this anxiety coupled with a less-than-strict enforcement of military discipline resulted in a mutiny among volunteer forces and several lethal duels among the men of the officer corps. Alas, the glory for the conquest of Mexico had shifted from northern to central Mexico and General Winfield Scott was placed in command.

For those interested in Mexico, Doubleday offers an account of Mexican life and society in northern Mexico during these turbulent times. The great fear among all classes of Mexicans was not the American occupation, but rather the extensive raids by warring bands of Indians from across the Rio Grande. They were disgusted with the lack of protection from these raids by their government far away in Mexico City.

The end of the war found Doubleday briefly stationed at Fort Brown, Texas, acting as quartermaster in charge of the mountains of surplus army supplies and equipment that were flowing out of Mexico with the returning troops. Under the command of the eccentric Thomas West Sherman, Fort Brown became a veritable prison for the officers and enlisted men of the garrison. A word of disfavor from the commanding officer became grounds for numerous charges to be lodged against the officers and men of the post. For refusing to obey an order to arrest civilians loitering in the vicinity of the post, Doubleday was arrested by Sherman for "the first and only time in my career." Doubleday had, on the face of the matter, violated the 9th Article of War, and might have had to face serious consequences: "Any officer or soldier who . . . shall disobey lawful command of his superior officer, shall suffer death. . . ."[4] However, an order to arrest a civilian by the military was clearly an illegal order, not a "lawful command." Doubleday most likely could have established his innocence in a court martial, and Sherman probably recognized that fact. Within a month, Doubleday was ordered to report to Fort Columbus, New York, and Sherman ordered to Fort Preble, Maine. Sherman evidently acknowledged the weakness of his case by dropping the charges against Doubleday.

While at Fort Columbus, located on an island in New York harbor, Doubleday met the soon-to-be-famous Thomas Jonathan "Stonewall"

Jackson, and documented several accounts of the eccentric nature of this health-conscious officer. It was during this time that Doubleday became involved in an incident during the funeral ceremonies in New York City of General William J. Worth: the anecdote of the little Jewish tailor from the Bowery, a story that is sure to bring a smile to the reader.

But Doubleday, a speaker of Spanish and by now an experienced traveler in Mexico, was soon sent on a return mission to that country. In the Treaty of Guadalupe Hidalgo, which ended open hostilities between the United States and Mexico, each country agreed to indemnify its own citizens for damages resulting from the war. A fraudulent claim for damages supposedly done to a silver mine in Mexico by the troops of Santa Anna had been levied upon the United States by a certain George Gardiner under the provisions of this treaty. Doubleday was appointed by the United States Senate as a commissioner to investigate the so-called Gardiner Mine Claim and sent as a member of a commission to investigate the mine site near the city of San Luis Potosi. His lively narration of this trip into a country still seething with hate for Americans after the late war and the unrest in the state of San Luis Potosi in the midst of revolution makes for exciting reading. A member of the commission, Joseph Davis Howell, brother-in-law of the famous Mississippian Jefferson Davis, created an incident in Mexico City during this trip that resulted in riot. But the commission was able to complete its mission and returned to the United States in time to testify in the criminal proceedings against Gardiner.

After this mission to Mexico, Doubleday was again sent to active duty against the hostile Plains Indians of Texas in 1854. He was ordered to Fort Duncan at Eagle Pass, Texas, on the Rio Grande. As a signatory of the Treaty of Guadalupe Hidalgo, the United States had promised to keep Indian war parties from crossing from the United States to violate the territorial integrity of Mexico. For this purpose, a chain of forts had been built across Texas from north to south to protect the settled portions of Texas and block Indian ingress and egress to Mexico. Military planners had envisioned that such a static line of forts, manned with infantry and artillery, would be sufficient to intercept Indian raiding parties. But such a plan did not take into account the nature of the Indian warrior on horseback, whose raiding parties formed perhaps the finest light cavalry in the world. An infantry soldier on foot was simply no match for an Indian on horseback on the plains of Texas. Raiding parties bypassed the forts on their way to and from Mexico and into West Texas. Doubleday saw no fighting at this site, but his account of a soldier's life on the Texas border is a valuable reminiscence. The inadequate protection of the Texas border against Indian raids by the United States government was a constant source of complaint by Texans to Washington. These complaints seemed to fall mostly on deaf ears, as little was done to guard effectively the frontier against incessant Indian depredations. This lack of protection was the first reason cited in the Ordinance of Secession, passed on March 5, 1861, by the Texas Legislature, removing Texas from the Union: "... Whereas, the Federal government has failed to accomplish the purposes of the compact of union between these States, in giving protection either to the persons of our people upon an exposed frontier or to the property of our citizens...."[5]

The last active phase of the Seminole War flared up again in 1856, and Doubleday was sent with the army to Florida on a mission to capture the few remaining Seminoles there and remove them from the state. Another fruitless and frustrating campaign began as heavily burdened United States infantry soldiers attempted to pursue the fleet-footed Seminoles through the heavily wooded tropical forests, savannahs, and swamps of their ancestral homeland. Doubleday's sympathy for the plight of the Florida Indian is evident in his anecdote on the surrender of a Seminole family and their exile to Arkansas.

Doubleday, who had himself been exiled from his country by tours of duty in Texas and Florida, rejoiced to receive an assignment that would place him in gentler society—as second in command of Fort Sumter, South Carolina, in 1860. But he had been sent into harm's way, as the fort was destined to become a focus of world attention in the upcoming War for Southern Independence. The first shots of the war were fired there on April 12, 1861, with Doubleday's aiming the first Union gun of the war. The shot was on the mark, but "bounded off from the sloping roof of the battery opposite without producing any apparent effect."[6]

So the Doubleday narrative which constitutes this book comes to an end. Doubleday wrote a book about his experiences in the siege of Fort Sumter, *Reminiscences of Forts Sumter and Moultrie in 1860-1861*, which was published in 1876.

Doubleday went on to achieve fame in this internecine struggle. He commanded a division at the battle of South Mountain, replacing his superior, General John Porter Hatch, who was severely wounded while leading a charge. Doubleday continued to command a division at the battle of Sharpsburg and for his bravery was promoted to the rank of major general of volunteers. Doubleday led his division at the ill-fated battle of Fredericksburg, and a corps at the battle of Chancellorsville. General Doubleday fought his most desperate, and as he remembered later, most bitter struggle at Gettysburg. With the death of General John Reynolds on July 1, 1863, General Doubleday led the First Corps in a sanguinary and desperate struggle against the Confederate forces of Generals A. P. Hill and Richard Ewell. Doubleday felt that the gallantry and leadership shown by him on this day fairly entitled him to continue to lead First Corps. But he was mortified to find, that evening, that General Meade had replaced him with a junior officer, John Newton. Meade apparently had made this decision without regard to the performance of Doubleday's command. An embittered Doubleday returned to command his division, and rendered signal service to the Union cause as a part of the forces which repulsed the Virginia Division of George Pickett on July 3, 1863. Doubleday recounted the highlights of his actions during the Civil War in his book, *Chancellorsville and Gettysburg*, published in 1882.

Gettysburg marked the last active duty by Doubleday in the Civil War; he was ordered to Washington shortly thereafter to preside over a military commission to investigate fraudulent contractors, deserters, and bounty jumpers.

With the end of hostilities, Doubleday's rank reverted to lieutenant colonel in the Regular Army and he was sent with his regiment, the 17th Infantry, to command the post at Galveston, Texas.

He was detailed as a member of a retiring board in New York City, in 1868, and presided over the cases of General Joseph Hooker and others.

Doubleday made his last tour of duty to Texas as colonel of the 24th Infantry, one of the first black regiments in the United States Army, assigned to garrison Fort McKavett, in western Texas. The frontier had been somewhat tamed by that time, but the perils of moving fragile household goods to the frontier of Texas were still present. General Zenas Bliss remembered that

> When General and Mrs Doubleday came out to the 24th. Infantry in 1870, they brought two casks of cut glass, very fine and expensive. When it arrived at Fort McKavett, there was but one whole piece in the two casks, all the rest were broken, and the glass was packed by an expert in New York.[7]

Doubleday remained at Fort McKavett until 1872, when the regiment was ordered to march overland to Brownsville, Texas, to relieve the 10th Infantry, which had been stationed in that city. On the march, Doubleday was "stung in the night by some venomous reptile"[8] resulting in a injury that impaired his already fragile health. The ailing Doubleday was offered an indefinite sick leave, during which he would receive full pay. But the old veteran could not reconcile the notion of receiving pay without work and retired from the service on December 11, 1873, with more than thirty years of service to his country.

Doubleday spent his declining years in Mendham, New Jersey, occasionally traveling to New York. A newspaper reporter recounted his meeting with Doubleday and gives us these impressions of the general, now in the autumn of his life:

> General Abner Doubleday who fired from Fort Sumter the first gun against the confederacy, was seen quietly strolling down Broadway the other day.... He is on the retired list of the army, and rarely ever wears a uniform. Though somewhat advanced in years he is well preserved. His face is clean shaven, except for a gray moustache. His hair is white and thin. Not quite six feet high,

he is broad shouldered, and has a well-knit frame, fast losing its symmetry from corpulency. The hat he wears has a military appearance. It has a somewhat funnel-shaped crown and the brim is stiff. The Grand Army men wears hats like it, except that theirs are slouched. His long black frock coat flaps open and reveals a massive chest....[9]

It was during his last years that Doubleday recorded the reminiscences and anecdotes found in this book. The manuscript must have been written mostly from memory; his memory was excellent, but he did on a few occasions err in historic fact. The manuscript ends abruptly with the firing on Fort Sumter, due perhaps to the loss or pilferage of the general's papers, but most likely due to his coverage of this and the Civil War phases of his career in his two other volumes.

Throughout his life, he had been a collector of anecdotes and stories, and the last chapter of this book is dedicated to the perpetuation of his stories of the great, the near great, and the forgotten military men of the United States. The editor combined two of the Doubleday manuscripts titled "Military Anecdotes" and "Some Experiences of Wit, Humor and Repartee in Army and Navy Life" to produce this last chapter. The two documents repeated many episodes and many stories were placed in a somewhat random manner. Duplicates were deleted and the text was reorganized into a more readable narrative. Accounts that dealt with non-military subjects were not reproduced. It is in this light-hearted spirit that the editor has included in the endnotes some additional military anecdotes from other sources. But the gentle Doubleday would surely have approved of the additions—their purpose is to perpetuate the memory of the "Old Army."

Abner Doubleday passed from this life on January 26, 1893, and would have most likely receded in the conscious memory of Americans if his name had not become associated with the invention of the great American pastime, baseball. How did this association come to be?

Albert G. Spalding, the sporting-goods mogul, who organized in the late nineteenth century the company that still bears his name, was a rabid supporter of baseball and had argued for years that baseball was a uniquely American game, having been invented in this country. After a world tour to promote the game in 1888 and 1889, he was convinced, having seen no other game played in other countries that "bore even the slightest resemblance"[10] to baseball. After an article appearing in 1905 authored by the British born Henry Chadwick claimed that baseball had evolved from "the English game of rounders," the baseball controversy began to heat up. An angry Spalding responded to the article by describing rounders as "that asinine pastime" which was about "as exciting as a game of Ring-Around-the-Rosy." With vital American interests at stake, Spalding convinced the baseball league presidents to convene a commission charged with determining the origins of the grand old game. The commission, which would become known as the Mills Commission, was chaired by Albert Mills. Mills was an avid supporter of baseball and had a record of service in the Union Army during the Civil War, having risen to the rank of colonel. Mills organized and even played in many of the baseball games staged between units of Union soldiers. Other members of the commission included James E. Sullivan, Alfred J. Reach, George Wright, N. E. Young, Senator Morgan G. Bulkeley from Connecticut, and Senator Arthur P. Gorman from Maryland. Each member of the committee was either intimately associated with baseball, being either a team or league president, or was associated with Albert Spalding's sporting-goods business. Spalding was thus in a position to exert influence on the findings of the commission, to say the least.

However, the findings of the Mills Commission were probably influenced the most by Mills' friendship with and admiration of Abner Doubleday. Mills met Doubleday in 1873 at a meeting of the Lafayette Post of the Grand Army of the Republic in New York City. Colonel Mills was charmed by General Doubleday, and a fast friendship developed. With Doubleday's death in 1893, Mills organized a memorial service in which Doubleday's body lay in state in the New York City Hall and was instrumental in having Doubleday's body interred at Arlington National Cemetery. Thus it was no surprise that the Mills Commission concluded, in the latter days of 1907, that baseball had

originated in the United States and that the game was devised by
Abner Doubleday. Unfortunately, the evidence that the Mills
Commission had supposedly amassed to support these two conclu-
sions had been consumed in a fire that destroyed the American Sports
Publishing Company. Perhaps that is what became of the section of
Doubleday's manuscript titled "Chapter 1" which is now missing from
the general's papers and might have explained his connection to baseball. A letter from Albert Graves, a resident of Cooperstown, New
York, and neighbor of Doubleday, is the only documentation remaining of Doubleday's connection to baseball. Graves asserted that
Doubleday had taught the Cooperstown boys his modifications of a
game known as "town ball." The changes to town ball included reduc-
ing the number of players, assigning each player a location in the field,
and replacing the wooden posts designated as bases by flat stones.

Thus a modest American war hero, who neither drank, smoked,
nor engaged in any other dissipative activities, the *beaux ideal*
American of the Victorian Age, would ironically become principally
remembered as the "father of baseball."

The voices of today's sports historians reverberate in strident and
accusing tones to attack the claims of the Mills Commission and even
the character of this kind and gentle man. Doubleday, it must be
remembered, never made any claims to the authorship of the game. A
reading of Doubleday's account of his role in the attack on Monterrey
must surely serve to convince anyone of his modesty, and, I think, can
be used to reasonably infer that he would have been just as reluctant
to mention his connection to baseball.

Debunking the supposed Doubleday "myths" on baseball has
become a national pastime for modern sports intellectuals, creating an
unpleasant odor that has permeated even to a regional level.[11] Sports
writers, functioning in our new order of "political correctness" now
claim that the first game of baseball played in Texas, supposedly at
Galveston, was not organized by Doubleday while stationed there in
1867! Doubleday was indeed stationed in Galveston on this date, serving as colonel of the 17th Infantry, sent to impose military rule on a
defeated nation. But the case against Doubleday's organization of

Texas baseball is certainly both circumspect and circumstantial; however, I feel sure that Doubleday himself, exercising his strong Christian virtue of modesty, would have willingly forgiven his critics—it matters not who is credited with organizing the Galvestonians into a game.

But as long as the subject continues to interest sports historians, I challenge them to prove that the first game of baseball played in Texas was not organized by Abner Doubleday and played in Brownsville, Texas, in 1848. After all, he was stationed there for several months during that year.

¿Quién sabe? But I digress from my real purpose in preparing these memoirs for publication. Through these pages, I have hoped to give you, the reader, a glimpse of the Old Army and the strongly individualistic men who filled its ranks. What better way to view this thin blue line of heroes than through the eyes of a wonderful storyteller: Abner Doubleday.

Praise be to his memory.

A final word on methods used to transcribe the text. The editor attempted to copy Abner Doubleday's handwritten manuscripts as he wrote them, retaining his spelling errors and unique style of punctuation. In a few places where the original was not clear, minor changes were made for clarification. Doubleday's reminiscences were not recorded in chronological order; the editor rearranged the original so that this volume presents his account in order.

The holographic text was taken from photo copies that were, in turn, copied from microfilm. As such, they are very difficult to read. The editor's transcription was reviewed by Megan Hahn, Richard Fraser and Melissa Haley of the Manuscript Department at the New-York Historical Society which houses the original papers. This last review brought to light my errors and Doubleday's penciled comments that were not clear on the microfilm copy. Special thanks are in order to the New-York Historical Society staff.

The editor, nevertheless, assumes the responsibility for all errors appearing in My Life in the Old Army.

Joseph E. Chance

1

FIRST ACTIVE DUTY

After the seclusion and hard work at West Point I enjoyed my three months furlough very much. Orders soon came for me to report as Brevet Second Lieutenant to Captain and Brevet Lieut. Colonel Thomas Childs[1] commanding Fort Johnson, Smithville, N.C.[2] The journey there proved to be very long and fatiguing, particularly that portion of it over the broken backed strap iron rail road which ran through the pine forests of North Carolina.[3]

The arrival of a new officer at a country village is always an event and I found myself among a very cordial and warm hearted people who held the army in high estimation. Colonel Childs was very glad to have another subaltern at his post. Second Lieutenant Sewell L. Fremont[4] was already there. He had been on duty for a year as he was graduated in the class that preceeded mine.

My first commander was a handsome man, of stately presence, and pleasing manners. He had gained laurels as a mere boy in the War of 1812 with Great Britain and in the war of 1836 which lasted several years against the Seminole Indians in Florida. He was a strict disciplinarian but his severity was a matter of duty, and always tempered with kindly impulses. Being extremely popular, his residence was the center of a circle which included some of the most influential families in the

Transcribed from the Abner Doubleday Collection at the New-York Historical Society—BV Doubleday, Abner, Chapters II and III of "My Military Biography, Including the Fall of Monterey." (See also Arthur J. Breton, A Guide to the Collections of the New-York Historical Society [Westport, Connecticut: Greenwood Press, 1972]).

state, for in the summer season the little village was much frequented on account of the cool sea breeze which swept across the bay. There was much gaiety and picnics, and pleasant excursions on the water were frequent. Our evening parades were a great attraction to visitors and residents, for we had a very passable band made up of Germans who had studied music and who had been selected from the recruits.

Our men as a general thing behaved well but on pay day, which came every two months, they gave us a great deal of trouble, for they were sure to be drunk and disorderly. These payments at long intervals, are, in my opinion, very demoralizing and destructive of discipline. It is much better to pay small sums weekly than large sums every two, four, or six months. The latter inevitably leads to gambling, drunkeness, and other excesses. In the British Army captains of companies formerly and I believe now paid their men by the day or week, and as the sums entrusted to them were small there was no temptation to appropriate them to their own use. Our system seems to me cumbrous, troublesome, and expensive, but the tide of patronage is too powerful in our country to be withstood and there is little likelihood that a change will ever occur.

The first payment that took place after my arrival I happened to be on duty as officer of the Day and was therefore responsible for the good order of the garrison. I soon had my hands full for the guard house was overflowing with delinquents who were drunk, noisy, and obstreperous. One of the prisoners who was quiet and inoffensive when sober was very violent when intoxicated. He undertook to whip all the men who were in confinement with him and succeeded in creating a tremendous uproar. It became necessary to tie him up and gag him, before any thing like order could be obtained.

These derelictions were, of course, soon followed by a garrison court martial. Captain Keyes[5] was sent from the headquarters of the regiment at Fort Moultrie as President, Lieut. Fremont was the second member and I was detailed as member and recorder which made it my duty to prosecute the case for the government. It was a new experience to me but by the aid of Captain Keyes I managed to perform the duty assigned me without any serious blunder. The culprit was a simple minded man named Raymond. He was charged with neglect of duty in allowing a man who was under sentence for desertion to escape from custody. As the latter was fettered with a cannon ball attached to his leg by a chain, the case looked serious to Raymond; the more so as the garrison was bounded by a fence nine or ten feet high. It was shown that the deserter had managed to get possession of a file, and to cut through his chain. As there was a barrel standing near the fence he was able to spring on it, after dropping his shackles and climb over, before the astonished sentinel could stop him. Raymond was an intensely stupid Irishman, and the trial proceeded somewhat after this manner.

Question by myself as recorder, Prisoner, you have heard the detail read to you; have you any objection to be tried by any member named therein?

Answer. Plaze yer honor, it was the barrel what deceived me entirely.

It was in vain that I reiterated the question, I could get no other answer.

I then asked him whether he plead guilty or not guilty but he still replied that it was the barrel that deceived him. When I asked him if he would like to ask the witness any questions he answered again, "It was the barrel." Nothing could induce him to vary from these words and I was obliged to proceed as if he had pleaded not guilty. I testified to his general good character and he was let off with a light punishment.

Several cases having occurred requiring the action of a General Court Martial, I was directed to proceed with a detachment by sea to Fort Moultrie in order that the prisoners might be tried there. Of course as there was a proper guard I was responsible for the safe keeping of the men entrusted to my charge. This reminds me of a similar case where some prisoners were sent from Hart's Island to New York to be tried and I am tempted to state it for the benefit of the younger members of the profession as on a previous occasion several of the guard had returned intoxicated and two or three prisoners had escaped. The young officer sent in charge received strict orders not to allow the men to leave the ranks. The detachment reached the city about 8 A. M. As the court did not sit until 11 A.M. the lieutenant thought he would take a stroll up town and he accordingly turned over the command to the sergeant saying Sergeant S____ I am obliged to go up town to attend to a little business. I will be back by half past ten. Be particularly vigilant and allow none of these prisoners to escape. No sooner was the officer out of sight than the Sergeant thought he could have a good time too and be back before the lieutenant returned; so he turned over the command to the corporal and soon disappeared. The Corporal began to feel lonely and find time to hang heavy on his hands so he called out one of the privates, told him he would be back soon and placed him in charge of the detachment. This process went on until only two men were left with the prisoners. On his return the officer found several of them gone and his guard in a very drunken condition. If I remember correctly he was court-martialled for the offense and suspended.

All this, however, is a digression and I must return to my narrative. The steamer entered the harbor as soon as it was light enough to see, and I was on deck determined to get a good view of the forts as we passed them. I was astonished to see at that early hour that the garrison were out and drilling on the beach. I afterwards ascertained that all drills took place at sunrise on account of the heat of the day.

I met with a pleasant reception from the officers of the regiment with several of whom I had been on familiar terms at West Point. Indeed, D. H. Hill,[6] Jasper Stewart,[7] and Charles L. Kilburn [sic],[8] who were there, were classmates of mine. General Armistead,[9] one of the heroes of the War of 1812 was in command of the Department; and Colonel William Gates[10] of the regiments and posts in the harbor. The general was considered a model soldier by the officers of his command, who all looked up to him with affection and respect. Our Army was so small at that time the rank of general inspired some thing like awe. They never called upon him except in full uniform.

Some of the officers whom I met, on my arrival, have won since then a world wide reputation. Our present Commander in Chief, General William T. Sherman was there as plain Lieutenant Sherman learning the rudiments of his profession. There too was George H.

Thomas the Rock of Chickamauga, the general who was never defeated. Thomas W. Sherman[11] was also present who lost his leg in a desperate charge against the rebels in Port Hudson. Braxton Bragg[12] who gained so much fame in the Mexican War and who afterwards became a distinguished general in the Confederate service. There too was John F. Reynolds[13] who commanded half of the Union Army and lost his life at Gettysburg, while defending his native state from invasion. Martin Burk[14] was there as a Captain, the gallant soldier of 1812 who was afterwards so prominent as the custodian of the rebel prisoners in Fort Lafayette, New York Harbor.[15] Daniel H. Hill distinguished in the Mexican War who subsequently became one of the great leaders of the Rebellion. Jasper Stewart another soldier of the Mexican War who in our late civil strife was Chief of Artillery to Genl McCall's Division[16] in the Peninsula. Three other officers who had made fine records in Mexico and Florida and from whom much was expected afterwards one Horace B. Field[17] was drowned at sea in 1853; Henry B. Judd[18] and William Austine[19] were both disabled and placed on the Retired List at the beginning of the Rebellion.

I do not believe there ever was a higher toned organization in service than the Third Artillery at that time; made as by the example of Sherman, Thomas, Bragg, and others. Each officer looked upon any stain upon the regiment as vital to himself. The command had just returned from Florida where it had spent several years campaigning in the swamps and hummocks against the most wily, treacherous and cruel of all the Indian tribes. The contrast of their late hardships and wild life, with the elegant hospitality of Charleston was very gratifying and acceptable.

After a few days spent in parties and festivities at Fort Moultrie I returned with my detachment to Fort Johnson.

Officers of the army in their varied careers are frequently called upon for all kinds of service. It is not uncommon to direct them to appear before civil courts and act as counsel for the government in cases where it is sought to release a soldier by the writ of habeus corpus. Once when looking for hostile Indians I was expected to navigate a sloop among the islands of the Bay of Florida and as I knew nothing about that kind of business it was a wonder that I did not wreck our craft or drown somebody. On the Mexican frontier questions of international law sometimes come up which require an immediate decision from the officer in command. Artillery officers have to be familiar with the operations of the wheelwright and blacksmith in order to repair broken down carriages and replace tires on the wheels. A lieutenant scouting for Indians is often obliged in cases of emergency to act as physician and surgeon to the men of his detachment. At posts where there is no chaplain officers frequently read the service at burials. On my return to Smithville I had to act as architect—make plans and draw up specifications for the erection of a new hospital. A young lady of the garrison assisted me in this duty and we held daily meetings but were very much puzzled to give the regulation amount of space for each room and get in the stair cases without making the partitions bisect the windows. We had a very economical quartermaster general[20] at that time and he did not choose to pay for the services of regular architects. Our post quartermaster Lieut Fremont although a man of varied attainments had no skill as a draughtsman and therefore turned the matter over to me. The system in vogue at that time of requiring lieutenant's to make these designs produced some curious results. Buildings were erected in the sunny south without piazzas and with very narrow staircases and others were built in the wintry north with wide verandahs which were never used. I did hear that an officer who had been a midshipman when called upon to construct quarters made them as far as he could do so on the principle of a ship. These things were better regulated under the administration of General Meigs[21] who is an accomplished architect who built the capitol extension at Washington.

I have no doubt that as regards this diversity of occupation our naval officers have a similar experience. During the rebellion when sailors and marines were landed to cooperate with our troops, Admiral (then Commodore) Preble[22] found that he had suddenly become a brigadier general and was required to throw out pickets, protect his flanks and take all the precautions incident to his new experience as an acting army officer.

Our doctor at Fort Johnson[23] went into new quarters and hospital we had designed for him with a good deal of satisfaction. He was a peculiar man, utterly unable to comprehend a joke. This had brought him in contact with some harem-scarem dragoon officers in Florida who had victimized him so often that he became desperate and would go for his pistols, if he suspected any designs against him. When he received his commission it was accompanied in the usual form with an order "to report without delay" to the commanding officer at Houlton, Maine, for troops had been sent there in consequence of a dispute with Great Britain about the North Eastern Boundary. The Doctor took the words literally and imagining there was some strong necessity for his presence hired extra stages and travelled night and day. This of course amused the garrison very much. After that he was ordered to a large post at Fort Jupiter, Florida, and there was made the victim of manifold jokes. He was threatened with being put in irons for some trivial offense, was made to believe the woods were full of monkeys; went out to hunt them and was driven in at full speed by sham Indians. Afterwards he was sent out in a boat to fish with a saber in one hand and a torch in the other. Upon finding he was adrift without oars he cried for help and the dragoon officers lay on the ground and rolled over in convulsions of laughter. Then he was tried by a sham court martial for trifling with the affections of a laundress who had followed the camp for many years and whose reputation was quite fragrant. He appeared in court with a long written defense and a crowd of witnesses to prove his innocence and the bad character of the laundress. It is sad to relate that these things worked on his mind and ultimately made him hopelessly insane. When I served with him at Fort Johnson he imagined every thing was intended as a joke. I went one day in full uniform by order of the commanding officer to arrest him. He took it all as a joke and said I could not fool him in that way.

A very important question vital to the discipline of the army came up about this time. During the service of our troops in Florida it became necessary to scatter them in small detachments all over the Peninsula in order to hold the numerous points threatened by the

Indians. Under these circumstances ordinary garrison courts martial could not be held without great danger, inconvenience, and expense. At the same time it was more than ever necessary that obedience and subordination should be maintained. A custom therefore sprung up of ordering men to be tied up and flogged[24] for flagrant derelictions of duty. When the troops returned to the forts on the sea-board where courts could be assembled, officers preferred the more expeditious methods they had learned in the field. General Scott then commander of the army thought private soldiers had some rights[25] and that the discipline of the service would be improved by regular investigations as to the guilt or innocence of prisoners. He issued a very stringent order on the subject, but it was in a great measure disregarded. Many officers however still think this power of summary punishment is essential to maintain order and obedience but I have satisfied myself by my own experience that it destroys the manhood of the soldiers and makes the service little better than the old fashioned slave pens. These capricious and irregular punishments are too frequently the result of bad temper. I have known sergeants to gamble with the men and then have them flogged for asking for the money they had won. Yet in such cases the private was not even allowed a hearing. General Scott's order was read on parade at every post in the army, and soldiers were authorized to report every violation of it. A case soon occurred at Fort Moultrie. Lieut. A___ [26] ordered a man to be tied up and flogged, who was drunk and disorderly, and when the man was released from the guard house he made a formal report to the commanding officer. The latter found an old article of war, which related to the money relations which existed in former days between officers and men when captains paid their companies once a week. In such cases disputes sometimes arose and the article in question read that these were to be decided by a regimental court martial with the right of appeal to a general court martial. The commander took the strange view that the case of the man who had been flogged came under this article of war. He said to his adjutant this article is to settle disputes between officers and soldiers; there is a dispute between Lieut A___ and Private G___. Order a regimental court martial to be assembled. This being done, the adjutant said "What is the court to do?" The colonel said a court must try some body for that is the object of courts. It cannot try Lieut. A , only a general court martial can do that; therefore it must try the man. So the latter was tried and punished. When the information went on to Washington, that the officer who had violated the order, had not been arraigned, but that the man who had made the complaint had been punished, General Scott was in a towering rage. He went to the Secretary of War and requested that Col. G be tried for not having carried out his instructions. The secretary did not like to do that but ordered a General Court Martial for the trial of Lieut A . The latter was found guilty and I believe was suspended for three months.

Although our post went by the name of Fort Johnson, it was wholly unfortified. The name came from an old work which had existed at the time of the War of 1812. One front rested on the Cape Fear River and the other three were bounded by a high board fence. One Sunday there was quite an excitement in the little town. For some time past there there had been rumors of secret meetings among the negros throughout the state with a view to an insurrection and as the blacks in our section of the country out numbered the whites in the proportion of six to one there seemed to be some cause for alarm. On the occasion referred to I was the only officer at the post. Lieut. Colonel Childs was absent on a court martial and Lieut. Fremont had been suddenly detached with twenty men to guard the U. S. Arsenal at Fayetteville, N. C. as thousands of muskets and cartridges were stored there. This left but thirty-three men remaining in the company. I was called out of church by an excited individual who related to me some suspicious circumstances indicative of a movement of some kind among the slaves. It was a novel experience to be called upon thus suddenly to make plans to protect a large section of country against a servile insurrection. I determined in case of necessity to send the women and children over to Fort Caswell—a strong work situated on the sea shore opposite at the mouth of the river, while I kept my men as a nucleus for the people to rally upon. Fortunately there proved to be no cause for alarm.[27] It was not the first time that apprehensions of this nature prevailed. I was told that a year or two before the officers one day heard a great screaming and to their amazement found the whole country full of families rushing towards the fort. They filled the houses and parade ground and created the greatest disorder and confusion for two or three days by which time the alarm subsided. During their short stay the officers were at their wits end to provide for them.

These dangers were not wholly imaginative. Several revolts it is alleged had occurred at the south but they were limited to certain localities and were of short duration. One in Southhampton County, Virginia[28] was the occasion of a forced march by Major Worth with the greater part of the garrison of Fort Monroe at Old Point Comfort, Virginia.

For my opinion, nearly three-fourths of the difficulties that occur in the army are the result of intoxication. It seems difficult to assign an adequate remedy. Several times during my military career when I was in command of posts I have attempted to stop the introduction of liquor but in each case I only made the matter worse. The men were sure to circumvent me in some way. It would come in in loaves of bread, in water melons and once numerous canteens were filled and brought in under the petticoats of one of the laundresses. Sometimes it would come in pails with false tops in which innocent milk seemed to float. The ingenuity of the men was boundless. When Inspector General Churchill[29] was a major in command of Fort Johnson he issued one of these prohibitory orders but it was of no avail. One day from an upper window of his house he saw a soldier approaching with two pails; one evidently containing water, and the other from its dark color he saw must be whiskey especially as he saw the man come out of a grocery where the article was sold. The major saw the man carefully cover up both pails and as he passed through the post garden hide one of them behind some bushes. The fact is the man had caught a glimpse of the Major and had easily guessed what he would do, so he hid the pail of water very carefully and passed by the Major into garrison with the pail of whiskey. The Major sent for the pail in the garden but contrary to his expectations it furnished no evidence which could be used against the man before a court.

Orders have been issued to recruiting officers during the last few years to be particular in regard to the moral character of recruits, but at one time men were enlisted without regard to any thing but their physical condition. The consequence was that the army was encumbered with a great many men who were mere nuisances. The theory in vogue at that time was that no matter how bad a man might be, he could be made a tolerable soldier by means of military discipline accompanied by severe punishments. Such men however, having no feeling of honor or self respect, were never trustworthy in the hour of danger. The popular opinion that the dangerous classes make good soldiers is wholly erroneous. It takes large sums of money to feed clothe and transport them and when they are needed at the front they will always be straggling in rear, out of harms way and ready to plunder every house that comes in their way. At one time in the Mexican War when recruits were scarce it is said the authorities of New Orleans freed the jails of the city on condition the convicts would enlist for the war. In regard to nationalities so far as my experience goes, Americans from the rural districts, who have pride, patriotism, and self respect, are the best soldiers in the world. A great part of our army, as at present constituted is made up of emigrants from Europe, who find themselves penniless and without employment in our great cities. They enlist for a livelihood. Of these the Germans are the most desirable. They have been accustomed to a stern military regime in their own country and hence are better fitted for service, than the others who are wholly undisciplined. As they rarely indulge in any thing stronger than beer they are always quiet and orderly. A rollicking devil may care Irishman who is fond of whiskey will keep an entire garrison in an uproar. He is always ready for a fight and may be depended upon when there is real danger, but these qualities hardly outweigh the serious disorder he occasions at times. He is warm hearted too, fond of his officers and somewhat reckless of consequences. His humor is inexhaustable. A man named Flory belonging to the Sixth Infantry was a good specimen of this class. He was a good soldier when sober, but obstreperous when drunk and always very penitent when the debauch was over. Then he

"Oh, it is not fit I am for the infantry...."

would go to the officer of the day, confess his derelictions and say "And I said to meself, if I went to the leftenant and tould him all about, sure he wouldn't be too hard on a poor bye; he would let me off asy." By taking this course he generally managed to escape the full penalty due to his offences, but finally his escapades became too frequent to be overlooked. He was tried by a General Court Martial for habitual drunkeness and found guilty and sentenced to be drummed out of service to the tune of the "Rogues March" with an empty whiskey bottle tied around his neck. Previous to this the officer of the day, Lieutenant O'Brien,[30] an Irishman like himself heard him making a frightful noise in the guard house, and went there to investigate. Flory had managed in some way to get some liquor and was singing at the top of his voice. O'Brien as he appeared at the door of the prison room called out "Stop that noise!" This command was echoed by Flory who called to the other prisoners to stop their noise. "Yes, but I mean you," said O'Brien. "And it is me ye mane," asked Flory? "Yes, you are the one who is making all this uproar" was the reply. "And it is Moore's melodies[31] ye call an uproar," said Flory. "Come," said O'Brien, "I have had quite enough of this and if I hear anymore I will have you gagged." "Did any one ever the loikes of that," said Flory. "Ye never could make them belave in ould Ireland that an O'Brien had gagged a Flory."

When the time came for the execution of his sentence Flory appeared sober and penitent. With tears rolling down his cheeks he turned to Lieut Robinson (now Major General on the retired list in the army and recently Lieutenant Governor of New York),[32] and said pointing to the bottle, "Lieutenant dont you think you could put a wee drap in it!" He afterwards soliloquized "Oh it is not fit I am for the infantry at all, at all, I must enlist in the Artillery," a compliment which that arm of service would no doubt have valued highly.

When I first resided in the South, I was struck by the negro idioms. As the slaves were not allowed to learn to read and write, it was impossible for them to improve in this respect. Their conversation was a parody on the English language. They never said a person was gone, but done gone. The word both was never used, all two was substituted for it. I remember soon after my arrival at Smithville my land-lady sent me a little boy to wait upon me. She did not charge anything for his services saying if he could learn to carry messages it would be an ample recompense. I had made a camera obscura[33] in a dark room and the inverted image was very beautiful. Some of the servants saw it and reported that I had a machine that turned every body upside down that passed my door. This excited much curosity and there was some hesitation on the part of the young ladies about passing my door. To show them it was harmless I appointed a day and sent this little sable messenger to invite them to come and see it. He delivered the invitation in this wise "*Moss Doubleday he send he complement and ax you to come and see de scomer.*"

The confinement by Lieut Fremont of a young boy who was living in the garrison and who was noisy and creating a disturbance at night and refused to obey orders raised some very important questions as to the extent of the powers of the commanding officer in times of peace, in regard to persons who were not in the military service. It was decid-ed that the confinement was illegal. I believe the rule is, that a citizen who infringes on the good order and peace of the garrison can be ejected from the grounds but cannot be held as a prisoner. Any other rendering would place citizens and their families living in the vicinity of a military post entirely at the mercy of the commanding officer there. The rising generation should be taught that while it is a matter of great importance to obey orders, yet there are times when the spir-it of an order is opposed to its literal fulfillment, for circumstances fre-quently arise which would have modified the order or reversed it in the mind of the officer who issued it. The true rule would be to do what the commander would wish done were he present; that is to obey the spirit of the command and not the letter. For instance an officer is ordered from A to B by a long circuitous road on the suppo-sition that a bridge on the direct route has been burned. The officer finds a new bridge has been built and goes by the shortest way. He is clearly justifiable in doing so. He is carrying out the spirit of the order. The subordinate who does this however must take the responsibility of his action and if it is wrong must expect to suffer the consequences.

Officers must refuse to obey *illegal* orders, for if they do so the civil law
holds them responsible. If a commander were to order his subordinate
to shoot down or rob a peaceable citizen the latter would be imprisoned and tried the same as if no such order had been given. There are
instances in our military history where soldiers have been hung for
shooting down citizens in time of peace who failed to give the countersign. This question has been thoroughly discussed in the recent Fitz
John Porter case.[34] In the Navy on ship board where the field of
action is more circumscribed, I believe the rule is more rigid for the
commander is supposed to be present to rectify all mistakes.
Somewhere in the naval records I am told however that there was a
case where a drunken officer ordered the ship to be steered in a direction that would have wrecked it on a reef. Under these circumstances
his subordinates took council together, disobeyed the order, reported
their action to the Naval Department and were, of course, sustained.

A naval officer related to me that on one occasion when his vessel
was off Smyrna,[35] Commodore Rogers,[36] who was a very strict disciplinarian, directed a midshipman to ask two Frenchmen who came
aboard if the Turks would interfere with the burial on shore of a warrant officer, a quartermaster named Marshall, who had just died. The
middy replied, "I dont speak French Commodore." "Ask them sir!"
roared the Commodore in a rage. The Middy blurted out in great trep-
idation to the French men:" *Si vous mettez old Marshall ici; pienza vous
the Turkeys come levee he.*" "That will do sir," said the Commodore,
"always try to obey an order in some way."

Note: A quartermaster in the Navy is a mere warrant officer; in the
army he is commissioned and frequently holds high rank. A midshipman who had just left the Navy and had been appointed a second lieutenant sent word to the major quartermaster in Baltimore that if he did
not fill his requisition more promptly he would put him in irons; he was
wholly unconscious he was addressing a superior officer.

Apropos of this subject of orders there are some helpless people
utterly unable to execute the simplest command without endless
detailed instructions. I once ordered an acting brigadier general to
guard a certain passage against cavalry, leaving him sufficient force for

that purpose. "But where am I to put my pickets," he asked, "and what am I to do." "Oh," was my reply," you desire me to act as Brigadier General in your place. If you do not possess sufficient knowledge of your profession to make the proper disposition of your force in this case then I shall be compelled to relieve you and put some more competent man in your place." He hastened to assure me that he could attend to it and I left him with more self reliance than he had before the interview commenced.

A lieutenant who was just graduated from West Point reported to General Eustis[37] during the Florida war. The General directed him to take a detachment and construct a road to a certain place some ten miles distant. This involved the construction of some small bridges over streams. The lieutenant replied :"I dont understand the process sir!" "Process be d___d" replied the general, "if you dont have that road done in ten days, I'll process you." The bridge was completed in the required time.

There is one point in the army intercourse of that day worth elucidating. The officers never would allow a superior to use insulting or abusive language towards them. They asserted that a reprimand could only be given by sentence of a court martial, and when off duty they were on an equal footing as gentlemen and although they fully recognized the right of any officer higher in rank to give them directions they did not admit he could accompany them by remarks of an offensive nature. He could of course inform the inferior that he had not carried out an order properly and could demand written explanations upon which he was at liberty to found charges and specifications for a court martial or to place an officer in arrest for a limited period. But the idea that any officer could vent his bad temper or exhibit his bad manners at the expense of those under him was not admitted. If a general in those days were to send for an officer and call him a fool or a knave he would simply be insulted in return and if he then submitted the case to the arbitration of a court martial it was ten to one that the junior would be virtually sustained. The same view prevailed in the Navy. An officer of high rank in that branch of service related to me an occurrence which illustrated this point. One of our war vessels was cruising off Smyrna, under a Lieut. Commander. The latter was very arrogant and insulting to one of the Midshipmen T___ for whom he cherished a peculiar and unnatural dislike. The midshipman chafed under these slights and constant snubbing for some months. One day while cruising in the Mediterranean off Greece, a discussion arose as to some point of classical history and T. expressed his opinion with the others, when the lieutenant said in reply, "*Oh you! You are an ignoramus.*" The midshipman blazed up at this and answered that no one but a coward would take advantage of his rank to grossly insult a junior officer without cause. He was at once arrested and sent below. But all the officers of the ship sided with him, taking the ground that the remark of the latter was personal and not official and that his junior therefore had the right to hold him personally responsible for it. The lieutenant took a different view and said he should bring T. before a court but upon finding that probably no officer of the Navy would uphold him—he was in a measure compelled to make a personal matter and after argument and expostulation until midnight with his officers he said, "well tell that d___d fellow I will fight him at daylight." The next morning the meeting took place and the commander was fatally wounded. He sent for one of his friends and said, "Do you know that d___d fellow got the shot on me after all," keeping up his animosity to the last. Not only were all officers regarded as social equals when off duty, but there was a marked difference in the mode of intercourse used on the two occasions. I remember on one occasion at our post when an officer, Brevet Captain Taylor,[38] was assigned to the command of the company in accordance with his brevet rank while Brevet Lieut Colonel Childs commanded the post, the latter said, "Taylor, how are you old fellow," and immediately afterwards, "Captain Taylor you will form your company, sir, march it to the parade and await further orders there."

The interminable quarrel between the staff and the line broke out about this time with great force. The staff were favored by the Secretary of War and had the best of it. When they ranked a line officer they did pretty much as they chose although the military theory was that the latter commanded every body at the post. Bragg, who

liked to force decisions on this point one day when he was a lieutenant and in command of the post reported the Captain quartermaster on duty at the post *as supposed to be present*: the staff officer[s]
insisted that when they ranked the commanding officer of the post
and he [the commanding officer] needed military supplies he must
send in a requisition for them and they were to judge whether they
would fill the demand or not. This, of course, destroys all unity of
command. If a commander thinks he needs certain articles for the
defense of his post he should have the power to order them and not
beg for them. The quartermasters of that day were noted for the very
liberal allowances they bestowed on themselves and the very scant
accomodations they gave the line officers. Once a new lieutenant
who came to Fort Clark,[39] Texas, upon being directed to the quarters
due to his rank sarcastically requested permission *to live in the post
quartermaster's hen coop* as that was a large and commodious structure.

   In 1844, I was detailed for a tour of duty with Ringgold's light battery[40] which was stationed at Baltimore. I spent several months there
but as the quarters were crowded and there were [more] officers on
duty there than could be provided for, the juniors were sent off and I
was directed to report to the head quarters of the regiment at
Charleston. There I became better acquainted with the officers
including our present commander of the army, then plain Lieut
Sherman who was a genial, studious, and spirited officer and a universal favorite. George H. Thomas was also there. He was one of the
pillars of the regiment; good humored, quiet but not reserved, with
quick perceptions—truth, honesty, and great repose of character.
Braxton Bragg however attracted the most attention. He had written
some brilliant articles for the reviews[41] in reference to the army organizations of different nations and was looked up to as quite a rising
man. General Wool, the Commander of the Division, regarded him
with great favor. Bragg was very honest and conscientious with regard
to the prompt payment of all dues incurred by him and he urged and
set an example to the younger subalterns of strict economy and self
denial for the purposes indicated. His only fault was the severity with
which he punished the smallest dereliction of duty. His best men suf-

fered in this respect so much as his worst. His men feared and hated
him for this. Once in Mexico a lighted shell was put under his bed[42]
while he was asleep. It exploded fortunately without injuring him.
Afterwards when he held high command in the rebel army he shot
more men for infractions of discipline[43] than all the other generals put
together. Sarcasm was his forte. He was fond of raising points with the
authorities at Washington and was very saucy and impudent in his
correspondence and managed to evade the penalties connected with
this species of writing for a long time. At last he was caught tried and
punished heavily by suspension and fine for his contumacy. It was said
that when he was a 2nd lieutenant on recruiting service at Governor's
Island he had a dispute with his commanding officer and managed to
entrap the latter into two divergent statements: whereupon he deliberate[ly] drew up and sent on charges against the aforesaid commander for lying. Genl Jones[44] who was then Adjutant General of the
Army was astonished that a raw subaltern should do such a thing and
did not answer the communication immediately. Then Bragg wrote an
impudent letter to Genl Jones to know why his letter did not receive
a reply. Jones endorsed in pencil a few remarks on the back of this last
epistle signed R. J. explaining why he had not replied to it and sent it
to Genl Scott who then commanded the army for his action. General
Scott was much offended at the disrespectful tone of Bragg's letter
and said, "Upon my word a very impudent communication. The
young man probably has had no experience in the army. Send it back
to him as reproof." Upon receiving it Bragg of course read the
endorsement in pencil which Scott had not noticed, and very coolly
wrote to Genl Jones informing him that after reflecting upon the matter he (Bragg) *had finally concluded to accept his (Jones) apology.*
Probably he received some sharp reply for he disliked Jones exceedingly and succeeded in giving him some more hits without being
hauled up for it. For instance once when a man was being tried for
desertion, Bragg was called on as a witness. He testified that the man
was not a deserter and would have been discharged from the army
long ago had it not been for the extraordinary stupidity of R. Jones
Adj Genl. U. S. Army. As this was said under oath as a witness before

a court Jones could not arrest him for the remark. He seemed to like quarrelling with his commanders. Once at Old Point [Comfort] General Eustis who was in command was making what is called the Grand Rounds at midnight. Bragg was officer of the guard and of course could not by rule and custom recognize Eustis until the latter had given the "*parole*", the secret word which shows he is entitled to command. Eustis forgot and called to Bragg to bring his men to present arms. Bragg replied, "Dont you dare sir to give me any orders until you have given the *parole*. If you do I will put you in the guard house!" This was rough for the general, but as law and regulation were on the side of Bragg he was forced to submit. It is needless to say that Bragg walked a very straight course after that so as not to give the general a chance to overhaul him.

In February 1845 I was promoted to be a second lieutenant in the First Regiment of Artillery and assigned to Company A at Fort Preble, Portland, Maine.[45] The contrast in climate was very great between that city and Charleston and the habits of the people were not less so. As all manual labor was done by slaves the inhabitants of South Carolina always seemed to be at leisure whereas in Maine every one seemed occupied. During the summer months I do not remember more than twenty days when thin clothing could be worn without discomfort. The appearance of everything about the post denoted the severity of the winters. All the windows were double and outhouses were provided for wood and coal where they could be reached without exposure. These northern latitudes differed very much from the south as regards the length of the twilight. After leaving Florida for Eastport, Maine, Lieut Colonel Childs gave the usual order that at the latter place reveille should be beaten at dawn of day. He was surprised to see all the men yawning and stretching and said to the First sergeant, "Haven't the men had enough sleep." "No sir," replied the latter, "I dont think they have." "Did not the reveille sound as usual at dawn of day, Sergeant?" inquired the Colonel. "Yes sir," was the answer, "but dawn of day comes here about 2 o'clock in the morning."

It is not perhaps remarkable that the long winters and severe weather should force people to remain in doors most of the time. This leads naturally to the use of books to pass away the time. At all events this is my explanation of the great reputation for literature that Portland has always enjoyed. Quite a brilliant coterie was always to be met at Mrs Little's hospitable mansion, for I believe she was universally recognized as the highest social authority in the place. Longfellow, Willis Seba Smith,[46] and John Neal[47] were among the celebrities associated with Portland in that day. As for Longfellow it was interesting to see the affection manifested for him by all his townsmen. They always spoke of him as Henry and his name was evidently a household word there.

Some two or three years before I joined the army the North Eastern boundary dispute arose with Great Britain and there was for a short time danger of a collision. Troops were hurried to Maine and posted on the frontier there in considerable numbers. An officer at the most distant station in the far north asked for a leave of absence to enable him "to go as far south as Quebec." The authorities at Washington could not believe we had a post of the regular army north of Quebec, but a glance at the map satisfied them of the correctness of the application.

When the international question was settled the British officers who were in New Brunswick and Canada became quite friendly and sociable and gave our officers some handsome dinners. Many of the British officers were younger sons of the nobility. The dinner services were radiant with costly gold and silver dishes for the messes having been established for a great many years had been the recipients of many costly presents of plate. Fancy the annoyance of our officers who had just come out of Florida and had nothing but cheap crockery to display. The attentions received had to be returned but there was a good deal of pride about the matter. In one case at Plattsburg I think the subject was discussed and Magruder[48] who was a leading spirit in our regiment at that time, told the mess to leave it to him. They did so and he borrowed on pledges, a goodly lot of plate from New York and added to it all the silver and gold dishes he could find in Plattsburg. He then gave a grand entertainment to the British officers and apologised for the poor show he made *on the ground that the regiment were just from Florida and the regimental plate had not yet arrived.* When he was asked by one of the officers what his pay was, he played the magnifico by replying, "My dear fellow, I have not the slightest idea. I always give it to my servant."

Portland is environed by beautiful scenery and the numerous islands in the harbor are gems of beauty. But the climate is too rigorous and the heavy fogs are so frequent that they are a great drawback to the place.

In the summer of 1845 there came from far off Mexico a note of arrogance and menace, and a refusal to recognize the right of Texas to form an alliance with the United States. Troops were at once hurried from all the northern seaboard to Governor's Island with a view to embark from there to reach their ultimate destination on the Texas frontier. The order soon reached us at Fort Preble and on the [date left blank] we reached the rendezvous at Fort Columbus where we found several regiments and detachments already assembled. There was much enthusiasm among us at the prospect of active service and the same devoted patriotism was displayed that had illumined the nation in its previous conflicts when young Washington met Lord Howe in 17 [blank]....

We set sail in the U. S. Store Ship *Lexington* commanded by Lieutenant Frank Elison, U. S. Navy on the [date left blank] of August, 1845 for the coast of Texas. The voyage under canvas was long and tedious nearly a month being consumed on the way. Our progress was enlivened by various amusements such as chess, cards, and a glee club was organized by M[agruder]. who was a very [good] singer himself. This was not the least of his accomplishments for he was noted for his conviviality and the anecdotes with which he entertained us at the dinner table when the cloth had been removed and the wine and cigars made their appearance. As he subsequentally became a very distinguished general in the Confederate service his characteristics have some historical value and I am tempted to give a speciman narrative, although the reader may consider it too trivial for a work of this nature. When it was decided to consider the Florida War with the Seminoles at an end, the artillery regiments which had been acting as infantry, were sent back to their usual posts on the seaboard. Charleston harbor was heavily garrisoned and M. was ordered there with his company to report to General Eustis who was in command. The order was obeyed with alacrity for the troops, who had been so long absent from civilization tramping among the pine and wading through swamps and everglades of Florida, were only too happy to share the gaieties and refinement of Charleston society. Immediately after his arrival M. determined to have one civilized meal as a contrast to the pork and hard tack which the government so liberally supplies to the troops in the field. He went to Lee's Hotel which was a kind of restaurant kept by a noted colored caterer who was celebrated for his skill in cuisine. The dinner was placed on the table the wine was uncorked and M. was about to enjoy himself. Unfortunately he was not on the best terms with his commanding officer and this possibly may explain the fact that he never partook of that meal. He had hardly seated himself at the table when there came a sharp rap at the door and an orderly appeared with an official communication from General Eustis directing M. to immediately return to Fort Jupiter, Florida, and temporarily assume command of the post there. The pretext for this was, that the young officer at that place, having just graduated at West Point, and never having previously been in command of troops, was too inexperienced to break up the post and dispose of the public property there. The moment M. read this terrible missive he rushed over to General Eustis' headquarters to cause the order to be revoked, if possible. He stated his case to the general who heard him unmoved and then simply said, "Sir, you will go!" M. told us that he displayed "the courtesy of a gentleman and the patience of a Christian by leaving the room in silence." Upon reaching Fort Jupiter the first question M. put to the officer in command was, whether there were any good officers in the vicinity. The young lieutenant replied that he did not know; that he had been very busy drilling the men and endeavoring to increase their efficiency. M. told us that he stopped all military exercises at once: "too much drilling you know injures the men," and set the whole command looking for oysters. Their quest was successful, and life became tolerable for a time. The next question was how to get away from the place comfortably. There was a miserable sloop there and that seemed to be the only mode of transit. M. had a strong desire to visit Cuba and now that he was in the vicinity he decided that the water at the post was unwholesome and he would take the sloop and run over to Havana to procure a proper supply for the voyage. He did not remain there long for although he registered his name as Genl. M., U. S. Army, and wore a fancy uniform, he did not receive any special attention from the magnates of the island. He ascertained too that there was an ugly law there authorising the detention of any foreigner who had contracted debts to the natives, until they were paid in full. As M's supply of cash was short he watched each days expenditures with a jealous eye and when his exchequer was nearly exhausted, left abruptly, and returned to his post. There he found a fine new steamer on a trial trip from Savannah which had entered the harbor for a supply of wood. M. offered the captain all the cut wood at the post to take him and his command as far as Jacksonville and the offer was accepted. M. remained at Jacksonville a few days and by one judicious entertainment to which some prominent citizens and the officers of the revenue cutter were invited, he succeeded in obtaining several excellent dinners in return. When these courtesies were exhausted he chartered a steamer and left for Savannah. As his party were going out of the harbor, they passed the revenue cutter the yards of which were manned to salute him. Unfortunately the steamer passed too near the vessel and carried away the bowsprit. The sailors rapidly tumbled down from the yards to repair damages. M. stood by the side of the pilot bowing profoundly towards the cutter with one hand on his heart, and shaking his fist with the other at the pilot to indicate that it was all his fault. The latter assumed a high tone, said he was a free citizen of Georgia and demanded to be put on shore. M. had him tied to the wheel and threatened to give him fifty lashes if he did not bring them safely in Savannah. When they arrived there M. still kept him in duresse until he could get all his men on board the Charleston boat. When this was effected and he was sure the man could not have time to swear out a warrant against him, he ordered him to be released. Upon reaching Moultrieville,[49] M. met General Eustis on his way to the wharf, formed his men and saluted him. The general made no remark. Thus the expedition ended.

2

THE FIRST SHOTS OF THE MEXICAN WAR

In 1821 Mexico invited colonists from the United States to settle in Texas. This may seem strange to those who like myself have lived among the Mexicans and know their deep rooted dislike to foreigners. The latter were always spoken of contemptuously as "gringos" from the verb geringar; meaning people who talk gibberish. This feeling was increased in regard to the Americans by the fact that nearly all of them were looked upon as heretics. Even since the period referred to and until recently our people were subjected to incessant robberies and personal indignities, for which they have never been able to obtain redress of any kind. Nevertheless the scant population of Texas and the fact that it was fast becoming depopulated from the incursions of the Comache, Kioways, Kickapoos, and other nomadic tribes finally induced the Mexican government to favor emigration from the United States as a barrier against the inroads of savages. But the American colonists who responded to this invitation under Stephen Austin soon had reason to regret their action. They had always had rights and were accustomed to see them respected. They were not prepared therefore to acquiesce in the military usurpations which were so prominent a feature in Mexican politics. The agent sent by them to the seat of government to remonstrate was seized and imprisoned, the territorial legislature was dissolved at the point of the bayonet, and orders were issued to the military com-

BV Doubleday, Abner. Chapters II and III of "My Military Biography, Including the Fall of Monterey."

mandant on the frontier of Texas to disarm the colonists, who were
looked upon with great jealousy by the military satraps in power.
There could be but one answer to such proceedings; the emigrants
flew to arms and in 1836 won their independence at the final battle
of San Jacinto in which [left blank] men under Genl Sam Houston
routed an army of [left blank] thousand commanded in person by
Santa Anna the virtual dictator of Mexico and captured him. To
obtain his release from confinement he signed a treaty guaranteeing
the independence of Texas but the Mexican government refused to
acknowledge or ratify it. Subsequently there were two raids into
Texas, one in 1837 and the other in 1843 with a view to reconquer
the country but both were failures as Texas was constantly increasing
in population and resources, there was but little probability that
Mexico could ever regain her lost supremacy. Nevertheless she
refused to acknowledge the independence of the new republic except
on condition that she would not annex herself to any other power
and to this the Texa[n]s as a matter of course would not agree; for
they had been nearly all citizens of the United States and were very
desirous of returning to the benignant rule to which they were accustomed. Congress at first refused to receive the new state into the
Union, but finally in 1845 in spite of the threats of Mexico, Texas was
formally annexed. There was bitter hostility and with reason against
this movement by the anti-slavery party of the United States who
thus saw a region as large as all New England added to the pro-slav-
ery territory of the country. As Mexico threatened reprisals it became
necessary at once to protect the new acquisition by sending a force to
the border. The small Army of Occupation thus formed consisted
entirely of regulars under Major General Zachary Taylor who had
won renown when quite a youth in contending against the British in
the War of 1812, and in the hostilities which terminated the contest
with the Seminole Indians in Florida. Our army was so diminutive
and widely scattered over the western frontier engaged in holding the
savages in check that it was no easy task to raise even 2000 soldiers.
By vacating a number of posts and by stripping the forts on the
seaboard of troops this was finally accomplished. General Taylor land-

ed his men at St. Josephs Island on the coast of Texas. From thence they were conveyed in lighters up the shallow bay to Corpus Christi at the mouth of the Nueces. The question at the time whether this or the Rio Grande was the true boundary of Texas was left to our minister who still remained negociating in the City of Mexico. President Herrera seemed willing to submit the actions of the United States to diplomacy but the people were not with him. He was obliged in the spring of 1846 to dismiss our minister without a hearing.

Even this concession was not sufficient to satisy the Mexican people. Herrera's administration was overthrown and the war party under Genl Paredes held the reins of power. This interval from the occupation of Corpus Christi by our army to the change of government in Mexico was passed by Genl Taylors force at Corpus Christi. The moment however that it became manifest that no boundary could be named that would be satisfactory to Mexico Genl Taylor received orders to advance to the Rio Grande, that claimed by Texas, and defend it if necessary against any advance the Mexicans might make. In stating these facts I have of course anticipated the course of events and now resume my personal narrative....

Our voyage was without special incident. We kept up as far as possible on ship board all the usual parades and inspections. Once there was a slight clash in the official routine. One day when I was on duty as officer of the guard all the drums and fifes were beating reveille together. A storm was coming up and the officer of the deck ordered that d____d noise stopped as the sailors could not hear his orders. Major Dimick [sic][1] who was executive officer for Colonel Erving[2] rushed on deck to know the reason why the usual calls were cut short and I explained the situation to him but he did not seem fully satisfied. We passed the Hole in the Wall at Abaso floated over the rose tinted sea bottomed with coral off Nassau, entered the Gulf of Mexico and in a few days reached our destination at Aransas Bay, Texas. We soon landed at Saint Joseph's Island. From there we were taken on steamers of small draft by the shallow inland passage at Corpus Christi at the mouth of the Nueces River, where the "Army of Occupation," as it was called, was stationed under General Zachary Taylor.

As the object was to defend Texas against invasion and as the authorities there claimed the Rio Grande as the true boundary line it may excite some surprise that we did not march there at once. General Taylor would probably have done so had not the Mexican President Herrera agreed to receive an American minister in Mexico. The latter had instructions from our government to negotiate the question of boundary for in truth there seemed to be a legitimate doubt as to whether the Nueces was not the true dividing line instead of the Rio Grande. The point proved to be of little consequence for the war party in Mexico triumphed. Herrera's administration was overthrown, our minister was sent home without a hearing and Mexico claimed the whole of Texas. These events however were not fully consummated before the early part of 1846; so that our army wasted all winter at Corpus Christi without making a movement of any kind.

There were about 2000 regulars assembled there; all that could be spared from our small army. They came from all parts of the country for owing to our long line of sea board and extensive frontier the troops were scattered everywhere in small detachments. This concentration was new to us and advantage was taken of it to instruct us in military evolutions on a large scale instead of the company and battalion drills to which we were accustomed. The force was divided into two brigades[3] one under Brg. Genl. William Worth and the other under Colonel David E. Twiggs[4] of the 2d Dragoons. Captain Porters company to which I belonged to Lieut Colonel Childs battalion [was] formed of eight companies from the different artillery regiments in service.

The officers of the army were now brought together with opportunities to acquire a knowledge of the service and of each other which had never before occurred. This gave rise to much emulation and esprit-de-corps which subsequently became a powerful impelling motive for noble deeds and heroism.

I fear our two brigade commanders were not very friendly to each other, one incident took place which might have been attended with serious results. A sentinel of Worths brigade was somewhat intoxicated and wandered from his beat. The officer of the Day of Twiggs brigade put him in the guard tent there instead of remanding him to the custody of his own officers. Genl. Worth was very much incensed at this and directed our officer of the Day to demand the man at once and if he was not surrendered to turn out the whole command if necessary and take him by force. The officer like a sensible man told the other officer of the day quietly that he had made a mistake and the man was sent back with an apology.

Soon after our arrival the question of brevet rank came up and created much feeling. Indeed it might easily have resulted in the partial disorganization of the army. Brevet rank at that time took place solely on detachments composed of different arms of service. Some officers who had brevets asserted that the artillery battalion being composed of different regiments came under the rule. Bvt. Lt Col. Childs took this view of it and directed some lieutenants who had brevets to assume command over their own captains. The latter sheathed their swords and walked off the parade. As it was evident that the enforcement of the order would create a mutiny the matter was finally referred to the authorities at Washington for decision. There General Scott stood up strongly for brevet rank but the Secretary of War held the contrary view. The great majority of officers holding no brevets were strongly opposed to the exercise of any increased powers in that direction.

Officers are directed by the President of the U. S. to obey all *lawful* orders of their superiors. Unlawful orders may be and sometimes are disregarded. If for instance a soldier was ordered by his commander to rob or kill a peaceful citizen he would be tried for the offence and the order could not be pleaded in justification. He would inevitably suffer the penalty. The officers who refused to obey Lt Col Childs command in relation to brevet rank did so on the ground of its illegality.

The Mexican army being largely composed of cavalry and a collision more than probable, our infantry were constantly drilled in forming square to resist cavalry. Discipline was strictly enforced and all disorderly conduct promptly punished. I remember one case which excited a good deal of attention at the time. A young officer named R was arrested by Colonel Twiggs and tried[5] for violating the [7th?] commandment in his tent. The Colonel was far from being a purist and did not care how many liasons his officers had outside the lines but within the encampment it was a very different matter. The offender in this case might possibly have escaped with a light punishment had he not committed the mistake of making a bitter personal attack through his counsel at his commander and fellow officers of the 2nd Dragoons. He was defended by a young Ordnance officer who prided himself on giving hard hits, and this ruined his client. The language of the defense was so extraordinary that I am tempted to give a few paragraphs from it as a speciman of juvenile eloquence.

"But gentlemen to show you how amusingly preposterous the facts set forth in this specification are considered throughout the dragoon camp from its commanding officer downwards, to show you that in the eyes of that immaculate individual the magnitude of the crime is made to consist solely in the smallness of the offence let us turn for a moment to the evidence upon your records.

Comment upon such facts is unnecessary. They exhibit the poisoned venom, the atrocious perfidy, the unmatched wickedness which have conspired in this prosecution as plainly as if written by a sun beam.

Yet with these examples staring him in the face, surrounding him in the hours of duty and of relaxation; visible to him at mid day and palpable to him in the hours of darkness, the immaculate purity of that individual is outraged by a solitary impropriety upon which the vigor and the vengeance of the laws.

Such was the school in which my practical military life commenced and such was the character of my instructor. It was in scenes like these that my principles have been tried, and it was through such a fiery ordeal of burning ploughshares that whatever virtue I possessed when I left the Military Academy was compelled to pass. I feel that I have not escaped from the trial unscathed.

I would fain hope gentlemen that this trial might have a beneficial effect present and prospective upon the regiment and its living impersonation; and if divesting himself of the decency that would avoid a disreputable action, he had retained the delicacy which would be ashamed of it; or if the blush of reproach could pierce the enamel of hoary profligacy or veteran vice, which nearly three score years of demoralization have fastened upon the furrowed visage of the commanding officer, perhaps a dim consciousness of guilt would glance athwart his countenance at the present exposure of his character and give him one moment of exquisite remorse. He might then retire from a station he never adorned, and abandon a profession to which he is no ornament. But in his bosom I fear there is no throb of pity; no pulsation of regret, no sensibility to reproach and no possible consciousness of shame. I leave with you gentlemen to denounce the author and executor of the crimes I have mentioned as he deserves. I have no doubt that if you have in your vocabulary any single epithet—any little syllabic formation—that will express with comprehensive brevity, the concentrated hatred and infuriate malignity of a thousand devils linked to a human form and a fiends propensities you will give the benefit of its application to the grand molock, the sovereign prince, the recognized governor of this modem pandemonium."

The latter clause was of course intended to represent the 2d Dragoons.

It is needless to remark that the council who wrote this defence was not serving in Twiggs' brigade and therefore not amenable to his authority.

The troops in addition to their drills and parades were busily engaged in fortifying their lines of tents not against an enemy but to shelter themselves from the bitter blasts which came from the north. No person who has never been in that region can appreciate the force and severity of a Texas norther. The change in temperature which sometimes occurs in the course of twenty minutes is incredible. Often while taking a siesta in consequence of the tropical heat which prevailed I have heard the roar of an approaching tempest. I would hardly

"A man of my well known virtue...."

have time to call to the men to come with axes to drive down my tent pins and hold the poles before the icy blast would be upon us. In fifteen minutes perhaps the rain would be hanging in icicles from all the bushes in the vicinity. Stoves and camp fires would be an immediate necessity. The storm would rage for three days and then all would be serene again. Not infrequently trains caught on the plains in these fierce winds where there is no fuel would be obliged to burn their wagons to keep themselves from freezing.

As I stated negociations were going on or it was supposed they were going on in Mexico as we had a minister there in relation to the boundary: so we remained quiescent at Corpus Christi until the result should be made known. To while away the time M. who was very enterprising in the way of providing amusement, sent for a theatrical company[6] who came on and gave some performances which were well patronized. I remarked to the star actress who took the principal parts that I was afraid she would find her surrounding rather uninteresting as there were not much beauty about a military camp and she must be an admirer of beauty to which she replied: "I adore beauty whether depictured in the flowing canvas or the lifeless marble!" As it was too great a strain on my intellectual powers to keep up much conversation of this character I did not attempt it. Just before the first performance was to take place M. told me he was going over to inspect the dressing rooms to see that all was right there. He added, "You look surprised Sir! A man of my well known virtue and morality can go any where. All doors are open to him." I learned afterwards that he returned from his expedition in a damaged condition. His coat was nearly torn off his back and his face was seamed with scratches, so that evidently some slight misunderstanding had occurred[7].

Our company did not remain at Corpus Christi for any great length of time. Captain Porter's[8] rank was such as to entitle him to a higher command than they cared to give him and we were sent back to St. Joseph's Island to guard the stores and public property there.

Before we left a body of Tonkaway Indians[9] came in to see General Taylor. They were wretched looking beings and I could well believe the Texan statement that they were all cannibals. Hunters who came upon their old camps asserted that they often found the half eaten bodies of the enemies they had killed. They were all mounted on mustangs,[10] or wild horses which they had tamed. A number of these were brought in for sale to our officers for the country was overrun with them in those days. The animals went in herds under regular leaders. They were very small in comparison with our American horses but were easily run down and lassoed by the Texans who offered them to us at two dollars and a half a piece. They proved to be very serviceable but were apt to break the bridle and dash off at the slightest alarm. The Texans, when their animals escaped in this way would follow them until they stopped to feed, and then were frequently able to "*crease them*" as it was called. That is, put a shot through the neck near the spinal marrow. This would temporarily paralyze them without occassioning a permanent disability. Owing to their cheapness General Jesup, Quartermaster General of the Army, wished Lieut Bragg who had applied for artillery horses to be sent him from New Orleans to take these animals in stead alleging that it would be a great saving of expense in as much as it was said they were able to live on the mesquit grass of the country to which Bragg replied that it was a beautiful example of the goodness of Providence in giving these animals the power of living upon grass since they had not strength enough to draw their own forage.[11] This was the same Bragg who gained our renown in the Battle of Buena Vista and who subsequently became a distinguished general in the Confederate service.

Speaking of Indians we had a Lipan boy for a short time to wait on our mess. His mode of announcing meals was "*Hey! Dinner!*" I believe he soon left us and ran off to his native wilds.

Corpus Christi must have been a charming place for people who dislike the restraints of civilization.[12] Before our arrival there was no law there but that of the Bowie knife and pistol. In fact, most of the inhabitants had fled in the first place from the United States to Texas on account of the crimes they had committed for the Lone Star State about that time became the refuge for a great many criminals. Questions concerning a man's antecedents were thought to be in very bad taste there. Now the inhabitants of Corpus Christi were generally

men who had found even the license of Texas too much for them.
They had therefore after committing fresh offenses fled to the frontier.
One of our officers remarked to me one day "Isn't it strange that every
gentleman to whom I have been introduced here has murdered some
body?" Another who went to a barber shop which had been opened
for the accomodation of the army heard a man remark. "Has Tom got
even with Bill yet?" The other replied, "Tom hasnt a bit of sense. He
fired at Bill right in the midst of a crowd of people, missed him, then
broke and ran for the chapperal. He might have waylaid him in fifty
places on his way home, but now he wont have much chance."

There was a Colonel Cook[13] residing in Corpus Christi at this
time. To settle some political question, he had shot his antagonist
while the latter was in the custody of the sheriff; hence his enforced
banishment to Corpus Christi. His house had once been beset by
Indians and after they had retired beyond rifle shot he astonished
them very much by sending a ball from a cannon into the midst of
them. He fired "his wagon" at them as they expressed it and did considerable execution. He was very polite and hospitable towards the
army. Once Charley May[14] then a lieutenant of Dragoons who afterwards gained much celebrity by the capture of the Mexican Colonel
La Vega, was invited to dine with him. It is said that May found a motley crowd of emigrants assembled who were probably all fugitives from
justice. Each man ate in silence with his revolver handy and a double
barreled gun between his legs. One of the party took offense at something May said and snapped his pistol twice at him but the percussion
cap did not go off. Other parties interfered, the assailant was convinced of his error and duly apologized but May himself became also
taciturn for the remainder of the dinner and it is needless to say was
glad when the festivities were over.

When we reached Saint Joseph's Island I found a much easier life
[than] before, as the greater part of the men were required for guard
duty to protect the extensive store houses of the army there was little
opportunity for the constant drills and camp exercises which took up
our time at Corpus Christi. As this was in the early days of Texas the
coast line was but thinly settled and I believe only two or three fami-

lies resided on the island, and these led a pretty wild life for wild animals and Indians were frequent visitors. Several of the latter claiming to belong to a friendly tribe came to one of these houses and begged for every thing they saw. The men were out hunting at the time and the wife of the settler was alone with her children. She gave up nearly all the food she had but at last seeing that the family would be left destitute of supplies, she got over the fear, refused to let them have anything more, and sternly ordered them to leave the premises. They went off grumbling but did not molest her.

There was an abundance of game on the island, deer, snipe quail, etc., and I occasionally took a small rifle I had, and went up the beach to shoot at the snipe quail etc. This occupation was not wholly unattended with danger for there was a species of tiger[15] roaming about the eastern part of Texas which was striped like the Asiatic animal but was smaller and less ferocious. Several of these had been killed by our hunters. On one of my excursions I came upon a kind of cave in the sand hills which was evidently the residence of one of these animals. The menagerie smell was unmistakeable and the bones lying around were very suggestive. As my gun was of very small caliber and merely fit for snipe shooting I did not await his lordship's return but made my way leisurely back to camp. It was getting dark and I had about three miles to walk. Great numbers of coyotes (little wolves) followed me, but as they are harmless, I paid no attention to their yelpings and howlings. Occasionally however a larger and more dangerous wolf is found among them. After getting some supper I went to my tent. It was quite dark and I unexpectedly found myself advancing on a large grey wolf[16] who stood at the entrance. He gnashed his teeth in a very suggestive manner and went off slowly; evidently doubtful as to the propriety of making an attack. It was useless to allow the sentinels to fire at these animals for the fusillade would be incessant and dangerous to soldiers who might happen to be in the vicinity.

At last the winter was over and on the approach of spring as every effort at negociation had failed, and the Mexican president Herrera, after agreeing to receive our ministers had, in obedience to popular clamor refused to recognize him. Our government took the decisive step of ordering our army to march to the Rio Grande. This was virtually taking possession of territory over which Texas should not have attempted to exercise jurisdiction. It was however the boundary claimed by the authorities of that state and as Mexico would not treat with us on any other terms than those of a complete abandonment of the whole country and a resumption of the old frontier at the Sabine the boundary question was of little consequence. Our people too labored under the delusion that the Rio Grande being a thousand miles long must form near its mouth a deep and wide line of defence and that it would be good policy to take possession of it as soon as possible. In reality it can be forded at a great many points during the dry season, and its convolutions are so remarkable that in a line of twenty five miles from Brownsville to the mouth of the river the distance is more than a hundred miles by water.

The only place where resistance might have been effectual against General Taylor's advance on Matamoros was at the Arroyo Colorado, a salt water lagoon which was about a hundred yards in width and barely fordable. Some Mexican cavalry did appear there and in the name of General Mexia the Commandant of that district announced that the passage of the lagoon would be treated as an act of war. Our troops however rushed forward with enthusiasm preceded by the skirmishers under Captain C. F. Smith[17] our former commandant at West Point who having taught war in theory was now prepared to demonstrate it practically to his former pupils. Contrary to all expectation the enemy made no resistance and our troops continued on their way. The base of supplies had been established at Point Isabel[18] in the Bay of St. Iago about twenty five miles from Matamoros.[19] General Taylor ended his march at a point about half way between the two places so as to cover his depots and threaten the city at the same time. Two companies under Captain and Brevet Major Jock Munro[20] of the 4th Artillery, his own, and Captain Porter's company of the First Artillery to which I belonged were sent to Point Isabel to guard the supplies there. We went by water while the main army marched across the country.

Although Mexico had resolved on war her system of forced loans and conscription proved to be a very slow and inefficient means of raising men and supplies and when Genl Taylor arrived on the Rio Grande her forces were not ready to take the field. There was therefore no immediate opposition to the advance of our troops. Ampudia, however was on his way from Monterey with an army to meet us.

Finding his depots were safe Genl Taylor took position on the bank of the river opposite Matamoros, threw up a large earthwork and awaited results. The first American flag was raised there by Colonel Belknap of the 8th Infantry on a pole cut out from a mesquite tree.

A motley crowd of sutlers with their clerks, camp followers, quartermaster's employees, and sailors now poured into Point Isabel and all the stores for the army were sent there. At first there was great confusion and some apprehension for it was thought possible that the enemy might steal a march on General Taylor cross the river below him and assail our position. Block houses were built on the ridge as citadels, a weak ditch dug and an embankment thrown up around the place. Where it is supposed that a place may be attacked there is sure to occur many false alarms. One of those is quite vividly impressed upon my memory. I was standing on the ridge by the side of Major Munro looking landward, for it was rumored that a detachment of Mexican cavalry had crossed the river and was going to make a dash at our depot. The major saw some movement in the road in the far distance and handed me his spy glass saying look and tell me what you see. I did so and replied, "I see some of our wagons coming in at a fast trot, now they have broken into a gallop." All the cattle out grazing and the cattle guards are alarmed and are making for the fort at full speed. The major turned around and called quickly to the drummers of the guard, "Beat the long roll at once!" When the alarm was heard there was great excitement. The two regular companies were rapidly formed in line and marched to the posts designated for them. Then the sutler's clerks and laborers were organized under a leader and were placed along the parapet. Then came the quartermasters employees. An officer of my regiment, Lieut Fowler[21] was just entering the harbor in a steamer. As soon as it came to an anchor he collected a body of sailors came in and reported with them. Lieut McPhail[22] of the [5th] Infantry who had just landed with a detachment of recruits made a stirring speech to them commencing, "Now is the time to show yourself men!" He then waved his sword and led them to the parapet.

The cavalry which had caused all this excitement proved to be Captain May's squadron of the 2d U. S. Dragoons who were returning from a reconnaissance.

The next day I went out hunting. When I was about two miles from the work I saw what appeared to be a company of Mexican cavalry with their serapes wrapped around them trotting leisurely along. To my great disgust I found they were between me and the fort and I was about to wade a wide lagoon to get away from them when they passed on. They were really a company of Texan scouts under Captain Walker and were dressed in Mexican costume to enable them to reconnoitre nearer to the enemies force without exciting suspicion.

After the alarm I have mentioned we set to work at the intrenchments with renewed vigor. All laborers and citizens who happened to be present were forced by our stern provost marshall Col. C.[23] of St. Louis to take a pick or spade and aid in deepening the ditches. The Colonel could not be charged with either inefficiency or lack of zeal. As I approached one part of the lines to inspect progress as officer of the Day the Colonel reported one luckless artist who had come on from New Orleans to make sketches, for mutiny. The man attempted to remonstrate but the Colonel replied, "You know, you scoundrel that you stopped work and refused to go on *until I gave positive orders to the guard to shoot you.*" I thought this was enforcing discipline with a vengeance.

Although the enemies main army had not arrived, predatory bands were roaming the country and lurking in the thickets, so that several untoward events occurred. Colonel Trueman Cross, Quartermaster General, having uncautiously rode out on the 10th of April a few miles from camp, was murdered.[24] Two parties of twelve men each [were] sent in different directions to look for him. One of these captured a Mexican camp but was waylaid by a large force on the way home, and the commander, Lieut Porter,[25] and one of his men were killed.

On the 12th, Genl Ampudia[26] sent an insolent message to Genl Taylor directing him to break up his camp and immediately return to the Nueces, threatening to drive him away in case of refusal.

On the 25th of April, General Taylor learned that 2500 Mexicans had crossed the river above and sent Captain Thornton[27] with a squadron of the 2nd Dragoons to reconnoitre in that direction while another squadron under Captain Ker[28] examined the crossings below Matamoros. Thornton's command met with a serious misadventure. He had proceeded a considerable distance without encountering any enemy. Coming to a farm house in an open space fenced around with logs stuck perpendicularly in the ground and surrounded with thickets he rode forward to question the inhabitants; intending that his command should remain outside the enclosure. Unfortunately, his orders were misunderstood and the entire squadron passed through the gate after him. About 1200 Mexican infantry suddenly surrounded the enclosure and opened fire upon the cavalry which had been thus entrapped. Thornton found a place in the fence lower than the general line of pickets and leaped over calling upon the others to follow him. His horse fell as he struck the other side and Thornton was made prisoner. Capt Hardee[29] of the same regiment now assumed the command and led his troop to the bank of the river which bounded one side of the enclosure with a view to swim the stream: but he found the ground so boggy that he was unable to do so. He therefore surrendered the entire command.

Captain Deas[30] of the 4th Artillery whose mind was somewhat affected swam the river and was made prisoner. He said he went over to reconnoitre on his own account. Genl Taylor was very much displeased and afterwards refused to exchange him. He was finally released by the Mexicans on their own accord.

On the 24th General Arista arrived in Matamoros and assumed command of the Mexican Army.

On the 28th, Captain Walker with his company of Texas rangers went out on a reconnaissance and captured a Mexican camp. On his return he was attacked by a large force[31] and lost a considerable portion of his command.

The new work opposite Matamoros was styled Fort Texas.[32] It was completed by the 1st of May and garrisoned with 600 men of the 7th Infantry and two light batteries under Lieut Bragg and Captain Lowd[33]; the whole being under the command of Major Brown[34] of the 7th Infantry. Leaving this force to hold the fort, Genl Taylor marched with the remainder of the army to Point Isabel. The Mexicans were highly elated at this apparent retreat and Arista complained that the Americans fled before he could get at them.

A heavy bombardment was at once opened against Fort Texas but the garrison stood firm and the enemy were unable to reduce the place. We heard the guns plainly at Point Isabel but the sound did not disturb the equanimity of our commander in the least.

The gallant Texan Captain Walker offered to make his way alone into the beleagured fort, ascertain the condition of affairs there and return. In spite of all dangers and obstacles he succeeded in executing his daring project.

Genl Taylor was dissatisfied with the weak intrenchments at Point Isabel and put all his forces in the trenches to deepen and widen the ditches. When this was accomplished he learned that a Mexican army of about 7000 men had interposed between him and Fort Texas and were now posted in order of battle at a place called Palo Alto (High Timber), about halfway between Point Isabel and Matamoros. He started on the 7th of May to meet them and halted that night about seven miles from Point Isabel.

The next morning he resumed the march after throwing up an entrenchment to cover his wagon train and leaving a squadron of cavalry to guard it. He soon came in sight of the enemy. The day was bright and fair and the Mexican army with its numerous banners shown resplendent in the sunlight. Their long lines of infantry with artillery in the intervals and cavalry massed on the flanks presented a very formidable appearance. To obtain a more critical view of their line of battle a daring personal reconnaissance was made by Lieut Blake[35] of the Topographical Engineers who rode along and quite near the entire front of their army, making accurate notes of their positions and estimates of their numbers. He gained great reputation by this feat but alas for the vanity of earthly fame. The night after the battle when taking off his revolver he accidentally shot himself and died almost immediately.

Genl Taylor at first formed with the right thrown back and resting on some ponds, and his left strengthened with his cavalry and artillery. He soon however brought forward his right to protect it by a piece of marshy ground in front of that flank; the ponds being a little to the rear of it. This made his line nearly parallel to that of the enemy. In this position he awaited the onset.

The Mexicans soon opened fire with their clumsy artillery. As no iron mines at that time were known in Mexico they used copper balls. The verdigris on these doubtless made them more deadly for the wounded. They did very little execution however as our men were directed to lie down and these missiles went over their heads. This fire was immediately answered by Ringgold's and Duncan's light batteries which rode close to the enemys lines for that purpose. Lieut Churchill,[36] too, of the 3d Artillery was in command of two long eighteen pounders guns which sent balls with deadly effect away back into the Mexican reserves. Tired of enduring this cannonade Torrejon's lancers asked to be led to the charge and advanced gallantly to charge the right flank.

The first news of this movement was brought to Genl Taylor by a Hungarian who for some time appeared unable to make himself understood in any known language. He kept repeating, "De Mexican, De Mexican," and pointing in the direction of Torrejon who was concealed by the intervening shrubbery. Col. Bliss, Genl Taylor's Adjutant Genl, fortunately understood German and the man knew enough of it to inform him that the Mexican cavalry was charging that flank. Genl Taylor said calmly, "I expected that!" and quietly said to Colonel McIntosh[37] who was on the extreme right, "Form your regiment against cavalry."

More than thirty years had passed since the Army of the United States had been drawn up in battle array to resist a civilized enemy.

This long silence was now broken by the clear ringing voices of McIntosh as he gave the command, "Fifth Infantry! Form Square!" The movement was executed as if on parade. "Fifth Infantry! Load at Will! Load! Fifth Infantry, Ready!" As Torrejon came on he was exposed to the fire of two sides of this square aided by a section of Ringgold's battery at the angles, under Lieut Ridgely[38] and by that of Capt Walkers Texan rangers. This was too severe for the enemy, instead of advancing they halted within 40 yards to return the fire but this spasmodic fusilade was almost wholly ineffective. They soon gave this up however and retreated in disorder. They subsequently attempted a charge on the left flank but were easily repulsed there by Colonel Belknap with the 8th Infantry aided by Duncan's light battery and Captain Ker's squadron of dragoons.

With the exception of one or two abortive attempts to gain our flanks which were met by counter movements, the remainder of the battle was simply reduced to a distant cannonade. When night came our army which had steadily advanced had gained nearly a mile on the enemy who retired before them. Towards the close of the action the Mexican artillery instead of being directed at our line generally as heretofore was concentrated against Ringgold's battery and Churchill's 18 pounders. One of the last shots struck Major Ringgold just above the knee cut out a piece of the right leg and twisted the pummel of the saddle so as to cause a similar wound on the left thigh. The disabled hero was transferred to Point Isabel for treatment. It is said he was not aware of the fatal nature of his injury and upon asking how long he had to live he expected an answer telling him he was in no danger. But the doctor to his surprise replied, "About an hour!" "Great God doctor!" he said, "Is that so." The latter answered "You cannot possibly live two hours!" He then made his will and died with calmness and resignation.

Another distressing wound was that of Captain Page[39] who was an excellent officer and universal favorite. He lost part of the upper jaw lingered a few days and expired.

Being only a second lieutenant at that time I was naturally more interested in minor details than in strategic movements. I remember that several officers who had quarrelled and who were not on speaking terms shook hands before the battle and fought side by side as friends.

In consequence of the rapidity of fire and perfection of our light batteries the enemys loss was far more severe than ours. Theirs amounted to about 200 killed and wounded while we had but nine killed and twenty wounded.

Councils of war seem generally to adopt a timid policy. One was held at General Taylor's head quarters that night. They recommended him to halt, intrench and wait for reinforcements. He refused to do either and said that he would relieve Fort Texas the next night or perish in the attempt. Preparations were accordingly made for an advance. In the mean time, Captain McCall was directed to go forward with the light troops and ascertain the enemys position.

McCall[40] found the Mexican army about three miles from Palo Alto strongly posted and covering the road to Matamoros. Their front was strengthened by earth works and protected by almost impenetrable thickets called *chapparal*. Their first line was sheltered behind the crest of a low ridge which bordered some ponds of water of no great depth. A strong battery was posted to hold the main road, an open space there rendering the fire of artillery effective. Two batteries farther back on the right and left assisted in holding this important point. Heavy supports of infantry were also accumulated there to defend what was regarded as the key of the position.

When Ringgold fell Lieut Randolph Ridgely of Baltimore, who had the reputation of being one of the most dashing officers of the army, assumed command of the light battery and with great audacity drew it up opposite and very near to the three Mexican batteries which commanded the bend in the road, and opened fire without hesitation. Captain McCall with his light troops was on each flank by way of support. Ridgely's guns could not possibly have remained there under ordinary circumstances: men and horses would have been swept away. Fortunately the enemy aimed too high and most of the shot passed over their heads. In front of Ridgely were drawn up the Guarda Costa of Tampico,[41] the elite of the Mexican army. They were mere youths and full of enthusiasm, but at every discharge of the light battery they were mowed down in swaths. Nevertheless they held their ground and did not give way. General Taylor now ordered Captain May's squadron to charge them and clear the road if possible. May rode forward and told Ridgely of the order he had received. The latter replied, "Hold on Charley until I draw their fire!" As soon as this was done, May made his celebrated charge. As he approached, the Mexican cannoneers abandoned their guns and took refuge in the thickets where his sabers could not reach them. The consequence was that although he captured the batteries he could not hold them for his men became very much scattered, and it was evident that horsemen could not contend with infantry under such circumstances. Upon looking around he saw he had but six men with him and therefore sounded the recall. He distangled his command and brought it back safely but with heavy loss. One of his officers, unable to control his steed which had become excited by the firing, dashed into the center of the Mexican cavalry and was lanced at once. As the troopers were threading their way back they came upon General La Vega of the Mexican army who had not left the vicinity of the guns. He defended himself with his saber until May came up and then surrendered.[42] Another account says he was captured by a bugler before May's arrival.

This famous charge made May a popular idol but its effects were neither lasting nor decisive. The moment May left the Mexicans stepped out of the bushes and resumed their places at the guns. Fortunately General Taylor had ordered an advance of the whole line to follow up the cavalry attack. The real contest had to be decided by the bayonet. Our troops dashed into the thickets and at once a very peculiar series of combats took place. Owing to the low chapparal trees and walls of thorny bushes which intervened in every direction it was impossible for the men to keep in line. Small squads would gain an open space and find themselves confronted by Mexicans. It was very difficult in these cases for either party to retreat without getting on all fours and crawling under the low branches which obstructed the way. The consequence was that each party had to fight to the last for there was no retreat. Lieut Jordan[43] of the 8th Infantry was in advance of his men and beset by several Mexicans. They got him down and were about to bayonet him when Lieut Sackett[44] of the Dragoons came up in time to rescue him. It is rare that officers of rank are engaged in regular melees of this kind but Colonel McIntosh of the 5th Infantry while leading on his men became separated from them and was assailed in one of the small open spaces referred to by several Mexicans at once. He was pinned to the earth with one bayonet through his hip another through his arm and still another through his neck. He was rescued just in time and fortunately survived his wounds. Colonel Belknap of the 8th Infantry had a similar but more successful encounter.

The guns in the road were taken with a rush by some men of the 5th Infantry under Sergeant Maloney[45] and were held with desperate tenacity until more force came up.

The loss of the batteries which commanded the road created a pause. The impetuous onset of our troops utterly routed Arista's[46] army and they fled in great haste towards the Rio Grande. As the water was high and there were but one or two ferry boats great numbers were drowned[47] in attempting to swim the river.

The joy of the garrison of Fort Texas may be imagined when they saw the flight of the Mexicans. They had heard the firing during the two days battles with great anxiety for if our army was defeated their ultimate capture seemed certain. So far they had resisted all assaults and had gained the commendation of their comrades. Unfortunately their gallant commander Major Brown was killed by a piece of shell almost in the moment of victory. Out of compliment to him the name of the fort was changed by General Taylor to Fort Brown; a name it still bears. The town of Brownsville[48] opposite Matamoros originated about this time and was also named after Major Brown.

Among the spoils of this battle were the head quarters camp of Arista with all his papers and military paraphernalia.[49]

The enemy were closely followed up by Colonel Childs battalion of artillery, Duncan's light battery, and Captain Ker's squadron of dragoons.

Our loss in the battle was 39 killed and 83 wounded. That of the enemy was estimated at more than 500.

The Mexicans were so disheartened that they gave up all attempts to hold Matamoros and concentrated the bulk of their forces at Monterey.

General Taylor remained with the main body of his army on the north side of the river at Brownsville but sent a detachment across to hold Matamoros.

As it was evident that our small army could not penetrate into the interior of Mexico without being largely reinforced, several months passed away before active operations were resumed.

3

FROM MATAMOROS TO MONTEREY

During the exciting period of the battles I had been stationed with Major Munroe's command at Point Isabel. I now obtained a short leave of absence to visit the captured city of Matamoros and gratify my curosity by learning something about the manners and customs of the Mexicans in their own country. The road to Fort Brown was not considered safe at this time for there were rumors that Mexican guerillas were hovering around the battle fields to plunder the wounded and it was said that they had cut the throats of some of our men who had straggled from the main body. I felt no apprehensions on this account however as a company of Texan cavalry were going in that direction and I had made arrangements to accompany them.

It so happened however that on this occasion I was destined to ride the whole distance alone. I was detained for a few moments at starting and told the cavalry to ride on and I would overtake them. I was not aware that there were two roads a mile apart separated by large ponds. The Texans went one way and I galloped on the other expecting every minute to overtake them and wondering that I saw nothing of them. When I reached the battle field of Resaca at the bend of the road where the batteries had been posted I suddenly found myself in presence of a party of Mexicans who were evidently there to despoil the corpses of the slain.[1] In the best Spanish I could muster I simply told them to get out of the way; that troops were close behind who would kill them and as I was in uniform they credited my statement and left me a free passage.

Upon my arrival in camp I received a warm welcome from Bragg, French,[2] Fremont and my other old comrades and became the guest of the officers of Ridgely's battery.

Matamoros had very much the appearance of a deserted town. Only the lowest part of the population remained and even they seemed afraid to venture out in the streets. A fandango was given to our officers every night, a catch penny affair. Of course it was not attended by the better class of females. I went there once with some of my friends, and came near paying dear for the entertainment. Hitherto these assemblies had been wholly deserted by the Mexican men but on the present occasion they crowded in in great numbers. Our officers had laid aside their swords in order to dance with more freedom. The Mexicans apparently out of curosity began examining these weapons and passing them to the rear. A foreigner who was present and who understood both English and Spanish called out to us that there was a plot to assassinate us with knives and told us our swords would soon be lost in the crowd. We came together, drew our pistols, reclaimed our swords and left in a body.

The news of the victories of Palo Alto and Resaca aroused the military spirit in the United States and created great excitement. An invasion of Mexico on a grand scale was at once projected and Genl Taylor was soon heavily reinforced with volunteer regiments from the different states. At that time our militia system was at a low ebb and a knowledge of military customs was entirely wanting. Many of the officers were politicans and were on such intimate terms with the privates that the latter were utterly regardless of the restraints of discipline. In fact they were more like organized mobs than military forces. They shocked us regulars by the gross familiarity with which they addressed their officers. There were too many militia majors, colonels, and generals thoughout the country for them to attach any special meaning to the title. One of them rushed up to Genl Twiggs tent looked in and said to the General, "Maynt I lie down on that bed, it looks sort o' nice!" Imagine his indignation. The men encamped near him became so very troublesome and familiar that on one occasion he rushed out frantically and called out to them, "Walk in! Make yourself at home! Bring your horses with you! Leave your dirt all around here! It is only old Twiggs tent! Never mind me! Ride right over me!"

I believe the first company that landed at Point Isabel came from New Orleans. They were called The Tigers.[3] One of them loaded with pistols and Bowie knives rushed up to me as I stood on the wharf and said with emphasis, "Now show me your Mexicans!" They were three months men. To call out volunteers for so short a period as this is absurd. Before they can be taught any military observances, or be brought into action their time is out and the great expense incurred in fitting them out is wasted. Another erroneous idea which prevailed at that time was that the worst criminals made the best soldiers. On several occasions men were let out of jail in New Orleans on condition they would enlist. So far as my experience goes these men always shirk danger. They are a constant expense and annoyance to the government and never render any real service. Regiments from the country where men are known to each other and have characters to sustain, are always trustworthy if properly commanded. I have known rascals sent out from the cities [to] take the mattresses for their own use out of the transport which brought them over. They were always committing depredations and were so careless of the public property that they would use their bayonets for candlesticks and leave them sticking in the ground when they marched away.

Soon after the battles there was a report that the Mexican army had reformed its lines and was about to attack Point Isabel. Commodore Connor came there with a fleet and landed all his sailors and Marines[4] as auxiliaries. They were armed and drilled in sailor fashion with phrases of this kind, "Foreward on the weather beam— ship your bayonets in." They petitioned if the enemy came that they might be allowed to board. Genl Taylor learning that the Commodore always wore his uniform [came] to meet him in full dress and Commodore Conner having been told that Genl Taylor never appeared in military costume took his off and put on a citizens dress.

While our government was thus making preparations for an advance the enemy were not idle. They were industriously engaged in fortifying Monterey and in bringing up troops and supplies from the capitol in order to hold it.

General Taylor prepared for the arrival of reinforcements by establishing another depot on the island of Santiago [Brazos Island] at the mouth of the harbor opposite Point Isabel and I was sent there with twenty [men] as a guard. The first regiment that landed there were the Kentucky Legion from Louisville under Colonel Ormsby.[5] They were an excellent body of men and the officers were high-toned gentlemen. Of course, they were ignorant at first of military customs and observances but they soon became good soldiers.

I had made the acquaintance of a boy named Carlos whose father was an Italian and mother an American. He was brought up on the lower Rio Grande and his knowledge of the people and country was of great service especially as he spoke both English and Spanish. He told me of a Mexican cut throat who had threatened to murder an American family who were still living among the Mexicans. So I sent out caught this man and directed a guard to take him over to the prison room at Point Isabel. He was on his way to the boat in custody of a sentinel and I went with them to see him safely embarked. The Kentuckians who had just landed caught sight of me and my prisoner and took up the idea that I had been out and captured him in single combat. They shouted, "He's got one of em! He's taken one of em prisoner!" and they looked at me admiringly for my supposed prowess.

After they [had] gone into camp I went to call on the Lieut. Colonel, the Colonel having gone over to Point Isabel. He had two tents pitched. As I entered the one in front I saw a soldier in his shirt sleeves with cowhide boots on asleep on a bed there. The adjutant who was conducting me shook the soldier to wake him up and said, "Orderly dont you know you must not go to sleep in the Colonel's bed with your boots on." The military reader will appreciate the want of discipline. Orderlys in the army are selected for being neatly dressed. They always follow the Commanding Officer at a respectful distance and never would dream of such a thing as lounging or lying down;

their business being to carry orders from the superior to his subordinates. These men were willing and obedient but they knew nothing of such things.

Through the exertions of the boy Carlos I began to obtain milk and eggs from the rancheros in the vicinity. As I saw that they were paid for every thing they brought a brisk trade soon sprang up. Another regiment of three months men arrived from New Orleans and went into camp. I think it is Genl Scott who said that when a militia regiment first receives its arms the number of casualties is almost equal to those of a pitched battle. This is an exaggeration but on the present occasion if I remember rightly there was one man wounded and another killed. The men were recklessly pointing their muskets in all directions and snapping the locks. Soon afterward I saw an amusing scene. The men of course looked upon every Mexican as an enemy whom they were bound to capture. Therefore upon seeing a blanketed Mexican approaching the camp they broke ranks and went for him, each ambitious to have the honor of taking a prisoner. When the Mexicans saw them all rushing towards him and heard the shouting he thought the idea was to kill him and fled. But some who were swift of foot headed him off and brought him in triumphantly to their Colonel's tent. There he showed a pass from the commanding officer at Burrita,[6] a post eight miles off on the Rio Grande. The man in fact had been sent as a messenger. The Colonel reflected for some time after reading and finally told his men to let the Mexican go. I saw at once that the traffic I had organized for the benefit of my mess would soon come to an end if this state of things continued. I therefore visited the Colonel and resorted to diplomacy. I told him if his people chased every peaceful Mexican that came in to trade with us they must be content to live on pork and biscuit, for no country produce could be procured under such circumstances. This appeal to his stomach proved successful. The matter was explained to the men and hence forward we had no difficulty.

New troops when they go into camp are always full of rumors and quick to imagine from any trivial circumstance that the enemy are approaching. The effect of this on the present occasion was that constant alarms were sounded. The long roll would be beaten in the middle of night and the troops formed to meet imaginary dangers. In one of these alarms which was caused by the supposed statement that a body of Mexican cavalry had been seen at the mouth of the Rio Grande some four miles distant. I knew nothing was the matter and offered to ride there before dark and reconnoitre. A Texan joined me [and] when we reached the river we met a party of our officers from Burrita who had been taking a ride in that direction. On our return after dark we found the whole command under arms. A hundred men were thrown out in advance. They challenged me and demanded the countersign a long distance off; the wind was against me but I luckily made myself heard just as they were about to shoot. It was a nervous escape for a hundred guns were pointed at us and the fingers were on the triggers.

It was now decided to make a new base of supplies at the mouth of the river and I was sent with my twenty men to guard it. I remained there about two months in charge of a great deal of valuable property. My friend Carlos told me that he had ascertained that a considerable body of men recruited for the Mexican army were at San Fernando about thirty miles south of us on the coast. He said they had heard that the stores were only guarded by my 20 men and had projected an expedition to capture us and despoil the depot. I transmitted this intelligence to General Taylor and he at once sent several regiments of volunteers to join me. Some of these men were quite lawless. Their officers in many cases were politicans, who kept up no sort of discipline as they wanted the votes and influence of those under them when they returned to civil life. One of the colonels sensible that his men needed some restraint wished me to punish them alleging that it devolved on me as I was permanent commander of the post and they were only there temporarily on their way to Monterey. I told him he must keep order in his own regiment; that my guard duty was as full as much as I could attend to. The commanding officer of another regiment, a Lieut Colonel told me with a chuckle that his men had cleaned out the sutler's stores[7] at the Brazos and he rather thought they would do the same here. I replied very gravely that I had the honor of a personal acquaintence with Genl Taylor and regretted very much that I would have to make representations to him accompanied by formal charges and specifications that would inevitably result in his (the lieut colonels) trial for open complicity in robbery. That the sentence of a court under such circumstances would probably be death for the perpetrators of such an offence. I frightened him so that he put sentinels to protect the store and visited them every half hour to see that his orders were enforced.

Of course the inequalities in military procedure were startling enough. One day a quarrel took place in the N.O. [New Orleans] regiment between a lieutenant and his subordinate sergeant whom he had scolded. The latter drew a pistol on his superior. Nevertheless as he had more influence than the officer he actually managed to have the latter tried for disrespect to him the sergeant. A regimental court of three members tried the officer[8] and sentenced him to be dismissed [from] the service, and he left accordingly for parts unknown. Of course the whole proceeding had no validity as only a General Court Marital can dismiss an officer, and the sentence then has no effect unless it has been confirmed by the General in command. In legal proceedings of this kind too each member of a court takes an oath not to reveal the vote of any other member. I was therefore a good deal astonished to hear each one discuss in my presence how the others had voted.

While at the mouth of the river, I was annoyed by a man who professed to have some consular authority from the British Government. He made threatening remarks against our army and as I thought he was acting as a spy I arrested him. He was subsequently released by General Taylor for lack of evidence against him. I shall have occasion to refer to him again.

In my new post I needed a cook for my mess and Carlos recommended a boy named Sancho to me. He said however that Sancho was a peon or slave after the Mexican fashion which was a very different system from that of the U.S. being founded on debt and not on color. Nor did it necessarily imply any inequality between the master and peon other than that of creditor and debtor. Sancho was beginning to go through the usual process in such cases. A man had loaned him $4 to go to a country fair. He agreed to work for his creditor until the amount was paid. While doing so he was to be charged heavily for clothing board etc. and tempted with fresh loans which it would take years to liquidate. In this way he would be bound to service all his life. I sent and paid the $4, but Carlos said the boy was afraid to come to me. His owner had told him I would treat him with great cruelty. However I got him at last and told him he could leave me whenever he chose to do so. Some of the superstitions he had learned amused me. Every time I sneezed he would say, "Jesus!" which is part of a formula "May Jesus aid you." He thought the devil was trying to enter me and this was his method of driving him away.

I did not look with much equanimity upon the prospect of remaining to guard the pork and flour in rear while my comrades were battling at the front. I therefore applied to [be] exchanged with another officer. General Taylor at once approved my application and was kind enough to compliment me for making it. So I soon found myself at Matamoros as a second lieutenant in company E which 1st Lieut James B. Ricketts[9] of my regiment commanded, the other officers either being disabled or on detached service. Just before I left the mouth of the river I came very near ending my earthly career in an unexpected manner. I undertook to swim to the opposite shore but the current was much more powerful than I had supposed and before I was a third of the way over I found myself a considerable distance below my starting point the river was so much wider there that I saw little hope of regaining either shore. I struggled until I was thoroughly exhausted. Carlos who was on the Mexican side saw my dilemma ran to some boys there who had a boat and urged them to rescue me. They demurred to this on the ground that I was a heretic and therefore it was better to let me drown. He suggested that I would pay them well for the service and this decided them. They arrived just in time to pull me in for I was utterly exhausted and would soon have been out to sea among the breakers.

I enjoyed our camp opposite Matamoros very much. The officers, Lt Ricketts and 2d Lt Weld[10] were genial and intelligent gentlemen and our relations were always friendly and fraternal. Everything was new to me. Lieut Haskin[11] of the 1st Artillery, a very efficient officer, was in command of a company on guard in Matamoros but he found great difficulty in keeping order on account of the tumultous crowds of volunteers which filled the streets. On one occasion he was obliged to form his company the whole width of the street and charge to clear the way. Our people tried to communicate with the natives but as neither understood the language of the other conversation was not very satis-factory. A Mexican lad on one of the principal stores learned to say, "How you do my friend." He was so proud of the achievement that he tried it on every one he saw. This reminds me of a padre who brought out a little boy of six years of age who he said could speak some English. It seems the lad had been present at a conversation between two teamsters and stuck with a remark given by one of them with great emphasis had committed it to memory. When I asked him to repeat it he said, "D___n your soul to hell." I told the padre it would be better for *his nephew* to stop learning English in that way. The mongrel lan-guage picked up by our men was not at all elegant but was useful in making themselves understood.... Our men used a lingo in which they made the words "bueno" and "vamos" answer for everything.... The word "vamos" played a very important part in every sentence. It means literally "we go" but has the also the sense of the French word "allons." I am going to Monterey, are you going there was rendered by "me vamos Monterey, you vamos Monterey." I like whiskey, "me vamos whiskey." Dont you like it, "you no vamos whiskey?..." "Bueno"—good was used to signify approval or to ratify a bargain. "No bueno" was the negation. One Mexican boy had learned to say "How you do my fren" and called it out vociferously to every body he saw....

One day as I entered a store I met the pseudo English Consul who had been released by Genl Taylor by pretending to be on an order. He was loud in his threats but when I pointed to my pistols and offered to walk out to the edge of town and settle it with him he subsided and said, "No you are fighting for liberty now but when the war is over I will follow you to the end of the earth to get satisfaction!" It so hap-pened that the next time I met him was at the close of the war. He

"Has she got any eggs?…"

was bidding then at an auction and remarked, "It is not worth a cent more *as my friend* Lieut Doubleday will testify."

The defeat at Resaca was a terrible blow for the Mexican people and as they would not attribute it to any lack of bravery in their soldiers they put the blame on Arista, who was relieved from his command by order of the new President Paredes and directed to report at the Capitol. I do not know how it is now but in those days Mexican officers of rank only carried out such orders as were agreeable to them. Arista declined to obey Paredes and returned to his hacienda near Monterey instead. A new army was assembled in the latter city under General Ampudia who set to work to fortify every avenue of approach. At last the welcome order came for an advance and the first brigade of Worth's Division, to which we belonged, led the way on the 17th of August.

On the [?] of September we started on our march for Monterey to drive the enemy away from there and take possession of the pass in the mountains which leads to Saltillo and the open country beyond. Our baggage was reduced to a minimum. We carried no tents of any kind. The officers of each company were only allowed one pack mule for their provisions blankets and mess arrangements. We made but eight miles the first day as we started late in the after noon. At night we found ourselves among hills and steep ravines covered with thorny bushes. The mule which carried our food and bedding got away in the darkness and was not recovered for several days during which time we had to depend upon chance purchases from the ranches for our sustenance. I did not find sleeping on the ground with out any blankets an agreeable pastime. The first night was very dark. About 10 o'clock when Ricketts and myself were turning over trying to find a smooth place on the ground where there were no stones or thorns—which seemed to be everywhere, a staff officer appeared and detailed Ricketts as brigade officer of the Day and me as officer of the brigade guard. The sentinels he informed us had been all posted some hours previous. He went away and I arose donned my sword and sash and started out to inspect my guard. It was of no use. I could not find any thing or any body in the pitch darkness. Occasionally I would stumble over some sleeping soldiers and once or twice found officers awake but they could give me no information. After tearing my clothes among the thorny bushes and nearly going over a precipice in the darkness I gave up the attempt in despair and managed with great difficulty to get back to the bush where Ricketts lay. If I was responsible to him and liable to be shot for absenting myself from my guard he was equally culpable for not visiting the sentinels. He upon hearing my narrative concluded not to venture out. I told him to turn over and go to sleep, and then he could not swear but what I had been with my guard all night. I expected to be arrested the next day on this very serious charge but I never heard of the matter afterwards.

At early dawn we resumed our march. Our company was in the advance which enabled us to stop at ranches along the route and get something to eat. A vol colonel also went ahead of the column accompanied by his orderly with the same praiseworthy intention. Unfortunately he could not speak a word of Spanish. He said to his Irish orderly, "Cant you make that female understand. I would like to buy some eggs if she has any." The orderly replied, *"I'll try sor."* He then went close to the woman, put his mouth near her ear and bawled out, *"The Colonel says, has she got any eggs?"* This method of bartering proved wholly ineffectual.

Upon ascending a hill an extensive view suddenly presented itself and made an impression which will never be effaced. The whole country seemed to lie beneath me and the mountain range of the Sierra Madre in its blue grandeur extended across the entire landscape. I had never been in a mountainous country before and the unexpected sight gave me a feeling of beauty and sublimity combined.

When we reached Seralvo [Cerralvo][12] we halted several days for the rest of the army to come up. We, that is Ricketts Weld and myself thought we would like to see something of Mexican home life and as we knew that the senor cure was the key of the place, we made his acquaintances and paid him some attention. I think Weld even went to church and splashed the holy water over himself in unnecessary profusion by way of making believe that he was an earnest Catholic.

The priest who had been a gay reveller in his early days introduced us to some of the better portions of the community, but we staid too short a time to render it of any avail. One custom surprised me very much. A clear stream runs through the center of the place. Upon taking a walk one day I saw a number of senioritas sporting and swimming about in the pellucid water in the costume of mother Eve.[13] They seemed generally to care very little for our presence and were not at all abashed with the exception of one who ran out and hid behind a very small tree.

Upon leaving Seralvo the army marched with an advance guard of cavalry and took the usual precautions against a surprise. Owing to the heat we usually started at 3 A.M. and reached our destination about 11 A.M. Then we went into camp and rested for our tents had come up. We saw Mexicans sitting in their doorways along the route to see us pass. They had lost all fear of us, now that they saw we had no intention of injuring peaceful citizens. They said to us "*Mucho fandango in Monterey*" which is equivalent to "They are getting up a dance for you in Monterey." They evidently looked forward to our discomfiture there for they knew great military preparations had been made to receive us. For some reason the day that we reached Marin the march was prolonged beyond the usual period until we had passed several miles beyond. As the heat was severe there were a number of sun strokes among the men. When we reached our halting places I saw a man run through the tents, and a crowd pursuing him. He was crazy from the effects of the heat.

Soon after leaving Marin we saw a white spot at the foot of the mountain in the far distance. Our guide told us this was Monterey. The day before the last march, our company had been detailed as rear guard. We rose as usual, had breakfast at 2 A.M. and formed at three. A very unwise proceeding for instead of fatiguing ourselves uselessly we might have rested several hours had we calculated the long time it took the army and its trains to pass by.

As we approached the city large bodies of Mexican lancers appeared in our front but made no hostile demonstrations. They appeared to be sent out merely to watch our movements.

As we came nearer we could distinguish the Mexican banner floating over the different fortifications and the English, French, and
Spanish and other flags had been raised over the consulates apper-
taining to those nations to save the houses from the effect of our bombardment.

At last when within about three miles of the city, we turned to the
right into the stately groves of St. Domingo along side of a clear
stream of water, and awaited there the result of the reconnaissances
which were going on in front by our Engineering Officers escorted by
our cavalry. It is unnecessary to say that these observations were very
important to enable General Taylor to fix upon proper points of
attack.

4

THE BATTLE OF MONTEREY

Our company commanded by Lieut. Ricketts were detailed as the rear guard for the day, still we rose with the rest at half past two in the morning, it being almost impossible to sleep amid the noise and confusion of breaking up the encampment. A breakfast of fried pork, hard crackers and coffee was soon dispatched, after which we amused ourselves by watching the Army as it filed past. The men were in the highest spirits and scarcely a company went by who did not have some light joke or badinage with our men, who were drawn up by the side of the road, under arms. There is something exceedingly romantic in these early marches. The sudden burst of martial music as the different bands strike up the reveille, and in the deep darkness of the forest, ending with the bugle calls of the light Artillery and Cavalry, the loud shout, the merry laugh, the hundred fires which spring up suddenly lighting up the green woods and glinting back from bayonet and sword; the bustle of preparation, the striking of tents, present a scene in the highest degree picturesque. It was long before all the Regiments had passed by, and when at last the different trains were under way it was broad daylight and the troops were several miles in advance. The intense heat made this march a tedious one, though the beautiful mountain scenery continually developing itself did much to enliven it. As we descended the high hill, previous to our arrival at Ramos, a Mexican Prisoner who was

BV Doubleday, Abner. "Memorandum Book of a Journey to Mexico to Look for Gardiner's Mine."

with us pointed to a white spot in the distant mountains and said, "there is Monterey." We looked with deep interest at the spot, which was to terminate our long march from Comargo, but how would we enter it. A cloud hung over the future which none sought to penetrate. In this march we passed a Mexican encampment where the fires were hardly cold, and when our advance reached Marin the lancers of Torrejon were seen retiring in the distance. As we entered the town, covered with dust, thirsty and weary we supposed we had reached our destination for the day, but to our disappointment we found the troops were encamped several miles beyond. We halted for about an hour, refreshed ourselves and the men with milk and pomegranates, and then resumed our route. About three o'clock in the afternoon we reached the main body and immediately commenced pitching our tents. The heat was intense. I tried while overseeing the men to procure a little shelter, under a thorny bush but to no purpose. A man suddenly rushed by, shouting for help. Several persons were in pursuit of him and I learned he had become insane in consequence of a coup de soleil. He was not the only victim. Two others had dropped dead during the day from the same cause....

Here we remained one day to enable the other divisions to come up and here we were joined by Lieut. Weld of our company who had been absent on pioneer duty. The final march was fixed for daylight but circumstances detained us until seven o'clock. We waded the San Juan which ran near our camp and then marching by sections proceeding so as to be able to form line of battle at a moment's notice. We had not gone far before we halted two hours to enable the pioneers to construct a bridge in front of us. Seeing several Rancheros standing near some *jacales* I asked one of them if there were many troops in Monterey, he replied "Oh, no! go on, you will have no difficulty in taking the place." This would have been very encouraging had it not been for a half ironical smile which seemed to indicate that none of us would ever enter the place alive. At *Agua Fria* another stopping place I saw a Mexican in tears who told me, an hour before two of his relatives had been shot[1] in the churchyard by order of Torrejon, on suspicion of having had dealings with the Americans.

After filling our canteens we again proceeded. At last we arrived at a high ridge about eight miles from Monterey which descended into a vast plain begirt with mountain ranges at the intersection of two of which the city itself lay distinctly visible. As I stood upon the summit by the side of Major Brown of the 4th Artillery he suddenly remarked; "Ha, they are coming out to meet us," and in fact three immense clouds of dust on the three roads which lead out of Monterey gave a strong color to the supposition. My heart beat quickly as I thought how soon we were to be engaged. But the dust came no nearer, we descended into the plain, joined the other division which was in advance and very shortly found ourselves immersed in a thick forest. Suddenly burst upon our ears the rapid booming of heavy cannon. Again and again we heard it, and all pressed forward with eager and excited steps, for those sounds told us a battle was inevitable. We soon reached the encampment of General Twiggs and filed to the right in the thick underbrush and stately trees of Walnut grove five miles from the city....

Here we remained until the next day at noon while our Engineers and Cavalry were making a reconnaissance. Several of us ascended to the top of one of the highest trees to obtain a view, but an intervening swell of ground almost entirely concealed what we wished to see. We noticed a white building upon a height in the far distance, which we learned was called the Bishop's palace[2] or castle, and several flags, one waving over the citadel Fort,[3] another over the Cathedral (Ampudia's Head Quarters) and another over the Spanish consul's house. In the evening we heard that our Major of Engineers, Mansfield, considered the works to be of great strength and it required little judgement to know they must be stormed at a heavy sacrifice.... The [west] side [of Monterey] was protected securely by strong forts on the hills. The series of these works were separated by a river which ran between them. It was decided that Genl. Twiggs' division should attack the nearest works while Worth's division was to make a circuit and storm the hill forts in rear. It certainly was assuming a great risk to divide our forces in this way, and it was somewhat audacious to attack 11,000 men in a fortified position with less than 6,000 but it seemed the only feasible way to take the town. For the whole army to march to the rear would be to cut loose from all its communications so that in case of defeat the disaster would be overwhelming. Hence Twiggs' division remained and Worth's division went behind the enemy, isolated itself, and ran the risk of being sacrificed....

At noon on the 20th we were ordered under arms. It was said our Division was to pass in rear of the city but whether to attack or only cut off the retreat of the enemy was still uncertain. As General Worth was unfortunately absent from the battles of Palo Alto and Resaca, all expected to be engaged in some desperate enterprise to revivify the laurels shaded on those occasions by the better fortune of his rivals. As we came out into the road I saw several of my friends among the volunteers who bade me farewell with a hearty shake of the hand which told their belief that we might never meet again and indeed how many a gallant heart full of fiery life and proud ambition now lies stiff and cold beneath the advanced redoubts. In the front of our column were the Texians employed as light troops, then came Duncan's battery then the Artillery Battalion. the 8th Infantry, then I think Mackall's[4] Battery, the 5th, and lastly the 7th Infantry. We proceeded for about a mile and a half on the main road to the city and then suddenly making a detour to the right we entered the cornfields and cultivated grounds of the suburbs. I knew we were somewhere in the vicinity of the Citadel Fort and every moment expected to hear its shot come crashing through our ranks but all was silent. Nothing could be heard but the crackling of the corn as we trod it down, and the occasional order to halt or advance. All conversation seemed instinctively to have ceased; each was wrapped up in his own thoughts and feelings. At last we halted near some hamlets and the men received orders to fill their canteens with water from a small brook near at hand. At the same time our skirmishers turned into the road which led towards the rear of the enemys fortifications. Whatever doubt we might have had before was now at an end. All saw that the stern heights above us, swarming with armed masses, must be stormed. As I turned a spy glass towards the Bishop's Castle the last rays of the setting sun were reflected back from a forest of bayonets. At the same time the sharp crack of the Texian rifles told that our advance had at last encountered that of the enemy. The dropping sound of musketry continued for about an hour. General Worth in the mean time ascended a high hill to obtain a better view. Had the enemy charged boldly they might easily have captured him. As it was they drove the Texians in upon us pell mell who shouted to us to stand to our arms for the Lancers were upon us.... The latter however did not make the assault and as it was getting dark we went into bivouac at the junction of the Saltillo and Cinegas roads. The enemys and our own exchanged occasional shots during the night. Every time the Mexicans fired they would shout "Viva Ampudia...."

The skirmishers were deployed again however and the road being clear we were ordered forward. The shades of evening were closing round us as we halted for the night. Darkness soon came down thick and palpable for a tempest brooded over the heights and deep recesses of the Sierra Madre, a true semblence of that wilder storm about to burst upon the devoted city and fill a thousand families with desolation. The position we had taken was a strong one. Our right rested upon a precipice, our left was covered by thick hedges and Duncan's Battery guarded the main road in advance. The ground was covered thick with thorny bushes, and broken pieces of limestone from a quarry in our rear....

Before we started there had been frequent roll calls and parades to listen to orders so when we fell in I did not expect to leave camp and therefore did not provide myself with rations or a blanket. The want of the latter proved to be a serious privation now for the ground was rough and rocky. In fact we had halted in a quarry on the side of the mountain and were altogether very uncomfortable. It had not occured to us when the order was given for us to fall in, that a long march was before us, or that we might be temporarily separated from our supplies. We were therefore utterly destitute of blankets and suffered severely from the cold and the difficulty of sleeping upon the rough ground without any protection from the inequalities of the surface. A severe neuralgia in the face prevented me from sleeping except at short intervals. From time to time wrapping a soldiers blanket around me I would make my way to a small fire which had been kindled in the yard of a jacal. Here I would find a group of soldiers of all arms conversing over the probable events of the morrow. They were the men of Palo Alto and Resaca and they jested as lightly over the future as if they were going to a festival. After listening to the conversation for awhile I would make my way back to my bed in the quarry and again endeavour to sleep. Duncan's men had their blankets wrapped around them and in the thick darkness looked like sheeted ghosts. They had their slow matches lit by the side of the guns. In the early part of the evening we knew from the frequent bugle calls that a large body of cavalry was bivouacked in our front. All through the night we could hear the long shrill cry of their sentinels shouting every half hour, "*sentinel alerte*." We had been in our position about an hour when the enemy in the citadel fort commenced throwing off rockets to light up around them probably in anticipation of a night attack, then came twenty one guns in rapid succession, then a fire ball sailed slowly through the air, and then again all was silent and dark. I felt at this time a feeling of security for which it is difficult to account. Although on the eve of a battle I could not realize my danger. The long night wore away at last and the battle morning dawned in the east....

At the first break of day, we stood to our arms and advanced towards the Mexican Cavalry on the Saltillo Road. For about half a mile we marched by a flank, but as we approached the enemy we deployed the Artillery Battalion on the right, Duncan's Battery in the center and the 8th Infantry on the left among the cultivated fields. I believe the remaining forces formed a second line or reserve. In this order with the Texian light troops in front we preceeded, the enemy slowly receding before us until they were entirely concealed by a spur of the mountain at the junction of the Monterey and Saltillo Roads. At this time I looked at our little band. Every face was flushed and seemed to wear an earnest and anxious expression. The half hour before an action is always the one when the men are most depressed. Once fairly engaged and the excitement prevents them from dwelling upon the idea of danger. We were rapidly approaching the spur referred to when suddenly the Lancers came thundering around the point, and charged our light troops almost unawares. A brief but sharp conflict ensued in which several Texians were lanced. Quick as lightning, Duncan unlimbered his guns and flung in a storm of cannister which soon sent the enemy to the right about. With loud cheers we rushed madly onward in the pursuit. The previous depression gave way to enthusiasm. It was like a sudden burst of sunshine in the midst of a dark sky. On we dashed, panting breathless, up the steep mountain. "Steady, men steady, dress upon the colors, keep up on the right." We were falling behind from the necessity of climbing the mountain in front while the left wing and center being in the plain could advance more rapidly. Half way up the steep slope we encountered two beautiful horses richly caparisoned, both killed from the effects of our fire. Near one of these a large handsome man apparently a Spaniard sat upon a rock. He was dressed in a rich scarlet uniform down which the blood was slowly trickling from a deep wound just above the heart. He was evidently dying and gasped out "misericordia" [mercy] from time to time to excite the compassion of our men. He also begged for a confessor which was something we did not happen to have with us. We had but little time to spare and pressed onward until we reached the other side of the mountain. Here the Lancers being almost out of sight we halted weary and exhausted with the long run. I looked around utterly unable to imagine where we were as I saw nothing of the city. We were in the midst of a beautiful valley begirt with sierras of the most picturesque description. The mountains did not slope gradually down but were bounded by a series of abrupt and rocky precipices nearly a mile in height, as if some convulsion of nature had rent them apart. Before us stretched a range of cultivated fields. Where were the main body of the enemy for those we had driven before us evidently formed but a small part of the entire force. Every moment I expected to see the glitter of their bayonets advancing through the woods in the distance. But all was still. There was some thing deeply impressive in this silence. The breeze played fitfully amid the rustling corn, the birds twittered in the bushes, the insect hummed as it flew by, but other sounds there were none. Nature peaceful and serene sympathised not with the stern passions of man. Again a feeling of depression came over me. It almost seemed as if the air were full of sad and solemn music, and the thought involuntarily occured how few of those around may live to see the light of another day. The silence was broken by an order from General Worth, who directed a company to be sent up the mountain we had just passed, to spy out and report the movements of the enemy. We were detailed for that purpose and accordingly retraced our steps, and clambered up the side of the ridge until we had obtained a sufficient elevation. The view from this point was grand and imposing beyond description. The landscape around Monterey with its cultivated fields of straw color, reddish brown and green bordered with hedge fences presented the appearance of a vast garden. On our left was the road by which we had arrived. On our right the magnificent valley of the San Juan begirt with sierras which resembled enormous granite rocks rent assunder by some convulsion of nature. In front was Federation and Independence Hills with batteries upon their summits which played incessantly upon our troops. Half way up the latter emminence was the Bishop's palace strongly fortified. Between these hills lay the city and still further on a mountain of singular and picturesque beauty called from the peculiar appearance of the summit the Comanche saddle. It was a spectacle which seen at any time could never be forgotten but on the present occasion, the marching of armies, the thundering of the batteries, the convulsive movements of the wounded and dying strewed around us gave it a thrilling and indescribable interest.

The first object which occupied our attention was the succor of the sufferers from the late conflict. We directed several of our detached parties to the points below where wounded Mexicans lay struggling but these last tried to avoid us under the impression we wished to dispatch them. The next thing we observed was a long white line near the palace which we at first supposed to be a white fence. It soon however broke into detachments and we then perceived it was a line of Mexican Cavalry. Some six or eight had entered the Monterey road at a distance of about half a mile from our position, when Duncan sent a shell which seemed to burst exactly in their midst. In an instant they rushed into the high corn and concealed themselves from view. We sent word to General Worth that a party appeared coming down from the palace, but a moment afterward our attention was attracted towards the Saltillo road upon which an almost interminable line of cavalry were advancing upon the city. For one moment it was supposed this was a new army under Santa Anna advancing to the relief of Monterey and Lieut Weld was sent down the mountain in all haste to communicate with General Worth, taking a private with him to assist in conveying orders. A closer inspection however showed the approaching force to be the same cavalry we had already repulsed in the morning. After Lieut W. had left we remained for some time watching the remainder of the division in its serpentine course beneath us. The enemy's batteries played on them incessantly but their march was as steady as if they were on parade. One of the balls had already killed Capt McKavett[5] and another tore one of the mule teams to pieces. As the forces gradually passed out of sight the guns on Federation hill directly on a line with us, for want of a better mark devoted themselves to us. One shot passed very near Lieut. Weld as he was returning. Another struck at the feet of Lieut Ricketts and myself covering us with gravel and dust, and several tore up the rocks in our vicinity without however striking a man. The sound of these projectiles was anything but pleasant. The roaring, rushing noise made by their passage through the air, being succeeded by a tremendous crash as they struck the rocks. While my attention was riveted upon the battery opposite, I suddenly heard a strange whistling for which I could not account. I at first fancied they were firing grape from the battery opposite but my comrades soon undeceived me. One of those white masses which at first we had mistaken for a fence, had drifted to the foot of the hill and there concealing itself in the hedges had opened a fire of *escopetas* upon us. Our men sprang to their feet and begged permission to return the fire. This was of course granted them. The enemy being hidden we could not say how much damage they suffered. One man was seen to fall from his horse and the rest beat a precipitate retreat. Our position was now becoming somewhat dangerous as General Worth had marched his division to the right, and the enemy's masses might easily be interposed between us. Col Childs sent up orders for us to descend and we proceeded to join the main body. Upon reporting to Genl Worth he said, "ah, gentlemen, I hope you did not find it too hot up there." We told him that we had only descended in obedience to repeated orders from Col Childs. We were then placed as an advanced picket from which in the course of half an hour we were recalled and ordered to join the Artillery Battalion. We found it bivouacking in a corn field. Some of the men were engaged in cooking the roasting ears and others were reposing on the stalks. I imitated the latter with a view of obtaining a little rest of which I was very much in need. In a few minutes my attention was attracted by the hasty funeral of some officer by the side of the road. I went forward and found it was Capt McKavett of the 8th Infantry who was killed quite early in the day. I had been quite intimate with him at Cerralvo a few days before. I was told he had prophesied his own death previous to the action and had made many gloomy speeches. As the column was advancing he looked up towards a small cloud in the sky and muttered, "*It is my evil destiny.*" A moment afterwards a ball from the battery on Federation Hill passed very near him, but he did not raise his eyes from the ground. He was cut down immediately afterwards by a ball from the same battery which struck him in the left side. I turned away when the body was brought up for I had no desire to see what lay beneath that bloody blanket. He was an orphan who had been educated by some charitable institution and sent to West Point. He sleeps his last sleep in a lovely spot. The corn waves above his tomb, the brook murmurs as it passes by and far above him the cloud capped sierras rear their heads as an eternal monument.

I now learned that while we were on picket duty, four companies of our battalion had been detached under Captain C. F. Smith to storm the battery which had annoyed us so much. By the time the burial was over this force had reached the foot of the mountain and soon the distant eddies of smoke and sound of musketry showed that the enemy were aware of the attack, and had advanced to repel it. For a long time it was impossible to say who had the advantage, the firing appearing at one period to ascend, at another to descend the height. For a long time we were unable to say which party had the advantage. The excitement of those below became intense. A faint cheer from the summit was answered with enthusiasm, and soon a loud hurrah accompanied with the waving of caps gave us the welcome information that the fort was taken. To our surprise the firing shortly afterwards re-commenced. Our troops had discovered a second fort in rear of the first, and this alas after a brief conflict surrendered or rather was taken by assault.

The capture of these two works was an important step towards the possession of the city. Captain C. F. Smith commander of the storming party was previously distinguished for his perfect knowledge of tactics and the minute details of his profession. On the present occasion he gained new laurels and confirmed the opinion of those who had seen him at Resaca that he possessed great coolness and bravery united to sound judgement. We were now able to approach much nearer the city than we had previously been, and by this time night coming on we took up a position in the yard of a deserted jacal. Having had but one meal in the last two days, Ricketts, Weld and myself set the soldiers who cooked for us to work, and having got out a tent fly we proceeded to make ourselves as comfortable as circumstances would admit. But the elements were in a conspiracy against us. By the time we had our meat fried a deluge of rain poured down and we found ourselves standing in a large pool of water. To sleep was manifestly impossible, and I went over to the jacal to see if there was any chance there. It was already filled with officers of all grades and there appeared to be no vacant spot. Col Childs however kindly loaned me his overcoat and displacing some saddles near him made room for me by his side. I was awakened about midnight by a new movement. It had been resolved to storm the height above the bishop's palace and Col C. took command of the storming party. As soon as I ascertained our company was not on the detail I went to sleep again knowing I would have need of all the rest I could get. In the morning we heard the height had been carried in gallant style, the enemy taking refuge in the palace. By a rapid movement our forces succeeded in building a new battery, by using the sand bags of the enemy's battery and a twelve pound howitzer having been hoisted up almost by main strength. Some shells were cast by Roland[6] into the castle itself producing an excellent effect. The castle was finally taken by sending a small party in its vicinity. The garrison sallied out to attack this party and being charged in their turn by a large force of our men in ambuscade, they turned and fled without re-entering the building and we thus obtained possession of it. Lieut Ayres was the first to spring in at a window, a very daring deed inasmuch as he did not know how many there were to receive him inside. It is said the wife of a Mexican officer who had dressed herself in male apparel and made many threats of what she intended to do with *Los Americanos* fled ingloriously at the very first attack.[7]

While these events were taking place we were on our way to a beautiful and romantic spot about eight miles or ten miles from Monterey on the Saltillo road, called "*Los Molinos.*" Bodies of cavalry had been seen coming from that direction and the object of our movement was to prevent any new inforcements from joining the already overwhelming force in the city. It was thought quite possible Santa Anna might be advancing with another army. We were accompanied by a section of Light Artillery under the command of Lieut Irons[8] and a company of dragoons under command of Capt Graham.[9] The valley at this point is about a mile in width. "*Los Molinos*" or the flour mills are at the very foot of the mountain which rises behind them in the form of an almost perpendicular precipice for several thousand feet. The white limestone buildings with the water works covered with highly polished cement contrasted beautifully with the rich green of the valley, through which a mountain torrent rushed with great violence. Here we rested until Capt Graham could make a report as to the amount of force in our front and the dispositions they were making. For one moment while gazing on the calm and lovely scene before us, I almost forgot the object of our being there. It was like a pause in a man's life when all his energies have been tasked to the utmost by some great event, before he has had time to form new plans. The very spirit of peace seemed to reign over the scene. The battle seemed far away as if it could never reach us again. We partook of the rich fruit that was offered us and rested our weary limbs without a thought of the future or the past. But our dream was soon broken. Capt Graham returned and reported the troops to be a mere handful of rancheros. We accordingly retraced our steps and left this little paradise with a sigh to mingle once more in the stormy excitement of the battle. Our movement we ascertained after wards had prevented the enemy from receiving 180 pack mule loads of flour.

As we approached our former position we met some Texian rangers who informed us that the castle had fallen. We hardly conceived it possible but the stars and stripes floating over the stern fortification in the vicinity confirmed the glad intelligence. The shades of evening were fast falling as we reached the foot of the hill and threaded our way up to the castle. From every side we heard the roars of laughter, the jest and the song. Merry groups were scattered around in every direction drinking their coffee and enjoying the first moment of repose they had been able to obtain for two days. The long line of arms stacked in rear of the castle showed where the post of the troops would be in case of a night attack. Our own destination proved to be the highest point of the hill. Here we found Lieut Martin[10] in command of the guns of Taylor's Light Battery. We were delighted to meet again in safety and after a few congratulations Lieut Ricketts proceeded to make his preparations to resist a night attack. As the point commanded the castle which in its turn commanded one third of the city, it was in fact the key of Monterey, and its possession was a matter of vital importance to us, as well as to the enemy. We had sentinels placed on all sides and were confident we could not be surprised. Martin then directed my attention to two wounded Mexican soldiers, but we had great difficulty in finding them in the dark. One was already dead. The other begged hard for water which I gave him from a canteen. As he showed a disposition to drink to excess I was obliged to take it away from him. He then asked for food and ate heartily from the few scraps I happened to have in my haversack. We then sent him to the place used as a hospital. As Martin and myself felt the need of something to eat, we stumbled down the side of the mountain until we reached the castle. We obtained a cup of coffee from some of the officers of our Regiment and then returned much refreshed. The night was chilly on the plain below but on the height above it was absolutely cold. There seemed to be no remedy for this, as our feeble fire was allowed to go out, to prevent its being a landmark to the enemy, and extra clothing or blankets we had none. Martin then proposed to pitch a Mexican tent captured in the morning's assault on the heights but this proved no easy matter, for never having seen one like it we found great difficulty in putting it together. The tent was erected at last and Lieut *Weld* and myself undertook to extract some sleep from it, of which we were very much in need. We found the rocky ground too hard for us and went to work making a floor out of an old Mexican sand bag battery in the vicinity. The wet sand was not much improvement, and we were chilled through, nevertheless the constant and excessive fatigue of the two previous days enabled us to sleep soundly at once. We or at least I was awakened by the whole tent with its heavy timbers coming down about our ears. I escaped by a miracle and as Weld never stirred we supposed him to be badly hurt. We extracted him from the wreck not at all injured but very much exasperated at being disturbed. The incident afforded us great amusement at the time. We had divided the company into three reliefs corresponding with three divisions of the night and there being three officers, each was to be on guard one-third of the night and sleep the remainder. I wrapped myself in the tenting and reposed in comparative comfort until twelve o'clock at night. At that hour I felt a hand upon my shoulder and sprang to my feet. It was Ricketts come to tell me it was my turn to watch. For a moment I could hardly realize where I was. I had been dreaming of home and I awoke in a foreign land with the dead strewed around me upon a battle field. He told me what was to be done in case Genl [P.F.] Smith who guarded the forts on Federation Hill should throw up certain signal rockets to indicate an attack. The amount and kind of force was to be shown by the color and number of the rockets and we were to send up other rockets as an answer to those we saw. After giving the orders from Genl Worth,

Ricketts flung himself down and was soon fast asleep. The first thing I did was to visit my sentinels to see that they were all vigilant. I then inspected the main body of the guard and found them all on the alert. Upon returning I sat down by the embers of the fire thoroughly chilled. The night was dark and cloudy and the winds whistled by in wild and melancholy blasts. Occasionally I raised my head to listen, but no sound was heard save the low murmuring of the guard conversing among themselves. Gradually my mind reverted to other scenes, to my far distant home and the many friends I had left behind. I was roused from this train of thought by the sudden challenge of a sentinel far below us on the plain. Well might he challenge I was assured afterwards by the Mexicans that a column of 3000 men was in his front. Having hailed the approaching steps three times he discharged his musket. The effect was electric. Our troops about a thousand strong, sprang to their feet, secured their arms, and sent by a scream of defiance that might have been heard for miles. The rocks rang with the uproar and the frightened foe retreated as swiftly as he advanced. As for us at first alarm our men on the height prepared for action. The cannoneers stood by the side of their pieces with lighted matches and the company formed in line. An orderly shortly afterwards came up breathless from the General to know if we had seen or heard anything and he was almost immediately followed by a drummer sent to beat the long roll in case of necessity. But all soon subsided into silence and daylight at last broke without the occurrence of any new incident. In my eagerness to wake up the company I was struck with the apparent deep sleep of one group of men. Stooping down to arouse them, I found it was composed of dead Mexicans. In the morning I took a better look at these corpses. They were dressed simply in uniform coat and pantaloons without under clothes of any description and their swarthy Indian faces wore every look which death can bestow. One had a laugh still upon his face, the muscles seeming to become rigid before the expression could change.

In the mean time the troops of the castle were engaged in getting up a nine pounder which had been captured from the enemy. It was a work of great labor but when it was mounted it commanded a large part of the city. While this was going on Lieut Martin borrowed a spy glass which gave us a much clearer idea of the place and its defenses. We saw frequent bodies of cavalry moving up and down the principal streets. Some of our men asserted the enemy had a white flag upon the citadel fort, but the glass showed it to be a faded Mexican banner. At last the troops below us moved down to attack the city. After waiting some half an hour we were ordered to follow and place ourselves as a reserve united with Lieut Bradford's[11] company, all deployed as skirmishers at the foot of the hill. After the expiration of another half hour Genl Worth rode back and ordered us to join the main body under Col Childs then fighting in the city....

It proved no easy matter to find Col Childs he being far in advance. After proceeding for about three quarters of a mile through a portion of the city deserted by the enemy, we at last arrived at a public square called the *Plaza de la Capilla*, from a chapel which connected with a cemetery, forms one side of the square. The latter was bounded by high walls with loop holes for musketry and embrasures for cannon. Here we found Capt Vinton[12] in command of the greater part of the Artillery Battalion. He directed us to fall in and take our place with the other companies. We then remained as a reserve for about half an hour to support the other companies in case they should be driven back. Nothing of the kind occurred however and we moved forward. As we were about to start Duncan rode up and told Capt Vinton he could save a large number of men by sheltering his command behind some projecting houses. This was really encouraging and seemed to show that we would soon have warm work. At length we put forward slowly, steadily and in silence, our platoons filling up the entire width of the street. Over the whole city in front of us was heard the continuous roar of cannon and dropping sound of musketry, indicating that the troops on the other side of the town under General Taylor were also engaged. As we approached the center of the city the fire became so hot we we were obliged to change our order of march and go by the flank at double quick on the side walk to escape the balls flying in the center of the street. The roaring rushing sound of the cannon ball, the "*whiff! whir!*" of the grape and the "*tsing*" of the musket balls could easily be distinguished from each other. We at last came to a store the door of which had been broken open, and sheltered ourselves within by order of Capt Vinton. We entered in good time but not before several were killed and wounded; one of these lay dying on the floor, and I saw another upon turning my head struck down by a shot and carried to the rear by two of his comrades. Before I went in two balls struck the wall by my head and another cut through the breast of the coat of the man on my left. One of our men named Ward walked back through the shot a distance of two hundred yards to get a light for his pipe at the slow match of one of the six pounders. He then sauntered slowly back puffing away while the Mexican balls flew thick about his ears. In front at a distance of eighty yards a barricade had been erected by the enemy who were driven from it by the advance of our troops. Still they commanded it by an *escopeta* fire from all the houses, and by batteries of grape converging from two streets. Genl Worth ordered Roland with a light piece to reply to the fire, but he could see no one to shoot at. The Mexicans were all concealed behind their parapet roofs. So after sending a few shells he was ordered back. How he escaped was a miracle to me, for the whole air was full of the hurtling sound of balls all seemingly directed at him.

After some delay it was resolved to attempt passage of the barricade and two companies, I think, were placed in a side street for that purpose. They rushed by at full speed and were followed by the remainder of the force at a run. We all took shelter under the wall of a bakery at the corner of a street. Behind this wall we remained several hours during which the Texians gained the tops of the houses and began to drive back the enemy with their rifles and Mackall's Battery and gallantly replied to the unremitting fire of the enemy. This part of the battle is associated in my mind with the memory of two young men who lived long enough to write their names in the annals of the war, and whose bloody deaths at Molino del Rey have consecrated them as heroes of the war: the gallant Ayres and the gay, light hearted Farry.[13] We remained under the shelter of the wall for some time and were then ordered into a house on the left having an inner court yard full of orange trees. Although the ripe fruit was hanging from the tree Capt Vinton directed none of it should be taken without the consent of the occupants. For men tired, hungry and thirsty I think this was carrying respect for private property rather too far. The Mexicans must have thought so too for they expected to be massacred without mercy. The only person I encountered was a half grown boy who was wild with terror. His knees were shaking, his eyes rolling and his tongue making inarticulate sounds. We occupied this position for several hours. During this time Genl Smith remained in the center of the street, directly in front of one of the enemy's batteries. The grape shot swept the street cutting into the houses on the right and left but the General by some miracle escaped uninjured. I stepped out and borrowed his spy glass for an instant and brought the swarthy faces of the Mexican gunners into a most interesting proximity. About this time one of my comrades advised me not to stand in the door way. I stepped back at his suggestion and immediately afterwards one of the grape shot struck the place where I had been standing. At this juncture Baille Peyton[14] rode up and asked us, "How goes the battle?" He wore his name in large letters on his straw hat, and had just come by a large circuit from Genl Taylor's camp. In the mean time [with] the shades of evening beginning to fall we were ordered to occupy a house with an important passage in it on the opposite side of the street. This passage communicated with the open fields and was the only one through which the enemy could gain the rear of our position in case we advanced further. We were ordered to cross to our new position two or three at a time at a run and one of our corporals was severely reprimanded for walking. Although the passage was open the doors of the building opening on it were locked and it became necessary to break them in to obtain an entrance. Weld had luckily picked up an axe at one of the houses and we set to work to force the fastenings but owing to the immense thickness of the panels it was a long time before we could succeed. As soon as the family found they could not keep us out any longer they opened the other doors at once probably expecting to be massacred. One little boy took down a picture of

Christ from the walls enclosed in a tin frame and held it up to me, as if to implore my compassion, exclaiming, "*It is our Lord, sir.*"

I found myself now excessively fatigued from the incessant excitement and want of rest on the preceeding nights. Not having eaten anything since the previous day my appetite was quite voracious. I satisfied it as well as I could with a cup of coffee and a bunch of grapes. The former was procured from the house across the way. We took advantage too of our privileges as conquerers and made them furnish also a bucketful for the men. The firing had now nearly ceased, it being too dark to aim with accuracy. Lieut Ricketts took every precaution to prevent a surprise, by stationing sentinels far in advance and watching himself during the entire night. I stood for some time, leaning against the door way thinking of the probable events of the morrow. The enemy greatly superior to us in numbers were now cooped up in a small part of the city. It was evident the morrow must decide the whole matter. To regain what they had lost it seemed probable the enemy would make a night attack and as we held one of the principal passages our position was both honorable and dangerous. Genl Smith himself came from time to time to examine it. He gave orders to defend it to the last extremity. After standing in the doorway some time my attention was attracted by an explosion from one of our mortars in the rear. I think Lieut Scarritt[15] assisted in the firing. Unfortunately the shell fell short of the enemy and entering the roof of a kitchen opposite to me, blew up there and covered me with fragments of adobe. The next attempt also fell short among our own troops who were very much annoyed at being bombarded in rear as well as front. The next shot however produced a tremendous effect. It struck the door of the main cathedral in which Ampudia had taken refuge. The building also contained a large quantity of ammunition. The coward immediately ordered the trumpets to sound a parley and innumerable rockets to be sent out in every direction probably thinking we were about to make a final assault. Unfortunately we did not know what a parley was and therefore answered all his demonstrations by increased firing. This again was answered by a bombardment from the Citadel Fort. The scene now became truly magnificent. The fiery shells crossing each other in the air, the sudden glare of the rockets, the shrill notes of the trumpets, the roaring of the cannon and crackling sound of musketry were all combined together.

I shall not soon forget the disagreeable night I passed in that narrow archway filled to overflowing with soldiers. It must be remembered I had hardly slept five hours during the two preceeding nights. I tried to procure sufficient space to lie down but the nearest approximation was a semi inclined position in which the body was brought in close contact with several sharp projecting stones. Even in this positon I might have obtained some rest had it not been for the passage being constantly thronged with Texians and Infantry soldiers passing backwards and forwards on duty. Then came a new excitement. It was said some wounded man had been left behind in the vicinity of the enemy. Fresh bodies were sent out to ascertain the fact and bring him in. The night seemed endless. When the morning at last arrived we were ordered to take up a new position in the plaza in front of us, from which our troops had retired the previous evening upon being bombarded in rear. Here we found Capt afterwards Col Miles[16] of the 7th, who pointed out to us the importance of the place and the advantage a ravine in the vicinity would afford the enemy in case he should attempt to drive us back. He also recommended to our attention the family of a Mexican Colonel who had unfortunately remained during the siege and were now shut up in an inner room in pitch darkness frightened out of their senses. We went at the Captain's request to try and reassure these people but our appearance was any thing but favorable. Our faces were much scratched from forcing our way through thorny bushes and our clothes from the same cause presented a very dilapidated appearance. They were stained too with specimens of every kind of mud from sleeping in road ways and on the wet ground. Add to this beards of several weeks growth, and we could not have been very prepossessing. Besides the Colonels family several others were also shut up in the out buildings. Among them were several Senoritas who bore fair claims to be considered pretty. In some surprise at the cessation of the firing we were notified officially that an armistice had taken place until twelve o'clock, which would terminate in a renewal of the attack on the center of the city, or in a complete surrender. We had therefore leisure to continue our conversation with the Colonel's family. One of the young ladies displayed a great deal of spirit and intelligence. I told her, her countrymen had fought well: she replied, "It was their duty to do so Senor, they were defending their homes and their country." She feared we would consider the females as fit objects of vengeance, and said, "do not class us with your enemies, we have done you no harm." I replied she had done great execution with her beautiful eyes. To this sally she hung her head saying half blushing, half laughing, "*quien sabe.*" I then turned towards a beautiful little girl and remarked that she resembled an American, but the child put up her little finger and waved it in front of her face saying she was a "*purita mejicana.*" The mother upon hearing me say the child was pretty, asked me if I was a bachelor, upon my replying in the affirmative, she said "does this child please you?" I said, "Yes very much." She replied "you may have her when she grows up."

The hours dragged along for all were impatient to ascertain the result. When it was nearly twelve I climbed up to the flat roof of the house to obtain a more general view. About two hundred yards in advance of me the Texians lay upon the roofs rifles in hand awaiting the signal to fire upon the dense masses in front of them. Upon descending I learned the gratifying intelligence that the armistice was to last for several months and the enemy to evacuate the town and forts in their possession. When I mentioned this to the Colonel's wife, she clasped her hands and poured forth her heartfelt thanks to the Virgen of Guadalupe through whose intercession in her opinion it had been brought about. She said, "Ampudia told me we were safe here; by no possibility could we ever be disturbed." The rest of the day passed without any peculiar incident. From time to time we saw Mexican officers galloping by with white flags. A body of our troops marched down to take possession of the Citadel Fort and as we had great curiosity to inspect the Mexican Infantry several of us went to the corner to see the garrison as it passed by. It came marching by platoons, with drums beating and colors flying and joined the rest of the Mexican force in the main plaza, the dark Indian faces of the soldiers presenting quite a contrast to our men. This show being over we made a requisition upon one of the families in our neighborhood for a dinner. This they cheerfully furnished but it was so mixed with their favorite condiment "*chile colorado*" (red pepper) as to be scarcely eatable. Having satisfied or rather burned our appetites the next thing was to procure some sleep. I threw myself down very thankfully on a cot without mattrass pillow or covering of any kind and never had a sweeter sleep in my life. I was awakened early the next day by Ricketts who found some little difficulty in rousing me. When my eyes were fairly opened he said to me laughing, "Here is a lady called to see you." It was the Colonel's wife who wished to avail herself of my knowledge of Spanish, to beg me to use all my influence to obtain permission from General Worth for herself and family to leave town. I felt little inclination to wake up the General at that hour but luckily the officer of the day was in the vicinity and gave the requisite pass. The lady departed at once with a thousand expressions of gratitude and invitations for me to call and see her at her country seat of Santa Catarina.

The first thing we did was to move into new and permanent quarters. The day passed quietly enough. In the evening I was detailed in command of a large guard. At night my patrols would come in and complain of having been stoned by the enemy, but as it was impossible to find the perpetrators of the outrage nothing could be done. The next morning after marching off guard, curiosity led me towards the grand plaza where the main body of the enemy were still congregated. I was without arms and soon found myself in the vicinity of the Mexican forces. Several of our men were sauntering about attracted like myself by a desire to see what was going on. One of them complained to me, that a Mexican had stationed himself at the corner of one of the streets with a huge knife avowedly to kill the first American who passed. I saw an officer coming who I was informed was General Garcia Conde and pointed out the man to him. Nothing could exceed the politeness of the General but there was something bitter in his manner. The Mexican as soon as he saw us looking towards him disappeared. I then continued my course until I found myself in the main plaza surrounded by a crowd of Mexican

Lieutenants and Ensigns who at once entered into conversation and were very polite. As we stood watching the preparations for departure I turned towards a large man whose complexion was very fair and who was dressed like an officer of rank, and said to him, "*En donde esta la caballeria.*" (where is the cavalry) He said "You speak English dont you?" I said "yes!" He said "Very well I am a Scotchman a surgeon in the Mexican Army. Do you believe that d____ scoundrel Ampudia never once left the church to see what was going on." After a short conversation I returned to my quarters and saw the Mexican forces file by in all their disgrace. They were allowed to retain six pieces of artillery each of which they ornamented with a small banner. They were accompanied by a perfect army of females on horseback. The soldiers were full of curiosity to see General Taylor and many asked if Genl Smith were not he.

In recalling the various incidents of the battle I forgot to mention two wounded men in the attack on Federation Hill. They came to me and made signs to show them the Doctor. One had his face mutilated by gravel flung up by a cannon shot which struck directly in front of him, and the other was shot while ascending the hill. A musket ball had entered his left cheek and came out low down in his neck. I was told he survived.

5

THE BATTLE OF BUENA VISTA

At length the hour struck which seemed about to become one of the darkest in our history. Santa Anna aware of the withdrawl of the Regular Regiments from General Taylor, and believing he could crush without difficulty the small army of undisciplined troops which remained, suddenly left San Luis and came rushing on with 20,000 men, confident in his power to regain at one blow the whole country to the Rio Grande. Urrea lay between Monterey and Cerralvo to cut off all retreat and the citadel fort at the former place was to be taken by bombardment. This news was too important to be long concealed. Influential merchants whose property was at stake and who possessed friends in the Army, knew the very day and hour of the proposed attack. In the mean time alarm succeeded alarm in Monterey. It was known that Urrea had passed the mountains at Victoria and every hour his Lancers were looked for in the vicinity of the city. The garrison at this period consisted of the Louisville Legion, Ohio Regiment, and Capt. Prentiss's Company of Artillery "E" to which I belonged. The Legion and our company were encamped at the Fort and the Ohio Regiment stationed in the city proper. The Fort itself in spite of its strong appearances was quite defective, the ditches being very narrow and containing large dead spaces. The relief of the parapet was the minimum and worse than all no bomb proofs existed except two very small

BV Doubleday, Abner. "Memorandum Book of a Journey to Mexico to Look for Gardiner's Mine."

magazines about ten feet square. It was necessary in fact almost to rebuild the work. The Engineer Officer Capt. Fraser[1] did his part to remedy these defects, but in spite of every exertion the works were far from being completed. The constant alarms showed the immediate necessity of finishing the magazines. One day a scene of great confusion was created by some drunken volunteers, who reported the enemy entering the suburbs of the city. The bells rang an alarm peal in the midst of high mass; the long roll was beaten in the main plaza and the troops were immediately formed. The first notice we had of this *stampede* at the Fort, was given by two citizens, who came on horseback at full speed shouting "to arms; to arms; the enemy are upon us." I was taking a siesta at the time and was awakened by Capt Prentiss who told me a Mexican force was reported to be within two miles of us. Our company was immediately turned out for the purpose of mounting the guns. All was confusion various kinds of private property was brought down and hastily flung into the Fort and the sick were hastily secured and placed in the unfinished magazine. Among these invalids was the gallant McClung[2] of Mississippi, who at first had been almost forgotten in the tumult. This alarm subsided only to give place to similar ones. Upon the same day an order arrived to send up the [1st] Mississippi Regt to Saltillo immediately. It accordingly started at dusk. I was visiting the city at that hour when I heard some voices calling me from the opposite side of the street. I found they proceeded from a Mexican family of the better class, with whom I was intimately acquainted. They clasped their hands and said, "Thank God, you are here, you can tell us the cause of these terrible alarms. We have been shut up the entire day frightened at every noise. Listen, Good God, what fearful shouts are those in the plaza; what does it all mean?" I reassured them as to the cries, which proceeded from the Regiment leaving town, and told them they had no immediate cause for alarm. I advised them however to quit the city the first opportunity as it was possible it might be the scene of a second battle. They accordingly prepared to move on the morrow. Hitherto our own prospect of sharing in the dangers which surrounded General Taylor was some what remote, but the next morning we received an order, to constitute ourselves into a company of heavy artillery and come on with all speed with two 18 pounders and 2 twelves. We at once applied ourselves with energy to have everything in readiness for the emergency. While Lieut Ricketts was engaged in turning over the public property in his possession, I was ordered to obtain all the men well enough to march from the Hospital and afterwards to make out a list of, and load the wagons with the requisite ammunition. As I rode through the deserted streets I was struck with the strange silence which reigned around. You might travel for hours through Monterey at this time without encountering a human being. It realized the fabled city whose inhabitants had been suddenly turned to stone. All around lay the machinery of life, but life itself was wanting. This contrast was more impressive to me than the solitude of the desert or the ocean had ever been. It was some time before I could find the Hospital. When I entered it, the sick came round me in crowds saying, "Lieutenant, you are going up to the battle, may God be with you; oh, that we were well enough to join you. You would not find us staying behind." All day we were occupied with the work of preparation. In the meantime the labor on the Fort proceeded with renewed vigor. Col. Ormsby's Regiment were encamped within, and above them floated a banner presented by the ladies of Louisville bearing the proud inscription "*Kentucky trusts you.*" A large number of Mexican laborers had been engaged and paid according to the amount of labor. Trunks of the largest trees were dragged in, hastily, to be hewed into shape afterwards in making bomb proof magazines. For ourselves, it was nearly dusk before we were ready to start, and then we were disappointed at finding the teams could not be hitched to the guns without extensive alterations and additions in the carriages. Blacksmiths were immediately sent for, and by extraordinary energy succeeded in having every thing ready by eight o'clock. Then came the usual annoyance in cases of this kind of hunting up drunken soldiers, it being a lamentable fact that men always think it necessary to be drunk at the commencement of a march. After some trouble the drunkards were safely deposited in the baggage wagons with their arms and accoutrements, and we set out. All was silent and dark. We travelled nearly two miles through the streets without hearing even a dog bark. As we passed the Bishop's Castle the men recalled the previous action and burned with enthusiasm to gather new laurels in the approaching conflict. Our train having taken another road separated from us but it made little difference as we were all to meet at "*Los Molinos*" some seven miles from Monterey. In this march short as it was we had a foretaste of the difficulties attending the transit of our heavy 18 pounders, one of which was overturned in a gully about three miles from the city. By sending back to the Ordnance officer Major Ramsey[3] a gin was procured and the piece remounted. Upon reaching *the mills* we found them apparently deserted. Upon a close examination of one of the doors I detected a light within, and after repeated knockings succeeded in gaining an entrance. The Miller was busily at work making flour. He furnished me with an empty room to sleep in and some *pinola*, for which he refused all compensation. Ricketts and myself lay down together on the counter of a deserted store. I had determined to get all the sleep I could so as to go into battle fresh. Our Captain Prentiss who slept outside was half frozen. At dawn of day we resumed our march and were shortly afterwards joined by General Marshall[4] with his staff and thirty of the Kentucky Cavalry. The road from Monterey to Saltillo is a complete pass from beginning to end the termination of which is at the defiles of Buena Vista. The sierras on our left were very remarkable in appearance being more than a mile in height. The ascent is a precipice which is almost perpendicular, so that it would be utterly impossible for any person to ascend it. Another feature of these mountains is their thinness. Near Santa Catarina there is a complete tunnel in the mountain through which the sun is clearly visible at certain hours. The sierras on the right were of the same character but are of less height and gentler slope. This scenery strongly attracted my attention as we passed along, and I was admiring in particular the color of the rocks when word was sent us to prepare to encounter a party of Lancers in our front. After making every preparation to receive them with ball and grape shot; they turned out to be a party of mounted Kentuckians escorting a

mule train. We met also some mounted Mexicans one of whom I suspected of being a spy, but the suspicion was not strong enough to jus-
tify his apprehension. We also started up a large gray wolf, who
walked away from us very slowly. This march seemed to me a severe
one for the heat was very great, and no water to be had. When we
arrived within five miles of the Rinconada as if bad luck had determined to persecute us, the axle tree of another 18 pounder broke
down. We however pressed on to our destination leaving a small
detachment to take care of the piece, until an axle tree could be
made and sent back. The men however had the ingenuity to lift the
immense weight by means of levers and jack screws and afterwards
bring it in on a waggon. Upon reaching the Rinconada I rushed up to
my knees in the little mountain brook which dashes by, and enjoyed
a drink which was perfect nectar. The village at this point must have
been a beautiful place at one period, but war is a sad devastator, and
now every thing was in ruins. The carcasses of dead horses lay all
around. The houses had all been turned into stables and were tum-
bling down on every side. The scenery itself is truly sublime. The
mountains which bound the valley contrast beautifully with each
other, some of moderate height, and gentle slope and others going up
to the very skies, like huge rocks sent assunder. They throw a deep
shade and give a dark and sombre appearance to the valley. We
encamped in a very disagreeable spot but after a long march one pays
very little attention to trifles, and I think we had as much sleep as we
desired. Capt Prentiss set all his mechanics at work to make a new
axle tree. This they had ample time to do on account of the reception of the following order which came by express:

Head Quarters, Army of Occupation
Camp at Agua Nueva, Mexico

Sir:

The Commanding General directs that you halt at the
Rinconada until further orders with Captain Prentiss' Company
and the troop of Kentucky horse.

He also wishes you to place the guns in position and be prepared to hold the place against any force, until you can hear again from Head Quarters.

I am sir
Very Respectfully
Yr Obedient Servant
W. W. S. Bliss
Asst. Adj. Genl.

[signed]
Brig Genl T. Marshall
at the Rinconada

The expressman stated that he had to take to the mountains to avoid the enemy whose numbers he estimated at 3000. They lay between us and General Taylor who had fallen back to Buena Vista. It had been falsely represented to Genl Taylor that Minon who commanded the 3000 men had cannon with him. It was therefore to be feared he would take the Rinconada and cut off Genl Taylors retreat, so that in case of defeat the entire army would be sacrificed. Hence the order for us to remain and defend it to the last extremity. Against an enemy coming from Monterey the pass is very strong as all the windings of the road are fully commanded by the summit of the hill; the Mexicans had accordingly built a redoubt at this point. Our force however was altogether too small to guard the heights and rebuild the redoubt which Ampudia had demolished nor could we with barely one hundred men guard a pass a mile in width over very rocky and uneven ground. We concluded at last to defend the main road at the village some four miles from the redoubt. The day was passed in preparation for battle. The gun carriages were repaired, rifles and cartridges issued to the teamsters and some twenty of the Ohio Regiment whom we met at the Rinconada were ordered to accompany us as a rear guard in case of a movement. To prevent a surprise cavalry picquets were thrown out on the Saltillo road. We frequently saw persons dressed as rancheros ride up to within a quarter of a mile in rear and pause apparently to estimate our numbers. To attempt to capture them would have led to no result except to encumber ourselves with prisoners. One of our men who was out hunting deer saw some 300 men at a distance of two miles from us. Besides the company of artillery who had enough to do to attend to the guns we had but 30 cavalry and 20 infantry. Of course we could spare none of these as all were needed to defend our position, which we thought would probably be attacked in the night. One third of the officers and men were kept on guard until midnight, another third until 4 A.M. and the remaining third from 4 until Reveille. I had the middle watch, and lay down fully determined to take four hours good sleep by way of preparation. Unfortunately the more I endeavored to sleep the less I succeeded, and twelve o'clock came without my having had any rest. I immediately put on my sword and walked out. Everything was silent as death except the conversation carried on by the guard almost in a whisper. The night was cool and dark, and the moon obscured by clouds. I walked the rounds of the various sentinels incessantly, occasionaly pausing to listen. No sound was there except the rush of the night wind through the leaves and the faint chirp of some birds in the distance. As I looked at one of the mountains which could scarcely be distinguished it became distinctly visible in a reddish light as if some watch fire had flared up strongly for a moment. I have no doubt at that time all the passes were full of armed rancheros ready to fall upon our defeated army and cut the throats of the fugitives. As soon as my tour was over I turned in to sleep but was awakened almost instantly. The want of this rest told upon me severely afterwards. During the night another express[5] from Genl Taylor arrived bearing the following order:

Head Quarters, Army of Occupation
Saltillo, February 22d, 1847, 8. P.M.

General

As the Commanding General understands that you have a respectable force at Rinconada, he has determined to bring forward the heavy guns, and therefore desires that you will take up the march for this place at sundown tomorrow and come through in the night. A considerable force of cavalry has been in rear of Saltillo to day, and may attempt to interrupt your march, but with proper vigilance the General thinks you will be able to come through safely. He desires me to say that your mounted men should be kept well in front, and on your flanks so as to give you timely warning of the approach or vicinity of any cavalry. Should you be menaced he directs that your waggons be parked, and the guns placed in position to drive off the enemy. The train for that purpose should be well closed up.

The General understands that it contains forty waggons, which will give the means of making a strong park if necessary.

The Armies have been in presence to day near Buena Vista, and there has been some skirmishing of light troops. We hold a very strong postition and cannot without difficulty, if at all be driven from it.

> I am Very Respectfully
> Your Obedient Servant
> W. W. S. Bliss
> Asst Adj Genl.
>
>
> Brig. Genl. T. Marshall
> U. S. Army
> Commanding at Rinconada

The above order I have understood was predicated on the supposition that Col Morgan's Ohio Regt had joined us. The expressman stated that Minon with his 3000 cavalry lay directly across our path. This was severe odds to be encountered by a force of 150 men defending a train of sixty waggons nearly a mile in length. It is easy to talk of preparing for the enemy by making a park, but as the road was not wide enough for two waggons it would be a work of time. Our heavy battery too was unwieldy. It was impossible to travel with the guns loaded and to load them would take a little time. The enemy knew the country and we were ignorant of it. If they had suddenly charged us the chances in their favor would have been overwhelming. We made every preparation during the day. This was the 23d February, 1847, the never to be forgotten day of the Battle of Buena Vista. The first notice I had of the action was from one of the old soldiers who said to me, "Lieutenant, if you will go down into that ravine and put your ear to the ground, you can hear distinctly the firing of artillery." What would we not have given to have been there, but as we were to start at 5 P.M. there was still a chance of our arriving in time to take a part. At last we set out slowly [to] climb the high hills until we reached [the] redoubt and then descended into the little hamlet of "*Los Muertos.*" Night had now come on, but we had a lovely moon to guide us. We supplied ourselves with water, and pursued our way, earnest and thoughtful. We were liable at any moment to be attacked by an overwhelming force of the enemy on ground chosen by themselves. They had sworn to give no quarter. If defeated every point of our backward path would be occupied by hundreds and thousands of excited rancheros thirsting for our blood. Even if we succeeded in joining Genl Taylor a doubtful battle was before us. In spite of all these circumstances I began after marching some fifteen miles to find an excessive drowsiness stealing over me, owing to want of sleep on the previous night, and the fatigue and excitement of the day before. We stopped at a small rancho named Ojo Caliente and rested for about fifteen minutes. We were too eager to reach our destination to wait longer. On our left at Capillinia 1500 rancheros were congregated under Don Jacob Sanchez[6] but they did not attempt to disturb our march. On the contrary the frightened inhabitants heard the heavy rumbling of our artillery and prepared to make a hasty flight. I found my drowsiness increasing so that I was unable to sit my horse and even when walking along I felt as if I were walking in my sleep....

Five miles further on we met an express from General Taylor, I need not say with what interest we gathered around him to learn the result of the battle. It was a scene I shall not soon forget. The huge watch fires of Minon on our left and front; the full moon sinking behind the distant mountains and the messenger of life and death in the center relating the events of the combat. The tale was incoherent enough. It could not well be otherwise. A soldier who has been fighting all day in one locality in the midst of smoke and noise is not a very good judge of what has been going on over a field of many miles. We ascertained that after fighting all day General Taylor still held his position and that was the main point. He said the battle would be renewed at daylight. It was already two o'clock and our men had marched on foot over twenty miles. Genl. Marshall thought they would be unable to fight without a few hours rest but all the men who were present implored the General to lead them against the enemy, without delay. We heard them with a good deal of pride. Again we set forward but the moon had already passed below the horizon and we had nothing to guide us.

At length we approached a small village about six miles from Saltillo. Our course had been bringing us nearer and nearer to the watch fires of the enemy. At last we encountered one of his picquets who first fired upon us, and then galloped back to join the main body, closely pursued by our cavalry. The night was fast becoming dark but many stars were visible. After a short consultation it was determined to proceed and we accordingly pushed on until we entered the village refered to. No molestation was offered us though bodies of the enemy were seen lurking in the vicinity. At this stage of proceedings while expecting an attack one of the 18 pounders became stuck fast in an *acequia* or irrigating ditch some 12 feet in width, and the utmost exertions of ourselves and the animals were required before it could be extracted. This was the last obstacle we had to encounter. Gen Miñon was fully apprised of our numbers but instead of attacking us, gave orders to his whole force to make a hasty retreat through Palomas Pass. I was told by a spectator that he bantered his picquets very much on their rapid flight calling them "*Los dispersados*." The entrance to Saltillo being now open we proceeded without furthur molestation. The excitement of passing Miñon's force having ceased, my drowsiness returned and being unable either to sit a horse or even walk I crept into a baggage waggon and entered Saltillo in that way. We saw

no signs of life until we reached the main plaza. Here I heard the cool
plashing of a fountain near which an Artillery officer was giving com-
mands. I recognized the voice and called out, "*Shover*".[7] We
exchanged hurried salutations and I passed by. On my left I saw a
magnificent church full of glancing lights, and I involuntarily
exclaimed what religious ceremonies are going on at such a time as
this. Some one standing on the pavement answered me, "That building is filled to overflowing with wounded and dying men. Lincoln, Yell,
Hardin, McKee, and Clay[8] have all fallen." A feeling of indescribable
solemnity and sadness passed over me. It almost seemed as if the
Angel of Death was singing a slow and solemn dirge. I made no further enquiries knowing that Capt. Prentiss would ascertain every
thing. In a few moments he galloped up and I asked him the result.
He replied, "This has been a terrible affair sir. Nearly a thousand men
are already killed and wounded. At daybreak the battle will recom-
mence. There is no hope of victory. All we can do, is to go out and
fight to the last." Even as he spoke an orderly dashed down the hill at
full speed, reined up and said, "Capt. Prentiss, the General directs
that your company proceed to the field of battle without delay." Major
Bliss came in person shortly after to reiterate the order. We reached
the high hill which overlooks Saltillo and took the road to Buena
Vista. The battle field was six miles from the city and as I said it is the
end of the long mountain pass which connects the lowlands with the
highlands of Mexico. On we dashed, our tired mules being whipped
into a desperate attempt at a gallop, for a body of the enemy's cavalry were on our left and it was reported a body of Lancers were
endeavoring to cut us off. We passed however without molestation.
Dead bodies and broken waggons strewed along our path told we
were nearing the destination. At last we reached the spot where
Washington's[9] battery was located. As we approached the field music
of the Army sounded reveille and shout upon shout which made the
welkin ring told that Santa Anna had fallen back. In consequence of
this news we were immediately ordered to return to Saltillo. It was
believed at the time that Santa Anna was merely taking up a new
position with a view of gaining our rear. We finally encamped on the

high hills above Saltillo after the almost unheard of march of 42 miles[10] between sunset and sunrise. Now that I had an opportunity of reposing I had lost all desire to do so. I had however a very heavy feeling about the eyes. Ricketts and myself descended into the city and went to a kind of tavern kept by a gigantic camp woman, who usually went by the name of the Great Western.[11] There we found officers of all grades, who having eaten nothing the day before, were endeavoring to procure some refreshment. We considered ourselves fortunate in being able to procure a cup of coffee and a piece of bread. After visiting one or two wounded officers Major Stein[12] and Lieut French we crossed over and entered the Cathedral directly opposite. The entire building was filled with wounded and the floor in many places was stained with blood. I did not remain long as I saw the surgeons preparing to operate. I was struck with the absence of all complaint on the part of our poor fellows. There was a silence amounting to solemnity about the place. In the employment of a merchant Monsieur Pelligrin in the city, there was a cook, who was born in New Orleans of French parentage. As she had left quite young she could not speak English. Considering us as her countrymen she came to offer her services at the church, in making broth, etc. She was much grieved at not being understood but at last she found an interpreter in Lieut Eustis[13] of the Dragoons. I saw with a sad heart the coffin lid screwed down over the brave and handsome Lincoln. A few days before I had met him in Monterey full of life, hope and eager expectation. We now returned to our station on the hill. The town was utterly bereft of its inhabitants. It was solitary as the grave. A tent having been put up hastily, I unrolled my bedding and threw myself down with the intention of indemnifying myself for the previous fatigue. All around me the soldiers lay like logs. The poor fellows had made a march almost unprecedented in war of forty two miles between sunset and sunrise, weighed down with their muskets accoutrements, etc. Notwithstanding a heavy feeling about the head and the strongest desire to obtain a little repose I found it impossible to sleep. I tossed about for an hour in vain. I then sprang to my feet procured a fresh horse from Shover (who was in command of a section of

a Light Battery) and we set out together. We passed many bodies of
men and horses in our ride of six miles and at last reached Buena
Vista once more. It was a romantic and interesting spot. Upon these
high tablelands of Mexico the mixed races of the septentrional had
contended with the Anglo Saxon for a great prize. The one was anti-
mated with all the hatred of caste, the animosity of religious bigotry,
and the old Spanish abhorrence of the invader: the other with all the
pride of former achievements and the presence of a General whose
name was victory. Yet there upon the greensward equal at last in
death lay the swart Mexican and the white northerner, the weapons
of destruction still grasped in their lifeless hands. As I entered the little village or rancho I came upon the Artillery Batteries. There were
Bragg, Thomas, and Reynolds leaning upon their guns surrounded on
all sides by the dead. It was a picture I shall never forget. We rode over
the whole field several miles in extent. In the ravines and upon the
plain above lay corpses doubled up in every attitude of death and
pain. Several of the wounded called out to me in their own language,
oh senor commandante, dont leave me here to die of cold and
hunger.[14] They were pleased at seeing the waggons approach to take
them in, but by far the greatest number preserved a stern silence and
endeavored to drag their mutilated bodies behind some place of con-
cealment evidently fearing we would give no quarter. On the brow of
the hill we notice many piles of flat rocks laid so as to make a shelter
and a loop hole for Santa Anna's infantry. Among the foremost
corpses that of a tall handsome man said to have been a Colonel in
the Mexican Army was very prominent. His leg had been completely
severed from his body by a cannon ball. I also observed a body which
had been stripped and which must have belonged to our army. It was
perfectly white and some naval emblems were tatooed on the arm. As
it was found in the midst of the Mexican lines it would seem to have
belonged to some poor prisoner, who had been carried there and then
murdered and stripped. The field of battle was very large in extent
and it took a long time to ride over the whole of it. I had seen similar
scenes before, and the force of habit prevented the suffering from
making a very deep impression upon me. But as I saw the long train

of waggons pass by laden with pain and agony and heard the low
piteous groans and faint shrieks of the wounded I felt as if I desired to
witness no more and putting spurs to my horse galloped hastily back
to Saltillo. Yet one waggon load which passed will never be forgotten
by me. It contained the corpses of Yell, Clay, Hardin and McKee.
Their faces were pallid as the paper I am writing on. Shover and
myself reached our camp on the hill at sundown, partook of a hasty
supper and were soon sound asleep. No alarm occured during the
night and I therefore awoke on the ensuing morning much refreshed.
As we were eating our breakfast an orderly rushed in, bringing an
order for Capt Prentiss to harness up his battery and proceed in haste
to Buena Vista, as the enemy were again approaching. Capt Shover
having been absent to Monterey he was ordered to leave an officer in
his place, and I was accordingly designated. In a few moments Major
Bliss came to re-iterate the order and shortly afterwards General
Taylor in person came to hasten the movement. He looked very anxious and well he might for the troops themselves were much dejected.
He told me himself to get out the ammunition I needed as soon as
possible. In a short time the battery was harnessed up and on its way
while I was left on the summit of the high hill over looking the city
and opposite a pass through the mountains which leads to Patos.
Upon approaching Saltillo from Buena Vista nothing is seen of the
place until the traveller finds it suddenly spread out at his feet far
beneath him. Beyond an immense plain is bounded by a vast amp-
itheater of mountains. The whole of this plain is studded with villages
and isolated ranchos and the effect is very beautiful. The point where
I was located commanded the city and was in a measure the key of it.
It also commanded the Patos pass. Here then I found myself in position with one piece of Artillery and three companies of Mississippi
Riflemen. These last were to be stationed in an adobe house which
the Engineer Officer, Lieut Benham was rapidly fortifying. Opposite
but separated by two ravines was a regular fort garrisoned by Major
Webster's[15] Company of my regiment and two 24 pdr. Howitzer. The
command of the whole was given to Col. Belknap of the 8th Infantry.
It will be seen that the proposed Fort would have had two of its sides

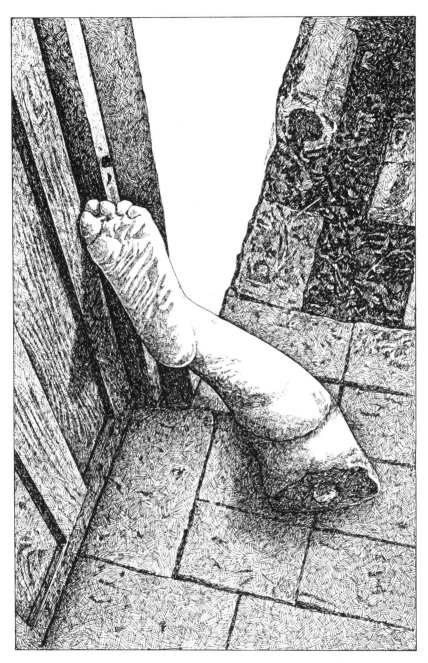

"It was no uncommon thing to see...."

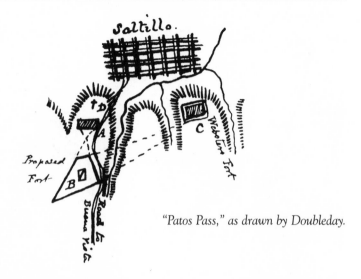

"Patos Pass," as drawn by Doubleday.

flanked by the 24 pdr. Howitzer at the corner of Webster's Fort and the other two sides by one or more Companies of Mississippi Riflemen in the adobe house at A. The adobe house at B was to answer as a citadel for the new work. My piece of artillery was at D. The prompitude with which this little piece of Fortification was designed by Lieut Benham showed in my opinion great *coup d'oeil*. Cavalry pickets were sent out to reconnoitre the Patos and Palomas passes and our glasses swept the country incessantly in search of an enemy. We soon discovered by the huge column of smoke arising from the direction of Santa Anna's Army that the prairie had been set on fire. Many thought it was to cover an advance others thought it was to hide a retreat. General Taylor was of the latter opinion and he was right. The battle was ended. For days long trains of waggons came in heavily laden with the wounded of the disorganized Mexican Army who had been abandoned by their own countrymen. For weeks in almost every house of the main street of Saltillo the Mexican surgeons were to be seen with bloody hands surrounded by crouching wretches waiting to undergo their turn at the amputating knife. It was no uncommon thing to see a leg or an arm leaning against the street door where it had just been cut off. Our own surgeons too were not idle. The entire street was one long hospital.

6

ROGUERY AND RASCALITY IN MEXICO

Duelling

After the retreat of the enemy was fully assured our company was ordered to take post with our heavy guns in a large yard belonging to an abandoned convent in Saltillo. We were located in the center of the town and were much more pleasantly situated than the troops in camp as we held a kind of independent existence and were not subject to the rigid rules at Buena Vista for Genl Wool was a very severe commander.

Capt Prentis being a man of refinement with a fine income gave a number of entertainments and was a general favorite. We had frequent visitors from the camp and our quarters became quite a rendezvous for our friends of the regular army.

One day Lieut. B.[1] came to pay me a visit of several days. We were walking up a street together near our residence when we chanced to meet a fiery specimen of the chivalry somewhat celebrated for the readiness to take offence and to call every one to account. He was dressed as a private soldier with the exception of a pair of straps on his shoulders and so when he passed us and said good morning gents we did not notice him particularly and as it seems did not return his salutation. He immediately turned about came up to us and said, "Gentlemen I said good morning to you as I passed. You can see by my straps that I am an officer and entitled to be treated with the ordinary courtesy of a gentleman. You did not answer my salutation and I think

BV Doubleday, Abner. The original text for this chapter can be found in two Doubleday Collection sources: BV Doubleday, Abner, "From the Mexican War to the Rebellion, First Rough Draft" and "Gardner's Mine...."

treated me in a contemptuous manner." B. a southern himself, somewhat hasty and choline, put himself in the wrong by saying, "I claim
the right to speak to such persons as I choose," or words to that effect.
Therefore M. said, turning to me, will you favor me with your residence, sir. I replied certainly I am living in that yellow house you see
there opposite the convent and this gentleman is staying with me as
my guest. You will find me very much at your service. He replied. I suppose so sir, bowed, and went on.

Brown and myself thought little of this occurrence and it soon
passed out of our memory. The next afternoon as we were taking a
siesta in my bedroom a thundering knock was heard at the street door.
Upon going to see what was wanted, several officers were ushered in
all in full uniform and with swords clanking at their heels. They presented a challenge in due form from Lt. M. to B. and I was notified
that when he was disposed of my turn would come. I do not know
what reply B. made as I did not see his note. One of the officers whom
I knew quite well took me aside and asked the origin of the difficulty.
I told him that we supposed M. was a private that we had no personal
feeling against him he was a stranger to both of us and we would have
answered his salutations as a matter of course had we known that he
was an officer; that it would have been answered under any circumstances had we not been preoccupied in conversation. He said that he
thought it a shame that a duel should come off for so slight a cause
and would do what he could to prevent it. The challenges were withdrawn and that was the last we heard of it.

Another affair occurred afterward which came near having a more
serious ending. Lieut. P.[2] a citizen appointment had joined our regiment of artillery. He was a capital fellow, but over sensitive. Being of
the same rank we were together a great deal. It seems he took a fancy
that I looked down upon him because he was not a graduate of West
Point. One evening when he was my guest there was a supper party
and he took more wine than he should have done. To my astonishment under the effect of the liquor he expressed a good deal of resent-
ment for the feeling he supposed I entertained toward him said he was
as good a man as I was and went on in a strain that became quite

offensive. It was at my own table and he was hardly in a condition to know what he was saying. The next morning I wrote him a letter simply calling his attention to the remarks he had made on the previous evening to give him an opportunity to make any explanation if he desired to do so. The next morning Col. August[3] of Va. who was celebrated for the number of affairs of honor in which he had been engaged called upon me in full uniform bearing an answer to my letter. This was to the effect that I had sent a demand for an apology by the hands of a negro messenger and that this was irregular and contramand [to] all the usual customs in such cases. The affair now began to look serious. I sent for Capt Mears[4] of N.C. a friend of mine, and handed him a letter to deliver to P. to the effect that my previous epistle had not been a demand for an apology, but was intended merely to call his attention to some incautious words he had used but now that he had formally selected Col August to represent him I did demand an explanation or apology. The affair thus went out of my hands into that of the two gentlemen referred to who sat up all night discussing it. At daybreak there came a knock at my door and P. walked in bowed stiffly and apologized by direction of Col. August who thought under the circumstances it was due me. P. and myself were fast friends after that and years afterward when his nomination for Genl was pending before the Senate Committee and about to be thrown out, I interceeded and had him confirmed.

Guerilla Activity and Spying by Mexicans

Becoming weary of the somewhat monotonous garrison life I made a trip to Monterey to see some of my old friends there. I went down with a paymasters escort and spent a week there. My leave being out I was obliged to return and as no troops were moving at this time I came back with a gentleman named Miller who was on his way to Saltillo on some business concerned with army supplies. He was only armed with a pair of derringer pistols and I had a revolver. We spent the night at the Rinconada and then resumed our way. When within ten or eleven miles of Saltillo we saw about three quarters of a mile ahead of us on the road a band of guerillas armed with guns and lances. There seemed to be about forty of them. They did not at first notice us. We were too few to contend with them and could not bear the idea of going back towards Monterey. A little ways off the main road there was a little village called Santa Maria. The Alcalde had often been in Saltillo and I knew him quite well so I resolved to throw myself upon his hospitality for the time being. I felt quite certain if we could gain his residence before we could be intercepted by the guerrillas we would be safe for the time being for he would scarcely provoke a contest in the presence of his own family. We accordingly dashed across the intervening fields and succeeded in reaching his house in time. The guerrillas drew up in a street about 200 yds. from the place as the main gates of the mansion opened and received us into the inner court. Don ____expressed great joy at our presence and exerted himself to make our stay agreeable. I had no intention of trusting him too far so I gave out that we would leave the next morning by a particular road and went off that afternoon by another route.

"This was the very life I had been desirous of leading. To mix with the rancheros...."

We were not molested and reached our camp in safety. A few days afterwards it was ascertained from some intercepted correspondence that Don ___ was the leader of this band of guerrillas and he was seized and imprisoned in consequence.

This same intercepted correspondence reminds me of another incident. We heard there had been serious battles on Genl Scott's line of operations and it was rumored that the Americans had been defeated at the very gates of Mexico and driven off. As this would forebode a concentration of force against Genl Wool he felt quite anxious about it and was very desirous of obtaining some reliable intelligence. It was ascertained that the Mexicans in Saltillo received almost a daily mail with all the latest news. The problem then was to capture that mail and the commander at Saltillo was directed to instruct the officers of the day to make every effort to carry out this design. I was the first officer to whom this task was assigned and set myself to work to accomplish it. I placed myself in the situation of the mail rider and tried to devise a method of bringing the mail in without being detected. I came to the conclusion that if I had to do it I should bring it in by Palomas Pass as that was unguarded and that I would choose the interval between dark and 9 P.M. when tattoo sounded. The next thing was to determine the time to bring it in town as daylight would almost ensure detection. The wait until 9 P.M. when tattoo was over and when all parties approaching the city were halted and examined would be very unadvisable. The best time was evidently between dark about 7 P.M. and tattoo at 9 P.M. Having come to these conclusions I took a small detachment with me stationed myself behind some houses on the Palomas Pass Road where it enters the town and examined every person that came in until it was about 9 o'clock. I found nothing and was about to return when I heard a man come jogging along on a mule. I halted him and made an examination. In a small bag attached to his saddle we could feel a small paper package which it was thought must be the letters. I ordered the man to be taken to the commanding officers office and there we all went to ascertain the result. The package was opened and found to be some four or five letters but they proved to be far from being satisfactory.

They were all from young ladies in the country to their families and associates in the city and were not at all edifying as they related merely to personal gossip and love affairs. All this time our prisoner had kept his blanket wrapped closely around him. I observed it and said we have not really searched him he may have other letters, take off that blanket and examine him. The moment this was attempted he fell upon his knees and begged for mercy for himself and his master. All this time he had been hiding a large bundle of letters and papers. These were examined for some time without any result. At last a paragraph in one of the epistles said you will find all the news in the letter to the Senor Cure. We at once opened this and it revealed the state of affairs in the city of Mexico and explained what was going on there fully to the satisfaction of Genl Wool who was pleased to compliment me for my successful endeavor.

One day the command at Palomas Pass secured some of the principal families including women of rank and standing and sent them in as prisoners on some foolish pretext. These people had many relatives and friends in Saltillo who were powerfully affected by the indignities heaped upon them. That night there was a serious insurrection and as I was officer of the day with a co of arty mounted as cavalry to back me I had a busy time.

Mexican Justice

John the English Pilot[5] at the mouth of the Rio Grande was once robbed of some $300. He succeeded however in detecting and apprehending the thief. In order to make him divulge where he had concealed the money he ordered his servants to take the rascal to the river and duck him until he restored the money. This produced the desired effect. John pocketed the $300, and supposed this was the end of the business, but he was mistaken. He was soon cited to appear before the Alcalde at Matamoros to answer the charge of attempting to take the life of a free born Mexican. He obeyed the summons and was confronted with his accuser. Although he proved all the circumstances it was of no avail. He was thrown into prison and the robber set free. The reason of this was simple enough, John had money to lose and the robber had none. To confine the robber would be merely putting an extra charge upon the state besides exposing the Alcalde to the vengeance of the robber's friends. After remaining in durance some two or three months John was glad to get off by giving the Alcalde the $300. In return for which he received this wholesome advice. Whenever you attempt to drown a man go through with it and then he can never appear against you.

Colonel Hamtramack of the Va. Regt.[military] Governor of Saltillo stated he had proofs in his possession that the President of the Ayuntamiento of the city kept a band of robbers in his employ.

Escrivanos

The *Escrivanos* or Clerks who record the proceedings of the Courts are great scoundrels and live by bribery. By altering the records the case goes up to the higher Courts and is presented in an entirely different point of view from what actually occurred. One of these men lived opposite to my quarters in Saltillo. His salary was only $20 a month—out of this he had supported a large family for years and was erecting a new and splendid residence.

Burglaries and Robbers

Scarcely a night passes in Saltillo without the houses of poor and unprotected widows are broken open, and their slender wardrobe[s] carried off.

In a short time after our arrival in Saltillo, a number of mules were extracted from a yard in our vicinity, by breaking through a great many adobe walls, and bursting open the doors of a deserted house. A patrol however accidentally came in contact with the Mexicans who immediately abandoned their stolen property. This robbery was committed within a few feet of a sentinel.

The horses belonging to the officers of our company being very large and superior animals, excited powerfully the cupidity of the

Mexican horse thieves. As our servants slept very near the animals it was supposed unnecessary to place a sentinel over them. The robbers however had the impudence to walk in at broad noonday while we were eating dinner. We were notified in time to save our horses but not our mules. The rascals escaped. This robbery having been effected through a garden which adjoined the stables, all connection with the garden was stopped up. Nevertheless the robbers made a second attempt at dead of night by cutting a place through the wall. The horses however balked at this place and made so much noise that we awoke. We pursued the robbers but they escaped by leaping the fences. I afterwards ascertained that the chief agent in the matter was the celebrated leader of a large band, named Valenciano De Leon. He had at one time kept the whole country under contribution. At present he was paid as a spy in our service, and had been of a great deal of use in various ways. Previous to the battle of Buena Vista he went into Santa Anna's camp and brought back an account of what was passing there. For this service he received eighty dollars. He afterwards went to Durango on a similar mission. When several sick volunteers were murdered he had pointed out the assassins privately, and they were immediately executed. He would frequently enter Col. Hamtramack's office (the Col was Governor of Saltillo) in disguise. Sometimes he would appear as one of our soldiers at others he would beg for charity in the garb of an aged beggar. But to return to our horses. Although we could ill afford it we now put a sentinel over the animals. Shortly afterwards we detected a robber secreted near him with a long knife. Another was seen loading a musket and still another was overheard on the roof of our house.

De Leon finally told our next door neighbor that he would extract them by making a way through her house. She assured him it was impracticable. Still he might be seen every day at the corner of the street with his face muffled in his blanket waiting for us all to leave the house in hopes some thing would turn up to favor his projects. Of course we did not ascertain these facts until we were on the point of leaving the country. Had our neighbor informed she would have met the fate of another person who lived near us, and who was cut to pieces one dark night by the robbers on suspicion of having been an informer. On this account every one is afraid to give evidence against them. They are always spoken of with as much respect as if they had a legitimate occupation.

The Executions

The first execution I ever witnessed was at Saltillo. Five notorious assassins and robbers of long standing were ordered to be summarily hung without trial[6] by Col Hamtramack of the Va. Regt. at that time Governor of the city. A few days previous they had murdered several sick Mississippians whose clothes were afterwards found in their possession. It was impossible to try the culprits, for no Mexican would dare to appear against them for fear of the remainder of the band. They would be able too to furnish any quantity of evidence in their favor, for few Mexicans consider perjury a crime when brought before Protestants. They were all well known however as having been convicted frequently of murder and robbery in their own law courts and as I said a portion of the effects belonging to the murdered men were found upon them.

As there were some rumors of a rescue all the troops in Saltillo were drawn up on the four sides of the main plaza. After waiting half an hour the waggon with the five culprits entered the square. They had their heads tied up with handkerchiefs and all were smoking the ordinary puro of the country. One only had confessed, the others determined to die impenitent. Of course, all the rites of the church were reserved for the former. The Padres stood in front of him dressed in rich robes and repeating a prayer to which from time to time he responded his thumb and fore fingers arranged all the time, to represent the cross and trinity. One lit his segar from that of his companion with great coolness and did not appear to manifest any emotion. He called out to different people in the crowd to bid them adieu. In another instant at a given signal the waggon drove on and they were all swinging and struggling in the air. At the same time all the bells in the city commenced ringing and the air resounded with the wild

shrieks and cries of the relatives of the dying. As soon as the last spark
of life was extinct the drums and fifes struck up a lively march and the
troops all returned to their respective quarters and cantonments.

A Midnight Ride

One day a man came dashing into Saltillo at full speed with his hat
off and every sign of having ridden hard. He reported himself to the
military Governor of the city, Major Washington, and reported that a
small party consisting of Col. Randolph[7] of Virginia, Capt.
Barksdale[8] of Miss. and Capt Deas of the Light Artillery with an
escort of a Sergt and five men had been attacked by a party in disguise, some 22 miles from the city at a deserted house called Ojo
Caliente, on the road to Monterey. He stated that he had left Capt
Deas wounded and bleeding, leaning against the house for support
and that the detachment had taken refuge in a corral and awaited
succor and re-inforcements. Lieut Evans[9] was in the office at the time
this communication was made. He had just come from the Rinconada
with 10 men, passing Ojo Caliente and remembered to have met Deas
and his party on the route. He says Deas was very drunk and riding
far ahead of his men, whooping and yelling as he went along. I happened to be in the office also. Major W. finding it would cause considerable delay to send to Buena Vista for cavalry ordered Lieut Evans
to turn about with his detachment and to join Col. Randolph at Ojo
Caliente. I also asked and obtained permission to go on the expedition. We set out at sundown and reached our destination about
eleven o'clock at night. As we approached the house we saw a number of groups of Mexicans congregated around some fires in front of a
building. Silently drawing our sabers we charged into the supposed
enemy, but finding them all peaceably engaged in cooking we
sheathed our swords again and asked an explanation. They told us
that Capt Deas and his party, finding the wound not so bad as they
supposed had kept on to the Rinconada: that the band of robbers consisted of about twenty men who had secreted themselves near the old
house knowing it was a favorite stopping place for travellers: that

most of them being from Saltillo to prevent being recognized had covered their faces with handkerchiefs. It appeared that Capt Deas who was riding in front of his men had come upon this band unexpectedly. Being very drunk, he had drawn his sword and charged them alone. They first made his horse swerve and then struck him with a lance in the back. Luckily the lance hit against the shoulder blade and did not therefore make a dangerous wound. The Captain then fell back on his friends who came up in time to fire one volley at the marauders. Capt Barksdale alleges that he hit one of the robbers. The latter retired a few hundred yards apparently awaiting another attack. This alarmed Col. R. who took it in his head the force in front of him was a portion of Urrea's Army. He accordingly sent back the man we had met at full speed for re-inforcements. Deas feeling somewhat better damned them all for a set of cowards and determined to continue his journey with own men whether Col. R. and Capt. B. accompanied him or not. Of course they had no inclination to remain behind and so all set out together. Upon entering the house a singular spectacle presented itself. The robbers had captured every Mexican who came along and after taking away his property had left him tied in the inside of the building. Quite a number had been used thus. They were all liberated by Capt. D and his party and these were the men who were now before us. As soon as we had ascertained these particulars we turned to retrace our steps, and here a ludicrous spectacle presented itself. It had been reported that a brush was about to take place with Urrea's force, and the consequence was that Webster's Battery and several hundred volunteer Infantry were en route for the scene of disturbance. The volunteers having borrowed miserable mustangs to come out with, were thoroughly disgusted at the idea of returning home without fighting on their broken down animals. Being well mounted I reached Saltillo about two in the morning. To my surprise I found picket guards out in every direction. Madame Rumor had asserted that the city was about to be attacked and there was considerable excitement which was still farther increased by Sergeant Kinnan of E Co., 1st Arty. firing into a party of Lancers on the edge of the town. The Sergeant was out with a patrol and the party he met were probably some of the robbers striving to return home. In their hasty flight they threw away their lances.

Trip to Parras in March, 1848

Finding time hang heavy on my hands in Saltillo, I resolved to make a trip to Parras. This town is on the frontier of civilization, is celebrated for its vinyards and is situated about 100 miles from the former place. Beyond this point the country is traversed by roving tribes of Indians, chiefly Comanches, Apaches, and Lipans, nearly all of whom are at war with Mexico. My companions consisted of Mrs. Major an American woman whose husband had been engaged before the War to attend to the factories in Durango, Mr. Riddle the interpreter, and a young man named Stevenson[10] whose father was a merchant in Chihuahua. Mrs. Major had a Mexican servant with her and Mr. Riddle another who was no less than the celebrated robber chief Valenciano De Leon. Upon my remonstrating at the risk we ran in taking so noted a character with us through an enemy's country, he assured me [that De Leon] had rendered many valuable services to government [and] had given hostages for his good behavior, and would be found trustworthy, as he was under pay in our service as a spy. With these reasons I had perforce to be satisfied. The dangers to be apprehended on our part were of two kinds, Indians and Robbers. All three of us were well armed with revolvers and I had a revolving carbine belonging to Mr. Gregg[11] the traveller. At least two thirds of the ranchos between Saltillo and Parras are occupied by professional thieves, and one of the villages San Miguel was the residence of the notorious Guerilla Chief named Refugio Gonzales, and entirely composed of his adherents. We were but three the Mexicans counting for nothing but as I said we were well prepared either to fight or run. At 9 o'clock in the morning we set out taking a short cut across the mountains, the regular waggon road being some fifteen miles longer. My companions having gone ahead Mr. De Leon and myself galloped on to overtake them. He seemed to know every body and as we passed the Indians of the Pueblo who were busily engaged in washing clothes in a brook two feet wide, he scattered his *"adios"* in every direction. We soon overtook our companions in a barranca on the edge of town. Up to this time I had supposed Mrs. Major to be a native of the country and accordingly addressed her in Spanish. It was an agreeable enterprise to find she was a native of Onondaga County, New York, for it was long since I had my own language from the lips of a female. The first thing that attracted my attention was the almost endless number of crosses which we encountered at every step, each one commemmorating some murder or violent death. It did not seem a very good omen for the commencement of our trip. The whole of the route was filled with these melancholy memorials, some pointing out of the scene of an Indian massacre but by far the greater part designating the spot where a combat with banditti took place. Our path soon became a mule track which in the course of five or six miles brought us to the foot of the Sierras. Here the road became almost impassable. It was tortuous, narrow and filled with the sharp points of stones projecting above the surface. At times we would be compelled to leap our horses over ledges of rocks, and in several instances the path was bounded by a precipitous rock above and a precipice below, so that the least stumble would have been fatal. For two hours we toiled slowly along. We were then rewarded by reaching a table land several hundred feet above Saltillo. The remainder of the day we were in one long elevated valley reaching to Patos. The few ranchos we encountered were of the most miserable description. Most of the houses were not even made of adobe but were constructed of reeds tied together and plastered with mud, and thatched with palm leaves. It was difficult to distinguish the adobe houses at any great distance as they are of the same color as the ground. The first peasant we met seemed to consider our expedition a dangerous one. He told us if we met with any robbers to give them a *"balazo"* [bullet]. After a very tedious ride we stopped at a small rancho called *Hediondita*, a name it probably derived from a mineral spring possessing a strong odor. Here we stopped to dine, water and feed our horses. The tortillas and fresh milk from the rancho joined to our own stores gave us a comfortable repast. These tamales are simply

rolls of corn meal put up in corn husk with a piece of meat in the center seasoned with chile. They are very palatable and convenient for a
journey. After an hours rest we continued our journey passing several
points where the robbers usually stop travellers. We were not molested however nor did we fear an attack as we considered ourselves
capable of managing any reasonable number which we considered to
mean at least ten to one. I learned a lesson in this journey as to distances in Mexico every Mexican from native politeness representing
the number of leagues to be at least one third of the reality. Near a
place in their vocabulary means forty miles from it, very near twenty
five and when you are right on it, you are at least twelve miles off. Our
days travel seemed endless but as the sun was setting we reached our
destination for the night the beautiful and picturesque village of Patos
forty miles from Saltillo. We stopped for the night in the suburbs of
the town at a house owned by some relatives of De Leon. They gave
us a room and we all spread our blankets on the floor and placed our
saddles at the head of them for pillows. Mrs. Major procured a kind of
settee. She had become inured to Mexican travelling and bore the
fatigues of the day wonderfully well. When supper was prepared I
found myself too sick to partake of it and lay down with the hope of
obtaining a good nights sleep. We were all much annoyed by two boys
who came in and sat down. Imagining none of us understood their
language they were entertaining each other with an account of their
love adventures, and of course were keeping us awake. In the course
of two or three hours I recovered from my indisposition and fell asleep
while thinking of our peculiar situation. We were sleeping with our
valuable horses under charge of the most notorious horse thief in the
whole country, in the house of his relatives and in a hostile village
where several hundred men could be brought to attack us, at any
moment. If they made way with us they would gain some of the most
valuable horses in the country and quite a large sum of money. At
dawn of day we were in our saddles and after partaking of a cup of coffee prepared by Mrs. Major we started quite refreshed. Upon leaving
Patos we found ourselves at once in wilderness. No isolated corn field
or adobe hut relieved the motonony of the way until after a ride of fif-

teen miles we reached a fortified place called *Macayeu* [Macuyu]. The
cause of this desolation was the incessant incursions of the Indians.
As we rode through the gateway a hundred savage dogs burst forth in
chorus and seemed anxious to tear us from our horses. We found the
Mayordomo profuse in his offers of hospitality. He offered to take
charge of our property and be responsible for every article. I had not
doubt of his sincerity as the town belonged to a friend of mine a member of the Mexican Congress whom I knew to be too cautious a man
to permit any outrages at his place. I therefore gave up even my arms
without scruple. We soon had an admirable breakfast of which we all
partook with great relish. This was the very life I had been desirous of
leading. To mix with the Mexican rancheros and see more of their
manner of living. We found chili mixed in large quantities in all their
dishes. After breakfast I started to take a look at the village. I found
it to be a square enclosed in a high wall overlooked by a tower which
they called a bulwark. As the Indians seldom fail to pay it several visits during the year, the people live in constant fear of being surprised.
Every season some one is killed or carried off and yet there seems to
be no adequate precaution against a sudden attack. The "bulwark"
was a two story building containing loop holes for musketry. The arms
only amount to about a dozen muskets and one wall piece. Some half
dozen of the muskets only are serviceable. They boasted much however of their skill with the wall piece which was nothing more than a
huge rifle mounted on a moveable frame. I was told it would carry a
mile with great accuracy, and had killed two Indian horses at that distance in the last raid. I found some of the people a mile from the rancho and yet they never know at what minute the enemy may be upon
them. The year before several persons were killed and two or three
children carried away. A discussion was now held as to whether we
should proceed any farther in that day. It was urged that by travelling
all day we would arrive in Parras late at night which would be both
troublesome and disagreeable as there are no inns in Mexican towns
and it would prove very annoying to seek quarters at such an hour. I
proposed to proceed to the next town of San Miguel but to this our
robber guide was strongly opposed. He said the place was full of our

enemies who if they did not attack us outright would make very strenuous efforts to steal our horses. They were much exasperated lately, Genl Wool having sent some dragoons to carry off all their corn as a punishment for their marauding expeditions. It was urged too that the Comanches or Apaches would not attack us by night, and that by delaying until evening we would render our journey much safer. It was accordingly determined to wait until the rising of the moon. Shortly after this my attention was attracted by a characteristic incident. A Mexican had just arrived on a mustang. De Leon took a fancy to the animal and claimed him as having been stolen from him a month before. The man showed his brand upon the hind quarter, but it made no difference. He was loud in his reproaches of the rascality of the claimant but De Leon only replied by playing with the handle of his long knife. At last he went to the Alcalde's house and said, there is a man here riding a horse which was stolen from me more than a month ago. Will you decide in my favor or shall I be compelled to take the animal by force. The Alcalde at once decided De Leon to be the true owner. Had he done other wise he would have made a powerful enemy. I saw him settle several other disputes in a very prompt manner summoning witnesses by sending them his cane. I tried to take a siesta but did not succeed. At 8 P.M. I fell asleep and was roused at nine by Mrs. Major who assured me that the moon had risen and it was time to start. In half an hour we were again on our way. Our ride for some time was through a very mountainous country but I could see little of the scenery. We passed San Miguel about midnight, but saw nothing stirring except the watch dogs who sounded the alarm as we passed by. At 2 o'clock we arrived at San Jose. From the fires burning in the fields we thought the laborers must be at work but we saw nobody. And now our journey began to seem interminable, for being constantly deceived as to the distance to Parras I was continually imagining we were approaching it and was of course ill pleased to find it farther off than ever. I remember one man told me it was two leagues, we then went four leagues and the next person we met told us it was very near only six leagues off. Finally they told us it was just over the mountain in front of us. It was a long time before we reached the mountain and when we did so I dashed ahead at full speed to obtain the first view. Upon reaching the top I saw no vestige of a town. Five miles ride brought me in sight of it at last and even then it was nine miles off. When we did enter the suburbs I was delighted with every thing particularly the endless lines of rose bushes in full bloom which bounded every dwelling. The houses too were handsomely painted, and the whole appearance of things was a great improvement on Saltillo. Until we could look up a house we took up our residence with the eccentric Captain Tobin,[12] who was apparently keeping open house. A huge bowl of whiskey punch sat on the center table which seemed to be well patronised. In this abode however there were some slight inconveniences. The Captain had been buying cattle for the Commissary Department, and his yard was full of them. The fence was not very secure or the servants were very careless, for from time to time a wild bull would charge into the crowd of visitors with decided effect. The results were a few sprained ankles and broken ribs. We consequently always kept one eye on the street door and the other on the *caballado*. One or two false alarms rendered us quite expert in beating a retreat. I finally concluded to accept the kind invitation of some members of the Virginia Regiment and took up my quarters with them. The people of Parras we found to be very friendly towards us, and to be possessed of strong American proclivities. This was owing to the fact that many of the young men were educated in Bardstown, Kentucky and were consequently strongly inculcated with our republican ideas. They had become highly dissatisfied with the despotism of their own government. Don Manuel Ibarra owned a large estate and was the chief man in the place. His relatives gave us a party almost every night and the fair ladies present seemed quite desirous of making conquests. All of this presented a pleasing contrast to the sullenness and hostility of the Saltillo people, who frequently shut their doors and windows at the bare appearance of an American. The officers of the Virginia Companies several of whom were temporarily stationed in Parras, could hardly tear themselves away when orders came to evacuate the place and the Senioritas are said to have wept bitterly. In Parras on the approach of an American every door would open at once with an invitation to enter. The effect of this was that the soldiers seemed to combine to preserve good order and protect the inhabitants while in Saltillo it was the reverse. One of the persons who pleased me the most in Parras was the Chief Judge Don Jose Maria Mier, one of the few upright men in Mexico. The liberality of his opinions and his native sense of justice were exemplified in more than one instance. Upon one occasion he encountered several poor Indians tied to mules. On enquiry he ascertained that Aguirre a Colonel in the Mexican service and a brother of the Governor had seized upon them without form of law as peons, and was about to dispatch them to his hacienda to work out a debt of a few shillings. Don Jose immediately ordered them to be set at liberty and the Colonel to be sent to prison for three weeks. The Aguirre family after this event averred with a great deal of reason that the place was altogether too much Americanised for them. It is said the Governor represented to the President of the Republic that the people of Parras ought to be punished for their cordiality to the Americans, but Pena y Pena gave him very little satisfaction.

About the time I arrived an incident occurred which created much excitement. Two of a band of robbers who had been committing many excesses disguised as Indians perpetrated a brutal murder upon two young Virginians who were out gunning. One of the latter having discharged his piece the robber induced the other also to fire at some object. This he did and then walked on leaving his companion in conversation with the two Mexicans. One of these placing himself behind his victim suddenly threw his arms around him and stabbed him in the breast. The other Virginian hearing a noise looked back and saw what was going on. Clubbing his gun he rushed upon the assassin and knocked him sensless. Unfortunately the other Mexican sprang upon him from behind and pinioned his arms at the same time stabbing him in the breast. The young man succeeded in loosening his arms but was overcome and killed by a deep stab in the neck. The robbers after wards stated that they had had a run of bad luck and were in hopes that it would change by killing an American. Through the prompitude and skill of Capt. Harper[13] both of the assassins were arrested.

One of them had been hung previous to my arrival and I was a witness to the execution of the other. He was brought out under the gallows, a noose fastened to his neck and the waggon was ordered to drive on without the slightest formality. The execution was attended by a large crowd of the lower class whose shrieks and cries accompanied his demise.

My leave having nearly expired I looked around for some opportunity of returning. At last, I ascertained that two Texian Express Riders were to be sent in a few days. They were well mounted and were each armed with a pair of pistols. They had just arrived the day before from Saltillo. On their route they had been attacked by a party of robbers but had succeeded in breaking through them after killing the foremost man. I concluded to go with these men and accordingly bid adieu to my friends and set out. About a league from the town on a small emminence I observed a cross which told its own history. The Comanches in sight, a long level plain in which there was no shelter and this small hill upon which a man could at least make a stand for a few moments all flashed before me. But the contention was soon over; the arrows had reached him and his bleeding scalp was torn off, ere his heart ceased to beat. As I have stated before there are no isolated buildings in this country, and we there fore journeyed on until we reached San Jose. Here I purchased a few tortillas and a little fresh milk. As I entered one of the houses with my gun in my hand the inhabitants took it into their wise heads I came to kill someone. The women shrieked and clung to each other in the greatest consternation, I looking on in great amazement utterly unconscious of what had caused the alarm. The next place was called Castanuelo. A short distance from it we encountered a magnificent large stone dam[14] erected under the old Spanish Government. It is a sad commentary on the Revolution that all works of internal improvement have long since ceased. Castanuelo and San Miguel were both equally near but we stopped at the former place in preference, as arrangements had been made to render it safe for Americans while the latter point was the head quarters of a Guerrilla party who had been outlawed by us, and whose property had been confiscated. We found the village to consist of about a dozen houses arranged in the form of a square, as a better defense against the Comanches who had nevertheless frequently ridden into the very center of the enclosure. My companions who were familiar with the place told me I could give up my arms without scruple and I accordingly allowed the rancheros to examine my eight shooting carbine which excited their wonder in a high degree. Upon entering the principal building I saw two young ladies and a girl who were white enough to be Americans. This was a phenomena I did not expect in such a place where it is rare that one meets anything but Indians. I said to one of these ladies in English by way of a joke, "Young lady cant you bring me a glass of water." I expected of course to be answered in Spanish but to my great surprise, she said, "Certainly sir, in a moment." I soon ascertained that her parents were Irish and that she was married to a Mexican who owned the rancho and had come out to look after his property. The other white woman spoke no English although she was born of French parents in New Orleans. She had come to Mexico at quite an early age, and was a native of the country to all intent and purposes, hating the United States most cordially. She too I found was married to a Mexican, a music master, who was seated in one corner of the room playing upon the bandelina [mandolin]. Her husband being present she had nothing to say to us strangers, but amused herself by playing checkers with one of her husband's friends. The whole party I found was on an excursion from the town of Patos. Some allusions having been made to matrimony the Irish lady said if it is mid day and your husband says the sun has just risen the wife must say so too. It is the only way to get along. She then commenced abusing Americans for taking away the arms of the rancheros so that they could not defend themselves from the Indians. I assured her nothing of the kind had been done. She said at all events it was our duty to protect the country, that the rancheros were so cowardly they could not be depended upon. For her part she intended to leave immediately under our escort. As her husband soon after arrived she concluded to remain. The Music Master and his American wife however concluded to go with us. He was one of the fiercest *patriotas* I had ever seen. His hatred was so bitter that he hard-

ly took the pains to conceal it, and his countenance whenever he
looked at us was full of sullenness and gloom. Nevertheless he was
very glad to accompany us to Macayu. In order to render the journey
less tedious, I took the liberty of conversing with his wife whom I
found to be a very entertaining person. She had travelled a great deal
in different parts of Mexico. She told me nothing could exceed her
surprise at revisiting the United States and comparing it with her
adopted country. We then proceeded to discuss many people known
to both of us in Saltillo and Monterey. The husband all this time was
riding a few paces behind and working himself into a frenzy of rage. In
order to show him how innocent the subject of our conversation was
I raised my voice but all to no purpose. One of the Texians rode up
and told me the man was quite beside himself. I therefore turned back
to see if I could not put him in a better humor. He smiled a ghastly
smile and checked his horse so as to fall behind the rest of the caval-
cade. It was fast becoming dark and the path could hardly be distinguished. His evident determination to allow the remainder of our
party to get out of sight and his strange behavior made me suspect
some ulterior design. I told him the others would soon be out of sight,
and it was full time we rejoined them. I then put spurs to my horse but
could see no signs of a path nor could I tell in which direction to go.
In this dilemma I threw the bridle on the horses neck and left it all to
him. He took the right course immediately and in about twenty minutes he reached the main body. The Music Master followed and rode
up by the side of his wife. She told him we intended to stop at
Macaya: that the night would soon be pitch dark and that they had
better remain at the same place. To this request, his jealousy being
excited he gave a very harsh refusal but as the difficulties to going on
were insuperable he was obliged to acquiesce. As soon as we arrived
at the rancho I and my companions went to the Alcalde's house, but
the Music Master took the most remote house he could find. I selected the Alcalde's bed room for my sleeping apartment next to which
was a hall and then another long room full of hides and jerked beef.
In this latter place the two Texians slept. None of the rooms had any
doors. After supper I observed a new arrival at the rancho. This was

no less than my robber guide Valenciano De Leon with thirteen companions. He had been hired in the first place by Mr. Riddle the interpreter to accompany him as far as Chihuahua for which he was to receive a certain sum. Upon arriving in Parras he demanded a portion of his wages alleging he had performed part of the contract. Mr. Riddle said he could not pay him a cent until the entire journey had been performed and there was nearly 800 miles further to go. De Leon of course was in a violent rage at making a journey to Parras and back without pay, and I have no doubt regretted he had not robbed us on our way, but it was not entirely too late. He asked me in Parras when I would return and now here he was with a fine opportunity of revenging his wrongs. He and two of his companions wrapped their blankets around them and lay down in the hall between me and the Texians, and some fifteen of his friends slept outside of the main entrance on the ground with their saddles under their heads. I immediately took every precaution. I told the Alcalde his life should be responsible for the loss of our horses. I procured a candle end and placed it in such a position that I could light it with some matches I had at a moment's notice. I then laid my pistols and carbine by my side and in a few moments was fast asleep. I had travelled fifty miles that day and found it impossible to keep awake. I should probably never have awakened again had it not been for a chair in the middle of the room. About one o'clock at night some one stumbled over this chair and awoke me. I immediately called out and cocked my pieces, but the step retreated as quickly as it came. In a moment I had lit the candle and commenced a search, but all was still as death. The three robbers lay in the hall motionless, and the Texians were asleep. I again returned to my bed, and in spite of every effort my fatigue overcame me and I again fell asleep. In about an hour I heard a loud cry from the Texians and rushed in as soon as I could to their assistance. One of them had been awakened suddenly by a hand feeling for his throat. He had suddenly flung it off, sprang to his feet and endeavored to grasp the assailant but without effect. Although as I passed through the hall I detected a movement of one of the robbers showing that he had just lain down. I did not think it expedient to provoke a combat which could be of no advantage to us, and which might end in the loss of our horses, if not our lives, for the odds against us was very great. We slept no more that night but kept watch together until daylight. I then called on the Alcalde to send for our horses which he did. As soon as they arrived we set out. At eight o'clock we arrived in Patos, we remained an hour to take breakfast. My friend the Music Master had arrived before us, and to my surprise seemed quite another man. He gave us a cordial reception and seemed full of fun. The price of our breakfast was as usual whatever we chose to give. At one o'clock we arrived at a miserable hovel called Rancho Grande where we obtained a few tortillas which with our own stores gave us a comfortable meal. Small as the house was, the whole of one side was taken up with an altar to the Virgen of Guadalupe. It was made like a stair case and every step was filled with pieces of colored glass and coarse flowers cut out of red paper. The walls of the room too were covered with rude pictures of the saints. By three o'clock I arrived in my own room in Saltillo, thoroughly satisfied to remain there. I had been gone eight days and had ridden fifty miles a day.

After peace was declared and our troops recalled from Parras the Comanches followed close upon their footsteps. I understand they made sad havoc with the ranchos killing nineteen persons in Macayu alone.

7

WE LEAVE MEXICO

When the news came that a treaty of peace had actually been signed with Mexico we joyfully turned our face homewards that is towards the sea coast, taking with us the heavy guns which had been an object of so much care and solicitude in the past. The first day's encampment an elderly dark skinned Mexican woman presented herself with her husband said they were going after a horse they had lost and begged us to give them seats in one of the wagons. Prentiss[1] answered, "*No Entiendo*" and she turned to Ricketts who gave the same reply. She then went at me—I also answered "*No Entiendo*" but she said, "Yes you do, for I heard you talking to Don Maniquila one day and I know you do understand." She then went on to say that she had washed clothes for some of the soldiers and thought it was very hard that she could not be permitted to have a ride; so Prentiss good naturedly gave the requisite permission. Her delight was so great that she threw out her arms and wished to give each of us an embrace which we carefully avoided. Had she been young and pretty we probably might have submitted gracefully to the infliction.

Upon our arrival at Camargo[2] we remained several days and turned in the guns which had given us so much trouble to the Quartermaster's Department. There we found Lieuts. O'Brien, Garesche,[3] Kilburn and several other artillery officers who united to

BV Doubleday, Abner. "From Mexican War to the Rebellion, First Rough Draft."

"in a spirit of fun at the head of the table...."

give us a banquet. The champagne flowed freely, every one was in the hightest spirits at the idea of returning home once more and the mirth was fast and furious when suddenly the same Mexican woman made her appearance. She wanted a free passage on the steamer down and inquired for Captain Prentiss. He was slyly pointed out to her. She rushed behind him at the table threw her arms around his neck and gave him a good squeeze. Poor Prentiss was utterly amazed at finding a pair of black arms around his neck projecting in front. He had not the slightest idea to whom the aforesaid arms belonged or the occasion of their being there. The officers at the table took in the situation at a glance and fairly yelled with delight. The laughter lasted for half an hour. Having embraced Prentiss she looked around to extend the same favor to Ricketts and myself but we fled from the place. When we came back the company had duly installed her in a spirit of fun at the head of the table and were paying her mock compliments and what was still better in her eyes loading her plate with eatables. She received everything in the most serious manner returned the compliments with interest and subsequently offered to make herself useful by washing the dishes.

Orders arrived for us to proceed to the lower Rio Grande and guard the stores there until the Mexican soil was evacuated. Our company accordingly went to Brownsville and remained there a few days previous to going to Point Isabel. While there the Chief Commissary came to see me and ask me if I would object to acting as an Asst. Commissary temporarily. He said he had only about 30 bbls provisions etc. in Matamoros and was desirous of leaving the country. If I would receipt for the stores and take charge in his place he would write to the Subs. Dept and have me receive a permanent appointment which would add $10 a month to my pay. I acceded to his request [and] receipted for the property. This kept me at Brownsville opposite Matamoros. I thought I had made a good bargain but soon changed my mind. It was true enough that there were but few stores in Matamoros but I soon found that as I was the only C.S. at Brownsville all the surplus stores of the Army which were on their way down the river were being invoiced to me, and that the money responsibility which would devolve upon me would become a serious matter.

Soon after my arrival I saw the same Mexican woman. She was having an altercation with some soldiers. She caught sight of me and said, "*Dichoso [los] ojos que lo ven*"—Happy eyes that see you once more; a rather neat compliment but Mexicans cannot be excelled by any other nation in greetings of this kind. They have a profusion always on hand. The woman now asked for a free passage up the river for her and she went off and persecuted us no more.

My commissary duties soon gave me considerable uneasiness. The guards had been withdrawn from Matamoros and there was [no] one to guard my store house but an old negro and a dog. I had orders to sell the stores there at public auction and succeeded in doing so, but a Jew who resided there bid for most of the articles and owing to the paucity of guards or to some misunderstanding they were sent to his warehouse before I received the money for them. In case he declined to pay I was aware that the Government would charge the articles to me. My anxiety was not lessened when he related some of his adventures in England and in New Orleans. He said on one occasion he desired to import a large number of French gloves as the fashionable world of London wore them exclusively although at that time the duties were very high on them. So the Jew purchased a great number of them in pairs marked each pair and then sent all the right hand ones to England. These were detained in the Custom House and as the duties were not paid, were ultimately sold to the highest bidder. Of course no one would bid anything but the Jew for a pile of right hand gloves so he got them for a nominal sum. He then sent over the left-hand gloves which underwent the same process. He was the only bidder. Having thus obtained his gloves free of duty he made a large sum upon them.

He told me too that he went to Cuba and bought several likely looking negro women out of jail for a modest sum. He dressed them up, took cabin passage for them and when they approached New Orleans he brought them into the cabin, put thick veils over their faces, and passed them off as Cuban ladies. He thus got them into the

Thomas West Sherman

city and sold them at a large profit. As the punishment for bringing
negroes in to the U.S. came under the head of slave trading which was
piracy he ran the risk of being hanged for this last exploit.

Under other circumstances these recitals would have been amusing enough but when I called to mind that he owed me a large sum of
money for the public property in his possession and that there very little likelihood of my ever receiving a cent my reflections were not all
all of an exhilirating character. To my astonishment the man called a
few days afterwards and paid his indebtedness in full.

About the same time numerous consignments of flour beans vine-
gar etc. came down the river and were landed on the shore at
Brownsville. There were no store houses as yet, no troops had arrived
and I was obliged to leave them there very much exposed to theft and
damage from bad weather. In a few days, Lieut Wooster's[4] Co of Arty
came and were assigned as the garrison of Fort Brown. There was
another arty company too located at Brownsville but I have forgotten
its name and designation.[5] I succeeded at last in getting a sentinel to
watch over my stores but as they stretched for a quarter of a mile
along the shore it was easy for Mexican or Texan thieves to get off a
barrel of flour from one end of the line while the sentinel was at the
other. The upshot was when I came to settle my accounts I found a
woeful deficiency. I at once called for a board of officers to examine
into my liability. When I laid the evidence before them they exoner-
ated me for all blame and the auditor at Washington credited me with
the deficiency.

The Commander of the Post at Brownsville, S. [Thomas W.
Sherman],[6] was a very arbitrary man. He took it very much to heart
that Genl Taylor on the eve of the Battle of Buena Vista had refused
to allow him to take command of Bragg's battery to which he had
just been promoted and had sent him to the rear. In doing this, Genl
T. did not intend to reflect in any way upon his bravery or skill as an
officer but was solely activated by a dislike to change battery commanders at such a time. S. was not therefore in the best of humor
and soon put every officer at the post under arrest for supposed mis-
demeanors. The Quartermaster [W. W.] Chapman[7] held the brevet

rank of Major and S. being only a captain Chapman gave it as his
opinion that he himself was by law entitled to the command. As this
opinion was merely speculative and Chapman did every thing that
was required by S. promptly and well, it would have been wiser in
the latter to let him alone especially as in the view he took of his
right to command he was sustained by Genl Scott the Commander
of the Army and by numerous officers who held brevets for services
in the Florida War. S. however, came to the conclusion that it was
not enough for Chapman to obey his orders, he must be forced to
recant his heretical opinions. He therefore placed Chapman under
arrest[8] and ordered me to relieve him. This was throwing immense
additional duties on me. It was bad enough to be responsible for all
the surplus Commissary stores of the Army but to add to this all the
Quartermaster's property including great numbers of horses mules
ambulances steam boats etc. was altogether too much responsibility
for my rank and pay. It was some consolation to know that I was
entitled to have all this property counted and invoiced; that I had
the right to see inspect and weigh every thing and that it would
probably take months to accomplish the transfer. Upon applying to
Chapman for a list of the property for which he was responsible and
showing him the order from S. placing him in arrest and directing
me to take his place he merely replied, "I do not recognize the order
of Maj. S. to either relieve or arrest me." Upon reporting this answer
to S. he got into a great rage and put a sentinel over Chapman with
orders not to let him leave his room. Thereupon Chapman balanced
his books by making a statement that as Maj S. had put him under
guard he Chapman was no longer responsible for any public property. Now it is a maxim of the authorities at Washington that somebody is always responsible for the care of public property. Manifestly
in the present case it could not be Chapman as he was in duresse; it
could not be me for I had not receipted for anything, and of course
it was Maj S. himself since he had produced this state of things. As
soon as S. saw it in that light he released Chapman and referred the
matter to Washington. I am not aware that any decision was ever
given in this case.

The next difficulty was in relation to Wooster's Company at Fort Brown. W. had his company ready to fall in for Sunday inspection as soon as S. made his appearance; but the latter went to the barracks which were concealed from W.'s quarters by traverses turned out the men and arrested Wooster for being absent, directing me to assume command in his place in addition to my other duties. W. was released in a few days afterwards.

There was some commotion in Matamoros between two factions and the party in power called the U.S. troops to keep order so S. gave directions for his companies to fall in at the beating of the long roll which was to take place whenever two rockets were sent up from the city. As every man in Mexico sends up rockets on his birthday the signal was soon given and the troops were formed and marched to the ferry boats. As Capt H.[9] objected to going over with his company to a foreign country and taking sides with one faction against another S. threatened to have him shot for mutiny. Luckily it was found to be a false alarm.

As there were a good many desperados in the country and very poor [civilian] jail facilities S. offered to feed and guard them at expense of U.S. Murderers and horse thieves were mixed in with soldiers who had been guilty of slight offenses. As Commissary I was ordered to feed these citizen prisoners. It was an illegal expenditure but it did not concern me particularly and I raised no objection.

Next came a sweeping order to arrest all Texans found on public grounds after tattoo and put them in the guard house. This was clearly illegal. We were living in a time of peace, the civil courts were sitting and by law they are in our country superior to the military. Cases of this kind had come up before and it had been fully decided that the utmost that we had a right to do was to put citizens off the public grounds by force if after due warning, they persisted in staying there. Some very respectable men, sea captains and others were put in the guard house under this order and were kept there several days. They were then let out with a reprimand. There was no definite boundary no fence between the public ground and that of the town and the main street ran through both. The men who were incarcerated with felons of the worst kind swore they would bring suit before the Texan court against the officer of the Day who used the guard to imprison them. S. detailed me as officer of the Day in spite of my staff position which should have exempted me from the duty. He then gave me instructions to arrest all citizens found on the public grounds after tattoo. I knew if I did I would be hauled up before a civil court setting at Brownsville and that I could hardly escape a heavy fine and imprisonment from which the Commanding officer would be powerless to rescue me. It has long ago been settled by the highest authority that an officer is responsible if he obeys an illegal order for all the damage done to persons or property. I attempted to explain to S. the situation but he refused to listen, with a wave of his hand he imperiously directed me to carry out the orders as he gave them and he supplemented them by adding that there were a good many Texans in the public grounds at that time and I would arrest every one who did not give a full and satisfactory account of his presence. It is probable I might by a little tact or by making a pretence of carrying out these instructions have escaped scot free but I was irritated by his refusal to hear me state the case and by his imperious manner and was sensible that no court martial when the circumstances were fairly stated could convict me. I refused to carry out the order and was sent to my tent in close arrest.[10] S. was very unpopular and the sympathy of the officers was all with me. When the question was referred to Washington I was released with out any decision being given in the case. This was the first and only time during my military career that I was ever placed in arrest and as there was a principle involved concerning the right of citizens I have never been ashamed of the occurrence.

About this time our Captain Prentiss[11] was taken with yellow fever at Point Isabel. He had been an attache of the American Legation in Paris and had travelled much in Europe and Asia. He was a man of culture and refinement and we were very much attached to him. Although Ricketts was not acclimated he nursed him carefully but could not save him. Fortunately he escaped himself.

Soon afterwards we were ordered to Fort Columbus, N.Y. Harbor. We put to sea in an old crazy sailing vessel the bulwarks of which were almost rotten. We encountered a severe storm off Hatteras and it was doubtful for a time whether we could weather the cape but we succeeded in doing so thanks to the skill of a very experienced Captain and finally ended our long voyage in the harbor of New York.

Only those who have been long separated from family and friends surrounded with death and danger can appreciate the pleasure we had in a reunion. The post of Fort Columbus was the most agreeably situated for enjoyment of any in the U.S. All the pleasures and treasures of the great Metropolis were accessible and as Fort Columbus at that day could only be reached by a row boat we could have quiet and rest without danger of being overrun by crowds and being made a public spectacle. Society welcomed us as the heroes of a great war and we were invited out in every direction to attend balls and parties. Our Commander Colonel Crane[12] was an old soldier a thorough gentleman and very much beloved by us. The fort was garrisoned at that time by the Company of Captain Winder[13] whose name has since been so sadly associated with the sufferings of our prisoners at Richmond—Capt French's Company, Capt Knowlton's[14] Company, under Lieut Seymour.[15]

We were generally in accord and led a very pleasant life. One day we were invited to attend a grand ceremony in the city of a national character at which all the citizen soldiers paraded. I forget the occasion of it now but it seems to me it was something connected with the funeral of Genl Worth....

I have referred to Winder who afterwards gained such an unhappy reputation as the goaler [sic] of our prisoners in Richmond. The cruelties practiced there were wholly inexcusable but here we saw no signs at Ft Columbus indicating that he had a tyrannical disposition. He seemed strictly temperate and honest in all his dealings. He would never borrow a postage stamp without returning it but he was fond of indulging in violent disputation and always carried his opinions to extreme limits. This probably was the cause of his horrible severity towards our poor prisoners, which was utterly inexcusable.

For the purpose of instructing every officer in turn in the duties of a Light Battery each was detailed for a tour of two years. I was sent in

1851 to Fort Hamilton[16] under orders to relieve 1st Lieut. Thos. J.
Jackson who had just completed his tour of duty with Brvt. Col. Frank
Taylor's[17] Company. He became afterwards the celebrated
Confederate General known as Stonewall Jackson. I remember him at
that period as a very staid quiet person clumsy or awkward in his
motions who never seemed to joke or enjoy any thing of a humorous
nature. At the same time he was cheerful and pleasant in his
demeanor but somewhat reticent. His clothes did not fit him very well
and he always wore uniforms even when he went to make purchases
in N.Y. which was unusual. The other officers always wore citizens
clothes on such occasions but Jackson was economical and would not
go to the extra expense of two kinds of garments. Unfortunately at
the time I saw him he was in bad health. He did know the cause of it
himself and as he had some strange symptoms he doctored himself in
a very extraordinary fashion.[18] Attributing his troubles to a want of
system he would indulge in precisely the same exercises every day at
certain hours. He would walk for instance a certain length of time
accurately by the watch. Then he would sit motionless for fifteen
minutes. Then he would rise and pound and kick a bag of sand with
his left hand and left foot under the impression that that side of his
body was dwindling. As Crawford[19] expressed it he thought all his
food ran down into his right leg. Again he would take it into his head
that he must not drink the surface water and would keep pumping for
a long time before he would take the pitcher away. It is said two of his
classmates jeered him about it as they stood by the entry of a casemate one day, both shouting, "Jackson, your pitcher's full." This
angered him and he walked over and challenged them after which
they let him alone. For his head was full of duelling in those days and
he had some curious ideas concerning the code of honor. A. P. Hill
who was also an officer of my regt and who knew him well said to me
one day, "Jackson is the last man I would ever ask to be second to me
in a duel for if he thought I had infringed the code in any particular,
he would shoot me without mercy." Subsequently when he joined the
church he opposed this mode of settling difficulties. Another trait of
his character which interested me was his strict honesty and consci-

entious attention to duty. Strangely enough as he would never mistreat any thing it was hard to convince him that any one else would do so. His trust and confidence in traders and horse jockies amazed the other officers. Lt. Tillinghast,[20] who was in the same company with him at Fort Hamilton gave me several amusing examples. Jackson had a fine horse but a horse jockey persuaded him to exchange him for a balky animal and pay him $50 to boot. On another occasion he went to town to buy a light horse carriage. He attended an auction and owing to the bad weather and few bidders he got an excellent vehicle at a marvellously low price. I think at $35. A man came along and asked him what he intended to do with the carriage. He replied it was to drive from Ft Hamilton to Brooklyn. The man told him it was unsuitable for that purpose and induced him to make an exchange for a poor establishment charging him $50 difference. The first day of my arrival at Ft Hamilton I took a late dinner with the officers mess. J. found that certain substances injured him very much and aggravated the symptoms of his complaint. He was especially desirous of avoiding pepper. As we were seated at the table his eyes flashed and he turned and said, "There Tillinghast you have put your knife covered with pepper right against my plate." T. replied mildly, "No J. my knife did not touch your plate. It may have touched your bread but not the plate and I dont think it has any pepper on it." J. seized the bread, tore it up furiously and threw it in the fire exclaiming, "Never mind, its of no consequence, it is not of the slightest consequence." But his actions and expression showed so much anger that they belied his words.

I have spoken of J.'s balky horse. It was a fine looking animal and as I knew he wished to dispose of it and I needed a horse I asked him what he would sell it for. The price he fixed was not unreasonable. I knew nothing about the beast but went down to the stable to try him before making the purchase. When I asked to have J.'s horse brought out I was surprised to see the interest excited. There was an immediate rush and a crowd of villagers gathered around. I thought there was an unnecessary amount of curiosity to see me mount him and could not account for it. I rode about half a mile found the pace was agree-

"*Circus?*"

able, came back returned the animal to the stable and the crowd dispersed. I then saw J. told him I found the horse was satisfactory and asked him if he had any faults. He hesitated and said not now. What did he use to have I asked. Formerly when I first bought him he would occasionally stop and throw out both his fore legs. Well said I, "I suppose you applied the spur then." "No," said he "that would never do for he would run off and would not be guided." I asked, "Is [he] all over this now?"; to which he replied in the affirmative. I then agreed to try him by riding him on a battery drill and if I was satisfied with him I would make the purchase. When I got on him again there was the same rush and excitement as before. Finding myself somewhat in advance of my section of Arty I halted to let it come up. Out went the fore legs and the horse refused to move. Tillinghast said, "Wait a moment Doubleday and I will get a lead on him." The horse then started again but the next time I halted, out went the fore legs. I then put the spurs to him and he dashed down a ravine into some brambles. I got him out of there called a soldier dismounted and sent him back to the stable. Upon narrating the circumstances to J. he simply said you made a mistake by halting. If you had kept him going you would have found him all right.

We had not been long at Fort Hamilton before the battery was ordered to march across country to Fort McHenry at Baltimore.

The first night out we were guests of Capt Philip Kearney[21] who gave us a banquet at his house near Newark. Jackson rode out with us and met with a very cordial reception for they admired the gallantry he had displayed at Chapultepec very much.

Capt and Bvt Lt Col Francis Taylor was of course in command. He was with reason proud of the record he had made at Churubusco and other battles in Mexico. That he was one of the permanent commanders of a light battery was a great gratification to him. At that day it was considered about as high a compliment as could be paid to an officer. Once however as we rode ahead on one of the country roads we passed a little tavern. A countryman stood on the porch and stared at us with a good deal of surprise for the troops were out of sight. He looked at the caprision of Taylor's steed examined his light jaunty cap and then made an enquiry which considerably lessened Taylor's idea of the dignified position of a Capt of a light battery. That one word put as an interrogation was "*Circus?*" This slight misadventure was followed by another when we arrived in the suburbs of Baltimore and encamped for the night. A middle aged man who belonged to one of the first families of Md. and was reported to be very wealthy came in to the room where we had established ourselves. He was very drunk indeed. He walked up to Taylor who was a man of severe morals who never drank nor gambled and who allowed no gambling in his command locked arms with him suddenly and said, "I say old boy I've given each of your men a bottle of whiskey and they are drunk as lords by this time and now you and I will go and make a night of it." Taylor had a good deal of trouble to get rid of his importunations.

We had a pleasant time indeed at Fort McHenry. Here were Sedgwick, Bragg, and others who were attached to another light battery. There was much good feeling and constant amusement in the city. Life passed pleasantly we were thrown much into society. The result was seen in the case of Lt Col Taylor who was a widower—by his marriage to the accomplished daughter of Chief Justice Taney. I was fascinated by the bright eyes of a Washington belle, Miss Mary Hewitt and my marriage took place on Jany 2, 1852.

Some three months afterwards I was more than surprised by receiving a confidential note from the Secy of War—Mr. Conrad—informing me that he desired to see me privately at his house. Now a Secy of War scarcely has any special orders for lieutenants and I could not fathom the meaning of this mysterious note which came to me direct and not through any of the ordinary channels.

8

THE GARDINER MINE CLAIM

I at once made my way to Washington and proceeded to call on the Secretary.[1] I was ushered into a private room and in a short time he made his appearance. He then proceeded to give me an account of what was called at that day the "Gardiner Claim". A man named George A. Gardiner[2] had just extracted by false statement and forgery about 600,000 from the U.S. Treasury. As he distributed about 2/3 of this sum to influential men, members of Congress, reporters, and others the justice of his claim was loudly vouched for by a great many people and the public press were very generally in his favor. As I think, a brief history of this case will not be without its use in the future. I will state the way this money was gained. Gardiner, who was a Cuban born in Pennsylvania, was living in Mexico during the war with the U.S. between the years 1846-48. Although there was a clause in the previous treaty with Mexico that in case of war the property of U.S. citizens doing business in Mexico should be respected the stipulation was wholly disregarded and I believe in all cases the property was confiscated. The Americans who had thus been despoiled consulted together and said Mexico has no money and it is useless to apply to her, our government must remunerate us for these losses when the war closes and take it out of Mexico in land. This was accordingly done when the Treaty of Peace was signed the U.S. kept Lower California and paid Mexico a certain sum for it, 3,000,000 of

BV Doubleday, Abner. "From the Mexican War to the Rebellion, First Rough Draft."

which was reserved to pay the claimants. Gardiner thought he would trump up a claim for a portion of this sum. He had some confederates in Mexico to whom he promised a portion of the money and they agreed to bear testimony to his statements. He spoke English perfectly for his mother was an American and his father an Englishman so that it was easy for him to pass himself off as a citizen of the U.S. He accordingly came to Tampico towards the close of the war and represented himself to the U.S. officer in command there as a fugitive from the State of San Luis Potosi. He said he was the owner of gold mines there worth $80,000: that Santa Anna had destroyed his mines or ruined the shafts that led down into them out of hostility to the Yankees. In due time he came on to Washington and consulted some claim agents. These told him that claims even when they were favorably considered were always cut down in amount. They advised him to claim a large sum and then he could secure the passage by giving the surplus to influential men. He at once acted on this advice and put in a claim of $800,000 for a silver mine destroyed by Santa Anna. At the same time he brought forward a claim as attorney for a certain John H. Mears for a quicksilver mine also destroyed in the State of San Luis Potosi by Santa Anna. These claims were absurd enough. It was quite conceivable that Santa Anna should seize valuable mines belonging to citizens of U.S. but that he should destroy them would make him out to be a simpleton. He would of course in such a case have had the mines worked for his own benefit. There were a number of English Cos seeking valuable franchises of this sort and they would only have been too glad to have taken them. Gardiner brought considerable documentary evidence to support his claim and forged the signature of the Gov. of San Luis Potosi and the seal of that state for that purpose. It is said he also managed by bribing up some clerk to get the signature of the Mexican Minister to attest his claim by inducing him to sign a paper folded over which he the minister supposed to be a mere routine paper, of no consequence. The large sums to go to individuals in case the claim was passed by the 3 Commissioners caused it to go through flying. The sums were reduced so that he only got 400,000 for his own claim and about 170,000 for that of Mears.

The way the cheat came to be discovered was this. The Secy of the Commission resigned and a Dr. Davis[3] who was then in Washington and who had resided 20 years in Mexico was chosen as Secy on account of his knowledge of Spanish and of Mexican customs. Davis had served in the war with Mexico as a Capt in the Qr Mrs Dept. He was a very honest and patriotic man. While assorting the papers of the Commission he came upon the claim of John H. Mears[4] for a quicksilver mine in San Luis Potosi which had been paid to Mears attorney Geo A. Gardiner to the extent of $180,000. He was astonished that such a foolish claim should have been passed and the money actually paid out of the treasury for it so happened that he was in San Luis Potosi at the time Mears claimed to have discovered the mine. He therefore personally knew the the falsity of the business for at that day no quicksilver mines had been discovered and all the quicksilver for amalgamants purposes was imported from Spain at great expense. The finding of a mine of this character would have created a great sensation and would have been known every where. He then called to mind that the claimant John H. Mears must have been the Vicksburg gambler who had barely escaped being lynched in that city by leaping out of a third story window and who had indictments against him in all the Western States for almost every crime in the calendar. Davis noticing that Geo A Gardiner was the friend and agent of Mears took a look at the Gardiner claim. He found it duly attested by the Great Seal of San Luis Potosi but soon saw that the seal was a clumsy forgery for he was familiar with the original. The claim too was full of absurdities. In it Gardiner alleged that he had owned a silver mine, the vein of which was 12 varas[5] wide, and which was ventilated with 3 air shafts. A vein of silver ore a few inches wide would be a great find in Mexico but one of more than 30 feet wide would have astounded the whole country. It would have been at once the center of an immense business. There were no silver mines at the place indicated and no such mine was ever heard of. Official lists of mines existed in Mexico with a view to taxes etc. but no such mine was on any of these lists.

A week or two after the money had been paid over to Gardiner some $480,000 for his own claim and that of Mears an article

appeared in *The National Intelligencer* of Washington exposing the
fraud. The President Mr. Fillmore was astounded that his administration should have paid out such a sum of money for so transparent a
fraud. He sent to the Editor of the paper [and] ascertained that Dr.
Davis wrote the article referred to and sent for him to appear and
make his statement before a Cabinet Council. When Dr. Davis had
clearly explained the fraud the President said to him, "You are sir I
understand an employee of my administration, for you hold an office
as translator in the State Dept. How happen it that you waited until
this money had been paid out before you gave notice of the fraud.
Why did you not notify me or some member of my cabinet previous
to that time?" "I did Sir," Davis promptly replied. "Who," asked the
President? "Your Attorney Genl Mr Crittenden,"[6] Davis said. Here
Mr. C. arose and said indignantly, "No sir I never heard of it." The
President said, "Sit down Mr. Crittenden I am going to sift this matter to the bottom." "Now, Mr. Davis, tell your story." Davis then said,
"You may remember Mr. Crittenden that one day as you were coming
out of the Supreme Court after arguing a certain case, I handed you
a letter containing a statement similar to the one I am now making."
"It is true," said Mr. Crittenden. "I remember it now but I had nothing to do with this business of Mexican claims and I thought it came
from some disappointed claimant and therefore paid no attention to
it." "You did very wrong," the President said.

The result of the Council was that instructions were sent to our
Minister in Mexico to proceed to San Luis Potosi investigate the
case and report. He and his secretary Mr. Bowes went to San Luis
and brought back ample testimony to show that no such mine existed. They did not go to the alleged place where the mine was supposed to be located for it was a very wild region and as Gardiner had
confederates there to whom he had provided a portion of the spoil
it would have been a very dangerous expedient for them. They sent
some Mexican witnesses to Washington to appear. Gardiner's
friends, and they were legion, at once indicted these witnesses and
said the whole thing was a Mexican conspiracy to obtain the money
for the Govt of Mexico.

The moment the U.S. Govt tried to right this wrong it found bitter opposition. Our Secy of the Treasury, Tom Corwin,[7] had recd $80,000 from Gardiner as Council fees in the matter, a former Minister to Mexico had $40,000, and so on [regarding] other influential men. The President now resolved to send a Commission to Mexico to collect evidence of the fraud, but the U.S. Senate Committee on Frauds of which Mr. Soule was chairman also resolved to do the same thing. To give the matter an appearance of fairness and take out of the domain of politics it was thought best that one officer of the army, one off[icer] of the Navy should go. I was selected from the Army because at that day I spoke Spanish with fluency. Hunter[8] was taken for the Navy—Mr. Partridge[9] who had travelled much in Spain was a fine Spanish scholar and particularly well versed in the law idioms of that language was also sent. Our Secy of Legation to Mexico Buckingham Smith[10] was added as another member of the Commission and lastly, Henry May[11] a prominent lawyer of Washington and brother of the celebrated Col. Charles May of the Army was chosen as head of the Commission to take depositions and collect evidence.

The object of my interview with the Secy heretofore referred to was to send me to Mexico with a single lawyer to collect the evidence but when the Senate concluded to send a Commission I was added to that.

May was furnished with funds and we proceeded at once to New Orleans. As the court for the trial of Gardiner would sit in about two months great promptness on our part was desirable.

The Navy was directed to furnish a vessel which would take us to Vera Cruz but the only small steamer available was the *Fulton* a nondescript affair built for harbor defense with very thick bulwarks and with[out] the means of attaining great speed. We were told that it was not sea-worthy and that a Midshipman and an Engineer had resigned rather than go to sea in her. The bow went partly under the waves instead of riding them. The last time she was out she came within an inch of sinking. Hunter and the naval officers on duty with the vessel corroborated this statement and said they were bound to go on board of anything and run all risks if they were ordered to do so but they thought it their duty to tell us if a storm came up it would be a matter of doubt if they could save the steamer. Nevertheless we had either to go in the *Fulton* or give up the object of our expedition and we concluded to risk the passage. The weather was fine and we reached Vera Cruz in three days. The first thing the Custom House Officer did was to lock up all our baggage indefinitely in order that we might bribe them to get it out. It was finally extracted after considerable difficulty though [by] our consul I believe and representatives. But we were not ordinary travellers but commissioners duly accredited to the Mexican gvt. We took up our quarters in the hotel on the main plaza facing the celebrated Castle of San Juan de Ulloa which was captured by the French under the Pursee de Fonteville.[12] The landlord who was a Spaniard hated Americans most cordially on account of the Lopez expedition recruited in the U.S. to capture Cuba. He imposed on us in every way and put us in a room on cots with some half a dozen other people so that we had to keep a sharp eye out to see that our money was [not] taken out of our pockets at night. Right opposite to us across the street was a large church and a chime of bells. The next day was some feast day and all these bells began to ring at daybreak with a noise enough to awake the dead. As the street was very narrow and they were directly opposite they sounded as if the bells were in the room. Every one sprang out of bed in amazement thinking something extraordinary had happened.

While at Vera Cruz our new minister to Mexico Judge Conklin (father of Roscoe and Fred)[13] joined us and accompanied us up to the capitol. It is unnecessary to describe our journey in detail which was not without danger for a revolution was going on and the insurgents had taken possession of the National Bridge where we had to pass. We resolved if they barred our way or attempted to levy contributions on us we would fight. All of us were armed with double barrelled guns. I was mounted on the top of the stage and Hunter being much my senior was to take command of the party. He said, "When I say 'lay by' go at them." Fortunately we found the pass in possession of the Govt troops they having driven off the others and as we had regular passes we experienced no difficulty. I shall not although describe the magnificent scenery of Jalapa or the grandeur of Popocatepetl and Orizaba, but it was not without a thrill of emotion that I stood on a spot where Cortes overlooked the vast valley of Mexico and fancied his feelings and aspirations at the sight. We spent the night at Perote and another at Pueblo making the [remaining] 80 miles to the City of Mexico in about 12 hours in the diligence [stagecoach]. We stopped at the Hotel Iturbide formerly the Palace of that emperor and being worn out with our journey were at once assigned to our rooms after partaking of a meal of chocolate and shortcake which is always served up at 8 P.M. As we approached the City of Mexico a guard of Lancers met us with a carriage for our minister and the Judge left us to enter the city in a more grandeous manner than we underlings could expect. He went to the same hotel room with us. We entered the city at night and could see nothing at all. The palace of the Emperor Iturbide turned into a hotel was an immense building with long corridors looking out on an inner court. The judge who was very much fatigued was shown at once to his room. He undressed and attempted to repose but was driven from his bed by myriads of fleas. To drown them out of the room the servants had flooded the floor with water and the fleas had fled to the judge's bed for shelter. He passed a sleepless night and at dawn of day made his way to the American legation lay down on a sofa there and gained some hours of rest. The rest of us were more fortunate. About 8 A.M. we were served with a cup of chocolate and some shortcake. The breakfast did not come off until 10 A.M. and then it was exactly like a dinner commencing with soup or rather sopa and ending with fruit and sweets.

I amused myself by a visit to Chapultepec and the battle fields but had to take two revolvers with me for the roads were very unsafe. All this and an inspection of the antiquities of the city was very interesting. I visited the Museo and was allowed to try on a part of the armor of Cortes and I tapped upon a drum made of serpent skin which was sounded all that terrible night called La Noche Triste in which the Spaniards were beset by multitudes of the natives. I shall not attempt to describe the various objects of interest in the city for my space will not allow of it and they have been often described by others.

May wished me to call on the Sec. of war and obtain from him some maps of our route to San Luis Potosi and the country where the mine was supposed to be located but I found nothing but guess work. There were really no maps worthy of the name for no two of them agreed. The Sec. of War was very polite and our conversation went on something like this:

Now you know you have in the City of Mexico a friend whose house and every thing he has is at your disposal.

I tried to answer in the same way offering my house in Washington where I had no residence at his disposal.

When we came to a door way he would refuse to pass and I could not think of taking precedence to him so we would stand bowing and scraping and insisting that the other should go first until finally we both slid through the door at the same time as it was wide enough for two. The struggle was renewed at every door we came to with the same result.

In due time we hired two ancient vehicles which must have been 100 years old and started on our long way to San Luis by way of Queretero. Each vehicle was drawn by 8 mules two abreast. The driver rode a off mule in rear. He had a very long whip and kept a bag of stones to throw at the fartherest mule whom he could not reach with the lash.

The Mexican travelling arrangements were peculiar. Great fields of large stone and difficult hills abounded. Whenever I asked a Mexican how the road was in advance of us there was one invariable reply, *Pues senor no falta de sin pedregalite ni de ni cuesteretas.*[14] If we succeeded in stopping at a place where there was a stage house we could get fair accommodations for these taverns were built especially for those who travelled in the diligencia. The ordinary fondas only furnish food at so much a meal and empty rooms. We provided our own bedding and the house provided the fleas. These were invisible and very lively. May and Hunter whose skins were painfully sensitive would lay awake all night and indulge reflections which were not all of a pious character. We stayed several days at Queretero. We lived quietly enough and as we wore Mexican dress did not attract much attention. Partridge had a tall hat which was rather a sign of authority and I think he received more attention in consequence. At Queretero one day the procession of the host passed me. Every one in the street got on their knees except myself. People looked at me in amazement evidently thinking I must be sick or crazy. I remember to have heard that an Englishman was once killed by a mob under similar circumstances. Had I worn the dress of a European I think [it] probable I might have met a similar fate. As it was, finding many eyes fixed upon me, I slipped into a cigar store and remained until the ceremony was over.

It would lengthen out these memoirs too much to give the details of our journey. I was amused at one little circumstance. We stopped to rest in front of a large country house which was back from the road some distance. A Mexican girl of about 20 summers very plain looking and marked with the small pox was gazing at us curiously. As we were about to start I turned and said in jest, "Wont you accompany us senorita." She put her hand to her forehead in an attitude of reflection for a few moments then to my surprise she assented and was preparing to take a seat in the carriage. I was obliged to explain to her that the invitation was not a serious one.

One night we stopped where there was a miserable ranch and the only sleeping accommodations were in a shed, too dirty for our ordinary bedding arrangement. So we put some ox hides down on the ground threw down our horse blankets on them and as it was said there was a band of robbers somewhere in the vicinity each of our party lay down with his revolver by his side. The door of the shed was off its hinges, but we placed [it] against the opening and went to sleep. Now it happened that a goat was in the habit of frequenting the shed and on this occasion he chose to resent our intrusion on his domain by going back some distance and charging the door. Goat and door both came in on us very abruptly. Each man grasped his revolver and sprang to his feet. Fortunately there was sufficient light to enable us to see the cause of the uproar. We drove the animal off, put the door up again and resumed our slumbers.

In due time we reached San Luis Potosi and after looking around for a short time we hired an empty house in one of the principal streets and moved our entire cortege in. We found before long that we had chosen a strange landlord.

We soon ascertained that he was the head of a party opposed to the Gov. of the state that an order had been issued for his arrest that he had escaped over the back wall of our house and was now in hiding. It was said that he had a good deal of power and influence but was utterly lawless. The year before a brilliant young Spanish actress had come to San Luis and was received with great applause. He made love to her but his advances were rejected whereupon he waited until she left town and then lay in wait with a party of his followers and carried [her] off to his country seat. Upon my making some uncomplimentary comments on this performance to a prominent Frenchman in San Luis he said with an air of profound conviction, "Oh women like that sort of thing."

As our mission was accredited to the Gov. and we depended on him for advice and assistance it did not look very well to begin by having a business transaction with the head of the opposition party. However we went in great state to call at his official residence in the Plaza the next day. Americans were not at all popular at that time in San Luis. It was too soon after the war and the feeling of hatred was very strong. The guard scowled at us and the sentinel at the main entrance called for the officer on duty and asked if he was to admit these people. Our names were sent up and the Gov. agreed to receive us. He was a small dark man and did not impress us at first as a man of mark but he spoke well, lamented the lack of education of his countrymen and said they were wholly unfitted for self government. Perhaps he was prejudiced by the local circumstances which surrounded his own administration. It was said that he had been duly elected to serve one term and now was usurping the place as he refused to give it up to its legitimate occupant. There was, to me, a look of deep melancholy about the man. Perhaps he then saw the gulf that was about to swallow him up or it may have been a presentiment of the sad fate which awaited him and which possibly may have been hastened by the fact of the favorable reception he had given the hated Yankees. Be that as it may, before a week had elapsed a party of men rode up to him with masks on their faces as he was walking on the Paseo sprang from their horses surrounded him stabbed him repeatedly and then remounted and rode off.[15]

We were received with great courtesy and hospitality by the foreign merchants in S.L. and were invited to the club they had established. The natives however had a deep feeling of hostility and it might have ended badly for had it not been for the audacity of one of our party, Capt Barry[16] of Washington. He had been in the Govt overland survey and had undergone much danger and hardship there. He was a dead shot and was not a man to be trifled with although he was a perfect gentleman in his manners. Upon learning that a certain native merchant was inciting the natives against us and that it might end in a dangerous note Barry went straight through the crowd up to the man who was speaking drew out a pistol and asked him what he was saying about us. The speaker apologized abjectly and Barry notified him that if he ever said another word on the subject he would kill him. He did this on 2 or 3 instances, as there were a number of us and well armed, people concluded to let us alone.

In one way however we came very near getting into serious trouble. The Secy of War had a wild brother-in-law[17] which he recommended to us as secretary for the expedition. He, I believe, had run away from home in early life and had led a rough life among the Texans on the border of Mexico. He was utterly useless as a secretary for his education had been very much neglected. His whole great desire was to ride about on a fine horse. When sober he was a very clever generous fellow but addicted to romancing and telling incredible stories. Unfortunately he drank too much one day at San Luis and began boasting in a garrulous manner that he had been a filibuster in some expedition into Mexico. The Mexican authorities looked upon us with suspicion and did not half believe that we came on the Gardiner Mine business. Some of them thought it was a ruse, that we were spies acting with reference to another invasion. Upon hearing H. talk in this way our foreign friends the merchants became alarmed. There was very little law and no protection for foreigners at that day. They told us in consequence of H.'s statement it was quite probable that not only we but they would be compromised and perhaps imprisoned. Fortunately H. had already gained the reputation of manufacturing stories out of the whole cloth and we treated his assertions in the present instance as another of his Arabian Nights lucubrations. This view of the case fortunately prevailed and we escaped any disastrous consequences.

In the mean time a revolution seemed to be going on in the State of San Luis. We noticed militia pouring into the town and cannon placed at the corners of the square so that we got away as soon as we could.

On our journey to Lagunillas[18] we met at one place several hundred people marching along in procession. We were dressed in Mexican costume so were not detained. One man, a peon, stopped me and asked me to drink to the health of his master in a glass of pulque. I did so passed on and was not molested.

Before we arrived at Lagunillas we received [a] letter from our friends in San Luis warning us that Gardiner had arrived in the country by way of Tampico, that he had two American friends with him, and that he had written to know how we were armed and what escort we had. This did not terrify us in the least for we felt fully able to protect ourselves against open violence.

We finally reached Lagunillas which we found to be a miserable little village of no account. We secured a vacant house made arrangements for our food and went to work to obtain the necessary evidence which we required. May first put up a number of handbills throughout the country offering a reward of $500 to any one who would show us the Gardiner mine. There were no mines however in Lagunillas and hence there were no applicants for the reward on the part of the natives. We soon found that Gardiner and his two American friends Abbott[19] and Slocum were located opposite to us across the plaza in the house of the Alcalde who was one of their confederates in the scheme of fraud. I spent my time very energetically in making surveys and reconnaissance of that part of the country for the information of the Govt. at Washington when the trial came off. After some days had elapsed Gardiner developed his plan of operation. The nearest mines were some 70 miles off in the State of Queretero. They had not been worked for a great many years. These he intended to claim as his. There were many difficulties in the way. His mining title called for one mine with three air shafts located in Lagunillas in the State of San Luis Potosi. These mines were in Queretero a long distance from Lagunillas, 60 miles beyond the boundary. Besides these were separate mines and one was 12 miles from the other two. His plan however was to swear that they were his, swear them all together, and swear that they were within the boundary of Lagunillas. For this purpose he stuck up various papers and proclamations relating to Lagunillas on the road to these mines to enable the parties with him to swear they had seen evidence they were still within the precinct of Lagunillas. Thus done Abbott appeared and said he was ready to show us the Gardiner Mine and take the reward. It was evident however that before going off into Queretero to look for a Gardiner mine we must have a statement from Gardiner that those were the mines he claimed, otherwise he would assert on the trial when we brought proof that these mines were never worked by him that we had gone to the wrong place. We therefore made a written demand on him to know if Abbott was his agent and if the mines Abbott proposed to show us were the ones he claimed. To this he made no answer. We could not afford to wander off in Queretero looking up mines and then have Gardiner report to Abbott: besides the trial would soon come off and May believed the judge would not wait for our return in such a case but would decide the matter in our absence.

The principal party associated with Gardiner in these frauds was Don Manuel Verastegui[20] who was a powerful chieftan residing not far from Lagunillas and owning an immense number of peones. When we mentioned his name to the Gov of San Luis Potosi as a confederate of Gardiner he was startled for Don Manuel had at one time put himself at the head of 3000 men and fought the government of Mexico: the strife was ended by his giving up some of his subordinates to be hung but he was pardoned and left in possession of all his power and property. May who was the head of our commission adopted a bold policy he went straight to see Don Manuel and laid the whole case before him. This was going into the lion's den but it proved our best policy after all Verastegui knew that Gardiner had received this large sum of money from our government but had seen him none of it. He was therefore turned against his partner in the fraud and did not hesitate to give up all the letters Gardiner had written him [self] on the subject. In one of these a proposition was made to assassinate our Minister to Mexico who with his secretary had been directed by our government to go to the mine but who had gone no further than San Luis. The words to this effect were if the party go to Lagunillas then blood be on their own head especially if your mountaineers get up a sudden row with them.

Having finished our explorations in San Luis we started to return home. There were two routes one the roundabout way by which we had come and the other more direct road lay directly over the Sierra Madre by a mere pathway which went by the name of the Highway for the Doves. The road was both difficult and dangerous but our sure footed animals passed over it successfully sometimes we hung over the brink of enormous precipices; we would journey down to the Tierra Caliente with its lemons and pine apples and again ascend to mountain heights where we were above the clouds. One day a tempest of wind and rains was going on beneath our feet while all around was sunny and serene. The country was in a state of revolution and one night it was thought we might be attacked. We therefore took turns in standing guard. Each sentinel was expected not only to watch over the safety of the camp but to attend to the boiling of our only ham the last piece of meat in our possession. I was amused to see Hunter put his naval ideas in practice on land. He made various wonderful knots to secure our tents with pegs and then lit a lantern and went the rounds with that in his hands. That would probably be a good plan aboard ship but would hardly answer in the Army. The light would blind the sentry and he would be a mark for every lurking enemy.

At one point we had a magnificent view. The whole table land of Mexico lay beneath our feet and the great peak of Orizaba rose up in the clear air in startling proximity to us. We passed many rich mines but had no time to inspect them.

Before we reached the City of Mexico we met some descendents of the old Aztec population and it was interesting to find the few that still spoke their native language. I looked upon them with a great deal of interest.

We reached the City of Mexico on a Christmas afternoon, and at once took up our old quarters in the Hotel Iturbide. Here H. met with a sad misadventure. He put his flute in his pocket and went out to the suburbs of the city. Everywhere people were dancing and playing on musical instruments. He went with one of the assemblies and was cordially received especially as he took out his flute and played for them. Unfortunately he got to drinking the miserable mescal of the country and soon became very drunk and combative. In this state he damned the Mexicans for a set of miserable peones and said he was a Norte Americano that he had fought against them on the border and could whip the whole crowd. A great row ensued. A foreigner who was there rushed to get the police. Two of the latter arrived just in time probably to save H.'s life for the whole crowd were at him. When the guards heard what he had said one of them slashed him across the forehead with a sword and came near putting his eye out. They then dragged him off to prison.

May was so indignant at this behavior that he discharged him from our service and refused to interfere in his behalf. However when he was seen the next day set to work to clean the streets with Mexican guards behind him prodding him with their bayonets it seemed too bad to desert him and our Consul Mr. Black[21] was requested to interfere. In consequence of his representations H. was brought before an Alcalde for trial. There he assumed a high tone, represented his imprisonment as a gross outrage for which the American Government would hold Mexico responsible said his brother-in-law was Sec. of War in the U.S. and that if he was not immediately released there would be another invasion of Mexico. The Alcalde smiled turned to Mr. Black and said if I let this foolish young man go will you give bonds in the sum of $10000 that he shall keep the peace. Mr. B agreed to this and H. was released. Upon rejoining us he did not meet with a very cordial reception, but he was so elated in getting out of prison that he soon forgot all his mishaps and commenced inventing stories as usual.

Upon arriving in Vera Cruz we found there was no direct line going to the U.S. and so we embarked in the British Treasure steamer for Havana. These vessels carrying large sums of money were built of great strength and were very carefully managed. I believe no accident of importance had ever occurred on one of them. Gardiner arrived in time to take passage with us. He was accompanied by a Jewish friend Levy and two gentiles Slocum and Abbott. On the voyage they represented him to be a great mine owner and a man of vast wealth and consequence. He soon became very intimate with the officers of the vessel while we were looked upon as people of no importance. We were accompanied by a number of witnesses who had known Gardiner's antecedents in Mexico. These were Americans and Englishmen with one or two Mexicans. One of our party was a mason and as the purser was also a mason they became acquainted and the true statement of the case was given. The British Officers dropped Gardiner and his friends at once and met their advances with chilling coldness.

Upon arrival at Havana we went on shore with our baggage to wait for the arrival of the *Isabel* which ran between that port and Charleston. I had worn a pair of pistols in Mexico and upon leaving the steamer attached them to my belt. I was told I would not be allowed to wear them through the streets as it was illegal. Nevertheless I thought I had the right to wear arms as a U.S. officer and as I did not desire to throw them away I determined to test the question. I was not interfered with. During my short stay in Havana I was surrounded with spies for every American that arrived there was supposed to be connected with some revolutionary scheme. I was amused at one circumstance. The gas was lit at 3 P.M. Upon inquiring why this was I was told that it was a perquisite of the Queen Mother it was desirable that she should receive as much lighting as possible.

There was considerable sickness in Havana at this time so that we were glad to leave. On our arrival in Charleston we found an epidemic of small pox raging there. We kept on and arrived in Washington Jany. 16, 1853.

Owing to our constant change of place and the uncertainty of the mails very few of our letters had reached our friends and they did not know whether we were alive or dead. My wife had been very ill and suffered greatly from anxiety but as soon as I arrived she recovered as if by magic and was happy once more.

Just before leaving the City of Mexico we had each purchased wax figures and other images as presents for our friends. Mr. Speyers told us that there was one thing which the ladies of his family appreciated more than any thing else. This was a certain style of petticoat deeply embroidered in the convents which were for sale. So we each concluded to buy one of them. We sent and procured 6 paying an ounce of gold for each. As our trunks were gone these skirts were thrust into my carpet bag at the last moment. Soon after my arrival in Washington I went out to purchase some clothing of which I stood very much in need. While I was gone my wife opened the bag and great was the astonishment of herself and the lookers on to see that I had gone into the petticoat business so extensively. There were many exclamations at the beauty and style of the embriodery which was a foot deep. She gave all the articles away but one. On my return however I explained the matter and reversed her decision as to the gifts.

At first there was a question whether an officer of the Army was entitled to any extra compensation for a trip of this kind but Congress finally voted me $2000. Our expenses were paid but the committee who audited the accounts struck out a great many articles that I thought were properly charged under the circumstances. Capt Barry said to me Doubleday you dont understand how to do this thing. You should have put in a lot of items for them to strike out; that should have satisfied them and they would not have objected to the legitimate expenses. Now I have charged them for $40 worth of sweetmeats which I bought in Havana under the head of nourishment. They will strike that out of course and some other items I have introduced and I shall receive what I am fairly entitled to. B. had put the item about sweetmeats in Spanish and as the accounting clerk could not read Spanish it was passed to his credit.

When the trial came off there was great excitement for many people were implicated who were men of importance and who did not wish to refund the fees they had received. After the evidence for the prosecution was in [the] Gardiner party swore the deserted mines they had visited were in Lagunillas and tried to change their location in reference to each other to fit his mining title as far as possible. He had some of the ablest lawyers in the country and they were well paid. The result was that there were 10 jurors for his acquital and only 2 for his conviction. This rendered a new trial necessary. Fortunately for the government there was time to send another commission to the Queretero mines. These returned with full information as to the facts so that on the second trial he was convicted. The judge sentenced him to 10 years in the penitentary but he had always said he never would serve a term there. He called for a glass of water which was brought him. I saw him put something in his mouth and swallow it. It was strychnine. He died that night in convulsions in jail.[22]

His property which had been enjoined, was some 200000 I believe, was thrown into Chancery and I doubt if the government ever got much of it. I think the lawyers got the lions share.

This trial lasted more than a year. When it was over I was ordered to rejoin my company which was at Fort Duncan, Eagle Pass, Texas on the Mexican frontier.

9

INDIANS IN TEXAS
AND FLORIDA

When I reached San Antonio I was delayed some two weeks before I could obtain transportation to my post. The state of things there was not regulated by law to any very great extent for the pistol and Bowie Knife were still the code of a good many of the population. One day when we were dining at Paymaster Desheil's[1] farm some two or three miles out of town the hotel where we were staying was raided by a party of roughs who went into every room and hauled out the inmates. Had I been at home there would in all probability have been one or two dead roughs for I was well armed. At last we started for the outlying post of Fort Inge,[2] two days journey. I was told I would not need an escort until I reached that point. In the mean time I had written to the Comdg. Off. at Fort Duncan[3] and a detachment of a Corporal and 5 men had been sent to meet me at Inge to escort me on the 3 days journey from there to Duncan for that part of the country is constantly infested by bands of roving Commanche on their way into Mexico to raid the settlements there.

A few miles out of San Antonio we came to a fine stream called the Leona, with clear pellucid water running over its pebble bed only one or two feet deep. I drove into the center of the stream and halted to let the horses drink. I observed several sturdy looking men heavily armed with revolvers etc. standing on the farther bank and called to one of them. He waded to me and I asked him if he had any objec-

"The hotel in Castroville was charmingly kept...."

tion to hand me a dipper full of water. He did so and asked me if this was a government conveyance. I told him yes it was an army ambulance. The men all left at once. Soon afterwards I ascertained from a San Antonio paper that these men were a band of robbers who had been plundering and killing people at that very point and supposing that my escort would soon come in sight they had thought it best not to attack us. It was a very fortunate escape. We arrived that night at Castroville[4] a charming little village. Lieut H. [Holabird] accompanied me on this trip, his Co. K of 1st Inf being stationed at Duncan.

The hotel at Castroville was charmingly kept.[5] The landlord having been the keeper of a restaurant in New Orleans. The food was excellent and every thing was extremely neat and clean. Lumber in that part of the country was very dear for there were no forests nearer than 80 miles and the labor of hauling was very great. Consequently, to separate the different bed rooms it was customary to use canvas white washed. I supposed it was a solid wall and we conversed pretty freely about Lieut H wondering why as he was just married he had not brought his wife with him. When my candle was put out I found the room as light as ever from the light that came through the partition. The light of my neighbor through [cast] his silhoutte in large dimensions on the wall so that we could see every thing he was doing. Of course he had heard our conversation and next day explained why he did not bring his wife.

One thing which had struck me in Mexico attracted my attention here. The great number of crosses on the hills around pointing out places where people had been killed by the Indians. Where men die suddenly in this way it is customary in Catholic countries to put up a cross in order that the passers by may pray for the soul of the deceased who died without confession or extreme unction.

At our next stopping place we came to a tavern of quite a different stamp. It was called Finger's and was the only house.[6] It was built of logs and very badly chinked and as the cattle were put in one room to keep the indians from driving them off in the night. The guest could put his hand out of bed and pat the cows on the head in the morning. We preferred to camp out in the open field rather than go in such a dirty place. The coyotes abound in this vicinity. These wolves keep up a constant yelping and crying all night but never attack the traveller. Capt. D.[7] who was an old campaigner brought his wife from Washington a short time previous to our visit and camped out as we had done. As he was within one days journey from his post at Fort Inge he had not brought a tent with him. He put his wife and her maid in the ambulance which was luxuriously fitted up for such emergencies and he slept underneath on his blanket on the ground. The coyotes soon began their uproar and the bride asked what caused all the uproar. Capt D. replied nothing but wolves. "Wolves," the bride shrieked with horror. He tried to convince her they would do no harm but about every 15 minutes she would look over the side of the ambulance and say, "Dear, are you there?"

The next day we arrived at Fort Inge and were very hospitably received. Capt D. informed us that after leaving that post we were liable to meet bands of Indians but my escort had arrived and we pushed on to Fort Duncan without being molested. We were fortunate for we came upon the fresh trail of a very large body of Comanches who had just passed by on their way to make a raid to Mexico.

Fort Duncan at this time was laid out in a large square, the officers quarters being some 200 yards from those of the men. It was tennanted by the 1st Regt of Infty under Col Plympton,[8] Major Morris,[9] and Capt Bainbridge.[10] Several officers who were stationed there with us gained great celebrity afterwards. Our present Lt Genl Phil Sheridan was then a 2nd Lieut who had recently joined the command. He was a perfect gentleman in his manners and very much liked even then. A. S. Johnston who afterwards became a Maj Genl was also with us. Col Wallace, May, Arthur[11] and others were all noted Army officers for services in Mexico and elsewhere. Our Co E of the 1st Arty was armed and acted as infantry.

Afterwards 2 cos of cavalry under Capt Walker[12] and Lieut Cass[13] were afterwards added to the force. Genl P. F. Smith who commanded in Texas directed that our company of Arty should hold the post while the others should at certain season be thrown out in a circle 30 miles off to try and intercept these roving bands of savages but as I said it is useless to use infy against mounted indians who have such keen senses that is almost impossible to surprise them.

On one occasion when only our little co of arty and the Regt band were left to guard Fort Duncan, where there never have been any fortifications, we received a polite message from a band of Seminole who were now under chief Wild Cat[14] in Mexico and who had fought our troops in Florida. They sent us word they would hang up the right arm of every one of us in the square of the neighboring town of San Fernando in Mexico.[15] There were several large bands of hostile indians at this time in our immediate vicinity. One of Mescalero Apaches another of Lipans who had been friendly but were now hostile and the Seminoles referred to. For a time there was considerable excitement in the garrison but no attack was made.

On another occasion some 14 Lipans attacked 2 herdsmen just outside of the post. One was a Mexican the other was an old soldier. The Mexican came in and gave the alarm. The long roll was beaten at once and our cavalry went out after the Indians who soon however escaped by crossing the river into Mexico where our troops were forbidden to follow. The soldier was found dead with 10 arrows sticking in him but he had killed 3 indians with 4 shots of his revolver.[16]

Certainly there are many more pleasant places than Fort Duncan. The thermometer reads 104 in the shade day after day. It was necessary to suspend all work from 12 to 4 P.M. Every body took a siesta and then every one was awake that being the only time when it was cool enough for comfort. The houses there were generally made of adobe and thatched with straw. Mine was all thatched. One day a person came in to my kitchen for a shovel full of coals; the wind blew strong some sparks and caught the thatch. All my house was soon burned to the ground with several hundred dollars worth of valuables.[17]

A new house was built for me but I did not occupy it long for on the 1854 [3rd of March, 1855], I was promoted to be a Capt in Co E at old Point Comfort. The change was a very agreeable one and I was soon on my way eager to revisit home friends and civilization once more.

An astrologer who cast my horoscope once told me that this was one of the pleasantest years of my life and he was not far wrong. The agreeable society and pleasant surrounding contrasted strongly with my recent abode in a barbarous frontier destitute of all comforts. Soon after my arrival at my new post the 9th Infy under Col. Wright[18] was sent to Old Point as a School of Instruction for the regiment. They had a very agreeable set of officers and many families were there. These, with frequent visitors from the elite of Va. society made the place very gay. The Secy. of War and Genls of high rank in the Army came there often on tours of inspection so that military drills parades and inspections in the day were followed by balls and parties at night.

Nothing occurred however at first of an unusual character. I was sent down to Florida with Capt Pickett, the celebrated general who led the charge at Gettysburg, Lt Carr,[19] Lt Childs,[20] and Capt Winder to sit as a court martial at Fort Capron. It was a long and difficult journey for after we arrived at Jacksonville we had to go by boat for several days down Indian River before we reached our destination. On our return we took passage in a steamer loaded with cotton which was to make a short outside passage by sea to Darien Ga. Several of our party were to leave on another steamer about the same time for St. Augustine, Florida. I was very much fatigued with our long journey in which we had bivouaked frequently and had had very scanty accommodations. I was therefore rejoiced to get on the steamer and I soon undressed myself and went to sleep. Winder had the upper berth in the cabin but he did not undress and he did not go to sleep. He had so strong a presentiment of danger that he begged me to join him in paying $80 for a conveyance to take us by land to Darien. I thought he was unnecessarily nervous and paid no attention to him. He lay down with all his clothes on. We were to leave the wharf at one o'clock at night. In spite of the success of pseudo scientific men who despise every thing that they cannot measure and weigh with their instruments there is a department of being in which they have never entered because they lack capacity to appreciate spiritual things. About half past 12 Winder sprang to his feet with a start gave me a strong slap on the shoulder to waken me shouted Doubleday the boat is on fire and was off. The flames proceeded from the cotton with which the vessel was loaded. This had been set on fire by the carelessness of a man who was smoking. I rose partly dressed myself and then looked out to see how near the flames were. In the mean time an attempt was being made to wake the passengers. Some ladies were so frightened they could not unlock the doors of their state-rooms and it was necessary to break in the doors to get them out. I met a lady in great distress about her children. By the time I had escorted her and her little ones off the boat it was too late for me to get back to my state room. I was decidedly in dishabille having only shoes stockings and a pair of pants on. The wharf was full of women in their night dresses and bare feet.

The other boat was well out in the harbor when it saw the flames and turned back to aid us. There were several young men aboard who had travelled with me and with whom I had become intimate. They had been sitting up and drinking to excess and one of them was maudlin drunk. He cried when he saw me threw his arms around me and kissed me and insisted on my taking his entire wardrobe. I accepted two or three necessary articles of wearing apparel borrowed some money from one of my companions and returned home in this way minus a gold watch and nearly all my clothing. Pickett was with me on this trip. Instead of going directly back to Old Point he wished to slip aside to his home in Va. and see his relatives. My going directly back would show that he was delaying his return. He urged me to delay but that I could not do in accordance with either duty or inclination. He said Doubleday it is our duty to go home I never slight my duty but attend to it thoroughly. Now in order to be sure that I get to Old Point all right I dont intend to hurry through it. I shall take my time to it and then I know it will be well done.

Soon afterwards the 9th Infy was ordered off to the Pacific Coast and Capt Brannan's[21] company and mine both of the 1st Arty were left to garrison this large post.

There were two candidates for the Presidency at this time, Fremont the young path finder as he was called was the nominee of the Republican Party and was opposed by the veteran politician and

Democrat Buchanan. The prelude to the great national storm which threatened to wreck the ship of state had already commenced and there was much treasonable talk. A party of Virginians threatened in case Fremont was elected to anticipate secession seize Old Point Comfort and hold Fortress Monroe against the government. I wrote to Fremont warning him of this plot and telling him that for one I intended to throw myself with my company into one of the barracks in case of any such attempt and hold out as long as possible. He determined the momen this election was announced to anticipate the revolutionists by occupying Fort Monroe with a party of his adherents headed by himself. Buchanan however was elected and the excitement subsided for the time being.

The new President was hardly inaugurated before his Secy of War, Mr. Floyd of Va., began to take action with a view to assist the secessionists when the moment came for them to act. He at once ordered our two companies to leave Old Point for Florida where there had been some recent outbreaks of the Seminoles but not to any great extent. I think they had murdered 2 or three settlers. This was sufficient excuse for Floyd to order the garrison of Old Point away and leave this large and important post merely in charge of an Ordnance Sergeant.

We, Brannan's Co and mine left Old Point in a steamer chartered for the occasion and were soon off the coast of Florida. Col. Justin Dimick[22] was our Comd officer a resolute and experienced officer who was determined to put down the Indian outbreak if it could be done and who neither spared himself nor his officers where duty was in question. When we came opposite our destination which was Key Biscayne Bay where Fort Dallas[23] is situated we had the misfortune to run aground. We were in a perilous situation for the bow of the boat was fast in the sand while the stern was free. Had any wind come up the thumping on the bottom caused by the action of the waves would have soon brought the engines through the bottom of the vessel. We got out our life preservers and as there was a light-house some three miles off we made all the signals we could think of to attract attention and get a pilot. I fired volleys of musketry from the deck but it was a dark night and we were neither seen nor heard. The idea of the vessel going to pieces on that shore was not an agreeable one for the sea is swarming with sharks. Fortunately the wind went down and there was almost a dead calm. When morning came the Captain suceeded in getting the vessel out. We proceeded joyfully on our way and were soon at our destination. The place had been held as a military post and all the requisite buildings were there to make us comfortable. There were no fortifications of any kind but it seems to be customary to call every spot in Florida and Texas occupied by a garrison a Fort. Fort Dallas was located on the west side of Key Biscayne Bay, the harbor being some 3 miles wide surrounded with pine woods with occasional patches of what are called indian hammocks which are dense thickets difficult to penetrate. There were several of them in the immediate vicinity of the post. A stream large enough to be called a river bounded one side of the post which was an outlet to the Everglades about ten miles distant.

One morning soon after our arrival just before breakfast I was standing near the stables when Col Dimick made his appearance in a soldiers overcoat and said to me, "Do you ride?" I replied in the affirmative and he said, "Get a horse from the Qtr Ms dept and let us ride out a little ways." I complied with his request and we rode out. It gave me a taste of his quality as an Indian campaigner. We scoured the country for a long distance were gone all day and did not return until night. I was very much fatigued and glad to break my long fast. The Indians might easily have cut us off for we took no precautions. We soon found that Dimick was addicted to these long excursions and whenever we saw him put on that overcoat we knew what we had to expect.

I am afraid if the statistics of the money spent in Florida were made out it could easily be shown that it cost more than $100,000 to capture or kill one Indian. I believe it would have been much cheaper to let the matter out by contract. In saying this I do not mean to disparage the skill or gallantry of the officers of the army for they were actuated by a strong sense of duty and did all in their power, but the material furnished us was not suitable for the business. The German and Irish emigrants who enlisted at this time composed the bulk of our forces and were almost necessarily ignorant of anything like woodcraft. How could a soldier loaded down with his musket and cartridge box his canteen and haversack succeed in catching wholly unencumbered Indians who knew every path and stream and culvert and who were not encumbered with any commissariat. They managed to find food enough where ever they were. The arrow root of which covered the country the inner bark of certain trees wild plums and the cabbage palmetto were always available. The waters swarmed with fish and the woods with game.

In order to send out scouting parties intelligently Brannan and myself were directed to make a road north to New River some 30 miles distant and I set myself to making a map of the surrounding country for I was fond of that kind of business and always liked to have all the localities around me on paper.

We did not see or hear anything of the Seminoles for some time and as their trail was frequently found fresh at a crossing about 3 miles up the river I was sent there to try and open communication with them. I put up a pole bent it towards the sun at 3 P.M. made 7 notches in it and leaving some tobacco and other presents then called wampum. I then put up a white flag and returned. All this meant that in a week from that day I would like to meet them then under a white flag. They looked at the arrangement and took the presents but did not meet us.

They knew they could outrun us and easily escape pursuit and they therefore were not at all afraid of us. One day one of them actually came to the edge of a thicket and was seen by some camp woman looking in at evening parade. The woman screamed the occurrence was reported the long roll was beaten and I put out with my co after that Indian. I deployed my men in open order and went into a hammock where the Indian had taken refuge. I soon found myself in difficulty. Some of the men went forward in open spaces and made rapid progress while others were detained by obstacles while several including myself were tied up in the wild vines and had great difficulty in moving at all. The Indians under such circumstances lay down and worm themselves down like snakes through the thickets for they have no impediments: no haversacks or canteens or cartridge boxes to bother them. I saw that my co was rapidly becoming dispersed and at last gave up the attempt in despair to catch this particular Indian. The bugles were blown a long time before I could reassemble the men.

Col Dimick now organized and kept up a set of scouting expeditions. He usually left one co to guard the post and went out with the other. He would keep along the road Brannan and myself had cut and we would examine the country east of the Everglades. We would tramp all day through the woods wading in the edge of the Everglades and return at night worn out with fatigue. Then we would cut a few palmetto leaves as a bed and lie down in our blankets heedless of snakes which were abundant or alligators which came around at night. We found plenty of these animals but no Indians.

An expedition was formed to go up to Lake Okeechobee and look there for them. On the way there I saw a long morass which runs parallel to the coast and is about 200 yards wide. On the other side there was a beautiful rolling country and as it had not been inspected I thought I would try and make my way over there. It proved an awful undertaking. The mud was very soft and deep and had it not been for the trees which were frequent we would not have got across it. Panting breathlessly and worn out we held on to the branches of these trees to prevent ourselves from going under. I was amused at the wit of 2 Irish soldiers who were floundering through the deepest part. One of them, covered with mud, said Denis "I think I'll stop here and open shop." "And what will you sell" said Denis. "*Artificial flowers!*" When I got over I found a beautiful country with plenty of game but no sign of Indians and it was not at all agreeable to return but we succeeded in getting over at a narrower and less difficult place. On this expedition I was struck with the different degrees of memory of localities in the soldiers.I tested them with my pocket compass. Some would lose the way before they had gone 200 yards, others seemed to have an almost magical power of direction: they never varied in their course and if awakened in the darkest night would start off unerringly on the proper route. And this reminds me of an incident which occurred on this expedition. We were on our way back for the lake and had made several days journey. Although we saw no traces of Indians Dimick kept up the scouting parties so zealously that he put one of my Lieuts on a mule gave him ten men on other mules that were disabled and unable to march and directed him to make a scout but to return to the command at night. The Lieut said to me, one of his friends, this is all nonsense. It is merely to look well on the map of an exploration which is to be sent to Genl Harney. We scouted this country before and we know there are no Indians here. I am not going to kill myself and the men for nothing. Our march is north east. Very well I shall take my men out of sight of you all then take the north east course and follow you into camp and get in early. Night came but the mule party did not make its appearance. Ten o'clock came and still there were no signs of them. We made huge fires to attract their attention and Dimick began to grumble. If I send my young men out on scouts I want them to be reasonable about it. They are altogether too zealous to keep their men out so late as this. About 2 o'clock that night the mule party made its appearance. The Lieut had kept going all day and as evening came on he thought he would join us. He had no sense of locality whatever and relied entirely on his compass but there was a bugler with him who had the faculty very largely developed and who watched his proceedings with a sorrowful eye. At last the Lieut said I think I will go over to that rising ground; the bugler forgot the restraints of discipline and said "Oh dont Lieut!" "Dont" said the Lieut, "why not I think our men are over there." "Oh no lieut we have been going away from them all day. We have got back to Lake Okechobee again. If you go over there you will see the lake." "Why bless me how is this" said the Lieut. Great Heavens I have been going N.W. all day instead of N.E.

Genl Harney who commanded the Dept now organized a large expedition to cross Florida from Tampa Bay making a considerable circuit to join us at Fort Dallas. This force was under command of Capt Pemberton[24] who had distinguished himself on Worth's staff in the Mexican War. He subsequently became the celebrated General who defended Vicksburg against Grant. A certain number of wagons were to be sent him to carry his provisions and tools but he would not wait for them and started without them. The consequence was that each soldier was loaded down with 10 days provisions. The weather was hot the marches fatiguing and the soldiers wasted or lost their provisions so that when five days had elapsed they still had a long distance to go and were out of food. They were obliged to eat one of the officer's horses and the tail of an alligator and they had a few palmetto cabbages. There was hardly any game in the vicinity at the time so that they were half starved and became very weak as they approached New River some 30 miles from Fort Dallas if I remember rightly. Brannan and myself had made a good road that far and had bridged all the streams but New River was wide and Pemberton's command had no way of crossing it. One officer, Lieut Lee[25] a relative of Robert E. Lee swam over and finding a good road on the other side kept on until he reached Fort Dallas and told us the plight Pemberton was in. Provisions were at once sent out and the men were so eager that they ate the meat raw. Lee who was excessively hungry and who arrived at dawn of day went to the sutlers store and ate crackers and cheese there until breakfast was cooked. He ate a very hearty breakfast and he went back to the sutler's store and ate whatever he could find then until dinner. He then ate a hearty dinner and it was said went back again to the sutler's store and kept on eating until supper time. A dangerous experiment but it did not seem to injure him in the present instance.

Before the expedition started our company was filled up with recruits from Governor's Island. To teach them to fire I put up a picture of an Indian on canvas leaned it against a tree and made them practice at it. They were mostly Irish and not used to firing and it was amusing to see their gratification when they hit it. I heard one of them say, "If that was ould Billy Bowlegs[26] himself, its little he'd trouble the country after this." The tree against which proved to be an india rubber tree the first I had ever seen.

We reached Okeechobee at last but saw no signs to indicate that our foemen were residing in that vicinity. The scenery was flat and uninteresting but the broad sheet of water was a pleasant sight after so much journey through pine forests.

After this expedition Pemberton's forces returned to the east side of Florida and we settled down to our usual drills, parades, and scouting.

Dimick who was afraid of nothing else had a great antipathy to snakes. The sight of one would make him sick and they are very abun-

dant in Florida. It was not at all an uncommon circumstance to see
them projecting their heads from holes under the roofs of the houses.
We made preparations one day to go on a scout and as the youngsters
thought they would have a better time and more freedom without the
comd. officer than with him they got up a conspiracy to scare him
with snake stories. They asked me what I was going to do with that
reata (long rope made of horse hair which I had brought from Texas).
I answered that I put it around my sleeping place at night to keep the
snakes off for they were never known to crawl over this kind of rope
probably mistaking for a snake of another kind. My answer opened
the way and they told some terrible snake stories apropos of the place
we were going to. Dimick shuddered but did not give up the expedition. After all they were not so far wrong for while he was out he got
caught in a narrow path with a huge rattlesnake on each side of him
and escaped by giving some prodigious leaps.

We had no success in the Indian question whatever. How could we
have. They kept out of our way and let us wander around. There were
only about 150 warriors in the whole vast peninsula and it was impossible to surprise them with the material we had principally as I stated
German or Irish emigrants who finding themselves penniless in our
large cities and had enlisted to get bread. These men were wholly
ignorant of wood craft and consequently were no match for the savages. The sensible thing to do would have been to organize some
bands of Western Indians discipline and feed them well and they
would have soon routed the Seminoles out of their nests.

However at last Dimick had a gleam of hope. He received information that Billy Bowlegs and his warriors about 120 men were congregated on a large island in the Everglades so he directed me to take
about 60 men and attack him. We were furnished with a supply of
boats for that purpose. The island we were to seek was said to be
marked with a large tree which rose from the top of a hill in such a
way as to be a land mark and overlook the whole country.

The Everglades is a curious fresh water swamp. Streams, rivers,
and lakes are every where interspersed with islands. For several days I
searched these islands as we penetrated the center of this inland sea

but we found no signs of an enemy. At last as we reached the central part I saw a large island which seemed to answer the description which had been given of the stronghold of the savages and prepared to attack it. There was a high place on it and a large tree there which overlooked the surrounding country. I waited at a small island for all my boats to come up so that I could organize a strong attack. Unfortunately I did not examine the small island where we were organizing for the attack, for I had examined all the others in vain and my attention was fixed on the large island. There was a dense thicket in this small island. Behind this thicket a party of Seminoles were in ambush. We did not know it at the time but ascertained it when we came back there. As soon as all was ready we started for the main island. As we approached it we saw plenty of Indian sign. The officers drew out their revolvers and we jumped into the water waist deep struggled through the high grass and charged up the slope but the Indians had left a day or two previously. They had made quite a residence of the place but probably their scouts had notified them of our coming. In order to ascend the large tree in the center I made a carpenter belonging to my company cut some short sticks and nail each one into the trunk of the tree so that we could go up this impromptu ladder. Every nail driven in brought out a milk white fluid which proved to be india rubber. We ascended to the top and had a fine view of the Everglades but saw no enemy. We then went back to the little island I have mentioned and there found very recent signs of them. Part of a deer had been cooked there arrow root was lying about on the ground and a number of small stakes showed that the indians had become civilized enough to use mosquito bars.

We found bear and alligators very abundant in this vast swamp. As we lay down at night the latter would come grunting around our boats and one of the crews said that one of these large creatures made an attempt to enter. At night as we lay down the uproar around us was fearful. Birds of all kinds were making the night hideous with discordant sounds. The alligators were grunting and occasionally the prolonged wail of a panther would be heard. We returned without having captured any Indians.

In a scouting party that took place up the country soon after that I was amused at the strong desire manifested by a German boy who had joined the band to go with us. The fatigue and discomfort of these expeditions were so great that all the men got off whenever they could but this boy was very desirous of seeing the interior of the country. He had formed an idea that it was full of strange birds and beasts. He had just arrived and was ignorant of the requirements of military discipline. The 3rd day out I saw him aiming his gun at a moccasin snake and as I had hopes of finding Indians and did not wish to alarm them by firing guns I said to him, "Dont shoot that snake." He very cooly answered me, "Oh I muss! I muss! he great big fellar!" and in spite of my prohibition he blazed away. His greenness saved him from a severe punishment.

I had in my command an old soldier named Pratt. He was a powerful hand at wielding an axe and was the best teamster we had. There was no enjoyment to him like the management of a six mule team. For some time after our arrival he was employed in ordinary company duty. He had been making cynical observations about the teamsters and their lack of skill so I said Pratt is dissatisfied he is an old soldier and I must humor him so I sent for him and told him I had had him detailed as teamster. He looked sad and depressed and did not manifest any pleasure. Nevertheless he took the team and attended to the duties. One day an accident occurred. He was thrown out of the wagon against a sharp stump and very much injured. He then said to me, "You know Capt when you wanted me to take that team, *something 'peared to be telling me I better not,*" and I didn't want it. I put this anecdote in for the benefit of my materialistic friends who dont believe in any thing that they cant measure and weigh with their instruments.

The Indian had frequented the islands in Florida Bay in the days of the old Florida War. Genl Harney thought as they were not found on the main land that they might have taken refuge here. So I was directed to take my company in boats and examine these islands which were very numerous. To aid me in the quest a Seminole woman an outcast from her tribe was given me as a guide. She and her Indian

husband had been employed for some time in that capacity. One day
he was shot. The story ran that their tribe and kindred having anath-
ematized them as enemies and spies for the white men, they became
tired of life and agreed each to commit suicide. She let him shoot
himself but did not carry out her part of the agreement. Another and
more probable story was that she quarrelled with him and killed him.
She received good pay from the government and this tempted a low
Spaniard to marry her. I do not believe she ever found any Indians for
us or intended to find them. She kept out of their way and did what
she could to prevent our troops from meeting them. On the present
occasion she presented quite a picturesque appearance straddling the
bow of my boat with one foot on each side occasionally dipping in the
water. There were many irreverent jokes about Polly[27] and myself on
the part of my lieutenants as we started out but young men will be
foolish sometimes.

At first the islands were pleasant camping places and fresh water
could be found but when we reached the middle of the large bay nothing but salt water could be obtained. Col. Dimick therefore came
down in a sloop to join us with the requisite supplies. I was sent to
make a circuit in boats of about 30 or 40 miles to examine all the
islands and was in constant fear that I would lose my connection with
head quarters. If I failed to get back there we would all perish for lack
of water and at last when we were several miles away it required great
attention not to lose the point we came from in the distant horizon
which was almost indistinguishable. Frequently several islands would
intervene and hide it from view. We found no Indians and no signs of
there having been any in the Bay for a long time. We were inside the
reef and the water was calm and clear as crystal. We were floating in
a vast tropical aquarium full of fish of every kind and we could look
down in the clear water and see them at a great depth moving around
in all directions. The calm water and June skies were exhilarating. A
gentle breeze came over us like the breath of a benediction. I have
always longed to go back there and float once more free from lifes
cares on those tranquil waters. Afar off we heard the roar of the angry
surf as it beat in vain against the barrier of the coral reef but this

added to the enjoyment by the contrast of the wild waves of the open sea and the calm water inside. Once however we were caught in the widest part of the bay which is some 20 miles wide. A violent storm came up and we barely escaped being swamped being obliged to row in the teeth of the wind to get to shore. We rigged up some impromptu sails and finally succeeded in reaching the land.

We at last retired to Fort Dallas our expedition having proved wholly fruitless.

I do not know that I ought to refer to a sad domestic tragedy; a woman's scream. I heard the scream while taking a siesta in the P.M. sprang to my feet rushed out half dressed and found two men in deadly conflict. One unarmed the other the seducer[28] armed with a large revolver with which he was trying to kill the wronged husband. At the earnest call of the latter for help I sprang to his assistance and with the aid of the guard who came up soon after succeeded in securing the criminal. The latter escaped the immediate penalty of his crime but died early in the war shot through the head at Fair Oaks.

My company had done a great deal of sentry and hard work and Seymour's men at Fort Capron 120 miles north of it had had comparatively a pleasant time. An order came from Col Loomis[29] who had succeeded to the command of the Dept in place of Genl Harney for me to march my co. to Fort Capron across Florida and exchange with Seymour's who was directed to report to Fort Dallas. The first 25 miles were easy travelling for Brannan and myself had made a good road but after that my ingenuity was taxed to the utmost for I had to make my way with a train of 12 wagons across large rivers great swamps and arms of the sea.

The first obstacle I encountered was at New River some 30 miles from the post. The problem was to cross a wide stream with a train of twelve wagons and about 80 animals without a boat of any kind. I sent a man to swim over with a small cord tied to his waist and the other end tied to a larger rope. The alligators were pretty thick but I have never known them to attack a man while swimming and the soldier was not afraid of them. When he was on the other side he pulled the large rope and fastened one end to the trunk of a tree the other end was tied to a tree on our side. I then took a wagon body covered it with a canvass tent and thus made it nearly water tight. Having done this I used my improvised boat to take my wife and her maid over, next the mules were unharnessed and harness sent over. Then I drove the mules into the water but instead of swimming across where men were waiting to take charge of them they swam up and down stream in every direction. After a great deal of trouble I collected them again on the shore. Knowing the habit of imitation that animals have I tied a rope to my horses neck strap and passed it to the men on the opposite side. I then thrust him into the water and the men pulled him straight across and he was obliged to swim. When the mules saw him swimming over one after another went into the water and followed him across. Now I had everything over but the empty wagons. I had ropes tied to the tongue and to the rear of each wagon in its turn. The men on the opposite side pulled on the tongue while the men at the starting point steadied it by means of the rope behind. The wagon sunk gradually down to the bottom of the river but as there were no obstructions it rolled on the bottom and came up on the other side. Knowing there was a more serious obstacle ahead in the shape of an innundation which had overflown the country and that the water was rising I pushed on without wasting a moment longer than was necessary. I soon came to a place covered with water which was about 300 yards wide and drove straight through it without the least hesitation. Fortunately the mules did not have to swim the water not being very deep but once or twice they were taken off their feet for short intervals. I was much relieved in mind when I had passed these obstructions and found myself in the endless pine forests once more.

In a few days we reached a place called Fort Jupiter[30] where troops were stationed in the old Florida war. There were still some remains of houses there.

What is called Indian River terminates at Jupiter. It is a kind of inner lagoon parallel to the sea coast very long and varying in width from a hundred yards to several miles. To pass a train of wagons and mules over it to attain the sea beach, the only practicable road, was a difficult operation. I found some old boards at Jupiter and the carpenters set up all night making a boat and making pitch from the pines to caulk the seams. It was finished by daylight. By means of this the animals and wagons were all passed over to the main beach. I also saw an old decayed flat boat lying at the bottom of the water. This was raised [and] caulked; blanket sails put up and while the teams made their way down the beach a small detachment sailed pleasantly down the river. We reached Fort Capron about ten o'clock at night. Seymour was very much astonished when I landed for he knew there were no roads to the south of him and he had not expected to be relieved. In a few days he went south by the same route I had taken.

There were only 3 or 4 people living in the fort country so we found it to be a very quiet post. About this time six vol. cos. of state troops were called out and ordered to report to me at Capron for the purpose of driving the Seminoles out of the country. They did not however have any better success. One co. however with a very earnest and energetic young officer was indefatiguable and captured several Indians. He came on the trail of an Indian family and at last caught up with them. I think there was one Indian his squaw and two children. As the troops came suddenly on them they all held up their right hands as a token of surrender. The Indians said to the officer when he drew near "How you do?" The latter answered "Thank you my health is pretty good How are you?" "How would you like to go to Arkansas (where all the persons were sent to a reservation)?" "Arkansas cold too much!" was the reply.

One of these vol. off. Capt Knapp told me an incident which amused me. He said he was brought up on the plantation of Genl Gaines of the U.S. Army who owned considerable property in Fla. When the war with the Seminoles broke out Genl G took the field at the head of a vol force. Knapp was about 18 then and he volunteered to go with the rest. At the end of the first days march they encamped for the night. The next morning the old Genl with his staff came riding along the lines and as he passed Knapp almost crying, went out to meet him and make a complaint saying Genl some dam rascal stole my blankets yesterday and I lay down with nothing to sleep on or to cover me last night. The Genl replied jocosely well really Knapp I dont see what can be done about it unless you steal somebody elses blanket, and rode on. That morning they did not march and Knapp as he was passing the Genls tents observed a very beautiful pair of blankets which were being sunned. There was no one around and he slipped off with them to his own tent and had a good nights rest. The next morning the Genl rode around as usual and as he passed Knapp's tent he drew rein and said my son the same d____ rascal that stole your blankets stole a pair from me yesterday evening. Knapp said I dont think it was the same d____m rascal who stole your blankets that stole mine. I think the man whose blankets were stolen took yours. What do you mean, said the General. Why Genl you advised me to steal somebody elses blankets and I did not know any one who could spare a pair better than you could. Now see here said the Genl. That is a very fine pair of blankets and I cant allow you to keep them you must give them back and I will send a plainer pair Good morning my son and off he rode.

At last the welcome order came for us to leave the solitudes of Fla. for the refinement of Charleston S.C. We were directed to go to Fort Moultrie and a steamer anchored outside to take us off. I was very much troubled in mind that night in relation to getting aboard the steamer. When the winds blows there is almost always a cross sea which swamps every boat on that part of the coast. In the old Florida war 16 soldiers were drowned at once.[31] One of our boats which went out in that direction was struck with one of these cross waves and nearly filled. I did not relish the idea of running such a risk with my co. and family. However there was no other way of getting off and we had to make the attempt. Fortunately the wind died away there was almost a dead calm and we had no difficulty.

It is needless to say we found Charleston society a very agreeable change from the wilds of Fla. There was great gaiety and many cor-dialities were paid the garrison until the great presidential contest again came on to disturb the peace of the nation and then came anger, bitterness, and hatred.

In the latter part of 1853 I took a long leave of 2 mo to visit my parents in the west. On my return in Dec. I spent some time in

Washington, and while there frequently visited the Capitol to hear the debates. Party feeling was excited to the utmost and it was evident the slave states would revolt since they considered their favorite institutions endangered by the election of a Republican president. An attempt was made to dissolve the government by refusing to elect a speaker, for the south with their northern allies made up a bare majority in Congress. On this occasion the Clerk presided over the deliberations if they could be called such, for there was a determination that no business should be accomplished. Mere nominal points would be raised under pretense of arguing them incendiary and threatening speeches would be made. Timorous northern men were offering to compromise on the slavery question and were ready even to place slavery above freedom to secure the peace of the country. Fortunately the south became more and more arrogant and demanded conditions impossible to realize in the state of public opinion at the north. *Mean dares will render persons demented.* At this perilous time Lovejoy[32] the great Abolitionist member from the west rose in the House and as he did not intend to mince matters there was intense excitement threatening bloodshed. Fearful of the result his own party tried to prevent his speech by parliamentry methods but did not succeed.

Soon after my return to Ft Moultrie there was an ominous silence and war clouds hovered over Charleston. Every effort had been made to propitiate them. Two millions of dollars had been spent on a new customs house to furnish them patronage, and a costly harbor improvement was going on, but nothing would answer. The Govt were called upon to kneel in the dust and bow to the ground before the nobility of slavery and the war spirit had been so far aroused that I doubt if compromise however degrading would have been possible to allay it.

10

SOME EXPERIENCES OF WIT, HUMOR, AND REPARTEE IN ARMY AND NAVY LIFE

"Some are born to greatness: some achieve greatness, and some have greatness thrust upon them."—Shakespeare

The abstract principles which underlie the philosophy of the ludicrous have been ably treated in Harper's Magazine and do not require any further elucidation by me. I propose herewith simply to give a few examples in the concrete of wit, humor, and repartee[1] as applied to Army and Navy life; more particularly to the former.

I was told by a talented literary lady that some years ago a Professor in a Western College wrote an article on the same subject in relation to occurances in the Revolutionary War. As I have never seen this essay and have at present no data to refer to, I cannot go back to that period.

Nor have I any information in relation to the witty sayings and doings of our army during the last war with Great Britain. When I left West Point there were many old officers still in service who had been engaged in that struggle. One of them told me an anecdote which seems to be worth relating as a specimen of the "retort courteous" and as it has a historical flavor I repeat it. A certain Colonel Loomis[2] who, if my memory serves me, was on the staff of General Dearborn on the Canadian frontier, was the hero of the episode. The Colonel was a great duellist, as a man had to be in those days, to obtain any standing in the Army, and he was very quick on the trigger where questions of honor were concerned. On one occasion he passed through the lines bearing a flag of truce for Sir George Prevost, who was Governor

BV Doubleday, Abner. " Military Anecdotes" and "Experiences of Wit and Humor."

General of Canada. Sir George received the missive, read it, and came out of his quarters in a towering rage. He said to Colonel Loomis angrily, "What is the meaning of this sir? The paper you have brought is of no importance. It refers to a mere matter of routine and should have been handed in at the outposts. Why have you come all this distance to bring it in person, conveying the idea that it was a matter of great consequence?" To this the Colonel replied with a low bow: "I had a strong desire to see the celebrated Sir George Prevost of whom I had heard so much, and I resorted to this method of doing so." This flattering answer somewhat mollified the British Commander and he said in a grumbling way, "Well stay and take dinner with us then." Colonel Loomis accordingly remained but did not find the British officers either sociable or polite. They evidently looked upon his presence as a Yankee intrusion. The dinner was an irksome affair and passed off in a constrained and silent way. At last, when the meal was over and the time had come for the usual toasts, one of the officers rose and in a grim voice proposed: *"The President of the United States—dead or alive."* All eyes were on Loomis who drank the toast without making any remark. He then rose in his turn and proposed: *"The Prince Regent— drunk or sober."* At this time George III, had been pronounced insane and his son George IV was setting in his stead. The British officers sprang to their feet and exclaimed, "Why this is an insult!" "It is a reply to one, at all events," answered Loomis taking out his card case and passing his cards out rapidly to each person at the table which was equivalent to so many challenges. The officers were about to accept the challenge by picking up the cards when the Colonel who presided over the mess interfered, saying: "The retort is a rough one, but we provoked it and as this gentleman is our guest, we will have to overlook it. I will hold anybody responsible myself who takes the matter up." So the quarrel ended peaceably and Colonel Loomis returned home with flying colors.

This "retort courteous" reminds of one that took place before our late war. Two officers of the regular army had had a disagreement. Although they were attached to the same company they never held any intercourse with each other except offically, in the strict line of duty. At last they separated mutually exasperated. After several years had elapsed the junior in rank happened to stop for the night at a post commanded by his old antagonist and called upon him in full uniform. The latter drew himself up and said haughtily, "To what sir am I indebted to the honor of this visit?" The other, stiff as a ramrod, replied: "*To Army Regulations, Paragraph 769 on page 265, which says that whenever a junior officer happens to be at a post commanded by a senior he must call upon him officially.*" As may be supposed the interview was rather embarrassing and did not last long.

A retort given by a lawyer in the case of a pretentious army officer who was a witness is worth recording. The former in the course of his argument said, "This soldier says so and so;" the latter interrupted him angrily and said "I am not a soldier sir; I am an officer." The lawyer continued without any change in his manner or expression, "*This officer who is no soldier says so and so.*" A reproof that seems to have been well deserved.

I believe that every man of experience will testify that fully two-thirds of the odd and witty speeches made during a campaign come from our Irish comrades. I can only give a few specimens at present.

In the Shenandoah Valley campaign an officer found that some of his men had managed to slip a demijohn of whiskey into one of the wagons in consequence of which they were becoming quite hilarious. He stopped the train, took the demijohn out and emptied it on the grass. An Irish soldier who was very much interested in this proceeding looked on ruefully at the sacrifice and said to a comrade, "*Dennis, if I'm kilt in the next battle bring me back and bury me here.*"

I once knew a Colonel who was highly distinguished in the Mexican War, and who was somewhat addicted to stimulants. As he was about starting out in an expedition against the Indians in Texas a young officer fresh from West Point came to him and said, "Colonel, I understand that we will be absent for several weeks. I have a small bundle of books I would like to put in one of the wagons if you do not object." The Colonel replied, "My young friend it would give me great pleasure to oblige you but we have hardly transportation for the food we are obliged to carry: every pound counts, so that I fear I cannot accommodate you." A moment afterwards another officer came up and said in a low tone; "Colonel, I have a barrel of excellent commissary whiskey; don't you think we could manage to take it along." "*Oh, certainly!*" replied the Colonel: "*any thing in reason! any thing in reason!*"[3]

This however is a digression for I was speaking of Irish wit.

A Naval officer told me that he overheard an Irish sailor say in reference to a very tyrannical officer who was thoroughly detested by the crew: "*Sure when the lieutenant dies there will be many a dry eye.*"

It seems to be a characteristic of the natives of the Emerald Isle to be always ready with a swift reply. At one of our army inspections an officer noticed a dark rim around a soldier's collar and said to him angrily

"Rafferty:"

"Sor:"

"How long do you wear a shirt?"

"*Two feet, three inches and quarter, your honor:*" was the unexpected answer.

I was told of another case which illustrates the same readiness. An officer of rank was dashing up Ninth Street in Washington in great haste to keep an appointment. Suddenly his carriage stopped. He put out his head to ascertain the cause, and was told that some laborers had just begun to tear up the street with a view to repair a sewer. The driver said, "There is only one line of stones in our way. Perhaps they will move them and let you pass." The officer called angrily to one of the Irish laborers and said, "Throw those stones to hell:" The man grinned and replied; "*Faith I'm afraid they'd be more in your honor's way there than they are here.*" But I fear this story has a suspicious flavor of Irish about it.

After our troops captured the City of Mexico they marched through the principal streets and occupied the main plaza. Not withstanding the capitulation and the surrender of the place by the constituted authorities, cowardly shots were frequently fired by Mexicans from the windows and roofs, and General Worth became highly incensed. He gave orders to break into and sack any of the houses that

"I'm standing for bait...."

violated the truce in this way. When quiet was partially restored an officer noticed an Irish soldier marching back and forth in the middle of the main street in front of the shop like a sentry, and asked him:

"Who put you on guard there?"

"I put meself, Sor"

"For what purpose?"

"I'm standing for bait."

"What do you mean by that?"

"The General says if they fire on us from any of the houses we can go in and sack them and *I'm standing for bait. Them's all jeweller's shops.*"

During a campaign by General Sumner[4] against the Navajo Indians, one of the enemy prowling around the camp in a dark night was shot by a sergeant of the guard. General Sumner was highly pleased. He complimented the sergeant highly which was all very well, but added that in the dangerous position in which the army found itself in the heart of the enemy's country, this was the only non-commissioned officer vigilant enough to be entrusted with the safety of the camp. Sumner accordingly kept him on guard for several nights in succession and the sergeant worn out with fatigue and lack of sleep said, *if the Lord spared him he would never kill another Indian as long as he lived.*

I have related this story chiefly for the moral it contains. Many generals during the late civil war, whenever a brigade distinguished itself by efficiency and gallantry, were in the habit of selecting that particular body of men to lead in every desperate enterprise and forlorn hope, until they were nearly all killed off or wounded. I heard one of the commanders of the Iron Brigade, which served under me in the Army of the Potomac complaining of this and I thought there was a great deal of truth in it.

This recalls to my recollection an anecdote of an Irish regiment which served under the Duke of Wellington on the Peninsula. The Duke had reprimanded them severely in orders for losing a position which they should have maintained. In the next battle, anxious to redeem their reputation, they went to the front and were sacrificed. As the Duke rode by after the action looking sorrowfully at the mutilated remains of the regiment, one of the soldiers who was desperately wounded raised himself up and shouted "*You ould hookey nosed villain! Does this satisfy you?*" The Duke sent his surgeon at once and made every effort to save the man's life, but did not succeed in doing so.

At the beginning of the late war when the North was sending troops to the field the governor of one of the Western States attempted to raise a regiment to be entirely composed of Irishmen. After filling nine companies, with great difficulty, all enlistments ceased. The men were kept in camp a long time waiting to complete their organization and at last became so riotous and unmanageable that the governor shipped them off to the seat of war. All this time they had not received *a cent* of pay. At last a paymaster was sent to give them their dues. But upon examining their papers he found he could not pay them as they had only nine companies instead of the ten which the law required; so he packed up his goods in the night and fled pursued by the curses and execrations of the men. The expression "*when I get me pay*" passed into a bye word in the regiment. Another paymaster who came met with the same difficulty and disappeared in the same way which intensified the excitement. Finally a company of Home Guards was attached to the regiment and as its organization was now complete a third paymaster was sent. On his arrival he asked to be directed to the Colonel's quarters and a large tent was pointed out to him. He found, however, when he reached it that he had not been correctly informed; that it was in reality a field tent. As he entered he saw a Catholic priest administering the last sacrament to a dying man. The priest said, "Patrick, are ye willing to lave this world with all its pomp and vanities to go to another and a betther world?" To the suprise of the paymaster, Patrick raised himself up and replied, "*Its a damned dirty world and I'm damned glad to get clear of it!*" The attendent said to him, "Don't say that Patrick! Sure you've had your own fun out of it." The priest turned to the man and said severely; "And when will you yourself be prepared to die?" To this the unexpected answer came, "*When I get me pay.*" A moment afterward the attendent sensible that this was not the proper time for jesting began howling, tearing his hair and going on in regular wake fashion.

The Germans are among the best and steadiest men in the regular army. They rarely indulge in attempts at wit, but their imperfect knowledge of our language frequently creates great mirth in others. At one time our recruiting officers enlisted numbers of them who had just landed as emigrants. Men were much wanted at the front and it was supposed that foreigners could soon acquire enough English for all practicable purposes. This proved a great trial for us junior officers who were obliged to instruct them. When I was stationed at Fort McHenry one of them was put as a sentinel over the magazine. After vain attempts to make him understand his duties generally I, at last confined myself to two points, which were, that he must salute all officers according to their rank and not allow any one to set fire to the magazine. When questioned subsequently with regard to his orders he said he was "*To shoot all officers according to rank and set fire to the magazine.*"

Recruits in those days were a source of endless trouble to us. They should have been retained at the large depots but as they were very much needed at the frontier posts and recruiting was not brisk, they were hurried off, frequently under a single officer, before they had acquired any knowledge of discipline. Their ignorance of rank and the great familiarity with which many of them addressed their commander was startling to West Point officers accustomed to the strict requirements of the service. We were much amused at the answer of one of these new comers named Martin at Fort Johnson, N.C. to the Inspector General Churchill who asked him if he was from Ticonderoga. The man replied, "Bless your heart, I live more than twenty miles from there." He always went afterwards by the name of "*Bless your heart, Martin.*"

A squad of these raw recruits had just arrived at a post commanded by Genl. G_____ in Texas. They were formed in line early in the morning for inspection in front of the general's tent, when an express came in with news of an Indian incursion. A company was at once ordered out in pursuit. The Captain formed his men immediately and reported for orders. He was asked if they had had their breakfast and replied that as the case was urgent he had not waited for that; to which the General who was occasionally jocular replied, "Well perhaps you may get a little *Indian meal* on your way. One of the recruits evidently appreciated this joke, for he called out, "Ha! ha! ha! Good for you General! Pretty good!" "*Sergeant take that man to the guard house,*" was the immediate reply; whereupon the recruit probably learned that it is not permitted to a private soldier to express approbation or disapprobation of his commanding officer's remarks.

As our volunteer soldiers are brought up in a republic where the doctrine of social equality prevails, it takes some time to inculcate the idea of Army rank among them, for they, in the words of Lowell:

"Would shake hands with a king upon his throne,
And think it kindness to his majesty."

When McDowell made his head quarters at the Arlington House, after the first battle of Bull Run, I had a desk in the room occupied by his staff, and was, by a special order of Genl. McClellan, assigned to the duty of arming the forts which environed the Capitol. An orderly from one of the new regiments was detailed to attend me. He had been a clerk in a store, and knew nothing whatever of the restraints or requirements of military life. A regular, when on duty of this kind, always keeps at a reasonable distance, stands attentively when spoken to, and salutes whenever he receives an order; but my new man lounged about in the most familiar way. On the third day he walked up to me, put one foot on the round of the chair, leaned over and said in a low tone, "Major, I'm tired of this orderly business. What I'm after now is a posish [position], see! a posish! That's what I want." I tried to instruct him in his duties without unnecessary severity and without hurting his feelings, but it had no effect. Next morning a British nobleman, or at all events a man who claimed to be one, and who was acting as Adjutant General, came to me in a state of great perturbation. It must be premised that he was very hard of hearing, which soon caused him to be discharged from the staff position he held. He had a desk near mine in the large room at Arlington House. When I entered at the usual hour he walked up to make a complaint and said:

"Upon ma word I'm indebted to your orderly for a vary delicate piece of attention."

"What is that Sir John?" was my answer.

"He came up to me this morning, gave me a poke in the ribs, point-ed across the room to a newcomer, a commissary whose hearing is defective, and fairly shouted in my ear, '*We've got another deaf man here now, Sir John!*' I was brought up in the British army, sir, and I'm not used to such proceedings." I sent the orderly back to the regiment and took another man in his place who proved to be more serviceable.

There were a good many stories at West Point in my day of the naivete of new cadets before they become accustomed to discipline. One of these who had just arrived received notice that the comman-dant desired to see him immediately. He replied, "Bother the com-mandant! I've just come from a long journey and I'm tired. I'm not going to run after anybody. If he wants to see me, let him come over here!" The surprise of the orderly at being charged with such a mes-sage was comical to witness. If one of the older cadets had replied to an order in that way he would have been locked up in the light or dark prison, but the inexperienced youth, received no worse punishment than a reprimand.

Doubtless our late enemies have many stories of this kind to tell in relation to their own experiences in the war and some one should col-lect them and put them in print. I heard one a short time ago from a Confederate lady in relation to General Magruder. When Sherman's operations and the action of our fleet had isolated Texas from the rest of the Confederacy Magruder was in command there and as he could receive no orders from his superiors he had full sway. One day he entered a restaurant in San Antonio dressed in citizen's clothes. A Confederate soldier who had been drinking came in soon after and seated himself without ceremony at the same table with the general. Magruder drew himself up angrily and said, "Do you know who I am sir?" "No," replied the soldier. "I dont care a continental who you are. When I first entered the army I was very particular about my associ-ates, but now I have become perfectly reckless. *You can keep your seat.*" Magruder enjoyed the joke and did not have the man punished.

This clemency was something like that of the French general Pelissier. In a fit of anger he had struck a soldier whereupon the man drew up his musket aimed at the general and pulled the trigger. The gun did not explode however and the general when the man was seized and confined wrote out charges against him for not *keeping his gun in proper firing order.*

This want of reverence for rank reminds me of an incident which occurred in the war with Mexico. In order to make a diversion in favor of our small force at Buena Vista, a body of the hardy backwoodsmen of Missouri were organized for service against the more Northern states of Mexico. These men were sent out under Colonel Doniphan and made a fine record for themselves gaining a complete victory over greatly superior forces at Sacramento. It was said that in this command there was little or no practice of discipline, and that every thing was decided by a kind of town meeting arrangement. One thing must be said in their favor however; they always voted to fight without regard to the number of their enemies. When their short enlistment was over fourteen of them came home by way of Saltillo, to see our army which was located near the town under command of General Wool. Now the general having taken such a prominent part in the battle of Buena Vista was credited with presidential aspirations. He was always a strict disciplinarian and exacted great deference for his rank and position. As these men from Doniphan's command were on their way home to Missouri he intended to be very gracious towards them in order that they might carry back favorable reports of himself and the part he had taken in the war. Unfortunately they had formed an unfavorable opinion as regards the latter point, blaming him severely for having lost two of his guns at Buena Vista. They gave us no credit for having whipped the best appointed army in Mexico 23,000 strong with our 5,500 men. Most of them declined to respond to the General's invitation to call at his head quarters but finally two more curious than the rest thought they would go and see what the old fellow wanted. The General received them in some state surrounded by his staff and complimented them on their achievements at Sacramento; but their manner was anything by cordial and they answered in a contemptuous way. *"Yes, we did not lose any of our guns."* This was rather a stunner for the general but he rallied and said "That's right men! stand up for your own victory." To this they replied, to the great astonishment and amusement of the spectators: "*General you dont know nothing about fighting Mexicans: you must crowd 'em general: crowd 'em; that's the way.*" They then turned on their heel and walked out of the tent. I was not present myself but this was the scene as described to me at the time it occurred.

The negro is not usually credited with wit although he too frequently amuses others by his misconceptions and want of general knowledge. In my experience I can only recall two instances of attempts at humor on the part of our colored bretheren.

In the advance against Monterey in Mexico we halted three miles from the city while the Engineer Officers supported by the Cavalry made a reconnaissance of the forts and other defenses of the town. When the fighting commenced one of the negro servants left the camp and went as far to the front as he dared, to see what was going on. On his way back he met several of his colored companions who were also going to the front on a similar errand. He said to them, "You go right ahead, and down dar at de turn of de road you will find six colored gentlemen waiting for you."

"What do you mean nigger?" was the reply.

"Never mind what I mean! You go right ahead, dey waiten for you."

So they kept on until they came upon *six turkey buzzards sitting in a row on a fence.*

At a 4th of July celebration at Fort McKavett, where I was in command, the negro troops had a grand dinner, and a colored orator was appointed for the occasion. One passage in his speech incited great hilarity. He said, "When all dese brave colored men went out to strike for freedom and de constitution, what did I do? *I struck for home!*" A remark that was highly appreciated.

A negro came into camp during the latter part of the war to apply for rations for his destitute family. He was told that he could have them, provided he took the oath of allegience.

"What am de oath of legia?" he inquired.

"You have to swear to support the constitution of the United States."

"Lord bless you Massa! Its more than I can do to support de ole woman and de chillun."

Another one complained to an officer that he had been told, *"dere was provision for de colored people in de constitution,"* and *"he hadn't had de first mouthful."*

I never heard of any attempt at wit on the part of an Indian but like the negro they make some very peculiar speeches at times.

An Indian in Arizona whose corn field had been trampled down by the troops said to General Cook: "Planting is good! Plant corn: soldier man come along with horse and eat 'em up! *Plant corn and son of a bitch locust eat 'em up."* The officers present laughed heartily, but the Indian preserved an impassive countenance and seemed surprised at the merriment he had occasioned.

There was an outbreak of the Seminoles in Florida just before our civil war began. I was in command of a post there and several companies of Florida volunteers were directed to report to me to commence hostilities with a view to capture and force the tribe to go on a reservation in Arkansas. One of the captains who was scouting on this expedition came upon an Indian trail which proved to be that of a warrior and his family. He surrounded them with his company at dawn of day and as he approached, the Indian held up his right hand as a token of surrender. The squaw held up her hand and the little children held up their hands. When he was near enough the Indian said to him, "How do you do?"

"Thank you," was the reply. "My health is very good at present. I trust you feel well enough to go to Arkansas." "Arkansas cold too much!" was the poor Indian's protest.

Another Indian incident has a touch of humor in it. About 1854 there was an uprising of the Sioux threatened in Dakota and a battalion of infantry and a light battery was hastily sent to the point where the savages were concentrating. The infantry officer ranked the artillery officer by brevet and was entitled to the command but he had been exhausted by the forced march had taken a drop too much [and] when they reached their destination and formed line opposite the hostile force he was not in a condition to give orders. The Sioux had on their war paint and were greatly excited. Some of their warriors were trotting back and forth in front of the line with ox-horns full of water with a view to make a dash upon the cannon and put out the port-fires which were used in those days to fire the guns. At this crisis when every thing betokened a bloody encounter a gallant young officer whose name if I remember rightly was [Hugh] Fleming,[5] did a very bold thing. He undid his sword and belt, threw them down with his pistols on the grass and walked over to the Sioux and offered his hand to the head chief. This softened them and they agreed to hold a parley half way between the lines and state their grievances. A conference took place which proved satisfactory but the Sioux chief who had been scanning the shoulder straps of the artillery officer and those of the infantry officer, who was sitting on the grass, asked the interpreter which of the two men ranked. The interpreter was obliged to confess that the artillery officer with whom the warrior had been making terms was only the second in command. The Indian drew himself up haughtily and said that he was the head chief of the Sioux and did not wish to deal with any sub-chief of the whites. The interpreter accordingly roused the infantry commander and said, "Major, he say he want to talk with you." "Talk with me," was the reply, "Tell him Bill d___n him!"

"Guess I better not tell 'em dat, Major."

"Yes, Bill tell 'em damn 'em! and Bill tell em the President who lives in Washington has more soldiers than the leaves on the trees and if they dont behave themselves he will whip them out in short order."

When all this was interpreted the Sioux drew himself up with dignity and simply replied: "*Great white war chief, whiskey too much!*" and peace was maintained.

There have been in times past a number of wits and humorists in the army, some of whom gained considerable celebrity in their day. I remember one of these named Forbes Britton[6] whose sayings and doings were a good deal quoted. He enhanced his jokes exceedingly by his perfect command of countenance and by the gravity of his demeanor. In the beginning of hostilities against the Seminoles in Florida a large force was concentrated on the eastern coast at Fort Jupiter and Britton reported for duty there. Soon after, the chief quartermaster, Captain Dusenberry, sent for him and told him that he knew he had but little experience in the service but owing to the scarcity of officers who were either absent or in the field he would be obliged to have him assigned as Post Quartermaster to take charge of several hundred wagons, ambulances, horses and mules, which had accumulated at the post. Britton listened to a long lecture upon the great responsibility that had devolved upon him, and the necessity of his devoting himself heart and soul to the duties of his new postion. He heard all this with his arms drooping, face flushed and with every indication that he was overpowered by the honor. At last there was a pause and Britton said, "Capt. Dusenberry are you entirely through?" Dusenberry replied that nothing more ocurred to him at that time. The young man answered, "*If you are entirely through Captain Dusenberry, I would like to hear you sing a couple of stanzas from the Star Spangled Banner.*" The Captain was very wroth and said afterwards, "I would have arrested the fellow and had him tried for disrespect; but the charges would have made me the laughing stock of the army and I gave up the idea."

Britton could be humorous in action as well as in words. When General Wool was in command of the Division of the Atlantic he went down to Key West to make an inspection of the post. After the military ceremonies were over, Lieutenant Britton accompanied the general on his way to the wharf [when] he was about leaving. He was most respectful and deferential in his deportment but the general noticed that whenever they passed a group of soldiers they were saluted with a roar of laughter. He inquired somewhat angrily the meaning of this ill-timed mirth. Britton answered that it was some nonsense of their own and turned towards them and made a gesture of reproof which added immensely to the hilarity. The fact was at all time he was conversing so earnestly with the general he assumed a hitch in his gait which was irresistably ludicrous.

By far, however, the most celebrated wit we ever had in the army was Lieutenant [George] Derby[7] one of the Engineer Corps. He wrote a book of jokes under the pseudonym of "John Phoenix" which was published a long time ago. It had an extensive circulation but is now out of print. Derby had been sent to California to improve the navigation of the San Diego River or as he said to dam the stream and he claimed to have done so mentally, in a very effectual way. About that time owing to the gold excitement prices rose enormously high and an officers salary became wholly inadequate for his support. There was great complaint and after a time Congress passed a bill to increase the pay of the army on the Pacific Coast. A claim agent who resided in Washington took advantage of this and sent a circular to all the officers interested. He asserted that the bill was passed wholly in consequence of his personal exertions and suggested that every officer affected by it should give him a gratuity of five per cent on the first months pay drawn by them under the new law. Derby's reply to this was republished in all the principal papers in the United States and occasioned great amusement. It began, as I remember it, by saying, "My dear Charles. I have received your modest request asking for five per cent of the first months increased pay which Congress has been kind enough to grant us and after deliberating on the matter for five seconds I have come to the conclusion to decline; for the following reasons: In the first place I do not know you Charles. You may, for aught I know, be some swindling fellow who seeing that the bill was about to pass thought you would levy a little innocent black mail on the officers. To be sure I see by your card which my wife has stuck up in the cracked looking-glass over our mantel-piece, that you are a general agent and a notary public. I take off my hat to that for I have a great respect for rank. I see too that you live opposite Odd Fellow's Hall. Why dont you move across the street?" The missive was humorous throughout and ended by saying, "Farewell Charles. Be virtuous and you will be happy."

It is said that the agent took two members of Congress with him to whom he had loaned money, rushed up to see the President and requested that Lieut Derby be dismissed the service. Mr. Buchannan simply lay back and laughed immodestly.

In the early days of San Francisco, Derby happened to be in a box at the theatre with some friends. He leaned over and said to a man in the parquette, "Won't you poke that man over there, two seats in front of you, with your cane. The man did so, and Derby turned away ignored the whole transaction and left the two men to settle it the best way they could. They came very near having a fight in the theatre. At last the individual who had been spoken to succeeded in attracting Derby's attention and said:

"I say you Mister! Didn't you tell me to poke that man with my cane?"

"Yes."

"What did you mean by it?"

"I wanted to see if you would be fool enough to do it."

This was very funny, but it is said that the aggrieved party waited for Derby outside and he had considerable difficulty to avoid a street encounter.

Derby said in one of his articles that disappointment had been his lot in life from his earliest years. When a mere child he went to the theatre to see the celebrated actress Miss Smith. She was advertised to appear in *two pieces*, but came out on the stage *"a whole and entire woman."*

While Derby was at San Diego the editor of the local paper there who had been a zealous advocate of the party that controlled the state administration, went to the capitol to get his reward in the shape of an office. Derby kindly volunteered to edit the paper in his absence. The editor thankfully consented to the arrangement, but upon his arrival at Sacramento was horror struck to find that Derby had changed the politics of the paper and was hurrahing for the opposite side. The next edition changed the politics again to a third party and in fact every time the paper came out it contradicted all the opinions and statements of the preceeding issue so the editor returned in all haste to regulate matters.

There was another man in the old army, Lieut. D____ [8] who was not looked upon as a humorist but whose eccentricities gave him a great deal of notoriety. He was a brave and capable officer but unfortunately he was too much addicted to censure his superiors. One day he accused the Commander of the Army, General Scott of cheating the Secretary of War in the sale of a pair of carriage horses. Two captains of the Fourth Artillery overheard him and preferred charges against him for defaming the General-in-Chief. Pending the trial he was confined in close arrest to his quarters which were in a casemate adjoining one that was used for the officers mess. The two accusers were obliged to pass D.'s casemate three times a day on their way to their meals. He was an accomplished musician and the moment they appeared in sight he seized his violin and played the Rogues March until they had passed by. They complained to old General Walbach who was in command but he nearly killed himself with laughing and gave them no redress.

The pretentious sayings of ignorant people are often very ludicrous. Professor Mahan, who had charge of the department of Engineering at West Point for so many years told me that on one occasion he went down to the army when it was in front of Petersburg to visit some of his former pupils. It was soon reported among the troops that the learned professor who had taught all our great generals the art of war was in camp, and a good deal of attention was paid him. A volunteer captain who had called to pay his respects said to him, "You have no idea sir what incompetent men the governor of my state is sending us. They have not the first idea of military science. Why sir he sent me a lieutenant the other day who is a perfect dunce. I ordered him to draw up the company in a horizontal line, and what do you suppose he did? He actually drew them up in a *vertical line*. The professor thought any man who could draw troops up in a vertical line must be a prodigy.

I heard a story in reference to the first battle of Bull Run which is credited to General Slocum.[9] It was said he saw a raw volunteer hiding in a ditch. The general directed him to get out of there and join his regiment at the front, to which he replied, "*Oh, yes! I know what you want. You want this place for yourself!*"

The officers of the old Army were generally very courteous and the occasion would have to be indeed an extraordinary one to induce them to break out in violent and abusive language. I knew the Confederate General Lee when he was a Captain of Engineers and must say in his favor that he was very considerate and careful in his intercourse with his inferiors. He never seemed to convey reproof [except] in the driest manner, but it had the same effect. When he was superintendent at West Point he thought one of his staff had not been sufficiently attentive to his duties. The latter asked for permission to go down to New York for the day. The General, who was then Major Lee, replied, "I have no objection but I would like to have you attend to one or two little matters before you go. He then gave him work enough to last a week.

He said to another officer who had been careless about fortifying his line on the heights of Fredricksburg, "I see you are riding a very spirited horse. Why not take some of the fire out of him by riding him over these hills where your men are laying out the earth works?" The officer colored. He felt the reproof as much as if it had been couched in stronger language.

General Worth too, of Mexican fame, acted in very much the same way. He inspected the post at Key West and found every thing in a very dirty condition. As he bade the officer in command good bye in the midst of a crowd of citizens he complimented him on the matchless cleanliness of the quarters and men. The officer understood the implied censure but the citizens did not.

General Twiggs, however, had the reputation of being the greatest master of the art of sarcasm in the old army. As he resigned at the beginning of the war to join the Confederacy, who by the way, seemed to have no use for him, his name is only known to most of our soldiers by his disgraceful order, while still on in our service, for all the troops under his command in Texas to at once surrender to the enemy. When he was stationed in New Orleans before the war an officer who had just graduated at West Point reported to him for duty and was assigned to a company in Texas. About a fortnight afterwards the general met the young man on the street and found he had not obeyed his order. The following dialogue ensued:

"Good morning Mr. S ___: Do you know that I was under the impression that I had ordered you to Texas?"

"So you did, so you did General; but I went down and took a look at those boats which run to Galveston and I did not think either of them was sea worthy."

Most officers would have met so serious an offense with the usual severe penalty but Twiggs resorted to another mode of punishment. He rushed up to the delinquent, shook his hand heartily and said,

"*Thats right Mr.___S! Dont you risk your life for the United States. I wouldn't do it if I was in your place. You needn't go to Texas. You shall stay here sir and I will watch over your safety. Mr. Adjutant take charge of this young man. See that he does not run in to any kind of danger. I shall hold you strictly responsible if anything happens to him.*"

The general walked off and S., who very soon found himself the laughing stock and butt of the garrison repented when it was too late that he had not obeyed orders.

When making a tour of inspection among the regiments in Texas where the troops were stationed to repel Indian incursions Twiggs came to one post commanded by a captain. He had a very strong prejudice against this officer regarding him as very inefficient and generally worthless. As this captain did not make his appearance on parade, the general inquired where he was and was told that he had been wounded by an Indian arrow. This the general promptly denied. His informant said:

"General I assure you it is a fact. Captain S_____[10] was wounded by the *Indians.*"

"Oh no! You are entirely mistaken. You cannot make me believe that."

"But general you can see for yourself. If you go to the hospital you will find him there now under treatment."

"Do you tell me seriously," said the general, "that he was wounded by *Indians?*"

"Yes general."

"*Why should they wound him? He has never done them any harm.*"

We had a young officer of Ordnance with us at the time named Kingsbury who was remarkable in the great abundance of caustic expressions and metaphors with which his mind was stored. Kingsbury volunteered to sit as lawyer and defend Ransom and the latter at once gratefully accepted the offer. Kingsbury could abuse Twiggs to his hearts content inasmuch as he was on the staff of Genl Taylor the

Commander in Chief and was not therefore subject to Twiggs orders. Besides he could be held legally responsible for what he read to the court as the defense of Ransom since whoever wrote it, the accused had adopted it as his own. The Court should at once have objected to every portion of it which abused Genl. Twiggs for as the latter was not on trial it was contrary to justice and precedent to paint him out as an unscrupulous libertine for even if it were true it would not excuse Ransom's fault and in truth had not direct bearing upon the case. But the court did not object and consequently this remarkable defense appeared, upon its record show of some of the worst passages.

I give the following extracts to show the extraordinary character of the document depriving it of certain objectionable paragraphs.

"But gentlemen to show you how amusingly preposterous the facts set forth in these specifications are considered throughout the Dragoon Camp from its Commanding officer downwards—to show you that in the eyes of that immaculate individual the magnitude of the crime is made to consist solely on the smallness of the offense let us turn to the evidence upon your records....

Comment upon such facts is unnecessary. They exhibit the poisoned venom, the atrocious perfidy, the unmatched wickedness which has conspired in this Prosecution as plainly as if written by a sunbeam.

Capt. H. reiterated the tale in all its deformity and the President of the Court interfered to prevent further testimony to the facts and to save its records from still further pollution. Well might be!—for not the harlotry of Babylon, not the licentiousness of a Borgia, not the revelries of a Charles the Second could equal this exhibition in the length and breadth of its depravity. Yet with these examples staring him in the face surrounding him in the hours of duty and of relaxation, visable to him at mid day and palpable to him in the hours of darkness, the immaculate purity of the commanding officer is outraged by a solitary impropriety upon which he invokes the vigor and the vengeance of the laws.

I would fain hope gentlemen that this trial might have a beneficial effect present and prospective upon the regiment and its living impersonations. And if in divesting himself of the decency that would avoid: disreputable action he had retained the delicacy that would be ashamed of it; or if the blush of reproach could pierce the enamel of hoary profligacy and veteran vice which nearly three score years of demoralization have fastened upon the furrowed visage of the commanding officer, perhaps a dim conscienceness of guilt would glance aftward his countenance at the present exposure of his character and give him one moment of exquisite remorse. He might then retire from a service he never adorned and abandon a profession to which he is no ornament. But in his bosom I fear there is no throb of pity, no pulsation of regret, no sensibility to reproach and no possible consciousness of shame. I have with you gentlemen to denounce the author and executor of the conduct which had been presented to you as he deserves. I leave no doubt that if you have in your vocabulary any single epithet, any little syllabic formation that will express with comprehensive brevity the concentrated hatred and infuriate malignity of a thousand devils linked to the human form and a fiend's propensities you will give the benefit of its application to the Grand Moloch, the sovereign Prince the recognized governor of this modern pandemonium."

It is almost needless to say that this defense dismissed Ransom.

Some time after this Kingsbury got into a quarrel with the commanding officer at Detroit on a question of quarters. The aforesaid Commanding officer was a veteran of the War of 1812. His name was Capt. Anthony Drane[11] and his reputation for bravery was far better than for sobriety. Kingsbury now resorted to quite an unjustifiable measure. He hired two soldiers to follow Drane about to collect evidence in regard to his drunkeness. He then preferred charges which resulted in the trial of Drane and his dismissal from the service for intoxication while on duty. On account of Dranes past services the President commuted the sentence to suspension for two years. So far Kingsbury was successful but the Secretary of War having ascertained from the record that K____ had obtained the evidence by placing enlisted men as spies over the Commanding officer ordered K____ to be tried by another Court.

When it came to the time for Kingsbury to make his written defense against the charges, Drane came into court in great glee to hear it. The following is that portion of the defense referred to which specially relates to Drane.

"It is on record and the record will outlast his epitaph, that for three months he was almost daily drunk in the presence of officers and men and unable to perform the duties that might have devolved upon him. Yet this man thus steeped in dissipation to the very lips; this man whose habits have made his name a reproach to the service, and a by-word to the community: upon whose head were the accumulated offences of years, and whose manifold derelictions have drawn upon him by a trial of his peers the highest penalty that the laws award; this man who bears upon his forehead the brand of his iniquity; who for years has been warring upon even loftier principles, who had been degrading the noblest energies of the mind and paralyzing the cardinal virtues of the heart: this man who had recently been the great Corypheus of vice and intemperance comes into this court in a paroxysm of propriety from the retirement to which he was sent by the justice of his judges and the mercy of the President as my accuser of a want of honor to the service and as a self chosen champion of morality and virtue. If the blush of shame could mantle a cheek crimsoned with alcoholic fires; if of dignity of mind or elevation of character were not wholly extinct; if the still small voice of conscious rectitude could longer operate upon one vibrating between the delirium of drunkenness and total intellectual darkness. Capt. Anthony Drane would never have appeared before this Court, but would have obeyed the admonishment of that conscience which must have been long thundering in his ears as to the Arch Fiend of old"

> "Back to thy punishment false fugitive
> And to thy speed, add wings"

If I remember correctly it was Kingsbury that gave Twiggs another hit in reference to the battle of Monterey. K. wrote a description of the action for the newspapers in which he said something to this effect, "Just as the troops were going into action the country was deprived of the services of Genl Twiggs who became suddenly indisposed and remained in his tent at Walnut Springs." When he came to the termination of the battle he said something to this effect, "Just as the battle terminated and the troops were rushing in to secure the place the country suddenly regained the services of Genl Twiggs who came upon the scene in excellent health."

It is certain that Twiggs kept out of the battle on the plea of illness and did not appear until the fighting was almost entirely ended. I heard that the only order he gave during the contest was to kill a poor devil of a Mexican prisoner who was trying to slip away from his guard.

Genl. Twiggs who so treacherously surrendered all the U. S. forces in Texas to the enemy at the beginning of the war, was very fond of devilling his officers particularly when they contested his military decisions. On one occasion a surgeon in Florida Dr. M. raised the point that his rank entitled him to go to head quarters where there were four companies instead of being stationed at a two company post. Twiggs acquiesced and the doctor was ordered to head quarters. When he arrived the General was very polite to him and offered to fit up a pleasant little cottage in the most comfortable manner for his accomodation, and this was not all for the interest of the commanding officer in regard to the doctors comfort was so great that he went every day to superintend the improvements that were going on and to suggest others. At last he said doctor your house is about ready but if you will allow me I would recommend a coat of white paint on the fence, and then it will be all in order for you to move in. The doctor gladly agreed to this and as as soon as the painting was done he prepared to occupy the place but alas he received an order the same day to move to another post a hundred miles off in the wilderness where there were no quarters whatever. He rushed to the General to complain but Twiggs said to him "Doctor you know you raised the point that you were entitled to be sent to a *four* company post, and as *two* companies have been sent away from here since your arrival, this is merely a two company post now. So you will have to go." And the doctor went.

Twiggs had another remarkable interview with a green lieutenant who had just arrived and reported for duty in San Antonio which was Twiggs head quarters at the time. Lieut. B. was ordered to one of the upper posts and upon applying to the Post Quartermaster for transportation received a spring wagon for his own conveyance and an ordinary road wagon for his baggage. Now on some occasions officers who had families and were changing stations had been allowed two wagons for their household furniture but of course this was a favor and not a right that could be claimed. Some one persuaded B. that to give him only one wagon was an outrage as it was making an invidious distinction in favor of other officers. He accordingly went to Genl Twiggs to make his complaint. Twiggs listened to him with great apparent interest and much sympathy, and said "Now stop one minute. Do I understand you correctly that this wretched quartemaster's department will only allow you one wagon to transport your baggage?" "I assure you general that it is the truth." "Why Mr. Black it is perfectly incredible. What is the service coming to? "Let me see, you have a trunk, of course?" "Well general I have a small ____." "Of course you have a trunk, every officer has a trunk. How much do you think your trunk weighs, I suppose about 300 lb."

"I dont know exactly general?"

"Then you have a mess chest?"

"I have a box with some cooking utensils." "Of course you have a mess chest. Every officer has one. How much do you suppose it weighs, shall we say 300 lbs?"

"Really General I dont know."

"Then you have a box of provisions," and Twiggs went on figuring until he had made up a load for him of about 2000 lbs. He then broke out in great apparent fury cursing the quartermaster's department and saying why here now is a second lieutenant going on to join his post with only 2000 lbs of baggage and these miserable wretches refuse to allow him but one wagon. (Black under extreme circumstances was only allowed 800 lbs by the army regulations.) I'll see to it Mr. Black I have got to make an example of some of these quartermasters and I might as well commence now. Leave it to me Mr. Black, I'll see that you get your rights." And Black went over with a great sense of his importance amid the suppressed laughter of the staff officers who knew that the general's remarks were to be taken in an inverse sense. The final result was that Black lost the road wagon and was obliged to content himself with the spring wagon alone.

About the year 1851 a grand celebration took place in New York in honor of some great public event which I have forgotten.[12] The U. S. Army and Navy were requested to participate in the ceremonies and prominent places were assigned to Genl. Scott our Commander in Chief, and to Gov. Fish. At that time I was a First Lieutenant in the 1st Regiment of Artillery and was stationed at Governor's Island in New York Harbor in company with Captain Wm. H. French,[13] Lieut. James B. Ricketts and others, most of whom were afterwards distinguished as Generals during the war. When the invitation came over for the Army officers to join in the procession no one desired to accept it, for we had attended two or three of these celebrations before, and had found them anything but pleasant. In the first place we were completely overshadowed by the militia who were riding about in their cocked hats covered with gold lace and wearing georgeous uniforms while we were dressed very plainly and not being field officers were expected to march on foot through the mud for two or three hours. It might have been some compensation if we had been sure of attracting the attention of the bright eyes of the ladies who were looking at the spectacle from the windows of the palatial residences up town but we were few in numbers and utterly lost in the crowd while the law of contrast made us appear quite insignificant, in comparison with those around us so we decided not to go. But our Colonel said this was an occasion in which it would scarcely be decorous or decent for Army officers to absent themselves and that some of us must be present. As his will was decidedly stronger than ours and he had many modes of enforcing it we gave up all resistance and prepared to sacrifice ourselves on the altar of public duty. We accordingly presented ourselves in due time at the City Hall and upon making ourselves known were conducted to what was called in those days *"the tea room"* and were directed to wait there until our turn came to fall in line. There were three of us, French, Ricketts, and myself, the others having managed to get off under the plea of sickness, duty as Officer of the Day, etc. The tea room was an institution voted by the City Aldermen for the purpose of refreshing themselves with food and drink. It was generally stocked with all the delicacies of the season, but on the present occasion, if my memory serves me, there was nothing but some remnants of ham and corned beef on the table, and the only liquid allowed was water. We found Commodore Eagle[14] and several other officers of the Navy already there and were greeted very cordially. After the lapse of about half an hour a very pompous individual entered the room and announced in a stentorian voice, "The officers of the U.S. Navy will now fall in the procession." A moment afterwards he came again and called out, "The officers of the U.S. Army will now join in the procession" and we followed the Naval officers who were all disappearing into comfortable carriages provided for their transit through the city. We noticed an extra carriage which they had not occupied and it did not take us very long to come to the conclusion that it would be a good thing to join the Navy, so we appropriated the vehicle at once. One corner of it however was occupied by a little tailor from the Bowery. He informed us that the carriage came from a livery stable near his shop, that he knew it was hired by the city authorities and that he thought it would be no harm for him to jump in and ride as far as the City Hall, as he had never been in a carriage in his life and wanted to see how it would seem but now he would get out at once and go home. His language showed him to be a well meaning but very simple and ignorant man. French insisted upon him keeping his seat and by way of amusement began to ply him with political questions, asking his opinions with great ceremony in reference to men and things with which he was wholly unacquainted. This puzzled the man exceedingly, and his mal apropos replies and attempt to assume a knowledge he did not possess caused much diversion. In this way we whiled away the time for an hour and a half until our part of the procession halted opposite Bleecker Street to give time to the troops who were in the rear to form in double line on each side of the street, for the purpose of saluting the dignitaries as they passed by on their way to the City Hall, to hear the oration. This long delay became at last very irksome. Immediately in front of us there was an open barouche drawn by six horses and escorted by a squadron of cavalry marching four deep on each side of the carriage in honor of the two Major Generals of Militia who were seated there in all the splendor of their military trappings.

One of these generals (Hall) being near his own residence in Bleecker Street concluded to get out and go home. This left the other general (Storms) all alone in his glory. A moment afterwards an aide approached us, and in a short curt manner informed us that the general directs that one of you regulars shall come and ride with him. This message was not very agreeable to us, for in the first place as we had not reported to Genl. Storms we did not consider ourselves in a position to receive orders from him and in the next place we did not like the words or the way it was delivered. In the regular Army it would have been worded in this way: Genl. So and So sends his compliments and requests that you will come and ride with him. We accordingly politely declined. We did not think it very appropriate either for officers of so little rank to be going through Broadway escorted in this way. A moment afterwards the aide returned and said, "The General thinks you could not have understood him. He wants one of you to come and ride with him. French now turned to the little tailor and told him that circumstances would prevent either of us from gratifying the general but that the case was different in regard to him, and he ought to go at once. He stared and said, "Do you really think so, sir." "I do" said French emphatically, "Courtesy demands it." "Well," he said "if you really think I ought to go, I suppose I must." He accordingly, to our infinite amusement, opened the door, but missed the step and came sprawling to the ground. He picked himself up and walked towards the general taking short quick steps and jerking his elbows in a ridiculous way that showed at once he never could have had any military training. General S. looked at him with an expression of doubt and astonishment. In a moment afterwards he had opened the carriage door and had clambered up by the side of the General. We could see the latter lean over and put some questions to him. The answers were evidently not at all satisfactory, for we saw the General in great wrath get out of the carriage slam the door after him and motion the cavalry to open their files to make way for him to pass up Bleecker Street. The little fellow found himself all alone and very much frightened. Before he could determine what to do the word was given, the whole cortege moved on, and as those in advance had gained a considerable interval the horses broke into a brisk trot to catch up. He now ran about like a rat in a cage and made an effort to climb out behind but was afraid of being run over and gave it up. To get out on either side would bring him among the cavalry horses which were very close to the carriage and beyond them was a double line of infantry. He finally gave it up and leaned back in his seat with his face as red as fire, for his prominent position made him the center of all eyes. It was not long before some office holder in the crowd observing the man and his escort took it into his head that the stranger must be Governor Fish.[15] He threw up his hat and gave three cheers for Governor Fish and the crowd responded handsomely. Word was immediately passed down the line that the Governor was coming and they must get ready to salute him. All the troops at once were called to an "attention" and directed to bring their arms to the shoulder in readiness. Imagine our amusement when we saw every regiment present arms. The drums were beaten, the trumpets blown, the flags lowered, and the officers saluted with their swords as the great man passed by. Far from appreciating the honors that were heaped upon him he seemed in a very unhappy frame of mind and cast furtive glances to the right and left in hopes he might find some avenue of escape but there was none. All things must have an end, and at last we reached City Hall. The Common-Council were drawn up on the steps covered with badges and in readiness to receive the distinguished guests of the day. When they saw the little fellow approach they went in a body to meet him, supposing he must be a Cabinet officer at least, as he came in such state, but before they could open the door he made a dive and came down on all fours. Very much astonished at this, they were about to help him up, when he crawled away with the crowd, rose up and dashed off at full speed evidently under the impression that his case would be turned over to the police for adjudication, if he waited any longer.

When we returned that night to the fort our comrades asked us if we had enjoyed the procession and we assured them we had been fully repaid for our patriotism in attending the celebration.

Practical jokes, I suppose, may come under the definition of humor. There is very little of that kind of amusement in the army for officers,

"Sure it's vegetable soup, sir…"

as a rule, do not like to be trifled with. I remember an incident of this kind told by a very intelligent gentleman named Downey,[16] who was formerly Mayor of Brownsville, Texas, but who been in the Dragoons under Lieutenant (afterwards our Major General) Kearney. The latter, in early days, commanded a company at the Cavalry School in Carlisle, Pa. under Captain (afterwards Major General) Sumner, who as we all know was a very strict disciplinarian. One day in passing along the line he turned to Downey and said, "I detail you for the cook room." Downey was dissatisfied and went to complain to Lieut Kearney. He said "Lieutenant, the commanding officer has detailed me for duty as cook. I know nothing about cooking and I will be very much obliged to you if you can get me relieved. I much prefer stand-ing guard and other company duties. There are any number of men who will be very glad to take my place in the cook-room." Kearney replied, "The difficulty is that Sumner detailed you himself and he will not let you off without some very good reason. However I think I know a way to manage it. He visits the kitchen every day at twelve o'clock. Put a little pot black on your face and hands and I think when he sees it he will order you out." Downey followed the advice and when Sumner came around and saw him he threatened him with terrific penalties if he ever caught him in that condition again. Downey reported the result of his experiment to Kearney who said "So that did not work! We will have to try something else. Get a watermelon. They are very plentiful around here now. Chop one up into pieces about an inch square. When Sumner comes around he will ask you what are you doing that for. You can tell him it is to put in the soup, and then I feel sure he will send you away."

Downey made his preparations accordingly to carry out this pro-gram. When Sumner saw him he roared out "What are you doing there?"

"I'm cutting up this watermelon sir."

"I see you are but what is it for?"

"It is to put in the soup sir."

"Where are you from?"

"I am from ould Ireland sir."

"Dont you know better than to cut up a watermelon to put in the soup?"

"Sure it's vegetable soup sir."

"Get out of this cook-room you infernal idiot!"

And Downey left triumphant.

Towards the close of the war when he had become a man of mark he called on Sumner at his residence in Syracuse and referred to his having served under him at Carlisle Barracks. Sumner said, "I remember you perfectly. I never have a watermelon on any table without thinking of you. You seem to be an intelligent man. Didn't you know better than to cut up that melon to put in the soup?" "To tell you the truth General," was the reply, "Kearney set me up to it."

Another case of practical joking will conclude this branch of the subject.

After the close of the war the late Col. George W. Wallace[17] was stationed in Washington. He himself appreciated a joke very quickly and could therefore easily forgive the same tendency in others even when it [was] made against himself. A grand military parade took place at the capital on the occasion of some great civic ceremony. In an account of the proceedings in the next days paper, the report stated that the troops were under Col. George W. Wallace commander of the 12th Infantry and garrison of Washington. The latter paragraph, however, did not appear as it was written. It came out in print "The troops were under Colonel George W. Wallace, commander of the 12th Infantry and a *grandson of Washington*. Whereupon the two adjutant generals M. and W. concocted a fierce letter to Wallace asking him by what authority he called himself a grandson of Washington. They signed the missive with the name of Peter G. Washington a noted politician from Virginia who held a high office under the administration at the capital but never claimed to be related to "The father of his country." Wallace took fire at once and wrote a scathing reply which he brought down to read to two staff officers; but happening to look at their faces which were full of ill suppressed merriment, he took in the situation at a glance. He said, "So you fellows have been selling me!" and went off enjoying the joke as much as they did.

There seems to be an element of the ludicrous in a certain mannerism of speech, when it is wholly unsuspected. I asked T_____, an old citizen of San Antonio if he knew C_____ our sutler at Fort McKavett who was an intelligent and large hearted man but somewhat irritable and impetuous at times. T_____ hesitated, and answered "I believe I do remember him. He is a large man, isn't he, and very excitable? When Santa Anna captured San Antonio he carried us both off as prisoners to Mexico. *My right leg was chained to his left leg for two years.* Now that you mention it, I have a distinct recollection of him."[18]

I suppose the Hon. Secretary of War may be considered as part of the Army and I venture therefore to relate an anecdote of Floyd who held that office at the beginning of the war. I must say that I had no very good will towards him for I was stationed at Fort Moultrie and Fort Sumter at the period referred to and if he did not make regular arrangements to have us all massacred his orders and mode of procedure tended to that end. He was a man of dark complexion which he attributed to his alleged descent from Pocahontas. He was very proud of his royal Indian blood and eager to proclaim it on all occasions. During the administration of Mr. Buchanan a party of Sioux warriors was brought to Washington by the agent in charge, with a view to a treaty of some kind which they were desired to sign. The diplomatic corps having expressed a desire to see these strange children of the forest, the President held a levee at the White House to accommodate them. Some time after it began Floyd made his appearance in evening dress, wearing a white choker and low shoes. He was introduced to the Sioux as the great war chief of the whites. The Indians scrutinized him closely evidently thinking his costume not a very suitable one for the field but they made no remark. To the surprise of every one Floyd struck an attitude, walked up to the head chief and said, "*Me Indian, Me-Pocahontas!*" The chief looked at him apparently much astonished at the statement, walked around him, felt of his short black curly hair and then exclaimed in great disgust: "*Naw Indian, Naw! nigger! heap nigger!*" This was pretty rough on a man who prided himself on being descended from one of the first families of Virginia. It is said the President lay back in his chair and laughed for half an hour.

I have no doubt our friends in the Navy could supplement this article by numberous incidents which have occurred in their branch of
the service. One of them, speaking to me of the strict discipline maintained in the old Navy referred to Commodore Rogers as a man who
never admitted any excuse for failure to carry out an order even when
it was impossible to execute it he would always insist that the attempt
must be made. On one occasion, when his vessel was anchored off
Smyrna a warrant officer named Marshall died aboard ship. The
Commodore desired to bury him on shore but was afraid the bigoted
natives might interfere in case he tried to do so. While he was cogi-
tating this subject two Frenchmen came on board. The Commodore
turned to one of the midshipmen near and said "Ask these gentlemen
if we bury Mr. Marshall on shore if the Turks will take up the body."
The midshipman saluted and replied, "I do not speak French, sir"

"Ask them sir!" roared the Commodore in a rage. The frightened
Middy turned to the strangers and said:

"*Si vous mettez old Marshall ici, piensez vous the Turkies come levy he.*"

"*Sh! That will do sir,*" said the Commodore, "*always try to obey an
order.*"

I will close with a few specimens of Congressional humor which
have come to my knowledge although they can hardly be considered
as germane to the heading of this paper which refers solely to the
Army and Navy.

Whenever a member of Congress gains a reputation for prompt
replies and sarcasm, very few care to meet him in debates of a personal character. Thad Stevens the uncompromising radical from
Pennsylvania who did so much to aid the cause of the Union is still
remembered gratefully by most of us. His tongue was a powerful
weapon and he had very little mercy on the copperhead element in the
House. Once a new man from Kentucky who was opposed to the war
interrupted him when he quoted a remark from "The distinguished
member from Kentucky" by saying: "Mr. Speaker, there are a great
many distinguished members from Kentucky here, and I would like to
know to whom the gentleman refers." Stevens replied, "*Mr. Speaker,
when I say the distinguished member from Kentucky, everybody in this*

House knows that I dont mean that young man." This was a pretty effectual quietus.

As Stevens was one of the great leaders of the Administration party
under President Lincoln and as heavy disabilities at the close of the
war weighed upon every one at the South who had been in arms
against the Government, several Southerners sought his influence to
free them from these restrictions. It is said that General McCausland
was one of these applicants and that the following dialogue occurred
between him and Stevens. The latter said:

"I believe General you are a graduate of West Point?"

"I am sir."

"You took an oath, did you not, to support the Constitution of the
United States?"

"I did sir."

"You left the service afterwards and went over to the enemy?"

"That is true sir."

Then said Stevens impressively: *"You commanded the party of men
who burned my iron-works just previous to the battle of Gettysburg?"*

McCausland was obliged to confess that this was also true.

"Well," said Stevens, *"I like your d___d impudence and I will get your
disabilities removed."*

I believe it is generally conceded that the greatest master of sarcasm our country has ever produced was John Randolph of Roanoake.
I heard several additional anecdotes of him from Mr. Stelle who was
librarian of the House of Representatives and who knew him well. I
am tempted to reproduce two or three of these here. The one that fol-
lows may possibly have been already in print.

Randolph, while in Congress, lost a very dear friend who represented the district adjoining his own. This friend was suceeded by an
enemy who boasted largely that the first thing he intended to do when
he took his seat was to put down that scoundrel Randolph. He carried
his intention out, accordingly, by making a very long and bitter speech
against R., full of personalities. Every one expected Randolph to make
a cutting reply but he paid no attention to it whatever. At last it
became his duty to announce the death of his friend in the House and

he did so with remarks so appropriate and so full of feeling that all the members were in tears. He began by saying, "There was one man, the playmate of my childhood and the friend of my maturer manhood," and then went on to state with much pathos the relations which had always existed between them. He ended by saying, "I refer to my deceased friend and colleague late of this House, *whose seat is still vacant*," looking directly, as he spoke, at the big fellow that filled it.

On another occasion he said, "Mr. *Speaker, isn't it a shame for the bull-dogs of the Administration to be worrying the rats of the opposition in this way.*" The opposition disgusted at the epithet applied to them, called him to order on all sides. He rose again as if he was about to apologise and said:" *Did I say rats?*" He pointed his long skinny finger at his enemies and said, "*mice! mice! mice!*"

The late General Charles P. Stone[19] told me another story of Randolph which he had heard in Washington. A lady there who had given a dinner party in honor of the great Virginian was disgusted to see him arrive very late and in his ordinary walking costume instead of the dress suit which etiquette demanded for such occasions. She manifested her displeasure very openly. This put Randolph in a bad humor and induced him to be disagreeable to his neighbor to the left, a young man named Parsons. He turned to him and said, "Mr. Parsons are you a descendent Sir, of that John S. Parsons who was hung at Bristol, England, in the reign of Queen Anne for piracy?"

"*No, Mr. Randolph*" was the reply, "*I am not the descendent of any British savage or of any Virginia savage.*" A rejoinder which delighted the hostess.

One of the men most thoroughly known in the old army was John Bankhead Magruder who subsequently became highly distinguished as one of the leading Confederate Generals.

He was a man remarkable for his humor and brilliant conversation. Indeed it is said that Daniel [?], after spending an evening with him, spoke of him as excelling in conversational power any body he had ever known.

Prince John as he was sometimes called was not at all scrupulous in his dealings with his tailors and tradesmen but laid them all under contribution without money.

His humor consisted rather in exaggerated statements of his own position influence in the army etc. than in any play upon words.

Every thing he said and did in his own peculiar line occasioned great laughter.

Once when he was a simple lieutenant stationed on the Canadian frontier where he found it hard to make both ends meet, he was asked by a British officer what pay he received per month. At this time he was playing the part of an officer of high rank to perfection. In reply to the query he said "My dear fellow I really dont know, I always give it to my servant."

Subsequently he travelled in Canada and was everywhere received by the British Commanders as an officer of great distinction and high rank while the major and two lieutenants of his regiment who were with him received no attention whatever, it being supposed that they were merely subordinate officers on his staff.

When the 1st Artillery was stationed along the northern frontier the officers of the regiment received a great deal of attention from the British officers in Canada and Nova Scotia. The latter were generally young sprigs of nobility enjoying large revenues and accustomed to heavy expenditures. Their messes were generally old institutions rich in fine silver ware and table appointments while our messes could only boast of plain crockery. Our officers felt the necessity of reciprocating the attentions they had received from their English neighbors but they were ashamed of the contrast between our poverty and their splendor. Magruder at this time was stationed at Sacketts Harbor and when it was decided that a dinner party must be given to the British officers on the opposite side of the line, he was fully equal to the emergency. He sent around to the different houses in the village to borrow every thing in the way of silver and ornamental ware that could be had so that when the table was set it presented quite a creditable appearance. When the titled guests arrived Magruder to the astonishment of our officers apologised for the poor reception he was obliged to give them, stating as an excuse that owing to the recent arrival of our troops from field service in Florida our officers had brought nothing with them but their rough camping and mess arrangements, the regular table service not having as yet arrived. The British officers commended every thing and the dinner was quite a success.

Immediately after this Magruder set to work to establish a regimental mess for Head Qrs and by dint of presents and laying a pretty heavy tax upon officers of the regiment he got up quite a handsome service of silver and was able to ask foreign officers to dinner with something like pride at the display. He even introduced in imitation of some British messes a highly embroidered mess jacket. One or two of the officers however refused to join in these expenses and Magruder led a crusade against them which engendered considerable feeling. The celebrated Confederate General D. H. Hill was a lieutenant in the 1st Artillery at this time and he left head quarters in consequence of his refusal to join in this jacket arrangement.

A sterling young officer from the back woods came on and joined the regiment in Maine while Magruder was introducing these innovations. He was quite struck with Magruder's manners and style. One day the new comer went to him and told him that having seen very little of good society he would like to have him (Magruder) give him some lessons and polish him off a little. Magruder replied to him *"Yes!—Yes! go and take a* bath *and come back to report to me precisely at 3 o'clock."*

During the Mexican War Magruder had a bright handsome lieutenant named Thomas Curd[20] assigned to his battery. One day Magruder said to him in the presence of several officers, "Thomas if this war lasts several years, it will be the making of you. You will be astounded at the promotion you will see. Let me see you are now merely a brevet 2nd lieutenant. Well if this war continues for five years I have not the slightest doubt that you will be—here he hesitated— you will by that time be a full second lieutenant." Imagine the disgust of Curd who expected him to say a colonel at least.

When Magruder was stationed at Newport he had two bachelor officers assigned to his battery to be available as beaux in the festive time he expected to have with the fashionable society there. One day in conversation he was talking loudly of his disgust at the fact that these officers had both become married men soon after their arrival. As he was expressing his anger at this untoward event he observed that one of the wives referred to had over heard his remarks but he kept right on without a pause "Yes sir as I was saying I was very angry indeed at these officers very until I saw the beautiful apologies they had to offer: the ladies they brought into the regiment: then I was forced to admit that they could not have done otherwise."

Magruder's battery of the 1st Artillery was stationed with a battery of the 2nd Artillery at Fort McHenry, Md. On one occasion about 2 o'clock at night the officer of the day was making his rounds and stopped for a moment before an open window where he saw Hayes[21] and Magruder sitting together and conversing. He heard Hayes say "Magruder it is out of the question. I cant sit up every night with you until 3 o'clock. I must go to bed" and he seized the candle and was about to retire. Magruder said, " My dear fellow if you must go you might at least leave me the candle." Hayes replied "you can have the candle but I must go" and left. The officer of the day who belonged to the 2nd Artillery overheard Magruder soliloquizing after this fashion: "Here have I been engaged for more than three months in trying to civilize this second regiment of artillery and I might as well have tried to polish a brick bat."

One day in Mexico Magruder asked Hooker who was an Assistant Adjutant General to give him an order on the quartermaster for a new pole to a limber of his battery in place of one that had just been broken. Hooker declined to issue the order as foolish and unnecessary. He said if you want a pole there is no difficulty about it. Go to the quartermaster and ask him for it and he will give it without an order. I dont propose to do any unnecessary writing if I can avoid it. Magruder sent a challenge to Hooker by an officer named Grafton[22] but he probably knew no fight would come off on a question of so trifling a nature. He said to Truman Seymour who was at that time a lieutenant in his battery, "you say it is a small matter. It may seem so to you but it is a very big matter to me I assure you."

On one occasion at a dinner party Magruder became very drunk and somewhat abusive towards a timid young gentleman who was present. His attention was called to it the next day by an officer who had been present at the dinner. The latter said, "Magruder you were not yourself yesterday at that dinner. You were quite insulting towards S___. who is a very inoffensive young man and who gave you no provocation." Magruder replied, "My dear fellow you dont say so. It must have been that d___d fish. I knew there was something wrong about it when I ate it."

I must give one more anecdote of Magruder. He was riding out one day in Texas with his orderly sergeant. There came up suddenly a furious thunder storm. A blinding flash of lightning caused Magruder's horse to swerve suddenly and throw him. The sergeant soon caught the horse and held him while Magruder remounted. Now M. would never admit that he could be thrown and for a moment was puzzled to explain what had occurred on any other hypothesis. After riding along in silence for a short time he suddenly turned to the sergeant and said, "Sergeant that was the most remarkable thing that ever happened to me in the course of my life."

"What is that Colonel?"

"Why I was struck by lightning and knocked off my horse without being injured."

Fort McKavett, Texas[23] is a large frontier post situated near the border of the staked plains. There are but a few settlers in that vicinity and they are a pretty wild set living in the midst of constant incursions from the Kiowas and Comanches. Most of these men have lived there all their lives and know little or nothing of outside civilization. An Army doctor at McKavett was called to attend a sick woman at a place called Kickapoo Springs. He performed an important operation and the frontiersman asked him how much there was to pay. He replied briefly $50. The man looked at him in amazement, pulled out three $2 1/2 gold pieces showed them to the doctor and said *"Doctor them's gold. It is all I've got. If you aint satisfied draw your weopins."* The doctor hastened to assure him that he was fully satisfied, and went off reflecting upon the Texas mode of settling bills.

Both officers and men in the Navy used to have a good many gibes at the Marines but it was rather a dangerous sport, as the latter were prompt to resent any indications of disrespect. One day a Naval officer called to a servant at the mess table, pointed to an empty bottle and said take away that Marine. A Marine officer happened to overhear him and promptly demanded an explanation. "I mean sir" the former said, "that that bottle has done its duty and will do it again if required" an explanation that was quite satisfactory.

My friend C. who lives in Galveston is a sturdy Englishman now quite advanced in age. He is very cholene [choleic?] impatient and combative. He is a man of a good deal of brain and ranks among the best chess players in the U.S. Before the war he was a sutler at Fort Duncan, Eagle Pass, Texas, which was at that day an extreme frontier post three days journey from civilization. After passing Fort Inge which was garrisoned by our cavalry the road became dangerous from numerous small detachments of Comanches and Apaches that were constantly going on raids into Mexico. C. had been down to San Antonio to purchase goods and was glad to find a small party of Texans there who were on their way back to Eagle Pass. He took advantage of their escort to rejoin his post. The first night out after passing Fort Inge it was determined to post a regular guard with the requisite number of reliefs. On this occasion Colquhoun called the Texans around him as he spread his blankets down for the night and made the following remarks. "See here. I wish you fellows to understand one thing. I cant hit a barn door at ten paces with a pistol and I am the greatest coward that every walked the face of the earth. I am not going to stand guard. You men that can hit the ace of spades at 100 yards every time and enjoy an Indian fight will have to do the guard duty. Dont come around waking me up about it for I wont go. And now d___d you, be off! Get away from here, for I want to go to sleep."

One day when I was a member of a Retiring Board in New York City an officer was sent to report to us with a view to being retired on account of sickness. He came in dressed in full uniform with a large sword dangling at his heels. To our astonishment we found he was stark mad and was there without a keeper. As he was very energetic in his language and actions and partly drew his sword by way of emphasis we did not feel very comfortable. We were wholly unarmed and he could easily have made quick work with us, if his violence increased. We were exceedingly polite to him and took care to coincide in all his views especially when he said he intended to put that rascal Guizot down who had attempted to write a history of civilization. When we were through the examination, the President of the Board directed him to return to Philadelphia but he said he preferred to go to Canada and very probably may have gone there for we heard no more of him.

Genl. Wool commanded at Saltillo during the Mexican War. One day a Mexican expressman came from the interior at full speed bringing important dispatches for the general. The latter looked around in vain for his interpreters. All three of them were absent. At last he saw a tall hoosier passing the window and called him in. The following dialogue ensued.

"My good man" Wool said "dont you speak Spanish." "No general, I am sorry to say I do not." "Cant you find me some one that does?" "Oh yes, general I kin do that." "Do it at once then."

The man very coolly walked up to the Mexican took him by the collar led him up to the astonished general and said, "*Here's a man that cant speak anything else.*"

Some amusing translations occasionally occurred in the French Class at West Point when I was there. Once a cadet who did not know his lesson was trying to guess the meaning of the phrase by the similarity of the words to those in English. He was called upon to translate "*Le sommeil du mechant*" which means "*the sleep of the wicked.*" After scrutinising the sentence for a moment he boldly pronounced it to mean "*Samuel the Merchant.*" The French professor fairly jumped out of his chair with amazement.

I remember under similar circumstances "*Leopold le Duc d' Autuche*" which means "*Leopold the Duke of Austria*" was translated by a cadet as "*The Leopard, the Duck and the Ostrich.*"

2nd. Lieut. M.[24] had joined the Army a short time after resigning from the Navy as Midshipman. In the Naval service the Quarter Master is merely a warrant officer and is of course ranked by all the Commissioned officers. M. supposed it was the same in the Army and not having received some stationary for which he made a requisition, he sent a peremptory message to the Quartermaster of the Post who held the rank of Major, that in case the stationary was not at his (M's) residence by 4 P.M. he should direct that the quartermaster be put in irons for disobedience of orders.

The regular fireman at West Point was sick one day and sent an Irishman to take his place. The latter appeared at 4 A.M. in a winter morning while it was still pitch dark, and entered the first room he came to, where four cadets were stretched out on their mattresses which were unrolled on the floor. In those days bedsteads were not allowed. The man was scarcely inside the room when he became confused forgot which way the fire place lay, took the wrong direction and ended by stumbling over one of the Cadets on the floor. This brought him down at full length with a coal scuttle in each hand filled with coal and kindling wood, upon the other three cadets. In an instant every one was on his feet striking out furiously to the right and left under the impression some one had made an attack upon him. They grappled together and rolled over in the dark every man hallooing at once and the confusion and uproar was increased by the noise of the coal scuttles which were banged about and by the coal rolling over the floor. At last after fighting some fifteen minutes quiet was restored and the frightened Irishman made his explanation heard.

The first night of our arrival at Fort Dallas, Lieut Tillinghast, one of our officers, slept in a wall tent. About 2 A.M. a large he goat walked in and stood motionless by the side of the bedstead. T. woke up and fancied he heard some one breathing. He put out his hand and encountered a long beard. This puzzled him exceedingly and he drew back wondering if he was fully awake. As there was no movement on the part of the intruder he put out his hand again. This time he encountered a pair of horns and drew back his hand still more quickly. For some moments he lay speculating as to whether the devil had really come to visit him or not. Fortunately for his peace of mind the goat walked out of the tent and betrayed itself by its bleating, so that he recognised him.

At the close of the Mexican war we had the misfortune to lose our Captain (P. [Prentiss]). The *we* in this case refers to Lieut. Ricketts and myself who were the two officers attached to the company. The Captain was a handsome man and a very accomplished gentleman. He had resided for some years at the Court of Louis Phillipe as an attache of the American Legation. Being a man of wealth he spent his money quite freely as his relatives were all rich and he was unmarried and therefore had no special reason for economy. He was taken sick at Brazos Santiago with yellow fever. Lieut. Ricketts was not acclimated himself but he nursed the captain faithfully, running the risk of taking the disease himself and he attended to the last wishes of the dying man. I was on detached service opposite Brownsville at this time.

Soon after the regiment was ordered to New York Harbor. After we had settled down into the ordinary garrison routine Ricketts told me he had a very painful duty to perform: this was to visit P's father and give an account of the last moments of his only son. He said he understood the old man idolised the Captain and that he anticipated a very melancholy interview especially as he had received a letter from P's sister who was perfectly heart broken. He accordingly went over called at the house and announced his presence to the old man who did not seem at first to remember his name. Ricketts said "I am the officer who attended your son in his last moments." Mr. P. replied "*Oh you are, are you? Then you are the very man I want to see. Now sir be good enough to tell me what you did with his money and other valuables.*" Very much taken aback at this rude reception and the fierce peremptory manner in which this inquiry was made, Ricketts explained the disposition he had made of the small amount of money the Captain had with him at the time and stated it was done in accordance with the Captain's dying instructions. "*Very well*" the old man replied "*what became of his watch?*" "*He told me to send it to his particular friend, Major Robert E. Lee of the Engineers, and I did so,*" Ricketts replied. "*You did, did you, now do you know that in doing all these things you have made yourself liable to a suit of prosecution.*" Ricketts said he was not aware of it, that he had acted in accordance with the wishes of the dying man and had nothing more to say on the subject. He then left thoroughly disgusted at his reception and at having been treated as if he was a thief trying to conceal stolen property. This interview was another illustration of the

French proverb that it is the unexpected that always happens. Ricketts
went there expecting to receive a sad and affectionate greeting and
the thanks of the family for risking his own life in the attempt to save
that of P. Instead of which he was treated like a pickpocket.

A case of decided presentiment was that of young Stewart[25] who
was a lieutenant in a rifle regiment in Oregon. He was a favorite son
of S. C. and had received the thanks of the Legislature of that state
for his gallantry in the Mexican war. Desirous of revisiting his home
and friends once more he applied for a long leave of absence which
was granted. As Phil. Kearney was going down the coast with a
detachment of cavalry Stewart accompanied him, that being almost
the only mode by which he could reach San Francisco in his home-
ward journey. To the surprise of all his friends he was suddenly seized
with a strong presentiment that he was about to die. As he was in
perfect health at the time and a very resolute brave and determined
man who was not troubled with weak nerves his friends were all
astonished and tried to talk him out of his conviction. He took leave
of all of them however asserting that they never would meet him
again as he would die in three days. On his way down the coast the
second day out he related to Capt Walker of the Rifles a strange
dream or rather vision which he had had. He found himself in battle
with a party of indians one of whom full of rage turned an arrow first
at Walker and then at himself uncertain which to shoot first. The
next moment he felt the arrow in his vitals and awoke. The command had hardly been out a few hours when they came upon a fresh
trail of Rogue River Indians who were at war with the whites.
Kearney was observed to step aside and hold a conference with the
surgeon who accompanied the detachment. When they separated
Stewart remarked to the Doctor "that was good advice that Kearney
gave you." "What was that" said the Doctor? It was to the effect that
we had just come upon a fresh trail of Indians and that as we had fine
horses and they nothing but poor ponies we must soon catch up with
them, and he asked you to have your instruments all in order. "Yes"
said the Doctor "that is what he said, but how did you know it?" "It
was very easy to guess" said Stewart. A short ride soon brought the

cavalry in contact with the Indians, a battle took place at once, and Walker assured me that Stewart was killed literally as foretold in his vision of the previous night.

At the battle of Buena Vista in Mexico a celebrated officer Lincoln who was acting as Adjutant General seemed to have a clear presentiment of his death which took place in the battle.

Genl. John F. Reynolds killed at Gettysburg expressed a similar feeling in the morning of the battle.

At the battle of Monterey Capt. McKavett of the 8th U. S. Infantry was killed by a cannon shot. I saw him fall at the time. In the morning before the battle he stated he should be killed and just before he was struck was heard to mutter, "It is my evil destiny."

President Lincoln a short time before his death made a speech in which he said in substance "in whatever way the war may be settled I feel I shall not long survive it."

I was returning on another occasion from Oswego where Winder and myself had been to attend a Court Martial, and as were going along in the cars Winder expatiated on the danger of crossing bridges, giving a number of examples, including the recent burning of one at Oswego and the giving away of an iron bridge on the Erie railroad which had just wrecked a train. A Yankee listened to him quite attentively looked at his uniform, leaned over and said, "*stranger are ye as 'fraid of gunpowder as ye are of bridges?*" Winder did not think it necessary to reply.

During the war, a somewhat illiterate Field Officer was detailed as a member of General Court Martial of which I was the President. This man paid very little attention to the testimony but whenever the time came to propose a sentence he would almost invariably say "*Oh, let's hang the cuss.*"

Charley May,[26] one of the heroes of the Mexican War, and a colonel in the regular army married a daughter of George Law[27] the celebrated New York millionaire. After his marriage he was stationed for a while at one of the frontier posts in Texas. Through some negligence of the staff officers the proper supplies did not arrive in time and May and his command were obliged to do without some articles of food for three or four weeks. He considered the quartermaster at San Antonio, Major B[28] as the responsible party, preferred charges against him and made strong efforts to have him tried by Court Martial. The quartermaster who came originally from the same regiment as May and who had been very intimate with him, was quite incensed at this proceeding. A few months after the occurrence May came to San Antonio on his way out of the state, for the purpose of going North on leave of absence. To travel with any degree of comfort he was obliged to ask the quartermaster to furnish a conveyance for himself and one or two wagons for his baggage to enable him to reach the coast. Maj B. now saw his opportunity. He drew himself up stiffly and said "that he was not aware that officers who were travelling for their own convenience were entitled to transportation." May replied, "Come B., dont talk that way to me. What would you say if I were to leave that splendid carriage of my wife's and those four elegant horses for you to use while I am gone. Wouldn't you make a sensation in San Antonio." B. smiled said nothing but went in. The next morning May received the transportation he had asked for and after sending the wagons on ahead, he drove past the quartermaster's office in handsome style. B. was standing in the door and May called out as he went past *"good bye, old fellow."* B. replied *"good bye; dont forget the carriage you promised to leave with me."* May answered *"Oh, B. you certainly did not suppose I was in earnest. My wife would never forgive me if I were to loan her carriage to any body. Good bye. Take care of yourself"* and the quartermaster went in, cursing all the cavalry officers that ever entered service.

A certain major in the staff who was a man of very large frame and a deep bass voice was particularly overbearing towards his inferiors in rank. On one occasion a puny looking lieutenant who had recently entered service came to B.[29] after office hours with an important requisition to be filled. The major, relying upon the man's youth and want of knowledge of the customs of service addressed him very fiercely. This attracted the attention of a crowd of officers and employees and as the young man seemed to take all he said very meekly he increased the violence of his language and finally became positively insulting. The lieutenant listened without making any reply until the major was through with his tirade of abuse, and then answered that he had come to the office on a matter of public business, that while there without having given the slightest cause for offense he had been grossly assailed in the presence of his brother officers, that he was not in the habit of receiving insults of this nature, and that now if he did not then and there in the hearing of all, make the fullest and amplest apology, he should insist upon the satisfaction recognized among gentlemen in such cases. The major who was always disposed to bluster but never ready to back up his words, saw, in this case, that he had caught a tartar. He immediately retracted every thing he had said claimed that it was the result of unusual irritation on his part and begged the young man to forget it, but it was a long time before the latter would consent to accept his explanations and apologies.

One more story of B. and I have done. He was stationed for some time in New Orleans. While there he made a call one afternoon upon the wife of one of the proprietors of the Galveston line of steamers as he had a particular object in view in cultivating friendly relations with these men. When he arrived at the door he found he had no card with him. The servant came to answer the bell and he directed him in a very magisterial way to bring him a visiting card immediately. The servant went in and picked up the first card he came to, on the card receiver, brought it back and gave it to B. who wrote his name upon the back and directed the servant to take it in to his mistress. This was done and he was directed to walk in the parlor. The lady of the house came in a few moments afterwards but was exceedingly stately in her reception of him. She seemed surprised at the visit and hardly made any reply to his observations and remarks in relation to the current topics of the day. She was so extremely frigid that he soon left the house.

In the evening her husband came home and asked her if Maj. B. had been there. She replied that no such person had called; that no one had been to see her except a very large portly French dancing master, who tried to be quite familiar in his manners and address.

It turned out on investigation that a French dancing master had called, when the lady was out, with the object of trying to induce her to send her two children to his school. The servant had brought B. the

"She seemed surprised at the visit...."

dancing master's card. B. had written his name on the back of it had sent it in, and the lady had looked at the printed side and not at the other.

In the days of Cortes the approaches to the City of Mexico were over narrow causeways through lakes of water. When our troops occupied the city these causeways still remained but the lakes had become swamps covered with luxuriant grass which concealed their true character. A wet ditch intervened between the road and the swamp but to all appearances the ground beyond the ditch was firm and solid. During the Mexican war Lieut. H. was on his way into the city across one of these causeways. At a particular spot where a sentinel was stationed belonging to one of the Volunteer Regiments the passage of heavy teams had worn the road into a gulley where the mud and water were about two feet deep. H. disliked exceedingly to wade through this slough and it occurred to him to leap the ditch into the beautiful meadow beyond, walk around the obstruction, cross the ditch again and then resume his way. He accordingly went back a short distance to get the necessary start and then ran to the edge of the ditch and leaped over;—but oh horror! When he was up in the air he saw that he was about to plunge into a dirty swamp instead of landing on solid ground. He struck on his feet but found himself up to his waist in mud and saw his hat some yards in advance of him. In making efforts to regain it the water came nearly up to his mouth. At last he succeeded in scrambling out and in regaining the causeway a sadder and a wiser man. Instead of warning him as a regular sentinel would have done the Volunteer roared with laughter and said Ha! ha! ha. You are the fourteenth man I have seen do that today!

When I was stationed with Patterson's army at Harper's Ferry there was a battalion of three months men there whose term of enlistment had nearly expired before they had seen any service. It was useless to attempt to drill or discipline them under the circumstances. I was very much amused at times by their utter ignorance of military rank and etiquette. As I had been at Fort Sumter and that was the only battle of the war they looked up to me with considerable admiration and respect which was much increased by the appearance of the 32 pounder Parrott guns in my battery. Some of these men overheard me say that we ought to have a fortification on the heights and ran to tell Mr. Patterson what Mr. Doubleday said. One of their officers to my astonishment came to me to ask for orders. I remarked did not the officer of the Day give you your orders. He replied, "*Yes, but what does he know about it. I'd like to have you tell me what to do.*"

On another occasion as the men of this battalion were marching by they saw me look through a reconnoitring glass at something in the distance. They all broke ranks and ran up to me with the most lively curiosity saying "*Maynt I look through that are thing.*"

I was once detailed on a Court Martial at Baton Rouge, La. A doctor in the army was seated opposite to me at table in the hotel in citizens clothes. I did not know him at the time but heard him remark to a companion, "*This steak reminds me of an old English poet.*"

I suppose he meant *Chaucer.*

Lieut F. H.[30] a wild young dragoon officer went through the Mexican war. He said one day there is a great deal of talk about the morals of these Mexican women but I have no complaint to make.

A certain commanding officer in Oregon, suspected a private of having stolen some of his chickens. The next morning this private reported to him as orderly. For the benefit of the uninitiated it may be as well to state that an orderly is a soldier detailed to remain around your house all day and to accompany the commanding officer whenever he goes out. On the present occasion when the man reported as Orderly the officer said to him, so you are my orderly are you. *The first thing you do go lock up that chicken coop and bring me the key.*

In the last war with Great Britain when the British invaded Baltimore a ludicrous duel occurred which had a fatal termination. There was a tailor in the city who started a military company not so much from patriotic ardor as from a desire to sell plenty of uniforms. He himself was got up in gorgeous style with epaulettes and plenty of embroidery. At the time of the battle of North Point he was sent out on a reconnaissance. Leaving his men behind he rode cautiously ahead until upon turning an angle in the road he suddenly found himself in the presence of a British Colonel who was on horseback and

accompanied by his staff. There seemed to be no chance for the tailor
to escape as he found himself right in the midst of his enemies and the
road in his rear occupied. The British officer who was a magnificent
swordsman thought this a fine opportunity to show his skill. He said to
the tailor, "An American officer I presume. It must be very annoying
to you to be made prisoner in this way without striking a blow and I
appreciate your situation. Now I will give you a chance for your freedom. We two will go around the angle in the road and there without
witnesses decide the matter by our swords. If you conquer me I am
your prisoner and if I conquer you you must be content to go with us."
The tailor agreed to the arrangement in the hope that he would find
some loophole for escape. Both rode around the corner and dismounted. The Colonel's staff remained where they were and the colored boy was sent out of sight to the rear. The Colonel now put himself on guard and commenced to make the usual complimentary salute
with the sword with which all fencers and duellists commence their
combats. The tailor instead of taking position and returning the salute
suddenly fell to the ground. The Englishman looked at him in amazement under the impression that he had a fit of some kind, but before
he could recover from his surprise the tailor had by a sudden upward
motion jabbed the unfortunate man in the abdomen giving him a fatal
wound. After attempting to staunch the wound with his shirt which
he had taken off for that purpose the tailor rode over to the Colonel's
staff and told them their leader was badly hurt and they had better
attend to him. He then returned to where he had left his horse called
his boy and galloped back to his company.

My colored servant Temple was a very religious negro and while
the battle of Antietam was raging, he knelt down in the bloody cornfield for which the two armies were contending and prayed for a long
time in a loud voice for the success of the Union cause. This supplication made in the midst of the flying bullets was a remarkable one and
deserves to be recorded.

One day at Old Point Comfort where a large artillery garrison was
stationed a new officer reported for duty who had just received his
commission and was entirely ignorant of the customs of service. He

was detailed as officer of the Day to go on the next morning after his arrival and after receiving pretty full instructions from one of the other officers he succeeded in getting through the parade without any startling blunder. After he had received his instructions from the commanding officer he took a walk around the post to see what the sentinels were doing. To his surprise he saw a boy in uniform following him whereever he went. This was one of the drummers who had been detailed as Orderly, that is to remain always near the officer of the Day in readiness to carry any orders or messages he may have to send. At last annoyed by the feeling that he had a spy put over him to watch him he turned around to the drummer and said sharply, "What are you following me about for?" The boy replied, "I am orderly to the officer of the Day, sir." This puzzled him still more as he did not know what the boy meant. At last he took it in his head that the boy must be the son of one of the officers for he supposed that no enlisted man would be impudent enough to follow him around. At last he entered a drinking saloon and as he noticed that the boy went in also he asked him if he would not have something to drink. The boy who was amazed at the request replied that he would. "What will you take" was the next question. "Anything the lieutenant pleases" was the answer. When they left the house noticing that the boy still followed him the officer went over to ask some of the other officers what it all meant. There was great laughter when they found out that he had been treating the boy as an equal and that he thought it was very *impolite* for the boy to follow him around in that way.

A soldier at Fort Dallas went to the sutler to get a quart bottle filled with whiskey. They filled the bottle for the stipulated price but he insisted it was not full. The sutler replied that the liquor came up to the cork and that the bottle would not hold any more. He said if you can get any more in it I will make you a present of the contents. The soldier turned the bottle upside down, pointed to the cavity in the bottom and said fill that. He won the liquor.

A recruiting officer in Utica, N.Y. was once tried for an assault and battery committed on a hackman who had been abusive to him. When the case came up the Recruiting Sergeant marched in with several

recruits touched his cap and said to the officer "I report to the lieutenant with three men." "What do you report to me for sergeant and
for what purpose do you bring the men here?" "*I have brought them to
swear to anything the lieutenant pleases*" was the reply.

One of our distinguished generals who knew nothing of art was
waited upon by a person who had just finished an elegant album containing engravings of the cartoons of Raphael the originals of which
are frescoed on the walls of the [Sistine] Chapel. He presented the
book to the general and asked him if he would object to giving him a
letter recommending the work. The general sat down and wrote "*that
it gave him great pleasure to recommend these beautiful works of art to every
one who was not able to procure the originals.*"

[Simon] Cameron was Secretary of War and [William]Seward was
Secretary of State at the commencement of the Rebellion.[31] We all
supposed that in the great crying need of the country nepotism would
no longer be regarded but officers of the Army would be promoted for
their knowledge and past services. Yet the first person promoted was
Cameron's son and the next was Seward's.

Toward the latter part of the war the number of bounty jumpers
and deserters increased to the extent that it was thought necessary to
adopt stringent measures. Many people of a low grade conscience and
intelligence considered it a good joke to enlist, receive the U.S. and
State bounties and then desert. One of this class tried the experiment
in a country place in Maine, was caught, arrested, tried by a Volunteer
Court Martial and sentenced to death. As the Volunteers in charge
did not like to carry out the sentence themselves they sent the condemned man to the regular garrison of the 17th Infantry at Fort
Preble, Portland Harbor, Maine. The man was a poor silly fellow who
thought his action would be treated as if he had engaged to work for
a farmer and had failed to carry out the agreement. He had no idea
that any serious consequences would result. In the mean time the day
assigned for his execution had nearly arrived when he was sent to
Portland and no one had communicated the terrible news to him. He
was full of merriment and every time he went out with the other prisoners he would keep them in roars of laughter by his antics and gri-

maces. The officer of the day observed this and said to him "My God! Do you know what that Court Martial that tried you did in your case?" The man replied smiling that he had not the least idea. The officer then said "You are sentenced to be shot to death next Friday, the day after tomorrow." Then the poor man realized the whole horror of his situation and became utterly unnerved. The Commanding officer of the post, Lt Col Andrews of the 17th Infy did every thing in his power to obtain a respite for him in order that he might have more time to prepare for the fate that awaited him, but there was some delay or derangement in the telegraph line and as the answer did not arrive in time the sentence was carried out on the almost inanimate body of the deserter at the time and place designated.

When I was stationed at Fort Preble in Portland Harbor Maine the commanding officer was an exceedingly tall and thin man with very long legs and a very long neck and as he was far from being a favorite on account of his excessive miserly tendencies the towns people commented pretty freely upon his personal appearance.[32] One drunken individual remarked that "*all he was good for was to whitewash light houses,*" which seemed to me quite an original idea.

One day a very bright young lady was conversing with one of our officers who was acting as Commissary at Fort Preble and who had just put an advertisement in the paper inviting proposals to furnish the troops with fresh beef. She had the paper in her hand and had just been reading the advertisement. Turning to the officer referred to, she suddenly asked, "*How does _____ _____ get in the fort?*" Get in the fort; why he is our Commanding officer. "*I know that*" she replied, "*but I dont see how he can get in without violating the conditions of your advertisement.*"

"*My advertisement! What has that got to do with it?*"

"*Why that says that 'necks and shanks are excluded,'*" she replied.

A young officer, Lieut B_____ who was quite a fancy man volunteered on one occasion for the first time in his life to accompany Lieut Holabird on a scout, the latter having had great experience among the Indians.

At night the following dialogue took place between the two officers, and as it amused me I have taken the trouble to record it.

"Great Heavens Holabird, here we are in the center of the Apache Country with only eight men."

"Well" said Holabird, "what are you going to do about it?"

"I think some body ought to sit up and watch."

"Very well sit up and watch" said Holabird rolling himself up in his blanket and preparing for a good sleep.

With many officers of the Army Chaplains are not considered as very desirable and indeed in view of the great number of sots and low politicans who have received these appointments as a reward for political services it is not to be wondered at that there should be considerable prejudice against them. Col. A_____ disliked them particularly on account of their constant interference with every prisoner put in the guard house whom they all desired to have released immediately for his supposed penitence.

One day a very ignorant man who had taken up the business of preaching and who called himself a hard shell baptist, was induced to apply to Col. A. for the position of Chaplain. The Colonel saw at once that some of his officers had sent the man to him as a practical joke. He gave him however a pleasant reception, listened to his application and finally said, "This is a very important appointment and you will have to preach a trial sermon before I can determine the matter."

"Oh certainly" was the reply, "I expect to do that of course."

"Very well sir, come with me to my friend Mr. Hall. He is a great biblical scholar and he will select a text for you."

They accordingly called on Mr. Hall who received them very courteously. He was a very able lawyer but he made no pretenstions to any theological knowledge.

Col. A. upon entering said, "Mr. Hall I have brought this gentleman Mr. Johnson, to see you. He has applied for the position of Chaplain to my command and we have come to you on account of your great biblical learning to ask you to select a text for him to preach from in his trial sermon."

It will give me great pleasure to do so said Hall taking down a large bible and slowly turning over the leaves. After considerable research in the Old Testament, he pointed to a verse and said "There is your text sir."

The minister put on his glasses and scanned the page curiously, but drew back with an expression of disappointment and amazement, saying "Well now really I dont think I can preach from that."

"It is an excellent text sir," said Hall, "and a beautiful sermon can be made from it." "Let me read it to you: *The waters of a separation were made from the ashes of a red heifer.*" "Observe it says a *red* heifer."

"Well now" said Johnson, "I'd rather have sumthin else. I dont see what good it will do to talk to your sogers about heifers. You know there are a great many texts in the Old Testament that aint good to preach from."

"Mr. Johnson" said Hall, "Are you aware you are talking of the Sacred Scriptures?" "Yaas, I know that. I didn't mean to say anything agin the scriptures but you know some things in the Old Testament are rather foolish to make texts of."

"Col. A." said Hall, "This man will not answer. He is a scorner of the scriptures" and the poor fellow went out with his head hanging down in considerable confusion and dismay, muttering something about a red heifer.

The punishment for desertion when I first entered the Army was very severe including 50 lashes on the bare back with a cat o nine tails, and a certain amount of imprisonment varying from six months to three years. On one occasion a deserter in prison at Fort McHenry escaped punishment in a very adroit way. He heard one of his comrades read an account of a burglary that occurred in one of the little towns in the western part of Maryland. He immediately sat down and wrote to the authorities there that he was connected with the burglary and could get the money back for them if they would make a requisition on the Military Authorities for him. The man had already been tried by a Court Martial and still had six months to serve as a prisoner. The requisition arrived in due course of mail, the man was surrendered to the civil authorities and was carried off to the remote village where the crime was committed. When he came before the court there he denied all knowledge of the robbery and proved an alibi. As they had already been put to considerable expense in bringing him on for trial, they did not feel much like spending an additional sum to put him back in Fort McHenry and as he could not be held longer under the civil process, they discharged him.

Lists of deserters were published in those days with full particulars including names, dates, color of the hair and eyes, height, etc.[33] One day a Philadelphia policeman arrested a man whose description corresponded with one of these old lists and brought him on to Baltimore to obtain from us the usual reward of $30. He had paid the man's passage and had fed him on the way, and was therefore hugely disgusted to learn that he had been at all this expense for nothing, as the man had been already punished and discharged from the Army. When the man, with a great deal of mock politeness, took off his hat and thanked him for his kindness in bringing him on to Baltimore where he desired to come, and for paying his fare by the way, the rage of the policeman knew no bounds. He went of swearing horribly that if he ever caught the man in Philadelphia he would arrest him anyway.

There is a sewer at Fort McHenry about 2 feet high made of masonry. It leads from the main gates through an outwork to the sea wall outside and is about 200 feet long. One day a member of the guard wanted to get out of the fort to have a bottle filled with whiskey. As the regular passage way was guarded he attempted to crawl through this sewer. Many years afterwards when the fort was repaired the sewer was opened and the man's dead body in full uniform was found in the center of it with his musket and an empty whiskey bottle lying by his side. He had gone half way when he was suffocated by the foul air, and as he did not appear again he was reported as a deserter.

Genl. [William T.] Sherman went to the theater one night in New York and said to the man who attended the parquet, "*Now I am quite late. I am General Sherman. I wish you would try and find me a good seat.*" The man replied, "*You are General Sherman, the h_ll you are. You are the man that chased me all the way through Georgia. Well! never mind! I'll do you a good turn this time,*" and the General was properly provided for.

When I was in command of Fort McKavett, Texas in 1870 the ladies had the utmost difficulty in procuring servants. Of course none could be hired in the wilderness and those that followed the camp were of the most worthless description. The Regimental Quarter Master N.,[34] of the 24th Infantry had been on recruiting service in Nashville and as the 24th was a colored organization his wife brought a colored girl on with her when she and her husband returned to it. A few days after her arrival the Sergeant Major of the regiment, a tall handsome mulatto, addressed the girl who became violently in love with him. The sergeant then came to me to ask my permission to marry. I told him I had no objection to his getting married, but as Mrs. N. had brought this girl on at a very heavy expense from Nashville, and as she could not get another in her place, it would annoy and embarrass her very much to lose her and that therefore he must see her in relation to the matter. He was unable however to come to any satisfactory agreement with Mrs. N., who would not consent on the one hand to have the girl leave her and was unwilling on the other hand to have a colored family in her house with all their train of visitors and other annoyances. The sergeant therefore was obliged to give up the idea of marriage for the present. The girl however soon became very restless and thought she could settle the matter by picking a quarrel with her mistress and suddenly leaving her. As soon as this was done she came to me and said, "Is you the Commanding Officer?"

I said "Yes, I am the Commanding officer." "Well I'm Mrs. N's servant. I wants you to send a waggon to carry my things across the creek."

The creek was the boundary of the public land and there were several houses outside and she proposed to go in one of these.

I replied "if you have left Mrs. N. after she has been to the expense and trouble of bringing you out here you cannot expect any favors from me. You must get your baggage carried the best way you can."

Mrs. N. now was becoming desperate at the idea of doing all her own cooking and washing and concluded to resort to strategy. She sent for the Sergeant Major praised his appearance and ability, told him there were colored cadets at West Point, she had no doubt that some day there would be colored officers,[35] and as he was already Sergt. Major which was the next rank to a lieutenant it was not unreasonable to suppose that he might become an officer some day. She told him under these circumstances he ought to be careful who he married and not fling himself away on the first colored girl he happened to meet. This tickled the sergeant's vanity and he told the girl he could not marry her, as some day he expected to be an officer and she had no education to make her a suitable wife for him.

The girl then returned to the house in despair and resumed her customary work. Mrs. N. supposed she had won the game, but the girl had a trump card in reserve which altered the case very soon. She walked in one morning with a tin dipper in her hand and informed Mrs. N. "that in this ere dipper" she had just taken 25 grains of strychnine; that she would be obliged to her, if she would be with her when she died, and would send her body afterwards on to her friends in Nashville. This was pleasant news. To pay the girls expenses on and be requested to furnish money for sending the body back. In addititon the girl's statement was literally true. It required the most unwearied attention of the two doctors at the post laboring day and night for ten days to save her life. All the chloroform and chloral in the hospital was used up in quieting the convulsions caused by the poison. She resisted all she could and said she knew that the Lord wanted her and stated that she had 25 more grains of strychnine in reserve which she should use as soon as she has recovered. Genl. Sherman paid me a visit about this time on his way to Fort Sill and when I told him the story, he said "By Jove it was too bad." "That fellow must be made to marry the girl right off." I said "Certainly General, if you order it" and sent for the Sergeant Major who was only too glad to carry out the General's wishes.

The marriage however did not prove to be a very happy one, and the remains of the poison in the girl's system finally brought on a cancer which killed her in the course of a couple of years.

My friend Genl. Z. Bliss of the regular army after a series of exciting adventures in Texas at the beginning of the war was finally captured and paroled in company with a number of other officers who were taken at the same time. Upon their arrival in Richmond on their way North they were suddenly seized and thrown into prison[36] in vio-

lation of the terms of their surrender. Upon learning this, the rebel officers in Texas sent on strong remonstrances and Bliss and his companions were finally released.

While in prison every now and then some zealous southernors
would rush in denounce and upbraid them as miserable yankee
hirelings etc. On one occasion a man came who made the whole
prison resound with his outcries. Indeed to all appearances he could
hardly be restrained from attacking them outright. He screamed out,
"Where are they?—let me see these people that dare to talk of con-
quering the south. I want to see what kind of looking men they are
that have undertaken to do that. Oh, you are the men are you! A pretty looking set of fellows you are, to talk of coming down here to sub-
jugate us. Waxing more wrathy he screamed out, "you ought to be
hung up like dogs every one of you without a trial." He then looked
cautiously around and seeing none of the guards were looking, he drew
a bottle out from under his coat slid it behind a box, and sinking his
voice to a whisper, said, "*there is some of the best whiskey you ever drank
in your life, and d___n you, if you ever tell on me.*" He then, as he went
out recommenced his tirade of abuse but they bore it very patiently as
they recognized him as a friend in disguise.

The celebrated Confederate General Bragg was at one time stationed at Fort Moultrie, S.C. together with Genl. Sherman, Genl Geo.
H. Thomas, Genl John F. Reynolds, and myself all lieutenants in the
3d. Regiment of U.S. Artillery. Owing to a scarcity of officers Bragg
commanded a company and was also obliged to perform the duties of
Post Commissary. One day the First Sergeant of his company came to
him to complain that the beef was tainted and unfit for issue to the soldiers. This probably resulted from the unusual heat of the season.
Bragg examined it and then sat down and wrote quite a sharp letter on
the subject stating that the condition of this beef showed great care-
lessness and inefficiency on the part of the Post Commissary. He then
signed it as Company Commander and addressed it to himself as Post
Commissary. He then wrote a spirited reply from himself as Post
Commissary to himself as Company Commander stating that if the latter had attended to his duty properly the thing would not have hap-

pened. The correspondence was kept up between the two functionaries and became quite volumnious and more and more insulting as it went on. At last the Post Commissary wrote that he would not put up with these attacks upon his character and military reputation any longer, but would appeal to the Commanding officer to do him justice. Bragg actually forwarded all these precious documents to the latter personage who being very thick headed puzzled himself exceedingly over the matter and then sent it on to Washington as being too deep a question for him to decide. Of course the authorities there enjoyed the joke very much but did not think it necessary to settle the important points at issue in the case of Bragg versus Bragg.[37]

Genl. Winder of the Confederate Army who gained such an unenviable reputation for his treatment of our prisoners at Richmond and Andersonville was formerly a Captain in the 1st Artillery while I was a Lieutenant in the same regiment. He had a pet parrot which we thought a great nuisance as its discordant screams were sure to wake us up at the hour of the siesta. One day it was placed on its perch and put out to get an airing on the ramparts of Fort Moultrie where its owner was stationed. A negro girl came along who had never seen or heard of a parrot. Nothing could exceed her surprise and amazement when the bird said, "*how do ye do, how do ye do.*" She remained silent for some time staring at it. Very soon it addressed her again and said "*good bye, good bye.*" Then she replied, "*I aint gwine yet.*"

The soldiers at Fort Columbus in New York trained a parrot to call out "*come back here you d___d old fool*" and placed it above the main entrance. One day it saluted the Commanding officer with this phrase after he had passed by on his way out. He turned around at once very angrily to find out who it was that dared speak to him in that way and his rage was increased when he found that the men to all appearance were laughing at him. As he noticed they were looking up he did the same and saw the cause of the disturbance whereupon his anger subsided. He ordered the bird removed but the men enjoyed the joke for a long time.

Genl. Eustis of the regular Army who died some years before the rebellion broke out, had the reputation of being a very rough officer but a very efficient one. A young officer just from West Point who had recently reported for duty in Florida was ordered by the general to construct a road between certain points. He replied "*I dont understand the process sir.*" "*Process be d____d*" Eustis replied "*do go and do it at once sir.*"

Once in Portland a countryman called at the General's Head Quarters and asked to see *Lieut Thomas.* The General informed him there was no such person there and asked "dont you mean *Lieut. Thom.*[38] The man answered "*it will do for you big bugs to call him Tom but I dont like to do it.*"

Genl. Eustis was a very strict disciplinarian. On one occasion at Portland, Maine he sent for Lieuts. Ricketts and Sid Smith[39] and asked them why they were absent from reveille roll call. They answered that all the quarters at Fort Preble were taken up by their senior officers and that they were located in a farm house about half a mile from the troops: that owing to the distance and a high wind blowing at the time they did not hear the drum call. The General remarked, "there is something in that. I will try and regulate it." He then sent for the quartermaster. Curious to know how he was going to regulate it, they waited in the anteroom to find out. When the quartermaster came they were horrified to hear the general ask him if he had not some wall tents on hand. Fortunately for them he had none. The idea of sleeping in a wall tent in that climate in the winter was enough to freeze anybody's blood. They did not miss a single roll call after that.

During the war with the Seminole Indians in Florida Fort Jupiter on the eastern coast was a very important military point. It had a fair harbor at that time although it has closed up since. A surgeon in the army had been stationed there for three years, until he was fairly wild to get north particularly as very important family matters required his attention. After repeated applications to the surgeon general of the army he was finally notified that another medical officer would be sent to relieve him. The steamer that brought orders, supplies, etc. came once a week but only remained long enough to unload its freight and then went on to the next post. The doctor kept a bright look out for his successor, and to enable him to turn over his public property in time to go off in the same boat, he had his receipts and invoices all made out in readiness to be signed. Several steamers came in succession but no one appeared to relieve him. At last he became wholly discouraged and would not take the trouble to go down to the boat anymore. One day, however, when it came in, a person who had just arrived passed the doctor and casually remarked that one of the passengers who came with him was a Medical man who was going to be stationed at Fort Jupiter. The doctor wild with excitement called to the hospital steward to have his papers ready and the property arranged so that it could be rapidly inspected and counted. He then dashed down to the beach but it was some time before he could find any one answering the description the passenger had given. At last he saw the person referred to, but he looked so coarse and unlike a medical officer in his immense cowhide boots and dilapidated hat and coat that the doctor hesitated to speak to him. Finally he rushed up and introduced himself as surgeon S. of the U.S. Army. The man bowed to the ground and announced himself as *"Doctor Mac Manus of the Quartermasters Department"* alas it was a horse doctor.

In the Navy it is or was customary for the officer of the Deck to send a midshipman at daylight to wake the Captain up and answer any questions he may desire to make with reference to the position of the ship etc. This duty was assigned to a new midshipman who had just reported for duty and was wholly inexperienced. He woke the Captain up accordingly and the latter said "it is daylight is it?"

"Yes sir."

"How does she head?"

Instead of replying as he should have done north west by half north the new Middy gravely pointed to the bow of the vessel and said *"She heads in that direction."*

This reminds me of another sailor anecdote. In the days of Jefferson during what was called the embargo nearly all of our sailors were thrown out of employment. One of them was hired by a farmer to do some plowing. He soon rushed back to the house at full speed with alarm on his countenance. The farmer asked him what was the matter. "Matter enough" he said "*the starboard ox has got on the larboard side; the plow is on its beam ends, and the old mare is afoul of the rigging.*"

"Paying with the top sail" is a phrase some times used in the Navy in reference to officers who suddenly sail away from a foreign port without paying their debts. The Duke of Edinburg was accused of running up a large indebtedness in New Zealand and then leaving the authorities to vote a sufficient sum to settle his accounts. One of our naval officers on that station remarked at the mess table that the Duke had paid his debts with the top sail. Another officer who did not understand the phrase said it was a perfect outrage for the Duke to sell one of the principal sails of a naval vessel to pay his private debts.

One of our Men of War was anchored off Governor's Island. Being very short handed the Captain thought he would borrow a few soldiers from the garrison to help him weigh anchor. He sent his compliments to the quartermaster of the post who had dined with him the day before, to request that he would render him some assistance in weighing anchor. The quartermaster was a recent graduate and had come from an inland town, so that he was quite ignorant of naval matters. He sent back a courteous reply that it would give him great pleasure to comply with the request, *but unfortunately there were no scales at the post large enough to be used for such a purpose.*

One of the Lieutenant Commanders of our Navy in 1840 was at one of the harbors in the Mediterrenean where there was a British fleet under an Admiral who had gained destinction under Nelson. The lieutenant had a great admiration for the Admiral which he expressed on all occasions. One day a British Midshipman came on board and the lieutenant as usual asked after the health of the Admiral. The Middy said the Admiral was in the dumps. The lieutenant asked what was the matter. The Middy evaded the question for some time and professed great unwillingness to say any thing further in relation to it. He said it was a ridiculous subject and he would rather not talk about it. The lieutenant who was one of those men who could never take a joke pressed the Middy to confide in him. The latter finally said the Admiral was inordinately fond of bean soup and never made his dinner without it. Unfortunately at present he had no beans that were good for anything and so he was obliged to dispense with his favorite dish. The lieutenant took this chaffing in sober earnest. He ordered several barrels of beans to be overhauled and the finest and largest to be carefully selected. He then had them placed in a bag and sent them with a polite note to the Admiral begging him to accept this slight testimonial of his regard. It is almost unnecessary to state that he never received any answer to his communication.

Capt Schenck[40] of the Navy was at one time in command of an ocean steamer. Upon arriving in New York the passengers were beset by an innundation of hackmen who came on board and for a time created such disorder and confusion that Schenck could not make himself heard. In a fit of passion he threw his speaking trumpet at the head of one of the most noisy and obstreperous of these men. He was immediately sued for assault and battery and the case came up before an Irish judge who owed his election in great measure to the exertions of the man who had been assaulted.

It soon became evident that the judge was strongly prejudiced in favor of the defendent. When the indictment was read he called out: "*I never knew a more outrageous case in my life.*" Schenck replied "*when your honor has heard all the particulars I think you may not think so.*" In answer to this the judge roared out, "*Silence you Schenck you or I'll commit ye for contempt of court.*" Schenck thought it best to make no further remarks and the case went on until noon when there was a recess taken until one o'clock. During the interval Schenck's lawyer said "this judge is not quite as bad a fellow as he seems to be. Let me introduce you to him." Schenck was accordingly duly presented. The judge shook hands with him very cordially and said "Schenck me boy I'm delighted to know you. You musn't think hard of me for what I say on the bench. These boys are my constitutents and I have to talk that way before them but I'll let ye off aisy, aisy." He fined him $500.00

Some years ago a brother of Senator Woodbury[41] of N.H. was on his death bed. He asked the doctor if he was going to die and the doctor said "*Why your feet are warm. You never heard of any one dying with warm feet, did you?*" "*Yes I have*" Woodbury replied. "Who was it" said the doctor. "John Rodgers who was burnt at the stake," replied Woodbury.

At a meeting of the bar in Philadelphia on some official occasion a distinguished lawyer (B.) who imbibe too much at times, came in quite late. A gentleman who was with him was invited to remain and take part in the proceedings although he was not a lawyer. He rose and made a very graceful speech in answer to the invitation stating that it was the highest compliment he had ever received in his life, etc. While he was talking B. was seen meandering out of the hall evidently for the purpose of getting more liquor. The gentleman went on to say it would give him the greatest pleasure to remain but he added, "When I see the condition my friend B. is in and recollect that he was the playmate of my boyhood and the friend of my manhood I feel that it is a duty both to him and myself to go and watch over him to see that he receives no injury and to use every exertion to prevent him from still further indulging in the intoxicating bowl. Under these circumstances gentlemen as the voice of duty and friendship calls me away I am sure you will appreciate my motives and excuse me from remaining." He accordingly went out. About an hour afterwards B. was seen reentering the room followed by his friend. Both were blind drunk and groping their way to their former seats. This commentary on preaching and practice afforded great amusement at the time.

When Genl. Jackson's administration came in power there was a clean sweep of all the office holders in Washington who belonged to the opposite party. All the officials connected with Congress were turned out except one old negro whose business it was to wash and clean the portico of the Capitol. Very indignant at being left in under the circumstances he immediately tendered his resignation saying, "I came in with gemmen and bress God, I'se going out with em." Having thus placed himself in the attitude of a political martyr he borrowed money enough from his former associates to set himself up as a hackman on Pennsylvania Avenue. He always went to the daughter of the former door keeper of the House to state his troubles and grievances, to ask for advice and occasionally to borrow money. One day he burst into her room in great agitation saying, "*I dont know what they will do with me, but the Lord knows I could'nt help it.*" He evidently was afraid of some fearful punishment and it was a long time before she could ascertain what was the matter. At last he said with tears in his eyes, "*I dont know what they'll do wid me, but I just done cuss a member of congress.*"

It seems a member of congress in a fit of drunkenness had seized his horses by the reins and had jerked them about in different directions, and the hackman in his own mind when he reflected upon the awful fact that he had actually cursed the man, thought he had been guilty of high treason.

At the commencement of the war and previous to the first battle of Bull Run Genl. McDowell[42] who was in command of the Army of the Potomac gave a grand review to President Lincoln in the vicinity of the Arlington House. The President had mounted his horse and was about to leave the White House with a large retinue when some sudden and pressing demand was made upon him to sign an important official document. Telling his escort to ride on ahead and that he would rejoin them in a moment he returned to his office. He was detained there longer than he expected so that he was obliged to gallop over the long bridge to Arlington by himself. When he arrived the review was formed and only awaiting his appearance. He saw McDowell in position and rode up to him to ask what he was to do as he never attended a review before and was ignorant of the mode of procedure. McDowell pointed out a man holding up a small flag and told him he was to place himself in front of that man and remain there until the troops had all passed by and saluted him. Just here a misunderstanding occurred. Mr. Lincoln supposed the man with the flag would give him full instructions. The marker, as he is called, did not know Mr. Lincoln and supposed some impudent old Virginia farmer was in front of him merely as a spectator to see the review. The President turned around and said to the marker, "Well my man, when I leave here where am I to go?" The marker astonished the President by replying, "*I dont care where the hell you go to, if you will only take yourself out of my way.*" The President said nothing but evidently thought there must be a great want of discipline in his new Army.

In one of Mr. Lincoln's visits to the Army of the Potomac to avoid making a considerable circuit he crossed through a back yard and entered the quarters of Genl Grant by the back door. He was accompanied by two or three citizens. The sentinel on duty looked at them very doubtfully not knowing whether they were intruders or not. Finally he concluded they must be members of the Sanitary Commission and let them pass with the warning "You Sanitary fellows will catch hell if you dont look out."

It is singular to note the numerous superstitions encountered by the traveller in Mexico. I have known several cases where men had been dangerously injured but refused to call in any physician. They simply bound a picture of the Virgin over the wound and relied entirely upon that. Almost every one of the lower and most of the upper classes wear a little medal containing the image of the "Virgin of Guadalupe" who it is said came down from Heaven to take charge of the Mexican people and who first appeared at Guadalupe in the suburb of Mexico. She became the patron saint of the country. It is a sorrowful fact however that ever since she took charge of them the Mexicans have been in hot water until now revolution has become chronic and all vestige of a permanent government has disappeared. One would think that the educated classes who have seen the world would not share in these superstitious beliefs. Our Minister to Mexico Tom Corwin told me an anecdote of Escandon the great tobacco monopolist which was very significant of Mexican usage and beliefs. Although Escandon had travelled all over Europe and was a man of immense wealth and extensive information he was still beset by all the early superstitions of his youth. He became violently ill in his palatial residence in the suburbs of Mexico and sent for the parish priest. He agreed with him that if the Virgin Mary would attend to his case and cure him, he would give $20,000 towards her shrine. By the aid of a skillful French physician he at last got well. He then sent for the priest and said, "It is very true that I agreed to give the Virgin $20,000 if she would cure me, but $20,000 is a very large sum and I think she ought to be willing to take $10,000. The priest replied that so far as he was concerned he had no objections to take the money but as Escandon had promised $20,000 the Virgin would be sure to look over the books and if she found he had only paid half the money she might be very

"I think she ought to be willing to take $10,000...."

angry and then the first thing Escandon would know, he would find himself sick again and then as the Virgin would be against him he would probably die. The matter was finally arranged by an arrangement between the two parties by which Escandon was to pay only $10,000 but the priest *was to credit him with $20,000 on the books*. It was supposed of course that the Virgin would merely look at the books and finding the amount to be correct would be fully satisfied.

The following story is from the Spanish. A sentinel on post heard some one approaching in the darkness of night and gave the customary challenge, "Who comes there?" To his amazement the man replied "Jesus of Nazareth" and then halted. As the sentinel could not leave his post he called the Sergeant of the Guard and reported the circumstance to him. The sergeant then went forward challenged in his turn and received the same reply. Furious at being trifled with in this way, he fell upon the man and beat him severely with his musket. He then sent for a lantern to ascertain who the intruder could be. When the light came he recognized a gentleman of high standing who lived in the neighborhood and whose mind was somewhat impared. Regretting his hasty action the sergeant asked him why he did not give his own name when he was hailed, to which he replied "I would have been a great fool to do that. If this is the kind of reception Jesus of Nazareth gets, I would like to know what I could expect."

An Irish laborer in one of the coal yards was ordered to be discharged by the head man who said "He dont know anything and he never will learn." "Be gorra" he replied "I know that in this establishment a ton of coal is only 1600 lbs." The head man replied, "Why he has learned something. He knows a great deal more than I thought he did. I think we will have to keep him."

Duncan McRae[43] was a celebrated N.C. politican and fighting man when I was stationed in that state. It was said that he revenged an insult he had received at a ball by shooting the man who gave it through the head in open court. He was put in jail for this but finally released. Afterwards it was reported he had fought a duel with another high blooded duellist across a table each holding on to the end of a pocket hankerchief. McRae was badly wounded in the encounter but recovered. I think the other man was killed or desperately wounded.

I was traveling once with McRae on the rail road through Virginia going south. He was escorting a young lady who had been placed under his care. I found him a very interesting and very entertaining man. In front of him there was a red headed Englishman who seemed inclined to be somewhat pugnacious in regard to the conductors etc. and at the same time very desirous of obtaining information about the country through which he was traveling. McRae amused himself by hoaxing him in every possible way. He referred to the young lady as his wife, spoke of the happiness of married life and the congeniality of two twin souls in a way that made it very hard for the girl to conceal her amusement. At last the Englishman asked "What is this thing you call the Magnetic Telegraph which has just been put up between Baltimore and Washington. I saw the wires as I passed by." "That sir" said McRae "is the most wonderful invention that ever existed. It has a thousand uses. *All the meat in the President's house in Washington is cooked by it.*"

This hoaxing went on for almost two days. As we were coming into [Goldsboro] N.C. the Englishman ascertained that he had been systematically hoaxed and came to me to know if McRae would fight him, evidently meaning with his fists. I took in the situation at a glance and assured him I would arrange it for him at once. I remarked casually that McRae was one of the most prominent fighting men in the whole country; that he had once shot a man through the head in open court and had fought a duel across a table in which he was desperately wounded. I ended my remarks by saying, "I'll just step over and tell him what you want." The Englishman turned white as a sheet and said "Oh my God, dont do that, I did not mean that kind of fighting. My dear sir, I will be everlastingly obliged to you if you will not say a word to him." I said "but it is no trouble at all to me. McRea is a man that is always ready." "My dear sir," he continued "dont, dont, dont, for heavens sake mention it," and he forthwith absconded and hid in the baggage car until we arrived at Wilmington.

I was amused by an anecdote related by a countryman who had come to New York during the war to buy some clothes. While passing a Jew shop in Chatham Street he was struck by the appearance of a jaunty looking coat which was displayed very conspicuously and which seemed to be about his size. Thinking he might get a bargain he went in and tried on the coat which fitted him very well. He asked the price and was told it could not be sold for less than $20. This he refused to give but offered $13 which he said was all the money he had. After considerable haggling over the price to induce him to give more the Jew requested his customer to follow into the back part of the store. There he led the way into a solitary room entering on tip toe and closing the door behind. He then said in a mysterious whisper, "I let you have him for $13." The man replied "All right, but why do you bring me here and act in this strange manner." The Jew answered "Mein brudder is mein partner and I dont want him to hear us. He has a disease of the heart and if he knew I sold dat coat for $13 it would kill him right off."

Quite a number of Irishmen were assembled one day at the City Hall in New York to be examined for the position of policeman. It was one of the requisites that the candidates should be able to write; pen, ink, and paper were placed on one of the tables, and each man was required to write his name. Some laboring men who were present expressed great surprise at seeing one of their number among the applicants. They said "just look at Mike! The idea that the loikes of him can get the place when he cant write!" Mike looked around him very contemptously, walked up to the table and wrote his name in full, very much to their amazement. He had been taking lessons and practicing incessantly and knew just enough to make his sign manuel and no more. When his companions saw him write they were very much astonished but one of them said "Ay but your honor ax him to write some body else's name." Mike turned around with a look of reproach and said "*An is it me just about going into the perlice that ye ax to commit forgery.*"

One of my old commanders when I was a second lieutenant had a way of reproving us with the expression "*when I was in the Army.*" He would meet us, for instance and say, "When I was in the army it used to be the regulation for officers to salute the commanding officer when he passed."

"I beg your pardon Captain I was not looking that way, and did not see you go by."

"Oh I dare say you may be right. Probably the regulation has been changed, but it used to be that way when *I was in the army*. Now that *I'm in the militia* I dont know how it is, perhaps the commanding officer salutes his juniors first.

Little K.[44] was an officer of my command who never took a joke. One day in Galveston a man came from a livery stable with a long bill in his hand charging him with numerous horse back and carriage rides. Some soldier had been there in citizens dress and had run up a bill by taking K's name. K. of course indignantly denied that he had had a single one of the rides charged against him, and appealed to the other officers to corroborate his statement, but by way of joke they all shook their heads and decided against him. One of them said "K. I always told you you would get into trouble about this riding business." His face was a study as he looked from one to the other in perfect amazement.

The B_____ family in North Carolina were blessed with ungovernable tempers. It is said two of the brothers had shot at their father and at each other. The one I knew always spoke in a very measured tone and in a low voice to avoid getting excited for then he was like a maniac. He married a very beautiful girl much younger than himself and of course became afflicted with jealousy. One day he had a handsome nephew staying with him. He heard him ask his (B's) wife to play for him on the piano which she consented to do. Unfortunately she had previously declined to play for her husband. This excited him at once and he went to the window put his head out and called to two of his negro men to come up and bring a cross cut saw with them which was lying in the yard. When the negroes entered the room he directed them to saw the piano in two and throw the pieces out of the window and it was done in spite of the entreaties of Mrs. B. who had received the instrument as a wedding present from her mother.

The same man used to hold his wife's hand, feel her pulse, and call over the names of every one who might by any possibility be a lover of hers. He would call out "Bill Jones" and look her straight in the eye. If she stood this he would go on to the next man, "Sam Kemper." If her

"If her pulse changed a little...."

pulse changed a little, he would begin to curse Sam Kemper and threaten to kill him at sight.

Having known his wife quite well before her marriage I called one day to see her as I passed through the place where they resided. The servant handed me a rickety chair to sit on and it broke down. After I left Mr. B. came home and asked how the chair became broken. His wife informed him I had made a call and a rickety chair had been given me for a seat. He flew into a fury at once, and said "I believe you were both sitting on the same chair or it wouldn't have broken down."

He had a sister who shared the family infirmity. She was internally a devil in her invention and malignanty but to all outward appearances was an angel of beauty. Her figure was tall graceful and commanding. She was courted by a very diminutive speciman of a man and managed to hide her claws long enough to marry him. After that it became the study of her life to make him as wretched as possible and she subjected him to every kind of wrong and indignity. On one occasion she playfully induced him to let her wrap him up in a long piece of cotton cloth until his arms were confined and he was helpless. She then beat him unmercifully. On another occasion she burned up a new suit of clothes which he brought home only retaining the end of one of the coat tails to convince him she had really done it.

At last he got a divorce, but wished very much to retain their only child, but she soon convinced him that he need have no interest in that subject.

In the old Florida war when a battle took place on the other side of a river some of the Florida volunteers refused to cross over.[45] An Army poet referred to it afterwards in these words

> O'er the ford and by the glen,
> Cowards watch the strife of men.

Capt. T. of the Artillery told me that on another occasion the captain of a company of Georgia Volunteers said to him, "*I am as brave a man as ever walked the face of the earth, but I am not going into that hammock*" which was the very place where the battle was going on and where his services were very much needed.

In the beginning of the war there was too much intimacy between the officers and men which resulted in a great want of discipline particularly among the three month's troops. One day a colonel was observed to shake his sword at a drummer and order him to beat his drum, but the drum remained silent. The Colonel then rode up to the man in great wrath and said, "Why dont you beat that drum sir." The man replied in a low tone "*Colonel I have got two turkeys inside this drum, and one of 'em is for you.*" The Colonel then called out in a loud tone, "*Oh if you are sick you can fall to the rear, but why didn't you say so in the first place.*"

At the battle of Antietam I was amused to see a German Sergeant trying to stop a runaway. He brought his gun to bear on the man and called out, "*Come back here or I shoots.*" The man turned around and pointed to a big spot of blood on his knee to intimate that he was badly wounded. The sergeant said, "*Oh, yes. I sees him. You got him off a dead horse. Come back here and vight vot you gets paid for.*" And the man thought it best to return.

In all army transports state rooms are reserved for the officers. One of these was assigned to an individual who signed his name "James Flanigan, M.D., U.S. Army." He was treated with great consideration and under the supposition that he belonged to the Medical Department, he had a free cabin passage. Upon calling him however to attend a case of sickness, it was ascertained that the M.D. attached to his name, stood for *mule driver*.

Many of the roads in Western Virginia are cut out of the side of the mountains so that there is a precipice below and another above. They are frequently very unsafe as owing to the washing away of portions of the road it becomes very narrow so that vehicles cannot pass in opposite directions. Genl. B.[46] was proceeding along one of these roads with troops and a train several miles long. He happened to be in the rear of the column when a long stoppage took place. After waiting about two hours for the train to proceed he sent a man to the front to find the Quartermaster. It was not a very easy task as the road was barely wide enough for the wagon and it required considerable management to get past the mules without being crowded over the precipice. Another hour elapsed and the general became very impatient. At last the Quartermaster made his appearance, and the General said "What is the meaning of this stoppage sir." The Quartermaster replied that a heavily loaded wagon had broken down in the narrowest part of the road: that on this account the freight could not be taken out and passed forward by the side of the wagon. Of course it could not be transferred over the heads of the horses and as all the teams in rear were closed up there was no room behind so that he did not know what to do. "I will tell you what to do," said the general, *throw the wagon over the mountain and go on.*" "Very well sir if you order it."

In a short time the train proceeded and after making about 10 miles further stopped for the night.

Now the general was very irascible and had a bad habit of throwing the first missile he could lay his hands on at the head of his colored servant when anything went wrong. One the present occasion he had not been in camp very long before he saw the servant approach him with considerable hesitation and reluctance. The General roared out "What's the matter now you scoundrel!" The man answered "*Your trunks sir.*" "Well what happened to my trunks?" The negro answered "*They done frowed 'em over the mountain ten miles back.*"

It was a sight to see the general dance about in his rage. When he found that he had ordered his own private baggage to be thrown over, he cursed the whole Quartermasters Dept. from top to bottom. A party was sent at once to the base of the mountain and by daylight he had recovered his trunks but in a very dilapidated condition, with almost every thing broken inside.

The next morning he was about to embark with his staff to go down to the Gauley River, when the same servant came in evidently with unpleasant news to communicate, as he did not advance beyond the door way and stood ready to dodge any hostile shot the general might send. "What's the matter now?" roared the General again. "*Your horse sir.*" "My horse. What's happened to him?" "*They done drowned him getting him aboard the steamer.*"

The general dashed off to see the Quartermaster in a great rage, which was considerably increased by some careless individual firing at a duck on the water, the charge just grazed the general's head as it passed him.[47]

Soon after I graduated at West Point I was stationed in North Carolina. In an adjoining county there lived a man named Ham Jones[48] who was somewhat celebrated in his day as the author of a very amusing story called "Cousin Sally Dillon." Jones and a young friend of his were visiting one evening at the house of an acquaintance and while there were introduced to two very beautiful girls who were the daughters of a presbyterian deacon. The deacon was noted for making very long prayers and for living in a very secluded way so that the young ladies were rarely seen in company. Jones and his companion thought they would call on these girls, for the novelty of the thing, and perhaps because they were somewhat smitten in their previous interview. They accordingly went to the house, soon after dark, inquired for the young ladies, and were ushered into the parlor. A few minutes afterwards the whole family came in and the conversation became general. In a short time the old man proposed family prayer and they all kneeled down. As Jones and his friend were not much accustomed to this they found it hard work, for their kness were tender and the floor was hard. The prayer was exceedingly long and when Jones thought it was over, the old man recommenced with great zeal and prayed for all the officers of the General Government from the President down. Jones thought this must be the end of the supplication and was rising up, when the deacon began again and prayed all through the State Government commencing at the Governor and ending with the Constables. He then started fresh on the County and Municipal officers. Anxious to know how long the thing was going to last Jones leaned over and woke up a little boy who was on his knees but who had fallen asleep with his head on his hands in a chair. He asked this youth if his father was not most through. The boy said "*has he come to the jews yet?*" Jones replied "*no.*" The boy said "*when he comes to the jews he is about half through.*" Jones and his friend concluded they had enjoyed their visit sufficiently, so they rose up softly and stole out of the house, without being observed, leaving the deacon still praying. They concluded that courting in that house was rather a tedious business and never went back there.

About 1850 "the mad poet" as he was called, C. Donald McLeod,[49] was a guest at the Astor House through the generosity of Stetson the landlord, who was a big hearted man.

One day a young Virginian seated himself at the dinner table directly opposite McLeod and called out in a loud tone, to one of his companions, "I have seen everything worth seeing in New York except C. Donald McLeod." McLeod leaned over and said, "I am C. Donald McLeod."

The Virginian stared at him intently for about a minute and then slowly drew a quarter of a dollar out of his pocket and passed it over to him. McLeod with great gravity pocketed the money and returned 12½ cents change saying *"children and fools half price."*

Political candidates in their discussions are quite sharp on each other. In a contest shortly after the war when each candidate took the stump in turn one of them said, "my opponent calls himself Colonel and claims to have been in the Volunteer service but my friends he never drew his sword but once *and that was in a raffle.*"

Soon after the close of the Mexican war my brother found himself at Brownsville, Texas near the mouth of the Rio Grande with a party of gentlemen on their way through Mexico to the gold fields of California. While stopping at Camargo to purchase mules for the trip the Asiatic Cholera struck them like a thunderbolt and killed or dispersed nearly all who formed part of the expedition. After burying a number of his companions my brother was struck down himself with the disease but finally by the aid of opium recovered. While still feeble and convalescent in Camargo he entered a building part store and part bar room. There were a number of Texans within drinking and trafficking. Pretty soon he saw a man enter with a double barrelled gun. This being a very common circumstance in that region he paid no particular attention to it. The man raised his gun to his side fingered the lock and immediately afterwards discharged the contents of the gun into the back of the man in front of him killing him at once.

My brother seized the murderer and called on the others for assistance but the prisoner made no resistance and took the affair very coolly. He was brought before an American judge who was about to take testimony in the case previous to making out a commitment when the prisoner said that witnesses were unnecessary: that he killed the man and went to the store for that especial purpose. The Judge asked him why he did it. He replied because the man had made a previous declaration to several parties that would kill him at sight. The Judge asked him if he could prove this and he called on several persons who testified that one day when the deceased was drunk he had said he would kill his antagonist on account of some difficulty which had occurred between them. The Judge then decided it was a case of self defense and released the prisoner from custody. My brother soon after came down the river to Brownsville where he made the acquaintance of a very pleasant young man named Moses who had recently arrived from Charleston, S.C.

A day or two after this Hickey[50] who was a noted desperado and man killer on the Rio Grande and who had been present at the trial of the prisoner referred to, came down the river to Brownsville. There he casually met young Moses who asked him what the news was above. Hickey told him the story of the killing and vindication of the accused party and Moses said, "I dont like that he did not give the man he killed any chance." Some days elapsed and Moses had forgotten the remark when the Judge who had decided the case came to Brownsville. As soon as he landed he walked up to young Moses accompanied by Hickey and said "I understand sir you say I am no better than a murderer since I let a murderer go free." Moses replied, "that is a mistake I have never spoken of you or referred to you in any way in my conversation." Hickey now spoke up and said "yes you did for I heard you." Moses said "I never made any remark in reference to this gentleman." Hickey says "do you mean to tell me I lie." Moses said "I mean to say that I never made any remark about this gentleman." Hickey then struck him and Moses challenged him on the spot. The matter was then left to the seconds of the parties who decided as the lie and blow had passed that the duel should be a bloody one; that they should fight at ten paces with double barrelled shot guns loaded with buck shot and that they should throw up for the first fire. Hickey won this and as he was a sure shot every body expressed pity for young Moses who had just come there, was a stranger to the customs of the country and had entangled himself in so deadly a difficulty.

My brother although very feeble from his illness crawled out to see the fight which took place behind a store. Moses although the odds were fearfully against him seemed perfectly calm and collected. The result of the duel proved to be very different from what every body anticipated. Hickey fired first but the two shots rang out almost simultaneously. Whether Hickey had overloaded his gun or was somewhat nervous will never be known but his shot passed over Moses head, a few of the buck shot making bloody furrows in the scalp without penetrating the brain. Moses fire was more sure and struck Hickey square in the face. The latter gave a frightful leap into the air and fell down dead. There was one less desperado in the country and Moses became the hero of the rough population who lived in that vicinity.

NOTES

INTRODUCTION

1. The biographical information on Abner Doubleday used in this sketch comes from the following sources: Cullum, *Register*, vol. 2, pp. 54-55; Heitman, *Register*, vol. 1, p. 380; Malone, *Dictionary of American Biography* (hereafter cited as *DAB*), vol. 5, pp. 391-92; "Father of Baseball Lived in Auburn 26 Years," *The Citizen Advertiser*, Auburn, New York, July 23-24, 1964; "Abner Doubleday," an unofficial service record in Abner Doubleday Collection, New-York Historical Society (see also Breton, *Guide to the Manuscript Collections*, p. 439).

2. *The Citizen Advertiser*, July 23, 1964.

3. Ibid.

4. "Trial Brevet Major R. S. Garnett, Captain 7th Infantry By A General Court Martial At Ringgold Barracks, Texas in May, 1852," published privately by R. S. Garnett (courtesy Verne D. J. Philips, Austin, Texas).

5. "The Texas Ordinance of Secession," appearing in B. P. Galloway, *Texas: The Dark Corner of the Confederacy*, p. 75.

6. *DAB*, vol. 5, p. 392.

7. Bliss, "Remininscences," vol. 5, p. 150.

8. Unofficial biography of Abner Doubleday, appearing in the Papers of Abner Doubleday, NYHS.

9. "The First Shot For the Union—The Man who Fired It—General Doubleday and His Early Adventures," undated newspaper article of unknown origin, found in the Papers of Abner Doubleday, NYHS.

10. For more information on how Doubleday came to be identified as the "father of baseball," see the highly fictionalized account in Nason, *Famous American Athletes of Today*, Chapter 5; for information on the Mills Commission's selection of Doubleday for this honor, see Spalding, *America's National Game*, Chapter 2 and Boston, *1939: Baseball's Pivotal Year*, Chapter 10.

11. Carroll, "The Doubleday Myth and Texas Baseball," *Southwestern Historical Quarterly*, pp. 598-612.

1: FIRST ACTIVE DUTY

1. Heitman, *Register* vol. 1, p. 299; *Register*, vol. 1, p. 135. Thomas Childs graduated from the United States Military Academy in 1814 and served in the War of 1812 at the Battle of Niagara and the defense of Fort Erie. In 1836, he was promoted to the rank of brevet major for planning the attack on the Seminoles near Fort Drane in Florida and his good conduct in that affair. For his successes against the Florida Indians, he was promoted to brevet lieutenant colonel in 1841. Childs was a member of Taylor's forces in south Texas and northern Mexico and participated in the Battles of Palo Alto and Resaca de la Palma, being promoted to the rank of brevet colonel for gallant conduct in those engagements. He was transferred to the invasion of central Mexico and fought at Vera Cruz, Cerro Gordo, and commanded the defense of Puebla. For his actions at Puebla, Childs was promoted to the rank of brevet brigadier general. Childs died on duty at Fort Brooke, Florida, on October 8, 1853.

2. Ross, *The Cape Fear*, pp. 43, 44, 104, 106; Cullum, *Register*, vol. 1, p. 27. Fort Johnson was located on the right bank of the Cape Fear River, three miles from its mouth, at the town of Smithville, North Carolina. The fort was built before 1748 to protect Brunswick from Spanish raiders, who were then at war with England. The fort was never very strong; the builders having mixed too much sand with the oyster shell binder "so that every time a gun was fired a part of the 'tabby work' parapet fell down." A hurricane in 1760 cut a new channel in the Outer Banks that bypassed the fort, and relegated this structure to an even more minor status. On July 18, 1775, to escape capture by a rebel Committee of Safety, the royal governor, Josiah Martin, ordered the fort destroyed. It was rebuilt at a later date.

3. Alexander, *Civil War Railroads*, pp. 39, 45; *The Daily National Intelligencer*, November 12, 1852. The strap-iron-and-stringer construction rail was a predecessor of the iron rail. Strap rails were made of timbers upon which sections of an iron strap were spiked. This type of rail persisted especially on Southern lines up to the time of the Civil War. Alexander includes an illustration of Union soldiers in the act of destroying such a rail. But progress in railroad engineering did occur in the South, albeit at a slower pace. *The Daily National Intelligencer* reported in 1852 that the Raleigh and Gaston Railroad had recently been relaid with heavy iron between Weldon and Gaston, North Carolina, the route likely traveled by Doubleday.

4. Heitman, *Register*, vol. 1, p. 436; Cullum, *Register*, vol. 2, p. 15. Sewall L. Fremont (named Sewall L. Fish at graduation) graduated from the United States Military Academy in 1841. Fremont served in the Florida War in 1841, and participated in the Battles of Palo Alto and Resaca de la Palma, May 8-9, 1846. In 1849, he served with a surveying party that determined the boundary line between the United States and Mexico. As a member of the 3rd Artillery, he was aboard the ill-fated steamer *San Francisco* on its way to California when it was wrecked off

the straits of Delaware on December 24, 1853, and was compelled to return to New York. Fremont resigned his commission on April 5, 1854, and was subsequently employed as chief engineer of the Wilmington and Weldon Railroad, residing in Wilmington, North Carolina. He served in the Confederate States Army at the rank of colonel, 1861-1865, and died May 1, 1886.

5. Heitman, *Register*, vol. 1, p. 596; Cullum, *Register*, vol. 1, p. 401. Erasmus Darwin Keyes graduated from the United States Military Academy in 1832, and was assigned to the 3rd Regiment of Artillery. He served as aide-de-camp to Winfield Scott from 1838 to 1841 in Florida. Keyes was an instructor of artillery and cavalry at the USMA from 1844 to 1848. From 1849 to 1859 Keyes served in California in garrison at San Francisco and in the Washington Territory to suppress Indian hostilities. Keyes served as military secretary to General Winfield Scott from 1860 to 1861. During the Civil War, Keyes rose to the rank of brevet brigadier general for "gallant and meritorious conduct" in the Battle of Fair Oaks, Virginia. He resigned his commission on May 6, 1864, and retired to his home in San Francisco, California, where he died on October 14, 1895.

6. Heitman, *Register*, vol. 1, p. 529; Cullum, *Register*, vol. 2, p. 57. Daniel Harvey Hill graduated from the United States Military Academy in 1838, and served variously in the 1st, 3rd, and 4th Regiments of Artillery before the Mexican War. He was promoted to the rank of brevet captain for gallant and meritorious conduct in the Battles of Contreras and Churubusco. For his bravery in the attack on Chapultapec Castle, Hill was promoted to the rank of major on September 13, 1847. He resigned his commission on February 28, 1849, and accepted a position as professor of mathematics at Washington College in Lexington, Virginia, from 1849 to 1854. From 1854 to 1859, he served as a professor of mathematics and engineering at Davidson College, where he authored the text, *Elements of Algebra*, and several religious tracts. He served from 1859 to 1861 as superintendent of the North Carolina Military Institute and later served in the Confederate States Army, 1861-1865, where he rose to the rank of lieutenant general. General Hill died on September 24, 1889.

7. Heitman, *Register*, vol. 1, p. 925; Cullum, *Register*, vol. 2, p. 51. Joseph Stewart graduated from the United States Military Academy in 1842. He served on commissary duty in northern Mexico at Cerralvo and Monterrey, 1846-1847. In central Mexico he was a member of the expedition from Vera Cruz to Orizaba in 1848, and participated in a skirmish with guerrillas. By the end of the Civil War, Stewart had been promoted to the rank of major, 4th Artillery. Stewart resigned his commission on August 25, 1879.

8. Heitman, *Register*, vol. 1, p. 597; Cullum, *Register*, vol. 2, p. 52. Charles Lawrence Kilburn graduated from the United States Military Academy in 1842. He was promoted to brevet first lieutenant for gallantry and meritorious conduct at Monterrey, Mexico, on September 23, 1846. A further promotion to brevet captain was awarded for his actions in the Battle of Buena Vista on February 23,

1847. Kilburn was further promoted to the rank of brigadier general in the Union Army on March 13, 1865, for faithful and meritorious service during the war, having served as a commissary of subsistence. He died on March 17, 1899.

9. Heitman, *Register*, vol. 1, p. 169; Cullum, *Register*, vol. 1, p. 91. Walker Keith Armistead graduated from the United States Military Academy in 1803 and was assigned to the Corps of Engineers. He was stationed at Fort Niagara during the bombardment in 1812, and served during the remainder of the War of 1812 in forces assigned to defend the mouth of Chesapeake Bay. Armistead commanded the Corps of Engineers and directed the Engineering Bureau at Washington, D.C., 1814-1821. With the reorganization of the Army in 1821, he was appointed colonel of the 3rd Artillery. He served in several sea coast garrisons until 1836, when he participated in the Florida War against the Seminole Indians and commanded the Army in Florida, 1840-1841. He was on sick leave in 1844-1845 and died at the rank of brevet brigadier general on October 13, 1845.

10. Heitman, *Register*, vol. 1, p. 449; Cullum, *Register*, vol. 1, p. 91. William Gates graduated from the United States Military Academy in 1806, and was assigned to the Regiment of Artillerists. In the War of 1812, he was engaged in the capture of York, Upper Canada, April 27, 1813, and the bombardment and capture of Fort George, Upper Canada, on May 27, 1813. Gates participated in the Florida Wars and was engaged in the defense of Fort Barnwell against the Seminole Indians on April 12, 1836. Gates was engaged in the Combat of Locha-Hatchee, on January 24, 1838, to subdue the Cherokee Nation during their emigration to the West. He participated in the Florida Wars in 1839-1841 and again in 1841-1843. During the Mexican War, Gates served as military governor of Tampico, Mexico. He was ordered to California and was aboard the steamer *San Francisco* proceeding to his destination when the ship was wrecked off the straits of Delaware on December 24, 1853. Colonel Gates was retired from the service on June 1, 1863, "having been borne on the Army Register more than 45 years." Gates died on October 7, 1868.

11. Heitman, *Register*, vol. 1, p. 882; Cullum, *Register*, vol. 1, p. 502. Thomas West Sherman graduated from the United States Military Academy in 1836 and was assigned to the 3rd Regiment of Artillery. Sherman was promoted to the rank of brevet major on February 23, 1847, for gallantry and meritorious conduct in the Battle of Buena Vista. During the Civil War, Sherman was promoted to the rank of brigadier general and major general on March 13, 1865, for his generally meritorious services during the war, highlighted by his command of Union forces in the capture of Port Hudson, Louisiana, where he was wounded and lost a leg. Sherman retired from the service on December 31, 1870, and died on March 16, 1879.

12. Heitman, *Register*, vol. 1, p. 240; Cullum, *Register*, vol. 1, p. 521. Braxton Bragg graduated from the United States Military Academy in 1837. During the Mexican War, Bragg was promoted to the rank of brevet captain for his gallantry in the

defense of Fort Brown, Texas, on May 9, 1846. He was promoted to the rank of brevet major for gallant conduct during "the several conflicts at Monterey, Mexico," on September 23, 1846, and again to the rank of lieutenant colonel for his meritorious conduct during the Battle of Buena Vista on February 23, 1847. Bragg resigned his comission on January 3, 1856. He sided with the Confederacy during the Civil War and commanded the Army of Tennessee at the rank of general, 1861-1864. Bragg died on September 27, 1876.

13. Heitman, *Register*, vol. 1, p. 825; Cullum, *Register*, vol. 2, p. 22. John Fulton Reynolds graduated from the United States Military Academy in 1841. During the Mexican War he was promoted to the rank of brevet captain for gallantry and meritorious conduct in the Battle of Monterey on September 23, 1846, and again to the rank of brevet major for his meritorious conduct during the Battle of Buena Vista, on February 23, 1847. Reynolds was killed on July 3, 1863, at the Battle of Gettysburg while "urging on his men with animating words." He was serving as colonel of the 5th Infantry at the time of his death.

14. Heitman, *Register*, vol. 1, p. 263. Martin Burke was commissioned as a second lieutenant of the 8th Infantry on January 28, 1820. He was promoted to the rank of brevet major for his gallantry and meritorious conduct at the Battles of Contreras and Churubusco, on August 20, 1847, and again to the rank of lieutenant colonel for his meritorious conduct at the Battle of Molino del Rey on September 8, 1847. For his services during the Civil War, Burke was promoted to the rank of colonel and brigadier general on March 13, 1865, for "faithful service to his country." He died on April 24, 1882.

15. Townsend, *Anecdotes*, pp. 50-55; Sandburg, *Lincoln*, vol. 4, II, pp. 153-59; vol. 4, III, pp. 55, 271; A Prisoner, *Two Months in Fort Lafayette*. Fort Lafayette, located in New York Harbor, on a diamond-shaped island surrounded by deep water, became known during the Civil War as the "American Bastille." While the Constitution was clear that writs of *habeas corpus* could not be suspended except when "in cases of rebellion or invasion the public safety may require it," it was not clear how this act of suspension was to be performed—by the president acting alone, an act of Congress, or some sort of joint action. Into this legal twilight ventured Secretary of War Edmund Stanton and Secretary of State William Seward, who began arresting "enemies" of the State and holding them in Fort Lafayette without formal arraignment or setting bail. Seward asked General Winfield Scott, commanding the Union Army, to name an officer to command Fort Lafayette who would obey the "extraordinary" orders he planned to issue. Scott immediately responded with the name of Colonel Martin Burke. "Colonel Martin Burke is famous for his unquestioning obedience to orders. He was with me in Mexico, and, if I had told him at any time to take out one of my aides-de-camp and shoot him before breakfast, the aide's execution would have been duly reported." Colonel Burke himself remained a virtual prisoner in Fort Lafayette, as he would allow no civilian visitors, fearing that someone might serve him with a subpoena

to appear in a state court, and he would not leave the guarded premises, lest he himself be arrested and held to answer charges of illegal incarceration. Possibly the most famous Fort Lafayette prisoner was Charles S. Moorehead, the former governor of Kentucky, who had struggled to keep Kentucky as a "neutral" state, and had criticized the actions of Seward. Moorehead was ordered arrested by the secretary of war and held in Fort Lafayette without arraignment or trial for four months. Only through the diligent efforts of John J. Crittenden was the governor released on parole. Seward was widely quoted as boasting to the British Minister in Washington that "I can touch a bell on my right hand and order the arrest of a citizen in Ohio, I can touch the bell again and order the imprisonment of a citizen in New York, and no power on earth but that of the President can release them. Can the Queen of England, in her dominions, say as much?" A Prisoner paints a grim picture of the life of a detainee in Fort Lafayette, listing the names of more than 179 persons who shared these meager quarters and rations with him. Many of these persons were arrested on the streets, held incommunicado, and hustled off to prison in secret. Families anguished over the sudden disappearance of a husband or loved one. In the election of 1864, anti-Lincoln placards appeared with the slogans, "Fort Lafayette to Let," and "We Demand the Habeas Corpus." But such was not to stand and Congress passed the *Habeas Corpus* bill on March 3, 1863, which specified that Congress had control over the *habeas corpus* writ, but authorized the president to suspend this writ. It further ordered that all persons now in prison should be released unless indicted by a grand jury, and that no one should be held in the future for longer than twenty days without being indicted. Finally the executive branch was directed to furnish the names of all persons incarcerated by order of the secretaries of state and war.

16. Heitman, *Register*, vol. 1, p. 653; Cullum, *Register*, vol. 1, p. 233. George Archibald McCall graduated from the United States Military Academy in 1822. McCall served in the Seminole War in 1836, on the northern frontier during Canadian border disturbances in 1838, and on frontier duty at Fort Gibson, 1839-1841. He was promoted to the rank of brevet major for gallant and meritorious conduct in the Battles of Palo Alto and Resaca de la Palma, May 8-9, 1846. McCall resigned his commission on April 23, 1853, and took up farming near West Chester, Pennsylvania. With the outbreak of hostilities in 1861, McCall served as major general of Pennsylvania Volunteers, a state commission. On May 17, 1861, he received the commission of brigadier general of United States Volunteers, and participated in the Battles of Mechanicsville, Gaines Mill, and New Market Cross Roads, where he was captured on June 30, 1862. He was placed in Libby Prison, but was exchanged from there by August 30, 1862. He resigned his commission on March 31, 1863, and died on February 25, 1868.

17. Heitman, *Register*, vol. 1, p. 419; Cullum, *Register*, vol. 1, pp. 604-05. Horace B. Field graduated from the United States Military Academy in 1840 and was assigned to the 3rd Regiment of Artillery. He participated in the Seminole War, 1840-1842, serving in Florida. During the Mexican War he was engaged in the

actions at Galaxara and Matamoras in central Mexico and was promoted to the rank of brevet captain for gallantry and meritorious conduct in the Battle of Huamantla, on October 9, 1847. Field was washed overboard and drowned while en route to duty in Calfornia on the steamer *San Francisco* when she encountered a heavy sea off the Capes of Delaware on December 24, 1853. Field and three other officers, as well as 180 enlisted men of the 3rd Artillery were swept overboard. All were lost save two.

18. Heitman, *Register*, vol. 1, p. 584; Cullum, *Register*, vol. 1, p. 580. Henry Bethel Judd graduated from the United States Military Academy in 1839 and was assigned to the 3rd Regiment of Artillery. He served in the Seminole War, 1839-1841, and in the emigration of Indians to the West in 1841. He returned to Florida, 1841-1842, to campaign against the Seminoles. During the Mexican War, he was engaged in the Siege of Vera Cruz and was promoted to the rank of brevet captain for gallantry and meritorious conduct in the affair at Medelin, on March 25, 1847. Judd participated in the skirmish of Amazoque, and the attack on the San Antonio Garita of the City of Mexico. He retired on November 21, 1861, for health reasons, but continued to serve as a volunteer mustering officer for the Union Army. Judd was promoted to brevet lieutenant colonel on November 13, 1865, for "faithful and meritorious service" connected with the organization of volunteer armies of the United States. He died on July 27, 1892.

19. Heitman, *Register*, vol. 1, p. 176; Cullum, *Register*, vol. 1, p. 560. William Austine graduated from the United States Military Academy in 1838, being known as William A. Brown at the time. During the War with Mexico, he participated in the Battle of Cerro Gordo, skirmish at Amazoque, the capture of San Antonio, and the Battle of Churubusco on August 20, 1847. For his actions at the Battles of Churubusco and Contreras, he was promoted to the rank of brevet major. From 1861 to 1865 he served as superintendent of mustering and volunteer recruiting for the State of Vermont. He retired from active service on February 20, 1862, due to a disability resulting from exposure in the line of duty.

20. Heitman, *Register*, vol. 1, p. 40. The thrifty quartermaster general was Brigadier General Thomas S. Jesup, who served in this position from 1818 to 1860.

21. Heitman, *Register*, vol. 1, p. 702; Cullum, *Register*, vol. 1, pp. 495-96; Coffman, *The Old Army*, p. 240. Montgomery Cunningham Meigs graduated from the United States Military Academy in 1836 and was assigned to the 1st Regiment of Artillery. By 1837 he was transferred to the Corps of Engineers. He was the designer of many civilian and military structures during his tenure in the corps. The civilian structures included extensions to the United States Capitol, the extension of the U.S. Post Office, and the Potomac Aqueduct. Military constructions included Forts Delaware, Porter, Niagara, Montgomery, and Jefferson. On May 14, 1861, he was promoted to the rank of brigadier general and appointed quartermaster general of the Union Army. For his successful efforts at supplying the many far-flung activities of this large army, Meigs was promoted to the rank of brevet major general on

July 5, 1864, for "distinguished and meritorious services during the rebellion." Meigs was an advocate of a harsh reconstruction for the South, even to the hanging of Jefferson Davis and Robert E. Lee. Some said that Meigs had become embittered with the South when his son, John Rodgers Meigs, was killed in Virginia by the guerrilla forces of John Mosby on October 3, 1864. General Meigs retired from the service on February 6, 1882, and died on January 2, 1892.

22. *DAB*, vol. 8, pp. 183-84. George Henry Preble was born in Portland, Maine, on February 25, 1816. His father was a sea captain and a nephew of Commodore Edward Preble. In October, 1835, he was appointed midshipman and in 1841 made passed midshipman. Preble commanded the first armed American landing party in Canton, China, in 1844. He accompanied Perry's mission to Japan, 1853-1856, and commanded a steamer operating against Chinese pirates. During the Civil War, while on blockade duty at Mobile Bay on September 4, 1862, he allowed the Confederate cruiser *Oreto* to break through and enter port. For this error, he was dismissed from the service. But the vigorous protests of his friends caused the secretary of the navy to return Preble to duty at his former rank as commodore in February, 1863. In September, 1864, he commanded the fleet brigade, a land force of 500 men who operated with the army to prepare Sherman's approach to the sea. For his command of land actions, he was commended by Admiral Dahlgren in general orders. In 1874, he was promoted to the rank of commodore and in 1876 was again promoted to rear admiral and commanded the South Pacific Squadron. He retired in 1878, and devoted his efforts to writing about naval history. Preble died on March 1, 1885.

23. DeAnne Blanton (National Archives) to Joseph E. Chance, August 29, 1995, editor's files; Heitman, *Register*, vol. 1, p. 322. The eccentric medical officer for Fort Johnston during Doubleday's tour of duty there was James R. Conrad. Conrad was appointed assistant surgeon on August 21, 1838, and was dropped from the service on June 28, 1853.

24. Coffman, *The Old Army*, pp. 196-98; Ganoe, *History of the U.S. Army*, pp. 173-74; Chamberlain, *My Confession*, pp. 192-96. Until 1812, a court-martial could authorize up to 100 lashes for the punishment of an enlisted man. The army abandoned this form of punishment during and after the War of 1812 as an inducement to recruit a better class of men. But by the 1820s, a strong influx of "the down-and-outer, the foreigner, and the adventurer," into the ranks caused the army to restore corporal punishment. In 1833, Congress authorized fifty lashes for the crime of desertion. But by 1861, needing to induce more recruits into the ranks of the Union Army, an enlightened Congress abolished corporal punishment. A graphic account of the abuses of the corporal punishment system is offered by Chamberlain in his description of actions taken by Captain Thomas "Battery" Sherman to punish enlisted men.

25. Scott, *Memoirs*, vol. 2, pp. 361-66. As general-in-chief of the army, Winfield Scott, concerned with the welfare of the enlisted soldier and the behavior of the

officer corps, issued General Order No. 53 on August 20, 1842. In part, these orders read:

> 1. Intimations, through many channels, received at General Headquarters, lead to more than a suspicion that blows, kicks, cuffs, and lashes, against the law, the good of the service and the faith of the Government, have, in many instances, down to the late period, been inflicted upon private soldiers of the army by their officers and non-commissioned officers.

> 2. Inquiries into the reported abuses are in progress, with instructions, if probable evidence of guilt be found, to bring the offenders to trial.

> 3. It is well known to every vigilant officer that discipline can be maintained (—and it shall be so maintained—) by legal means. Other resorts are, in the end, always destructive of good order and subordination.

> 7. Harsh and abusive words, passionately or wantonly applied to unoffending inferiors, is but little less reprehensible. Such language is, at once, unjust, vulgar, and unmanly ....

> 8. Government not only reposes "special trust and confidence in the patriotism, valor, fidelity, and abilities" of army officers, as is expressed on the face of commissions; but also in their self-control, respect for law and gentlemanly conduct on all such occasions. A failure under either of those heads ought always to be followed by the loss of a commission.

26. Cullum, *Register*, vol. 1, p. 96; vol. 2, p. 11. The parties thought to be involved in this court-martial were most likely Lieutenant George W. Ayres of the 3rd Artillery and the commanding officer of the garrison at Fort Moultrie, Colonel William Gates of the 3rd Artillery. This trial probably occurred between 1842 and 1844. Ayres was killed on September 8, 1847, while leading an assault on the enemy's works at Molino del Rey. Gates retired from the service in 1863 with more than forty-five years of faithful service.

27. Herring, *Fort Caswell*, pp. 1-14. Fort Caswell, at the west side of the mouth of the Cape Fear River, on the southeastern coast of North Carolina, was completed in 1838. The fort, named for North Carolina Revolutionary War hero Richard Caswell, was built to protect the entrance to the river which was wide and deep. Potential invaders of the state could sail on the river up to Fayetteville and from there could disrupt the internal canal and lock system of the state and gain access to the coal fields in Chatham County. The fort was described in records as being "an enclosed pentagonal work, with a two tiered loop-holed escarpment flanked by [cannoneers] galleries extending from the main body of the fort which provide fire, with emplacements for 61 channel bearing guns, mounted en-barbett."

28. Oates, *The Fires of Jubilee*, pp. 1-156. The abortive slave insurrection led by Nat Turner began on August 22, 1831, in Southhampton County, Virginia. About sixty men, women, and children were put to death by a mob of slaves that

marched from one plantation to another along a line from Cross Keys to Courtland, Virginia. The mob was dispersed by Virginia militia, with citizens murdering many innocent blacks in acts of hysterical retribution. The ring leaders were tried and hanged. White slave holders for the first time began to fear their slaves, and subsequent rumors would cause many panics among the white population of this region.

29. Heitman, *Register*, vol. 1, p. 301. Sylvester Churchill was commissioned as a first lieutenant in the 3rd Regiment of Artillery on March 12, 1812. On June 25, 1841, Churchill, at the rank of colonel, was directing the inspector general's department. During the Mexican War, he was promoted to the rank of brevet brigadier general for gallantry and meritorious conduct in the Battle of Buena Vista on February 23, 1847. Churchill continued as inspector general of the Army until September 25, 1861, when he retired from the service. He died on December 7, 1862.

30. Heitman, *Register*, vol. 1, p. 754; Cullum, *Register*, vol. 1, p. 503. John Paul Jones O'Brien graduated from the United States Military Academy in 1836. O'Brien served in operations in the Creek Nation in 1836, and in the Florida War, 1836-1838, where he participated in the Combat of Locha-Hatchee against the Seminoles. In 1838 and 1839 he was engaged in emigrating Indians from Florida to the West. From 1839 to 1841 he was stationed on the Canadian border to quell border disturbances. O'Brien served in Wool's column in 1846 and marched into Mexico to capture Chihuahua. He was promoted to the rank of brevet major for gallant and meritorious conduct during the Battle of Buena Vista on February 23, 1847. After the Mexican War, O'Brien served as quartermaster at La Vaca, Texas, and died at Indianola, Texas, on March 31, 1850, at the age of 32.

31. "Death of the Poet Moore," *Daily National Intelligencer*, March 16, 1852. The lyric poet Thomas Moore was born on May 28, 1780. He studied the law at Trinity College, but his heart was with the lyrical music and song of his people. He was an unabashed lover of Ireland, although when he composed his "Melodies" it was both unsafe and unfashionable to be an Irish patriot. This collection of songs accomplished many of the goals that agitators and Irish nationalists had advocated for centuries. His skill in music, his wit, his knowledge, and his charming conversational powers placed him in the first ranks of his literary contemporaries but he was never ashamed of his country or his origin. He could never resist an occasion to plead the cause of Ireland, especially among the influential persons of his time. Among his many famous compositions are "Believe Me If All Those Endearing Young Charms," "The Last Rose of Summer," and "Oft in the Stilly Night." His friend Lord Byron recorded his thoughts of Ireland and Moore in these few lines:

> My voice, though but humble, was raised for thy right;
> My vote, as a freeman's, still voted thee free;
> This hand, tho' but feeble, would arm in thy fight,
> And this heart, tho' outworn, had a throb still for thee;

For I loved thee and thine, though thou art not my land;
I have known gallant hearts and great souls in thy sons;
And I wept, with the world, o'er the patriot band
Who are gone; but I weep them no longer as once.
But if aught in this bosom can quench for an hour
My contempt for a nation too servile, though sore;
Which, though trod like worms, will not turn upon power.
'Tis the glory of Grattan and genius of Moore.

Thomas Moore died on February 27, 1852, mourned and missed by the world, and especially so in his beloved Ireland.

32. Heitman, *Register*, vol. 1, p. 838. John Cleveland Robinson was a cadet at the United States Military Academy from 1835 to 1838. He joined the service in 1838 at the rank of second lieutenant in the 5th Infantry. During the Civil War he was colonel of the 1st Michigan volunteer regiment and was cited for his actions at Gettysburg, the Wilderness, and Spottsylvania. On March 24, 1895, he was awarded the Congressional Medal of Honor for his actions on May 8, 1864, at Laurel Hill, Virginia, where he "placed himself at the head of his leading brigade in a charge upon the enemy's breastworks where he was severely wounded...." Robinson retired in 1869 at the rank of major general and died on February 18, 1897.

33. Hammond, *The Camera Obscura*, pp. 1-7. The camera obscura is a device for creating the image of an object on a planar surface known as a screen for tracing or other applications. A pinhole aperture creates an inverted image on the screen. The camera obscura was used by many artists as an aid in reproducing images. Later improvements included a lens system that converted the image to an upright position and produced a brightened and enlarged version of the image. In the nineteenth century, the camera obscura became popular with the general public and was used to create shadow drawings and plays for an audience, the forerunner of the modern motion picture. The basic design of the camera obscura was incorporated into the development of the first photographs.

34. Heitman, *Register*, vol. 1, p. 799; Cullum, *Register*, vol. 2, p. 118. Fitz-John Porter graduated from the United States Military Academy in 1845. Porter served in central Mexico with the forces of Winfield Scott, where he participated in the siege of Vera Cruz, and the Battles of Cerro Gordo, Contreras, Molina del Rey, and the capture of Chapultapec Castle. He was promoted to the rank of brevet captain for his actions at Molino del Rey and to the rank of brevet major for gallant and meritorious services in the capture of Chapultapec Castle on September 13, 1847. Porter was wounded, September 13, 1847, at the Belen Gate during the assault on the City of Mexico. With the advent of the Civil War, Porter participated, 1861-1862, in the major battles in northern Virginia, rising to the rank of major general of volunteers on July 4, 1862. For his con-

troversial actions taken while commanding the 5th Corps of the Union Army during the Battle of Second Manassas, Porter was cashiered from the army on January 21, 1863, for violation of the 9th and 52nd Articles of War. He was "forever disqualified from holding any office of trust or profit under the government of the United States." (For more information on Porter's court-martial, see Sandberg, *Lincoln*, vol. 4, pp. 545, 625-26.) Porter vigorously fought to be reinstated and was successful on July 1, 1886. On that date he was reinstated at the rank of colonel. He retired on August 7, 1886, and died on May 21, 1901.

35. Izmir, or Smyrna, is a Turkish city on the eastern coast of the Aegean Sea, about twenty-two miles southwest of Istanbul.

36. *DAB*, vol. 15, p. 75. John Rodgers, the famous American naval officer, was born in 1773 at Havre de Grace, Maryland. Rodgers spent eleven years in the merchant marine, rising to the rank of master by the age of 20. He joined the United States Navy on March 8, 1798, as second lieutenant aboard the *Constellation*. During the naval war with France, Rodgers participated in the capture of the *Insurgente*. Rodgers commanded the *Insurgente* in a cruise, was later transferred to the *Maryland*, and from there sailed on a cruise to the West Indies. From 1802 to 1806 he was in the Mediterranean and participated in the Barbary Wars. Rodgers was commander in chief of the squadron blockading Tripoli on three occasions and as such earned the rank of commodore. He and Commodore Preble negotiated the treaty of peace with Morocco that ended the wars. While on his mission to protect American shipping from British interference, his frigate, *President*, forty-four guns, engaged the British sloop, *Little Belt*, twenty guns, in a fifteen-minute duel that severely damaged the British ship. In the War of 1812, Rodgers was the ranking officer in active service. He commanded the *President* and sailed shipping lanes, capturing eight British merchantmen on one cruise. He led a party of sailors and marines against the British invaders of Washington, but arrived too late to be of service. His last active service was a tour of duty in the Mediterranean, 1825-1827, commanding the American squadron from his flagship, *North Carolina*, seventy-four guns. On May 1, 1837, poor health forced Rodgers to resign his commission, and he died on August 1, 1838.

37. Heitman, *Register*, vol. 1, p. 408; Cullum, *Register*, vol. 2, p. 38. Henry Lawrence Eustis graduated from the United States Military Academy in 1842 and was assigned to the Corps of Engineers. Eustis was involved in the building and repair of lighthouses, forts, and harbor improvements, 1842-1849. He served as assistant professor of engineering at the United States Military Academy in 1849 and resigned his commission on November 30, 1849, to accept a position as professor of engineering at Harvard University. During the Civil War, Eustis served as colonel of the 10th Massachusetts Volunteers and fought at the Battles of Fredericksburg and Gettysburg. Eustis was promoted to the rank of brigadier general of volunteers on September 12, 1863, participating in the Battle of the Wilderness, the battles

around Spottsylvania, and the Battle of Cold Harbor, on June 3-5, 1864. Eustis resigned his commission on June 27, 1864, and died on January 11, 1885.

38. Heitman, *Register*, vol. 1, p. 946; Cullum, *Register*, vol. 1, p. 274. Francis Taylor graduated from the United States Military Academy in 1825. He served in the Florida War against the Seminole Indians, 1836-1837, and fought in the Battle of Wahoo Swamp. He served in Plattsburg, New York, in 1838 and 1839 during the border disturbances with Canada. During the War with Mexico, he participated in the Siege of Vera Cruz and the Battle of Cerro Gordo on April 18, 1847, where he was promoted to the rank of brevet major for gallantry and meritorious conduct. He participated in the skirmishes of La Hoya and Oka Lake. For gallant and meritorious conduct at the Battle of Churubusco on August 20, 1847, Taylor was promoted to the rank of brevet lieutenant colonel. He participated in the capture of the City of Mexico on September 13 and 14, 1847. After the war, Taylor served on a board to devise "A Complete System of Instruction for Siege, Garrison, Sea-Coast, and Mountain Artillery." The board's recommendations were adopted by the service in 1851. Taylor died while serving at Fort Brown, Texas, on October 12, 1858.

39. Ferris, *Soldier and Brave*, pp. 319-20. The site of Fort Clark, Texas, is located in Kenney County on the southern edge of Brackettville. The post was founded in 1852 to guard the San Antonio-El Paso Road and protect the Mexican border from Comanche raids. From this fort in 1873, Colonel Ranald Mackenzie launched a raid into Mexico against Kickapoo and Lipan Indians who were using that country as a sanctuary. The fort remained active during World War II as a cavalry training center but was closed at the end of the war. More than twenty-five buildings remain, three of them of vertical log construction dating to the early 1850s; the remainder are of stone construction dating from the 1850s to the 1880s. The buildings are now used by a privately owned guest ranch which occupies the site.

40. Dillon, *American Artillery*, pp. 14-20; Scribner, *Camp Life*, p. 20; Curtis, *Mexico Under Fire*, p. 8; Rayburn, *Century of Conflict*, p. 41. Company C of the 3rd Artillery, led by Major Samuel Ringgold, developed the tactics for the light battery or horse artillery that would lead the American army to victory in the Mexican War. The bronze six-pounder guns could be rapidly deployed by a team of galloping horses, and subsequently unlimbered and made ready to fire in less than three minutes. In the ammunition box were a variety of munitions: solid shot, shell, spherical case shot, canister, and grape shot. Secretary of War Joel Poinsett was quick to see the potential of this strategy that had been so devasatating in the Napoleonic Wars. In contrast were the Mexican artillery pieces pulled by slowly moving oxen, laboriously placed into firing order and using only a solid shot made of iron or copper. Poinsett designated one company from each of the four regiments of artillery as a company of light artillery. In 1839 Poinsett established a training center at Camp Washington, New Jersey, and designated Ringgold and Company C, 3rd Artillery, to train the other three companies in the new tactics of highly mobile light artillery. These companies in turn returned to

their respective regiments and trained the remaining companies of their regiments. Major Ringgold saw the fruits of his labor at Palo Alto on May 8, 1846, when American horse artillery pounded Mexican forces into a retreat. The much-captured Mexican General Romulo Diaz de la Vega reported sadly to his captors that during the opening of hostilities on May 8, his brigade band had just struck up the lively aire of "Las Zapadores de Jalisco" when an American artillery shell exploded in their midst, killing the band members. Unfortunately, late in the afternoon, while deploying his battery on the field, Ringgold was struck by a Mexican cannon ball that pierced both legs, tearing away most of the flesh from above each knee. Ringgold died the next day after learning of the great American victories in south Texas. Ringgold was interred in the cemetery at Point Isabel, and a volunteer from Indiana, B.F. Scribner, reported that his grave was "enclosed with a wooden fence, the rails of which are filled with holes, so as to admit musket barrels. These form the palings, with bayonets serving as pickets." Ringgold's body was later reinterred in Baltimore, Maryland. A popular lithograph of the period depicts the death of Major Ringgold and his horse, Davy Branch. The big thoroughbred, was reputed to be the fastest horse in the army, and the sporting Ringgold used his speed as a source of extra income.

41. A Subaltern [Braxton Bragg], "Notes on Our Army," vol. 10, pp. 86-88, 155-57, 246-51, 283-87, 372-77, 510-12, 750-53; vol. 11, pp. 39-47, 104-09, in *Southern Literary Messenger*; McWhiney, *Braxton Bragg*, pp. 26-51; Grant, *Personal Memoirs*, p. 343. McWhiney, in his biography of Bragg, appropriately titled the chapter dealing with Bragg's life, 1837-1845, as "Naturally Disputatious." Bragg had taken the army to task in a series of nine anonymous notes published in the *Southern Literary Messenger*, 1844-1845. Following an organizational chart, Bragg began by criticizing the office of secretary of war. The office was regularly held by a civilian with no practical knowledge of field operations who made policy often on the advice of staff officers quartered in Washington. Bragg then pointed out the disproportionate number of staff officers as opposed to line officers and suggested that many of the duties assigned to staff had been routinely done a few years earlier by the line in addition to their other duties. Bragg criticized the duties assigned to the quartermaster and commissary departments: "... drivers of mules and slayers of bullocks clothed with military rank...." Officers in the ordnance department stationed at arsenals could be found in "their fine buildings, pleasure grounds and flower gardens ... enjoying themselves in sweet repose ... and occasionally looking into their workshops, as much from curosity as a sense of duty...." Bragg saved his best ammunition for his attacks on his arch foe, General Winfield Scott, whom he characterized as having an "aspiration for political honors." Scott, according to Bragg, had authored an "indelicate and ungenerous attack" upon a brother officer, General Edmund P. Gaines. McWhiney is careful to point out that several of the changes in the army administration advocated by Bragg were significant and important and were finally adopted in 1903, nearly sixty years later. Perhaps the reluctance for adoption was due to Bragg's venomous style

of writing and caustic, undiplomatic references to "unnamed" military officers that everyone in the military knew by name. These notes were a model for how to offend colleagues and superior officers. Only the superior leadership, resourcefulness and personal bravery that he exhibited in northern Mexico at Monterrey and Buena Vista saved his career.

42. Magoffin, *Down the Sante Fe Trail and into Mexico*, p. 257; Stewart, *John Phoenix, Esq., The Veritable Squibob*, p. 87. Susan Magoffin, while traveling through Monterrey, Mexico, records in her diary this observation of Braxton Bragg:

> Tuesday [August] 31st [1847]
>
> The Gen. invited us out today to see his light artillery under Maj. Bragg reviewed. I was pleased with their manueverings which were both expeditious and beautiful. The Maj. is called a great disciplinarian drilling his men twice a day much to their dissatisfaction, they a few nights since placed a shell with a slow match, intending to kill him, but fortunately tho' it exploded about 11 o'clock shattering the roof of his tent, his trunk, part of his cott, and even piercing the bed-clothing, *he was unhurt*.

Lieutenant. George H. Derby, corresponding with a citizens committee formed to purge San Francisco of criminals, wrote them to request that they keep an "eye" out for a man who had stolen his prize race horse. The letter perhaps exposes the identity of one of the Bragg conspirators:

> Sonoma Cal. June 24 1851
>
> Secretary of the "Vigilance Committee" Sir I have the honor to inform you that a most notorious villain is now in your midst whose arrest I as well as very good citizen must most earnestly desire. His name is Samuel R. Church a deserter from the U.S. service. This man enlisted in Mexico where (if we are to believe his own boastful confession) he had long been connected with a band of robbers, has since his entry into the service been guilty of a continued series of crimes which has caused him to be kept for the majority of the time with a ball and chain attached to his leg. He asserts that he was the man who endeavored to murder Capt. Bragg by placing an exploding shell beneath his bed at the camp near Saltillo.... The man Church is about thirty years old, five feet nine inches high, strongly built, freckled face, light red hair & has lost two or three of his upper front teeth....

By February 12, 1852, the eye of vigilance had focused clearly on Samuel Church, and in a letter to his mother, Derby reported that, "I heard the other day that Church had been arrested again in Stockton for stealing another horse and hung, and I am very glad of it!"

43. Watkins, *"Co. Aytch": A Confederate Soldier's Memoirs*, pp. 48-50. Sam Watkins, a private in the Confederate 1st Tennessee Regiment, remembered the harsh discipline of General Braxton Bragg, and its impact on the enlisted men:

They had no love or respect for General Bragg. When men were to be shot or whipped, the whole army was marched to the horrid scene to see a poor trembling wretch tied to a post and a platoon of twelve men drawn up in line to put him to death, and the hushed command of "Ready, aim, fire!" would make the soldier or conscript, I should say, loathe the very name of the Southern Confederacy. And when some miserable wretch was to be whipped and branded for being absent ten days without leave, we had to see him kneel down and have his head shaved smooth and slick as a peeled onion, and then stripped to the naked skin. Then a strapping fellow with a big rawhide would make the blood flow and spurt at every lick, the wretch begging and howling like a hound, and then he was branded with a red hot iron with the letter D on both hips, when he was marched through the whole army to the music of the "Rogue's March." It was enough. None of General Bragg's soldiers ever loved him. They had no faith in his ability as a general. He was looked upon as a merciless tyrant. The soldiers were very scantily fed. Bragg was never a good feeder or commissary-general. Rations with us were always scarce.... No coffee or whiskey or tobacco were ever allowed to be issued to the troops. If they obtained these luxuries, they were not from the government. These luxuries were withheld in order to crush the very heart and spirit of his troops. We were crushed. Bragg was the great autocrat. In the mind of the soldier, his word was law. He loved to crush the spirit of the men. The more a hang-dog look they had about them the better was General Bragg pleased. Not a single soldier in the whole army ever loved or respected him.

44. Heitman, *Register*, vol. 1, p. 582. Roger Jones was commissioned as second lieutenant in the Marines Corps in 1809. During the War of 1812, he was promoted to the rank of brevet major on July 5, 1814, for distinguished service in the conflict of Chippewa, Upper Canada, and again promoted to the rank of brevet lieutenant colonel for his participation in the sortie from Fort Erie, Upper Canada, on September 17, 1814. Jones was promoted to the rank of colonel on September 17, 1824, and brigadier general on September 17, 1832, for "ten years faithful service in one grade." He was promoted to the rank of major general on May 30, 1848, for "meritorious conduct particularly in performance of his duties in the prosecution of the War with Mexico." Jones died on July 15, 1852.

45. *DAB*, vol. 8, p. 182. Fort Preble was named for Commodore Edward Preble, famous for his actions against the Barbary Pirates. Preble was a native son of Portland, Maine.

46. *National Cyclopedia*, vol. 8, pp. 118-19. Seba Smith, the editor and author, was born in Buckfield, Maine, on September 4, 1792. He was a graduate of Bowdoin College in 1818 and practiced law in Portland, Maine. He was editor of *Eastern Argus*, a state-wide journal, and in 1830 started the *Portland Daily Courier*. He is probably best remembered for his humorous and satirical letters and books about the mythical Major Jack Downing. Major Downing was a character devised by Smith to cast humor on politics and politicians, especially the administration of

President Andrew Jackson. Smith, however, considered his best effort to be *New Elements of Geometry* written in 1850 as a spoof on this time-honored branch of mathematics. Smith and his talented wife Elizabeth Prince Smith, who wrote under the name of E. Oakes Smith, greatly added to the intellectual climate of Portland, Maine. Smith died on July 29, 1868.

47. *DAB*, vol. 13, pp. 398-99. John Neal, born in Portland, Maine, on August 25, 1793, was the son of a Quaker schoolmaster. He was noted for his literary prose and poetry, his work as a literary editor, and as an entrepeneur. The subjects in his romantic novels were often unflattering caricatures of his fellow Americans. He was, on occasion, challenged to a duel for pricks given by his sharp quill and threatened repeatedly for his reflections on the local characters that appeared in his novels. But Neal was fearless and would not suffer a fool. He was dismissed from the Society of Friends, in his own words, "for knocking a man who insulted him head over heels; for paying a militia fine; for making a tragedy; and for desiring to be turned out, whether or no." He remained vigorous and healthy throughout his life; at the age of seventy-nine he physically ejected a local tough from a horsecar for refusing to extinguish his cigar. From 1823 to 1827, Neal lived in England, and published several articles on American politics in *Blackwood's Magazine*. On his return to America, he edited the *Yankee*, a literary magazine published in Portland. He encouraged contributions from young writers such as Whittier and Poe. Poe remarked that "the very first words of encouragement I ever remember to have heard" came from Neal. Neal became wealthy by his investments in real estate and the granite quarries of Maine. Neal was a lifelong friend of Longfellow, who undoubtedly encouraged and stimulated his literary production. He died in Portland on June 20, 1876.

48. Heitman, *Register*, vol. 1, p. 684; Cullum, *Register*, vol. 1, p. 367; Freemantle, *Three Months in the Southern States*, pp. 34-37. John Bankhead Magruder graduated from the United States Military Academy in 1830 and was assigned to the 7th Infantry. He was transferred to the 1st Artillery in 1831, and served in coastal garrisons until 1837. From 1837 to 1838 Magruder participated in the Florida War. The Canadian border disturbances brought him to Fort Columbus and Plattsburg, New York, 1838-1840. During the Mexican War Magruder participated with Taylor's forces in the Battles of Palo Alto and Resaca de la Palma. He was transferred to Scott's forces and participated in the Siege of Vera Cruz. Magruder was awarded a brevet for meritorious conduct at the Battle of Cerro Gordo, and served in the skirmishes of La Hoya and Oka Lake. Magruder saw action at the Battles of Contreras and Molino del Rey and was awarded a second brevet for participation in the storming of Chapultepec Castle. He completed his active service in Mexico by participating in the capture of Mexico City. After the war, he served on frontier duty at San Diego, California, 1850-1851, in Texas at Fort Clark, 1855-1856, and at Fort Leavenworth, Kansas, 1859-1860. He was stationed in Washington, D.C., on garrison duty, when he resigned his commission in 1861. Magruder rose to the rank of major general in the Confederate Army, and died on

February 19, 1871. Lieutenant Colonel Arthur J. L. Freemantle, of Her Majesty's Coldstream Guards, had a notable dinner party with Magruder on the plains of Texas on April 15, 1863, and offers this description of the man:

> General Magruder, who commands in Texas, is a fine soldierlike man, of about fifty-five, with broad shoulders, a florid complexion, and bright eyes. He wears his whiskers and mustaches in the English fashion, and was dressed in the Confederate gray uniform.... He asked after several officers of my regiment whom he had known when he was on the Canadian frontier. He is a Virginian, a great talker, and has always been a great ally of English officers.... The General, who spoke of the Puritans with intense disgust, and of the first importation of them as "that pestiferous crew of the Mayflower;" but he is by no means rancorous against individual Yankees. He spoke very favorably of M'Clellan, whom he knew to be a gentleman, clever, and personally brave, though he might lack moral courage to face responsibility. Magruder had commanded the Confederate troops at Yorktown which opposed M'Clellan's advance. He told me the different dodges he had resorted to, to blind and deceive the latter as to his (Magruder's) strength; and he spoke of the intense relief and amusement with which he had at length seen M'Clellan with his magnificent army, begin to break ground before miserable earthworks, defended only by 8,000 men. After dinner we had numerous songs. Both the General and his nephew sang.... On these festive occasions General Magruder wears a red woollen cap, and fills the president's chair with great aptitude.

49. Swanberg, *First Blood*, pp. x, 7; Doubleday, *Reminiscences of Forts Sumter and Moultrie*, p. 161-62. Moultrieville was located on Sullivan Island; located just north of the main channel into the harbor of Charleston, South Carolina. The resort town took its name from Fort Moultrie, also on the island. Abner Doubleday, a defender of Fort Sumter during its famous bombardment at the onset of the Civil War, remembered this incident concerning Moultrieville:

> There was a large, first-class hotel, near the shore, on Sullivan's Island, called the Moultrie House ... a favorite resort, for planters and others, to enjoy the fresh sea-breeze.... Since the rebel occupation of Fort Moultrie, this hotel had been used as a depot and barracks for the troops in the vicinty.... I therefore aimed two forty-two pounder balls at the upper story. The crashing of the shot, which went through the whole length of the building among the clapboards and interior partitions, must have been something fearful to those who were within. They came rushing out in furious haste.... When we left Fort Sumter, a South Carolina officer, who seemed to feel aggrieved in relation to this matter, asked me why we fired at that building. Not caring to enter into a discussion at that time, I evaded it by telling him the true reason was, that the landlord had given me a wretched room there one night, and this being the only opportunity that had occured to get even with him, I was unable to resist it.

2: FIRST SHOTS OF THE MEXICAN WAR

1. Heitman, *Register*, vol. 1, p. 374; Cullum, *Register*, vol. 1, p. 188. Justin Dimmick graduated from the United States Military Academy in 1819. He was promoted to the rank of brevet captain on May 1, 1834, for ten years faithful service at one grade. On May 8,1836, Dimmick was promoted to the rank of brevet major for gallant and meritorious conduct in the war against the Florida Indians. In a skirmish near Hernandez Plantation, Dimmick killed two Seminole Indians in personal combat. He was stationed on the Canadian Border, 1838-1840, to suppress disturbances brought on by the border dispute with Great Britain. During the Mexican War, he participated in the Battles of Palo Alto and Resaca de la Palma. In central Mexico he was active at the skirmish of La Hoya, and promoted to the rank of brevet lieutenant colonel for his gallantry at the Battles of Churubusco and Contreras on August 20, 1847. He was wounded in the assault on Chapultepec Castle and promoted to brevet colonel for his actions in that engagement. Dimmick participated in the capture of the City of Mexico on September 13 and 14, 1847, and was appointed the military governor of Vera Cruz, 1847-1848. He returned to Florida, 1848-1849 and 1856-1857, to suppress Seminole Indian hostilities. Dimmick was retired from the service on August 1, 1863, being "over the age of 62 years." On March 13, 1865, he was promoted to brevet brigadier general for "long, gallant, and faithful services to his country." Dimmick died on October 13, 1871. His son, Justin E. Dimmick was also a professional soldier. He graduated from the United States Military Academy in 1861 and died from wounds received at the Battle of Chancellorsville on May 5, 1863.

2. Heitman, *Register*, vol. 1, p. 407. John Erving received his commission in 1809. He was promoted to brevet major on April 25, 1828, for ten years faithful service at one grade. Erving retired from the service on October 26, 1861, at the rank of colonel and died on October 26, 1862.

3. Grant, *Personal Memoirs*, pp. 47-48; Dana, *Monterrey Is Ours!* p. 103. Taylor had divided his Army of Occupation in Corpus Christi into two brigades. The 1st Brigade was commanded by Brevet Brigadier General William J. Worth, and the 2nd Brigade by Colonel David E. Twiggs. Twiggs was the senior of the two at the rank of colonel, but Worth claimed seniority by virtue of his brevet rank of brigadier general. When Taylor scheduled a review of the army prior to their departure for the Rio Grande, he gave the command of the troops to Twiggs. Worth protested and refused to participate in the review until the question of brevet rank could be resolved. The issue was hotly debated among the officers of the army with petitions sent to Congress asking for redress. Taylor, not wanting to start a feud that would divide the officer corps, wisely cancelled the review and forwarded the question of brevet rank to Washington for resolution. The response, in favor of Twiggs, arrived a few days after Taylor's arrival on the Rio Grande. An indignant Worth resigned and left the army by April 8, 1846. With

time to rethink his position, Worth subsequently tendered his services again to the army and was accepted at his former rank. He rejoined the army at Camargo on July 29, 1846.

4. Heitman, *Register*, vol. 1, p. 976; Kenly, *Maryland Volunteer*, p. 119; Diary of Sgt. James Mullen, Jr., Entry for Sept. 15, 1846 (Justin Smith Transcripts, Latin American Collection, University of Texas, Austin). David Emanuel Twiggs was commissioned as a captain in the 8th Infantry in 1812. By 1846, he had risen to the rank of colonel, commanding the 2nd Dragoons. He was promoted to the rank of brigadier general in June, 1846, and received a brevet for his actions at Monterrey on September 23, 1846, and was voted a sword by Congress on March 2, 1847, "in testimony of the high sense entertained by Congress of his gallantry and good conduct in storming Monterrey." Kenly remembered, however, that:

> on the day of battle I saw General Twiggs when he came upon the field riding from the direction of camp, but well out of the range of the guns of the citadel. This was, I think, about noon; it might have been a little earlier, but it was after the repulse of our first assault. I was so struck with his coming almost alone and in such very unmilitary garb, that he noticed me, and, approaching, said, "I expected a battle to-day, but I didn't think it would come off so soon, and took a dose of medicine last night, as I always do before a battle so as to loosen my bowels; for a bullet striking the belly when the bowels were loose might pass through the intestines without cutting them." I was very much interested at hearing all this from so old a soldier ....

Twiggs' late entry into the Battle of Monterrey was noted by his highly verbal nemesis, Charles Kingsbury, in an acid letter appearing in the press, under a pseudonym (see Chapter 10). Twiggs was noted among his fellow soldiers for his rich and inventive use of profanity. Sergeant James Mullen, Jr., noted that, "Twiggs is a horse he can Curse a man right out of his boots." The white-haired Twiggs, known as "Old Orizaba," was a very robust and active man. Twiggs was dismissed from the service on March 1, 1861, for his handling of the surrender of the Military District of Texas to the Confederacy. He was later commissioned as a major general in the Confederate States Army, but was too old and infirm to take the field. He died on July 15, 1862.

5. Heitman, *Register*, vol. 1, pp. 593, 601, 816; Cullum, *Register*, vol. 1, p. 592; Hitchcock, *Fifty Years in Camp and Field*, p. 203; "Orders of General Zachary Taylor to the Army of Occupation in the Mexican War," Order No. 17, September 30, 1845, Order No. 22, October 14, 1845, Order No. 24, October 17, 1845 (National Archives, Washington, D.C.); I. Smith, *Reminiscences of a Campaign in Mexico*, pp. 40, 99; *New Orleans Tropic*, March 31, 1847. Charles Peoble Kingsbury graduated from the United States Military Academy in 1840 and was assigned to ordnance. From 1840 to 1845 he served as assistant ordnance officer variously at the arsenals of Watervliet, Fort Monroe, Washington, D.C., and Detroit. During the Mexican War, he was with Taylor's command at Corpus

Christi assigned to ordnance and served as chief of ordnance for Wool's column on the march through Chihuahua. Kingsbury was brevetted for gallant and meritorious conduct in the Battle of Buena Vista on February 23, 1847. He served briefly in the ordnance department at Point Isabel, Texas, in 1847. After the Mexican War, he commanded the ordnance departments of several arsenals. In 1861 he served as superintendent of Harper's Ferry Armory and ordered the destruction of this arsenal to prevent it from falling into the hands of the advancing Confederates. Kingsbury served as a staff officer in the Army of the Potomac until 1863. From 1863 until 1865, he engaged in arming and equipping volunteers from the states of Iowa, Wisconsin, and Minnesota. He was brevetted for "gallant and meritorious services during the rebellion" to the rank of brigadier general, but reverted to the rank of lieutenant colonel after the war. Kingsbury retired from the service on December 31, 1870, and died December 25, 1879. He was an author of *Elementary Treatise on Artillery and Infantry*, a contributor to the *American Whig Review*, *Putnam's Monthly*, and the *Southern Literary Messenger*. Ethan Allen Hitchcock, ever the moralist and prude, wrote from the camp at Corpus Christi in his diary:

> 3d Oct. It is noteworthy that since the arrival of the 2d Dragoons there have been several disgraceful brawls and quarrels, to say nothing of drunken frolics. The dragoons have made themselves a public scandal. One captain has resigned to avoid trial, and two others have had a dirty brawl. Two others are on trial for fighting over a low woman.

Kingsbury had agreed to defend Captain Croghan Ker of the 2nd Dragoons against charges that Ker "did strike and fight with first lieutenant Owen P. Ransom of the 2nd Regiment U.S. Dragoons—this at the Dragoon Camp, Corpus Christi, Texas on the 29th day of September, 1845." Captain Ker was convicted of "conduct to the prejudice of good order and military discipline" and sentenced to be suspended from rank and pay proper for three months and confined to the station of his company during this period of time. Ker, however, was found not guilty on the more serious charge of violation of the 27th Article of War, due to the extenuating circumstance brought on by Lieutenant Ransom's attempts to renew a "personal contest" even after Ker had been placed under arrest. The object of this "personal contest" may have been the favors of a woman, as delicately suggested by Doubleday and Hitchcock, but the official records do not sustain this claim. Owen P. Ransom was dismissed from the service on November 3, 1845, an action quite likely taken as a consequence of this incident. Ker resigned his commission on November 10, 1851. Isaac Smith wrote an account of the campaign in northern Mexico from the Indiana volunteer soldier's point-of-view. Smith accused Kingsbury and other regular officers of slandering the American volunteer soldiers' services in Mexico.

The next attack that was made upon the Indianians was from the pen of Lieutenant Kingsbury, over the anonymous signature of "BUENA VISTA." "It is unnecessary to refer to this extraordinary letter .... We may expect such an one to slander us, without cause, and we envy not his praise."

Smith replied to Kingsbury in like kind by accusing him of selling ordnance supplies to volunteer officers that should have been issued routinely.

6. Jefferson, *Autobiography*, pp. 49-50; Mahone, *History of the Second Seminole War*, pp. 277-78; Peters, *The Florida Wars*, p. 201; *The American Flag*, July 19, 1846. This was not the first American war in which theatrical groups performed for the troops. During the Seminole Wars, William C. Forbes led a company of actors into Florida. Around May 19, 1840, this troupe was attacked while moving from the steamboat landing at Picolata to St. Augustine by a band of Seminoles led by Wild Cat. Three actors were killed, and three escaped. According to Jefferson:

> The theatrical wardrobe [eighteen trunks] belonging to the company fell into the hands of the Indians, who, dressing themselves up as Romans, Highlanders, and Shaksperean [sic] heroes, galloped about in front of the very fort, though well out of gunshot, where Forbes and the more fortunate members of his company had fled for safety. Several of the Indians were afterwards taken, and as they were robed and decked in the habilments of Othello, Hamlet, and a host of other Shaksperean [sic] characters ... their identity as the murderers was established, and they were hanged in front of the garrison.

General W. J. Worth was surprised at a scheduled meeting between American forces and the Seminoles on March 5, 1841, when Wild Cat appeared in the "nodding plumes, sock and busk" of Hamlet. From among the accompanying warriors in his party, one was dressed in the "simple garb" of Horatio, while another sported the royal purple and ermine of Richard, III, and others were decked in spangles, feathers, and crimson vests. Wild Cat solemnly greeted Worth and no one from the American delegation dared even to smile.

In an article titled, "My Lord, the Players are Come," the editor of *The American Flag* announced the arrival in Matamoros of the acting troupe that had previously entertained the troops in Corpus Christi. The troupe consisted of Mrs. Hart, Mrs. Jefferson, Mrs. Irwin, Miss Jefferson, Miss Christian, Miss Bradley, Miss Irwin, and Messrs Hart, Jefferson, Wells, and Smith. "Mrs Hart has long been a favorite with the army, and her admirers muster strong about Matamoros at this time. She has great versatility of talent and knows well how to please the public taste ...."

Young Joseph Jefferson remembered that the troupe, which he characterized as "our gallant band of comedians," was given permission to occupy the old Spanish theater. "The soldiers, settlers, gamblers, rag-tag and bob-tail crowd that always follow on in the train of an army ... were ready for amusement. Here we acted to the most motley group that ever filled a theater." By mid-September, the troupe's manager skipped town with all the cash and back salaries, leaving the actors "on [their] own resources."

7. Longstreet, *From Manassas to Appomattox*, p. 20; *Corpus Christi Gazette*, January 8, 1846; Meade, *The Life and Letters of George Gordon Meade*, pp. 43-44. Lieutenant Longstreet remembered that:

> The officers built a theatre, depending upon their own efforts to reimburse them. As there was no one outside the army except two rancheros within a hundred miles, our dramatic company was organized from among the officers, who took both male and female characters. In farce and comedy we did well enough, and soon collected funds to pay for the building and incidental expenses. The house was filled every night. General Worth always encouraged us, General Taylor sometimes, and General Twiggs occasionally. We found ourselves in funds sufficient to send over to New Orleans for costumes, and concluded to try tragedy. The "Moor of Venice" was chosen, Lieutenant Theodoric Porter to be the Moor, and Lieutenant Grant to be the daughter of Brabantio. But after rehearsal Porter protested that male heroines could not support the character nor give sentiment to the hero, so we sent over to New Orleans and secured Mrs. Hart, who was popular with the garrisons in Florida.

The reviews of these performances were mixed at best. Complimentary notices included "a fair company of actors," and "very clever," to the harsher verdict of Lieutenant George Gordon Meade that the performers were "a company of strolling actors, who murder tragedy, burlesque, and comedy, and render farce into buffonery … a low flung company."

8. Heitman, *Register*, vol. 1, p. 799; Cullum, *Register*, vol. 1, p. 177. Giles Porter graduated from the United States Military Academy in 1818 and was assigned to the 1st Regiment of Artillery. He was engaged during the Florida War at the Skirmish at Okihumphy Swamp on March 30, 1836, and the Battle of Wahoo Swamp on November 21, 1836. In 1838, Porter participated in the emigration of the Cherokee Nation to the West. He was stationed on the northern frontier during the Canadian border disturbances, 1838-1841. Porter served on garrison duty at St. Joseph's Island, Point Isabel, and Fort Brown during the Mexican War. He served as commander of the Artillery Battalion, 1849-1851, and again in that capacity, 1853-1856. Porter was reported ill, 1860-1861, and retired from active service on September 3, 1861, after having served for more than forty consecutive years. Porter died on May 31, 1878.

9. Newcomb, *The Indians of Texas*, pp. 133-53; Ferrell, *Monterrey Is Ours!* p. 13. The Tonkawa Indians roamed central Texas and lived by hunting, gathering, and fishing, practicing no agriculture. The expedition of Alonso de Leon in 1690 made contact with Tonkawas in the area of Victoria and Lavaca Counties. The Tonkawas were not cannibals but did consume the flesh of their enemies as a ritual practice. They believed that the consumption of parts of an enemy's body might allow them to either destroy or control his spirit. That is, if the enemy were brave, the consumer of his flesh would become brave, or if the enemy were strong, then they might become strong by this ritual. Finally, the ritual was considered as

an insult to the kinsman of the dead warrior, who had not been courageous enough to prevent his death. The tribe became extinct by the end of the nineteenth century due to disease and the consolidation of their tribe with larger tribes. Lieutenant Napoleon Jackson Tecumseh Dana recorded an Indian visit to the army camp at Corpus Christi:

> September 21 (1845)—Yesterday we had a visit from some Lipan Indians, regular wild, fierce warriors, fine-looking Indians, mounted on horseback, painted red and brown, and dressed off with buckskins, buffalo tails, and other ornaments. One fellow had a pair of leggins I would much liked to have got, but I was afraid to ask him for fear he would want to eat a piece of me. Their dresses were very funny. One fellow had his navel painted vermillion, with black around it. They are a bold set of fellows, but their tribe is small. The Comanches are the sovereigns of the prairies of Texas.

10. Warnock, *Texas Cowboy*, p. 23. A real Texas horse wrangler who worked the ranches of the Texas border in the early twentieth century, Roland Warnock, had this to say about the famous mustang:

> Our horses were all raised in the brush country. A real good cowboy—a man that makes his living that way—thinks a lot of his horse and takes care of him. A horse has got to be raised in that brush country to make a good brush horse. They are a smaller horse, but they are quick as lightning and can do most anything except talk. These little horses were awful tough and could stand lots of hard work in that heat. It gets awful hot down there. I don't believe thoroughbred horses could stand the hard work that the little Spanish horses used to do down on the border. They know exactly what you're after when you start out in there after those cows. Their ears are pointed forward and they're looking for cattle just as hard as you are. When they see one, they'll take out after it—quick—and if you don't watch out, you'll fall off.

11. "From the Army in Texas," *New Orleans Picayune*, November 5, 1845. Braxton Bragg, addressing a letter signed with his familiar *nom de plume* "Subaltern" to the *Picayune*, titled "Correction of an Official Misstatement," strived to set the record straight. In a fuming response to a letter published in September, which attempted to explain the organization of the artillery as a branch of the army, Bragg launched into an attack on the inefficient use and supply of field artillery in Taylor's Army of Occupation, then wintering at Corpus Christi. Bragg closed his caustic letter of rebuke by pointing a finger of guilt:

> Every attempt to equip these companies for field service has been thwarted by our ponderous and inefficient Quartermaster's Department. When ordered to supply horses here, by General Taylor, they have purchased the mustangs, or wild horses of the prairies—animals about one-third the size the average size of our horses—and about as suitable for artillery as goats would be for carriage horses. It is charitable to suppose this originated in ignorance ....

12. Ferrell, *Monterrey is Ours!* p. 13; Croffut, *Fifty Years in Camp and Field*, pp. 206-07; Briscoe, *City by the Sea*, p. 111. After a short stay with Taylor's forces camped near Corpus Christi, Lieutenant N. J. T. Dana, reported on September 22, 1845, that "All the people around here [Corpus Christi] are rascals. There is not a man of them who is not a renegade from justice from our country, some for crime, some for debt." The city had grown by January 1, 1846, and, according to Croffut, Ethan Allen Hitchcock wrote on that date:

> Mild and balmy. The day will go as other days—drinking, horse-racing, gambling, theatrical amusements. A ball is advertised for this evening in Corpus Christi. Colonel [Henry L.] Kinney thinks there are 2000 people here besides the army. They are nearly all adventurers, brought here to speculate on events growing out of the presence of troops and the uncertain state of things between the United States and Mexico. There are no ladies here, and very few women.

Many of the officers of Taylor's army felt the same way about the residents of Corpus Christi. Lieutenant Richard H. Wilson, adjutant for the 7th Infantry, considered Corpus Christi "the most murderous, thieving, gambling, God-forsaken hole in the Lone Star State or out of it...."

13. Webb, *Handbook of Texas*, vol. 1, p. 406; *American Flag*, September 16, 19, 23; October 17, 21, 31; November 7, 1846; April 3, 1847; C. Smith, *Chile Con Carne*, p. 341; Dana, *Monterrey is Ours!* p. 13; Chapman, *The News From Brownsville*, p. 93. Louis P. Cooke was born in Tennessee in 1811 and was a student at the United States Military Academy but left before graduation to come to Texas and fight in the revolution. He arrived too late to participate in the Battle of San Jacinto but stayed in Texas to serve in the Army of the Republic. Cooke rose to the rank of lieutenant colonel in the army before seeking political office. He was elected and served in the Third Congress and in the administration of Mirabeau B. Lamar, served as secretary of the navy from May 2, 1839, to December 13, 1841. Cooke served in the Sixth Congress, where he introduced the Texas Homestead Exemption Law and served on the committee to select a site for the capitol. Cooke was a trader and moved from Corpus Christi to Matamoros with the American Army in June, 1846, to open a store on the corner of Calle Teran and the Public Square in partnership with a man named Humphreys. To retaliate against Mexican guerrilla attacks on American travelers in northern Mexico, Cooke organized a retaliatory raid in September, 1846. Cooke and his party burned the Rancho de los Animos, Ranchos de las Masa, and the Rancho Surestio, supposedly owned by the bandits Juan Antonio Byene and Chica Trevino. A man captured at Ranchos de las Masa, one Marteas Garza, was identified as a bandit and murdered by the Cooke party. Cooke's men were never punished for this banditry by the American occupiers of Matamoros, but on September 23 a lone Mexican rider entered Market Square in Matamoros, rode up to Señor Jesus Garcia, the guide for the Cooke party, and shot him dead in broad daylight. Onlookers were too stunned by the sudden action to respond, and "The assassin, a large fine looking Mexican,

wheeled his horse as soon as he had discharged his pistol and galloped to the further corner of the Square, where he halted and turned round to see if he had made sure his aim; being satisfied, he cooly replaced his pistol in his belt, put spurs to his horse and was soon out of sight."

Compton Smith, a surgeon with Taylor's army in northern Mexico offers this brief description of Cooke: "He has figured largely as an Indian fighter; has carried as evidence of his acquaintance with the Camanches, in an ugly scar, made by an arrow-head, which crashed through the cheek bone, had entered his right eye, tearing it completely from the socket." This disfiguring injury might partly explain Cooke's intense dislike of Indians. Dana reported an incident that documents Cooke's dislike:

September 22—The chief of the Lipan tribe of Indians was shot by some rascal last night in a very cowardly manner. I should think the old fellow had nine lives, for he will not die from this, and he was shot enough to kill a half a dozen men. Some rascal got him out in the dark to take a drink, and then drew a six-barreled pistol and shot the chief in the forehead. He fell, but the ball did not penetrate. It traveled round the skull. He was again shot in the breast, when miraculously again the ball struck a rib and instead of penetrating it traversed around and came out at the back. He then got up and ran, when the ruffian took him in the neck and shoulder with a load of buckshot. A Colonel Cook here, a leading man at this place, but an outlaw from the States, with ten-thousand dollars reward on his head, was suspected, but he stoutly denies it to General Taylor and says he had gone to bed. A long time ago this colonel had his eye put out in a fight by an Indian arrow, and he says this is the man who did it. For which he swears to kill him if he finds him on the altar.

Cooke was constantly in demand for transporting trader's goods from Matamoros to the lucrative markets at Monterrey because his wagon and mule trains were seldom raided by Mexican guerrillas. By the end of the war, Cooke had settled in Matamoros; and from across the Rio Grande at Brownsville, Mrs. Chapman commented in a letter dated December 10, 1848, on his choice of residency:

Colonel Cooke, a Texan, who entered at West Point, but left and who held some high office in the State Government is also living in the same city [Matamoros], a fugitive from justice and is, if things may be called by their right name, a cold blooded murderer. He was tried and eleven jurors were against him but the twelfth refused to hang him. He was remanded and broke jail. Cooke and his wife, Mary A. Cooke, were both victims of a cholera epidemic that swept Brownsville in 1849, and died there.

14. Heitman, *Register*, vol. 1, p. 698; *New Orleans Picayune*, June 16, 1846; Chamberlain, *My Confession*, pp. 106, 108, 111, 126; Curtis, *Mexico Under Fire*,

pp. 70-71. Charles Augustus May joined the 2nd Dragoons on June 8, 1836, at the rank of second lieutenant. By the eve of the Mexican war, he had risen to the rank of captain. He was promoted to brevet major for his services in the Battle of Palo Alto, to brevet lieutenant colonel for actions the next day at Resaca de la Palma, and to the rank of brevet colonel for actions at Buena Vista. After the war, he received a promotion to major in 1855, and resigned from the service in 1861. He died on December 24, 1864. Charles May was lionized by the penny press after the first battles of the Mexican War to satisfy the needs of an American public for a war hero. A correspondent at Matamoros described May as:

> such a man as one would expect to meet after hearing so much of his gallant exploits on the battle-field. He is a soldier heart, hand, and soul. In height he is about six feet four inches, rather slim but bountifully supplied with bone and sinew, with a beard hanging down upon his breast and his hair resting upon his shoulders—his figure as straight as an arrow, clear blue eyes, handsome teeth ... his appearance is as distingue [sic] as the most romantic could desire for one whose courage and activity has won for him so high a name.

Samuel Chamberlain, private soldier of May's regiment, did not think of his captain in such flattering terms, referring instead to May in Aesopian terms as a classic case of the "Ass in the Lion's skin." General de la Vega, reported by the press to have been captured by May, was in fact captured by a bugler, asserted Chamberlain. What's more, May had shown an extreme amount of timidness at Buena Vista, more than Chamberlain thought proper for a man referred to throughout America as the "Hero of Resaca." However, May could react with heroism against the arbitrary orders of a humbug volunteer general. Franklin Smith, not an admirer of General Robert Patterson, recorded this scene from the caliche streets of Camargo:

> The General issued an order that no wagons or horsemen should pass the street facing his palace door.—It is the principal street leading to the landing and one side at least very inconvenient to go round.—Twenty times a day he and his orderly and the sentry on his pavement have been thrown into spasms at ignorant teamsters and horsemen endeavouring to pass.—He has consequently lost a great deal of sleep, had to swallow much unmilitary dust, and he's doubtless had a fit of indigestion .... Col. May and Lieutenant [Forbes] Britton affecting not to understand the order or to forget it gallop past the palace door a dozen times a day with lightning speed and raising a devil of a dust lost in the clouds of their own creation before the sentinel has time to call a halt. Now to send Britton to the guard house would be an easy matter but to imprison the gallant May now the darling son of America and dear to all the hearts for galloping down in a public street in a town which he helped to conquer must give the Comdg. Genl pause ....

15. Starker, *Wildlife of Mexico*, pp. 464-70; Henry, *Campaign Sketches*, pp. 41-42. Doubleday was describing *felis onca, el tigre*—the jaguar, a cat native to coastal and

near inland Mexico that ranges as far north as the Texas coast. The adult male can reach weights of 250 pounds and can be dangerous if wounded or cornered. The color can range from solid black, to tan, to a golden tan that is spotted with black rosettes. The jaguar will make ground dens or seek shelter in caves. Their principal diet consists of deer, javelinas, and cattle when possible. The jaguar presents a threat to the cattle ranchers of Mexico, and many large ranches retain professional hunters to thin the jaguar population. Henry reported that American soldiers in Taylor's command killed a "panther" while hunting near Corpus Christi, Texas, in 1845. The cat weighed 160 pounds, was seven feet eight inches from tip to tip, and stood four feet in height. According to Henry, "The spotted tigers are terrible animals, and the fiercest hunting-dogs cower at their approach." A documented sighting of the jaguar in south Texas occurred as late as 1953 along Petronila Creek, south of Corpus Christi. The sound of the roar of *el tigre* at night in the monte must still give rise to thoughts of a more primeval time when man was not only a hunter, but sometimes the hunted.

16. Starker, *Wildlife of Mexico*, pp. 399-405. *Canis lupus, el lobo*—the wolf has probably been exterminated in south Texas and exists in Mexico only in the Sierra Madre Occidental and the arid mountains of western Coahuila and eastern Chihuahua. The wolf is brown or gray in color; the adult male can reach weights of 100 pounds. Even a small wolf is quite a bit larger than a coyote; they should not be confused. The wolf's consumption of domestic animals such as cattle, sheep, goats, burros, and horses has brought about its widespread extermination by ranchers.

17. Heitman, *Register*, vol. 1, p. 895; Cullum, *Register*, vol. 1, p. 280. Charles Ferguson Smith graduated from the United States Military Academy in 1825 and was assigned to the 2nd Artillery. He served at West Point, 1829-1842, as instructor, adjutant, and as commandant of cadets and instructor of infantry tactics, 1838-1842. During the Mexican War, he was awarded a brevet for gallantry at Palo Alto and Resaca de la Palma and a second brevet for distinguished conduct during the capture of Monterrey. He was transferred to Scott's Army and participated in action at the Siege of Vera Cruz, Cerro Gordo, skirmish of Amazoque, and the capture of San Antonio. Smith was awarded a third brevet for meritorious conduct at the battles of Contreras and Churubusco and in the field for the storming of Chapultepec Castle and the capture of Mexico City. During the Civil War, Smith served in the Union Army at the rank of major general of volunteers and participated in the attacks on Forts Henry and Donelson. Smith was taken sick before the Battle of Shiloh and died on April 25, 1862.

18. Point Isabel was a small village on the Laguna Madre, about five miles northwest of the Brazos Santiago Pass. This village, originally named Fronton, was a Mexican customs station serving as a port of entry for the city of Matamoros and a large portion of northeastern Mexico. An extensive supply depot was established there during the Mexican War and an earthen defensive structure, Fort

Polk, was thrown up around the depot. The city of Port Isabel exists today on the original site. The only remaining wall of Fort Polk forms an embankment upon which the old lighthouse stands.

19. Kearney and Knopp, *Boom and Bust*, pp. 15-25. The city of Matamoros was founded in 1774 by ten powerful ranching families living in Camargo, farther up the Rio Grande. By 1796 the growing village was known as Nuestra Señora del Refugio de los Esteros (Our Lady of Refuge of the Lakes). In 1826 the city received its current name in honor of Padre Mariano Matamoros, who had been killed in the Mexican struggle for independence from Spain. Matamoros grew and became the official government port of entry for all trade goods entering northeastern Mexico. The actual port was Fronton, near Brazos Santiago, from where goods were carted overland to Matamoros. By 1844 Matamoros had been laid out in the Spanish style of squares, filled with many governmental buildings, markets, and a large and attractive church. The city had a population of 11,823 on the eve of the Mexican War.

20. Heitman, *Register*, vol. 1, p. 736; Cullum, *Register*, vol. 1, p. 133. John Munroe, born in Scotland, was graduated from the United States Military Academy in 1814 and assigned to the 1st Artillery. Munroe was awarded a brevet for "conduct uniformly meritorious and efficient during three campaigns against the Florida Indians" in 1838. During the Mexican War he was awarded brevets for his actions in the capture of Monterrey and the Battle of Buena Vista. Munroe served as military and civil governor of New Mexico, 1849-1851. He commanded the Department of Florida, 1853-1856, and the Department of the Platte, 1858-1861. Munroe died on April 26, 1861.

21. Heitman, *Register*, vol. 1, p. 433. William Henry Fowler graduated from the United States Military Academy in 1833 and was assigned to the 1st Artillery. He won a brevet in 1838 for actions in the war against the Florida Indians and was promoted to the rank of captain in 1848. Fowler died in 1851.

22. Heitman, *Register*, vol. 1, p. 681. Daniel H. McPhail joined the service as a second lieutenant of the 5th Infantry in 1837. He won a brevet for meritorious conduct in the Battles of Contreras and Churubusco. He resigned his commission in 1849. McPhail rejoined the volunteer service of the United States as paymaster in 1861 and won another brevet in 1865 for faithful and meritorious service. He died in 1884.

23. Heitman, *Register*, vol. 1, p. 335. This person was most likely Colonel Ichabod Bennet Crane.

24. Henry, *Campaign Sketches*, pp. 81-82. Colonel Truman Cross left camp on April 10, 1846, for a ride and failed to return to camp by nightfall. Extensive searches failed to discover any clues as to his disappearance in the thick brush that covered the area. A Mexican reported the location of the body of an American officer on April 21, 1846, and a search party was dispatched to retrieve the body of

Cross. A board of officers convened on April 23 to report on the circumstances connected with this death. The officers accepted the testimony of a Mexican witness, who claimed that Colonel Cross had been captured by a band of guerrillas led by Romano Falcon. Cross was murdered by a blow to the head delivered by Falcon with a pistol. "There is no proof of this tale; but the hole in the skull was evidently made by the butt of a gun." On April 24, a service was held for Colonel Cross, whose remains were interred at the foot of the flagstaff. The escort was composed of a squadron of dragoons and eight companies of infantry. The service was read, three volleys were fired, and the flag was raised. "[T]he escort marched off to a gay and lively tune, and left the dead in silence. Such is a military funeral: we have no time for grief."

25. Heitman, *Register*, vol. 1, p. 800; Dana, *Monterrey is Ours!* pp. 85-87; F. Smith, *Mexican War Journal*, p. 96; *New Orleans Picayune*, August 27, 1846. Theodoric Henry Porter was a cadet at the United States Military Academy from 1835 to 1836. He entered the service as a second lieutenant of the 4th Infantry in 1839. Porter was killed on patrol by Mexican guerrillas on April 19, 1846, near the Rio Grande. He had led a party of ten men on a search for the body of Colonel Truman Cross when he encountered a party of armed Mexicans and was slain in the ensuing battle. Dana reported that Porter's body had not been found until June 5, 1846: "Two skeletons have been brought in today for burial, which have been recognized as those of Lieutenant Porter and the man who was killed with him." Porter's remains were interred with military honors at Chester, Pennsylvania. He was a son of Commodore David Porter and widely respected by his peers for his courage. Porter faced down General Zachary Taylor on one occasion. Taylor was known for his sense of justice, but could on occasion fly into a rage of passion. When the passion was on the old general, his officer corps were careful to avoid any potentially unpleasant confrontations. But not so for Lieutenant Porter. According to Dana:

> On one occasion he [Taylor] became enraged at the delays of some men and rushed among them thumping with his fist first one then the other. Lieut. Porter was looking on and enjoying the sport mightily but presently the general took hold of a sick man and began pummeling him with his fist. The man crying out "General I am sick." "No you are not you d____d son of a b____h" thump "You are drunk you rascal" thump. Lieut. Porter knowing the man to be sick stepped up to him and said "Genl. the man is sick and not drunk—I know him to be sick"— "I say it is a d____d drunk and not sick"— "I know him to be sick"— "I say it is a d____d lie" said Genl. Taylor shaking his fist in the Lieutenant's face "I say it is a d____d lie and G__d d____n you I will throw you into the river." The Lieut. shook his fist in the General's face exclaiming "You throw me into the river try it you d____d old rascal and I will throw you into the river." The General put his hands behind him and walked into his tent. Soon afterwards Lieut. Porter made his men take up the sick man and brought him to the General's tent and laid him down saying "I wish

to satisfy you General that the man is sick"— "very well" Mr. Porter said the General "I was too hasty sir I was too hasty all right sir I was too hasty."

26. *Diccionario Porrua*, vol. 1, p. 101. Pedro de Ampudia was born in 1805 in Havana, Cuba. He came to Mexico in 1821 and fought against the Spanish, participating in the assault on the St. Juan d'Ulloa Castle at Vera Cruz. After Santa Anna deposed Bustamente in 1840, Ampudia became a general in the army. He participated with General Adrian Woll in an invasion of Texas in 1842 and led the troops that captured Colonel William S. Fisher and his Texans at Mier, Mexico, on December 26, 1842. Shifted to southern Mexico, he fought against separatist forces in the Yucatan, commanding the siege of Campeche. During the war with the United States, Ampudia commanded the defenses of Monterrey. After the fall of that city, he proceeded to San Luis Potosi, where he was appointed quartermaster general of the forces raised by Santa Anna for the defense of Mexico and fought in the Battle of Buena Vista. After the war, Ampudia was active in politics, becoming governor of the state of Nuevo Leon in 1854. He died in 1868.

27. Heitman, *Register*, vol. 1, p. 959. Seth Barton Thornton entered the service as a second lieutenant of the 2nd Dragoons in 1836. Thornton was killed by Mexicans while on patrol near the San Antonio Valley of Mexico on August 18, 1847.

28. Heitman, *Register*, vol. 1, p. 593. Croghan Ker served as a captain of Louisiana volunteers in the Seminole Wars in 1836 and later in the same year joined the regular service as a lieutenant of the 2nd Dragoons. He rose to the rank of captain in 1840, but resigned his commission in 1851.

29. Heitman, *Register*, vol. 1, p. 499. William Joseph Hardee graduated from the United States Military Academy in 1834 and was assigned to the 2nd Dragoons. He received a brevet in 1847 for actions at Medelin, Mexico, and a second brevet the same year for meritorious conduct at St. Augustine, Mexico. Hardee resigned his commission at the rank of lieutenant colonel in 1861 and joined the Confederate Army. He rose to the rank of lieutenant general in that service and died November 6, 1873.

30. Heitman, *Register*, vol. 1, p. 363; Meade, *Life and Letters*, p. 63; Nichols, *Zach Taylor's Little Army*, p. 60; "Correspondence Between The Secretary of War and Major General Zachary Taylor," 30th Congress, 1st Session, House Ex. Doc. No. 60, pp. 143-44. Edward Deas graduated from the United States Military Academy in 1828 and was assigned to the 4th Artillery. He was promoted to the rank of captain in 1847 and dismissed from the service on April 11, 1848; being reinstated on June 15, 1848. Deas was drowned in the Rio Grande on May 16, 1849. Meade's letter to his wife on April 19, 1846, mentions Edward Deas:

> An officer by the name of Deas from South Carolina (whose family resided some years in Philadelphia), a rather eccentric fellow, undertook of his own authority to ascertain the fact, of whether or not he [Colonel Cross] was in Matamoros, and without any permission or authority from General Taylor, or

even informing him of the step he was going to take, deliberately swam the river a few nights ago, and went into the town. He was, of course, made prisoner by the first sentinel he came across, and is now detained over there a prisoner of war. The manner in which he left, being entirely voluntary and without permission, prevents General Taylor from demanding his release. A newspaper correspondent thought that Deas had become enamored of a Mexican beauty on the opposite side of the Rio Grande, and like another "Leander he plunged into the Mexican Hellespoint after his Hero."

General Taylor took a dim view of the affair, and in a letter of April 23, 1846, to the adjutant general in Washington, D.C., expressed the opinion that Deas was "laboring under mental alienation at the time he committed this unfortunate act." On May 11, 1846, prisoners were exchanged, but General Taylor did not request Deas. However, he was exchanged along with all other American prisoners.

31. Connor, "Maurice Kavanaugh Simons." The attack on Captain Samuel Walker's camp by Mexican rancheros on the night of April 25, 1846, resulted in the death of five Texans. Of the eight posted to guard the camp, only three escaped; George Washington "Wash" Trahern, Maurice Simons, and the colorful Texan G. K. "Legs" Lewis. Simons related that the incident was brought on by Creed Taylor, an irascible Walker volunteer soldier. "[Creed] Taylor killed an old Mexican," much against the wishes of Simons, and in an act of revenge that evening, "...we were attacked in camp by 200 Mexicans." Simons's widow, writing in later years to her daughter (the letter is reproduced by Connor), said of the episode:

> Once they [Maurice and Wash] and six men went with them to drive the beeves were camped out when they heard Mexican soldiers. They ran undressed and barefooted, scattered in every direction. Maurice hid under some cactus and saw one of his men killed. A Mexican officer cut him open with a sword. The prickly pear was so dense that while he was there two of the Mexican soldiers stopped near enough to him to light their cigars and he could hear what they said. They were saying that they would rather have those 2 blackheaded devils (he and Wash) than all the others. He staid there until dark then made his way to headquarters where he found Wash who had made just as close an escape.

32. J. Smith, *War With Mexico*, vol. 1, pp. 467-68; Dana, *Monterrey is Ours!* pp. 58-71; *New Orleans Picayune*, May 21, 1846; Henry, *Campaign Sketches*, p. 103. Fort Brown, originally named Fort Texas, was a large earthen fort built across the Rio Grande from Matamoros prior to the opening engagements of the war. As described by Smith, the fort had:

> six bastion fronts, which made a perimeter of 800 yards, a strongly designed wall of earth 9 ½ feet high from the natural ground, a parapet 15 feet thick, a ditch about 8 feet deep and from 15 to 22 feet wide, a gate and a drawbridge … the magazine was built of pork barrels filled with sand, seven tiers thick and four tiers high, with a timber roof covered with 10 or 12 feet of sand.

The fort was manned by the 7th Infantry and Companies E and I of the 3rd and 4th Artillery Regiments respectively, a total of 550 men under the command of Major Jacob Brown. On May 3, 1846, the fort began to receive cannon fire from Fort Paredes and other Mexican emplacements on the south side of the river. A lively artillery duel ensued with the Americans scoring some hits on Mexican batteries. The fire ceased from the American side though, when it was discovered that half the ammunition reserve had been expended in this brief exchange. American cannon would hereafter only be fired to repel invaders. Constant shelling from the Mexican side continued until May 9, 1846, when Taylor's forces lifted the siege with their brilliant victory at Resaca de la Palma. It was estimated that during that period Mexican cannoneers fired 2,700 shells and shot at Fort Brown, killing Sergeant Horace Weigert, Major Jacob Brown, and wounding thirteen privates. The half-forgotten remains of the earthen walls of Fort Brown can be seen today adjacent to the Brownsville City Golf Course, a unique relic of the Mexican War.

33. Heitman, *Register*, vol. 1, p. 644. Allen Lowd joined the service in 1814 as a second lieutenant in the artillery corps. He received a brevet for his gallant conduct in the defense of Fort Brown. Lowd died on November 25, 1854, at the rank of major in the 1st Artillery.

34. Heitman, *Register*, vol. 1, p. 252. Jacob Brown joined the service as a private of the 11th Infantry in 1812 and by 1814 had risen to the rank of sergeant. Brown was commissioned as an ensign in 1814 and rose, by 1843, to the rank of major in the 7th Infantry. Major Brown died on May 9, 1846, from a wound received in the defense of the fort opposite Matamoros now known by his name.

35. Heitman, *Register*, vol. 1, p. 223; Thorpe, *Our Army*, pp. 75, 90; Curtis, *Mexico Under Fire*, pp. 54, 240. Jacob Edmund Blake graduated from the United States Military Academy in 1829 and was assigned to the topographical engineers. On May 8, 1846, as Taylor's forces faced Arista's army at Palo Alto prior to action, Blake made a daring reconnaisance of Mexican forces then in line of battle. At a distance of 150 yards, Blake made a galloping inventory of the Mexican army and reported the tally to Taylor. His bravery was the object of American and Mexican admiration. On the evening of May 8, after the success of American arms at Palo Alto, an exhausted Blake retired to his tent. While preparing to rest, he dropped his pistol, which discharged a ball, striking Blake and killing him. Thomas Frost composed a poem, "The Guns in the Grass—An Incident of the Mexican War," to memorialize Blake's heroic act:

> Old Rough and Ready scans the foe;
> "I would I knew," says he,
> "Whether or no that lofty grass
> Conceals artillery.
> Could I but bring that spot in ken,
> 'Twere worth to me five thousand men!"

Then forward steps Lieutenant Blake,
Touches his hat, and says,
"I wait command to ride and see
What 'neath that prairie lays,"
We stand amazed; no cowards, we;
But this is more than bravery!
...
He turns, remounts, and speeds him back.
Hark! what is that we hear?
Across the rolling prairie rings
A gun? ah, no—a cheer!
A noble tribute sweeps the plain;
A thousand throats take up the strain....

Samuel Curtis records in his diary entry for October 23, 1846, that on a scouting party, "Lieut. L. Chase has ordered a wagon to accompany us for the purpose of bringing in the body of Lieut. Blake who was accidentally killed on the 8th May, and buried on the battle ground."

36. Heitman, *Register*, vol. 1, p. 301; Cullum, *Register*, vol. 1, p. 597. William Hunter Churchill graduated from the United States Military Academy in 1840 and was assigned to the 3rd Artillery. He was awarded a brevet for distinguished service at the Battles of Palo Alto and Resaca de la Palma. Churchill died at Point Isabel, Texas, on October 19, 1847, while serving as an assistant quartermaster.

37. Heitman, *Register*, vol. 1, p. 668. James Simmons McIntosh joined the service at the rank of second lieutenant in 1812. He was promoted to the rank of colonel of the 5th Infantry for his actions at Palo Alto and Resaca de la Palma on May 8 and 9, 1846. McIntosh died on September 26, 1847, from wounds received at the Battle of Molino del Rey, Mexico.

38. Heitman, *Register*, vol. 1, p. 830; Henry, *Campaign Sketches*, p. 235; Kenly, *Memoirs of a Maryland Volunteer*, p. 46; F. Smith, *Mexican War Journal*, p. 155. Randolph Ridgely graduated from the United States Military Academy in 1832 and was assigned to the 3rd Artillery. He was awarded a brevet for gallantry and distinguished conduct at Palo Alto and Resaca de la Palma, but modestly declined a brevet for his actions in the capture of Monterrey. On October 25, 1846, Ridgely was severely injured in a fall from his horse while riding through the streets of American-occupied Monterrey and died two days later. His death was a severe shock to the army and to the nation, who had read many accounts of his bravery in the penny press. Henry remembered that "his dauntless courage and reckless exposure of person, combined with the most perfect coolness and judgement in the hottest fire, won golden opinions for him from all." His love of horses and riding was legendary. Kenly reported, on July 26, 1846, a famous horse race at Burita, Mexico, between two prominent sportsmen and admirers of the

American thoroughbred: "After dinner we had a horse-race between Colonel Bailie Peyton, of the Louisiana Volunteers, and Randolph Ridgely, in which Peyton's horse won: which he would not have done, as Ridgely laughingly said, if the race-course had been the road toward the enemy." Henry thought that Randolph Ridgely was the best rider in the world, and the famous orator Thomas F. Marshall, said, "As well might one expect to hear of an eagle dying from the fall of his own wings as to hear of Randolph Ridgely's dying from the fall of his horse."

39. Heitman, *Register*, vol. 1, p. 765; Grant, *Memoirs*, p. 45; *New Orleans Picayune*, July 8, 1846; Henry, *Campaign Sketches*, p. 126. John Page entered the service in 1818 at the rank of second lieutenant in the 8th Infantry. He was promoted to captain of the 4th Infantry in 1831. Page participated in the Battle of Palo Alto on May 8, 1846, and was greviously wounded by a Mexican solid shot that whizzed through the ranks of the regiment. According to U. S. Grant, "One cannon ball passed through our ranks ... it took off the head of an enlisted man, and the under jaw of Captain Page of my regiment, while the splinters from the musket of the killed soldier, and his brains and bones, knocked down two or three others ...." Page survived the disfiguring wound for several months. His wife came to Brazos to accompany him back to his home and was reported as passing through New Orleans on July 8, 1846, on the steamboat *Missouri*, bound for Jefferson Barracks. Captain Page died on board the *Missouri* on July 12th, near Cairo, Illinois, universally mourned by his comrades.

40. Heitman, *Register*, p. 653. George Archibald McCall graduated from the United States Military Academy in 1818 and was assigned to the 1st Infantry. He received two brevets for his actions at Palo Alto and Resaca de la Palma. McCall resigned from the service at the rank of colonel in 1853. He joined the volunteer service in 1861 and served in the Union Army until his resignation in 1863. McCall died on February 25, 1868.

41. E. Smith, *To Mexico with Scott*, p. 52; Clayton and Chance, *March to Monterrey*, p. 49. On May 9, 1846, a battallion and a company of soldiers of the famous Costa Guarda de Tampico were posted on the crucial site where the road from Point Isabel to Matamoros crossed an old channel of the Rio Grande. The Costa Guarda was made up of professional soldiers and considered to be one of the finest Mexican military units. They held their ground against the United States 5th Infantry, refusing to desert their post even after it had been overrun. E. Kirby Smith noted that here, "the most desperate hand-to-hand fighting ensued. The enemy here fought like devils." Only twenty-six of the Costa Guarda survived the sanguinary struggle for control of the road. A young Mexican lieutenant of the regiment captured in the battle reported that rather than retreat, their regiment had been cut to pieces. Before capture, he had placed the regimental colors in his hat, and when taken prisoner, rather than surrender them, had thrown them into the chaparral. The colors were recovered and became a part of the war prizes taken for exhibition to Congress in Washington, D.C.

42. Chamberlain, *My Confession*, p. 108; Muster Rolls, 2nd Dragoons, April 13, 1846, through June 30, 1846. Chamberlain, not an admirer of Charles May, expressed the same opinion. "All the buglers of the two Dragoon regiments hated May for claiming the capture of General La Vega at the Battle of Resaca de la Palma, when it was one of their own—Winchell of Company H, 2nd Dragoons—who took the Mexican prisoner." Chamberlain's memory of this name was probably faulty, the only bugler whose name corresponds is Private Frederick Wonsell of Company F, 2nd Dragoons, the company led by Captain May against the Mexican artillery emplacements at Resaca de la Palma.

43. Heitman, *Register*, vol. 1, p. 583; Cullum, *Register*, vol. 2, p. 65. Charles Downes Jordan graduated from the United States Military Academy in 1838 and was assigned to the 8th Infantry. He was awarded a brevet for actions at Palo Alto and Resaca de la Palma, where he was wounded. He was serving as a captain of the 8th Infantry in Texas at Fort Duncan when that state seceded from the Union in 1861. His company was captured by Confederate forces under the command of Earl Van Dorn, and he was paroled. Under the conditions of his parole, he could not serve in a military capacity until exchanged. This exchange did not occur until 1863. Jordan resigned his commission in 1863 and died on January 5, 1876.

44. Heitman, *Register*, vol. 1, p. 856; Cullum, *Register*, vol. 2, p. 131. Delos Bennet Sacket graduated from the United States Military Academy in 1840 and was assigned to the 2nd Dragoons. He was awarded a brevet for his actions at Palo Alto and Resaca de la Palma. After the Mexican War, Sacket served on the frontier in Kansas, Idaho, and Utah. During the Civil War, he served in the Virginia Peninsular Campaign and the Maryland Campaign in 1862 and at the Battle of Fredericksburg. He served in staff assignments for the remainder of the Civil War. Sacket died on March 8, 1885.

45. Heitman, *Register*, vol. 1, pp. 686, 762; *American Flag*, July 19, 1846, April 18, 1847. Maurice Maloney, a native of Ireland, entered the service in 1836. He rose to the rank of sergeant major, the highest ranking non-commissioned officer in the army, by 1846. Sergeant Maloney of the 4th Infantry and Sergeant Michael O'Sullivan of the 3rd Infantry were recognized for their heroic actions at the Battle of Resaca de la Palma on May 9, 1846, when they charged Mexican cannons guarding the roadway and aided in the capture of General La Vega. Americans living in Matamoros collected a fund for "presenting Corps. O'Sullivan and Farrell, and Sgts. Maloney and McCabe with some token of public approbation ...." Both O'Sullivan and Maloney were commissioned as second lieutenants in their respective regiments and fought in both northern and central Mexico. O'Sullivan resigned his commission on October 31, 1847, but Maloney rose through to the rank of lieutenant colonel, retired in December 15, 1870, and died January 8, 1872. Maurice Maloney was cited for actions at the Battle of Molino del Rey, again at Chapultepec, and finally for gallantry in the Civil War during the Siege of Vicksburg.

46. *Diccionario Porrua*, vol. 1, 139. General Mariano Arista (1820-1855) was a noted Mexican cavalry officer born in San Luis Potosi and educated in the United States. He commanded the forces defeated by General Zachary Taylor's army at the Battles of Palo Alto and Resaca de la Palma. Arista was the president of Mexico from 1851 to 1853.

47. E. Kirby Smith, *To Mexico with Scott*, p. 52; J. Smith, *War With Mexico*, vol. 1, p. 159. Two ferry crossings were in operation on the Rio Grande near Matamoros, the upper crossing (Anacuita) near Fort Paredes, and the lower crossing (Paso Real) near Fort Brown. On May 9, 1846, the Rio Grande was out of banks with rapid currents and difficult to swim. The two ferries were crowded with panic stricken Mexican soldiers and camp followers, eager to escape the oncoming American forces. One ferry was capsized by a Mexican officer who jumped his horse from the bank onto the ferry. E. Kirby Smith reported that 300 were drowned attempting this treacherous crossing including a priest and several officers. When the waters of the Rio Grande subsided several days later, bodies were found hung on the branches that extended into the water. The priest's body was recovered from one of the trees, his beads still tightly clutched in his hands.

48. *American Flag*, June 24, 28, 1848; Coker, *News From Brownsville*, pp. 102-03. With the ratification of a peace treaty, American governmental and commercial interests in northeastern Mexico began an exodus to the Rio Grande. Under the protective guns of Fort Brown, just across the Rio Grande, a settlement of government storehouses and private establishments began to spring up.

> The Quartermaster's Department here is busily engaged in erecting buildings and temporary sheds on the opposite bank of the river, preparatory to the transfer of quarters from this city [Matamoros]. The place ... is about half a mile from Fort Brown, on an elevated ridge beyond the reach of overflow from the river .... Uncle Sam, being a large capitalist, a public spirited, liberal and enterprising old gentleman, will give such a start to this new city that its future importance requires no prophet to foresee— "Athens" (the embryo city is so christened) already appears to us with its thousands of magnificent houses, its thousands upon thousands of industrious and enterprising inhabitants....

> However, the name "Athens" was not to be selected. This letter of practical advice, signed "C." and thought to have been authored by Helen Chapman, appeared in the next issue of the *Flag*:

> Gentlemen:—You are rather too fast in giving a name to the location of the Quarter Master's Depot on the other side .... [A] national name for it would be more befitting than the stale and worn out name of "Athens"—a name given to so many country Post offices and "Cross Roads" in the United States, that a letter directed to Athens, generally makes the circuit of the whole Union in search of its proper destination— "Brownsville" occurs to me as being the most appropriate name for this place, in memory of the gallant Major Brown....

And so the name was chosen. By January, 1849, the building of the city was underway. Helen Chapman gives us this view on the building of Brownsville:

> As I saw it that morning, the history could easily be read in the scene. Everywhere was bustle and animation—hammers ringing merrily—logs being prepared as foundations for other buildings—workmen in great number, all hurrying with their utmost speed—the new, fresh, comfortable looking buildings appearing in contrast to the five or six ruined Adobe walls of Mexican houses that the ravages of war had spared.

49. Coker, *News From Brownsville*, pp. xvi, 14, 371. On May 9, 1846, the rapid retreat of Mexican soldiers from the battlefield at Resaca de la Palma exposed the camp of General Mariano Arista to capture by American soldiers. The general's personal and military papers, his military chest, and his personal silver service were captured. The military papers yielded a valuable map of northeastern Mexico that accurately indicated water holes and distances between locations. Known as Arista's map, it was the first accurate representation American soldiers had obtained of northeastern Mexico and was widely copied. American officers wrote home for many months on the captured personal stationery of General Arista. Arista's silver service, marked with his name, consisted of a dozen silver dinner plates, two large platters for meat, one dozen table and tea spoons, two coffee cups "shaped like china," a large drinking cup, and a chocolate cup. After the end of the Mexican war, on instructions from General Arista, the silver service was to be sold with the proceeds to be distributed among the Mexican soldiers who were wounded at Resaca de la Palma. The sale to John E. Gary was arranged by Major W. W. Chapman. Arista's silver service is now the property of the Museum of New Mexico in Santa Fe.

3: FROM MATAMOROS TO MONTERREY

1. Henry, *Campaign Sketches*, p. 107. General Taylor, at a meeting with Mexican General Ricardo under a flag of truce just prior to the American occupation of Matamoros, complained about the treatment of American wounded and dead. Taylor protested that the enemy had stripped American dead and mutilated their bodies. General Ricardo shrugged and replied that the women who followed the army and the rancheros were guilty of the crimes and that the Mexican Army could not control them. Taylor replied sharply, "I am coming over, and I'll control them for you."

2. Heitman, *Register*, vol. 1, p. 437; Cullum, *Register*, vol. 2, p. 81. Samuel Gibbs French graduated from the United States Military Academy in 1839 and was assigned to the 3rd Artillery. He was awarded brevets for "gallantry and meritorious conduct" at Monterrey and at Buena Vista where he was severely wounded. French resigned his commission in 1856, and later served in the Confederate Army, rising to the rank of major general.

3. Curtis, *Mexico Under Fire*, p. 13; *American Flag*, July 19, 1846. Doubleday may be confusing this unit with the famous Louisiana Tigers, a Confederate Zouave Regiment originally commanded by Roberdeau Wheat. General Persifor F. Smith commanded the Louisiana Volunteer Brigade, mustered illegally for service on or about May 15, 1846, by General Edmund P. Gaines. The brigade consisted of the George Washington Regiment (1st Regiment), commanded by Colonel James B. Walton, the Louisiana Regiment (2nd Regiment), commanded by Colonel James H. Dakin, the Andrew Jackson Regiment (3rd Regiment), commanded by Colonel Samuel F. Marks, and the Montezuma Regiment (4th Regiment), commanded by Colonel Horatio Davis. General Smith was a strict disciplinarian, and forced the young men from New Orleans and environs to perform manual labor in the hot sun, some for the first time in their lives. Samuel Curtis reported that:

> The Louisiana troops seem to have got dispirited because they were required to clean the ground of their encampments. It is said they gave their General (Genl Smith) the cognomen of Genl Chaparrel had circulated—The report that he had [gotten] 5 cents an acre for clearing land.

> The brigade was disbanded by order of Gen. Zachary Taylor by July 4, 1846, because the men, who had been mustered for only 90 days service, refused to extend their period of service to a year. The volunteers were returned to Louisiana without performing any service except that of eating up Gen. Taylor's scarce rations.

4. Parker, *Recollections*, pp. 50-55. Commodore Connor had sent 1,200 sailors and marines ashore from the Home Fleet standing off shore to reinforce Fort Polk at Point Isabel on May 7, 1846. The regular "blue-jackets" were issued muskets but most had not been drilled in their use. A prejudice against the small-arms drill was strong on board the ships of the line, and sailors had made little progress in the company drill. Each ship relied on its company of marines, who were well drilled, to form a nucleus around which the sailors could rally in land engagements. Young midshipman William Parker, ordered onshore to Fort Polk, remembered that:

> As soon as we got on shore at Point Isabel we expected we might have to march to join the army, so the lieutenants went immediately to work drilling their companies; and I thought the army officers who looked on would die of laughter at the sight. One lieutenant would persist in giving the order double up, when he wished to form two ranks; and we were all performing the most remarkable evolutions.

The sailors remained at Fort Polk, while Taylor advanced to battle the Mexicans at Palo Alto on May 8, 1846. The sound of the guns was heard throughout the afternoon at Point Isabel, but, to the chagrin of the sailors, did not appear to be advancing. "We were in a great state of excitement, and the sailors were dying to go to the assistance of the army." About midnight a black servant rushed into the walls of the fort and announced to all that General Taylor had been defeated with a great slaughter. But Commodore Connor would not allow his sailors to advance to Taylor's aid. Due to their ignorance of small arms and their lack of formations, a regiment of Mexican cavalry could have easily cut them to pieces. Young Parker was quite disappointed, "… in my opinion, he [Connor] made his first mistake of this war …." Parker noted that the American victory was later celebrated by the tars in the way they celebrated all successes: with whole-sale drunkenness.

> When General Taylor returned to Point Isabel after his victories, he was received with great enthusiasm, especially by the sailors, who were generally drunk. They had gotten the run of the sutler's stores by this time, and knew where to get whiskey; but even without sutler's stores they would have known where to have found it. I heard a lieutenant say that he once sent a watch of sailors ashore for recreation on an uninhabited island in the middle of the Pacific Ocean, and they all came back drunk! I don't know about that, but I know that our men were drunk, and when General Taylor arrived the sailors almost carried him in their arms and could hardly be kept out of his tent. The General was very tolerant of them….

5. Heitman, *Register*, vol. 2, pp. 63, 67. Stephen Ormsby was colonel and Jason Rogers was lieutenant colonel of the 1st Kentucky Volunteer Regiment. The 1st Kentucky Volunteer Regiment, known as the Louisville Legion, was mustered into service in May, 1846, for one year of service. The Legion marched on Monterrey but did not particpate in the fighting that resulted in the capture of that city. The Kentuckians spent the balance of their time in Mexico in garrison at Monterrey.

6. F. Smith, *Mexican War Journal*, pp. 48, 216. Burrita is a small Mexican village sit-uated on the south side of the Rio Grande located about ten miles from the mouth of the river on a bluff. An 1847 vintage map indicates only about eight huts in the village and a small American army camp. This remote camp, away from the scenes of action and glory must have been quite a tedious assignment for a volunteer soldier from the United States. Franklin Smith related that:

> An officer in one of the volunteer regiments while stationed at Burrita went round to look to the sentinels—the night was very dark and raining and the mud deep. Coming along cautiously he heard a sentinel soliloquizing thus— "Well this is the G_d damnest shot of work I ever saw yet. I voted for old Polk G_d d___n him and here I am in mud and rain and misery. I came out here to fight and instead of fighting I have to tread this mud for four hours what a d___d fool I was—I ought to be in Hell for a d___d fool. Who comes there?" "James K. Polk" was the officer's reply. "Well" bringing his gun down and tak-ing aim "Stand James K. Polk for I'll be d___d if I dont shoot you if you give me the least chance."

7. Heitman, *Register*, vol. 2, p. 63; McCaffrey, *Army of Manifest Destiny*, p. 96; Edwards Journal, January 23, 1846, Indiana Historical Society; Wallace, *An Autobiography*, p. 116. The 1st Regiment of Indiana Volunteers was stationed either at the mouth of the Rio Grande or at Matamoros during its entire year of federal service. Doubleday was probably talking to Lieutenant Colonel Christian C. Nave, about the misdeeds of that regiment. The first three regiments of Indiana volunteers were mustered into service near New Albany, Indiana, in May, 1846, and formed a camp of instruction at that location. Sutlers formed temporary stores near the camp to sell merchandise and food to the recruits. A conflict developed. Henry Edwards, one of the new recruits camped at New Albany, remembered that:

> There was a number of Booths and sheds erected on the camping ground with cakes and pies ... segars, lemonade and various articles in the confectionary line but the men "got in a breeze" and on the night of the 19th they demolished most of the Booths and helped themselves to such as suited their tastes .... This outrage on the property was perpetuated by the sanction of some of our officers.

8. "Orders to the Army," June 3, 15, 18, 1846. A court-martial was convened for the Washington Regiment of the Louisiana Volunteers on June 15, 1846, with Major J. P. Breedlove as president. Charges brought against Second Lieutenant J. H. Kelly included disobedience of orders and neglect of duty. The court found Kelly guilty of both specifications and sentenced him "to be reprimanded in General Orders." On June 18, the same court found Private William M. Wilson of the Alabama Volunteers guilty of mutinous conduct and sentenced him to be placed in stocks for four hours each day for seven days and to be "kept at hard labor during the balance of each day." Private George Ray was found innocent of the charge of "Highly disgraceful conduct to the prejudice of good order and military discipline." Private Philip Schmidt was found innocent of the charge of desertion, but guilty of the lesser charge of being absent without leave. He was sentenced to walk in front of the guard from five to seven o'clock in the morning and from four to six o'clock in the evening with his knapsack on his back loaded with four six-pound balls and with his musket at "shouldered arms" for six days. The remainder of the time to be kept at hard labor in charge of the guard.

9. Heitman, *Register*, vol. 1, p. 830. James Brewerton Ricketts graduated from the United States Military Academy in 1835 and was assigned to the 1st Artillery. Ricketts joined the volunteers in 1861 and by the end of the Civil War had risen to the rank of major general of volunteers. He was in action at Bull Run, Cold Harbor, and with Sheridan in the Shenandoah at Opequan, Fisher's Hill, and Cedar Creek. Ricketts retired at the rank of major general in 1867 and died on September 22, 1887.

10. Heitman, *Register*, vol. 1, p. 1016. Thomas Bradford Jones Weld graduated from the United States Military Academy in 1840 and was assigned to the 1st

Artillery. He was promoted to the rank of first lieutenant in 1847 and died on September 10, 1850.

11. Heitman, *Register*, vol. 1, p. 509. Joseph Abel Haskin graduated from the United States Military Academy in 1835 and was assigned to the 1st Artillery. Haskin was awarded two brevets, the first for actions at Cerro Gordo and the second for meritorious conduct at the capture of Chapultepec Castle. During the Civil War he rose to the rank of brigadier general in the Union Army. Haskin retired in 1870 and died on August 3, 1874.

12. J. Smith, *War With Mexico*, vol. 1, p. 89; Scribner, *Camp Life*, p. 49. Cerralvo is about fifty miles southwest of Camargo along the main line of advance of the American army to Monterrey. During the war the town claimed about 1,800 citizens. Buildings were mainly of stone; many private residences contained formal gardens watered by the numerous springs of crystal clear cold water that emerge from the ground south of the town and are circulated throughout the city by a system of canals. American volunteer soldier B. F. Scribner offered this view of Cerralvo in 1846:

> We pitch our tents near the old Spanish town of Ceralvo, which bears the impress of an antiquated fortress, and reminds one of the dilapidated castles we read of in romances. The houses are built of gray stone, with loopholes for windows. Through the centre of town runs a beautiful clear stream, spanned by bridges and arches. There is also a cathedral with chimes and a towering steeple. It is said to be 166 years old.

13. Dana, *Monterrey is Ours!* p. 144. The custom of nude public bathing was apparently most prevalent on the Rio Grande and Rio San Juan. To the young men of mid-nineteenth-century America, where the glimpse of a young lady's bare ankle could bring on a blush, this cultural practice was much commented upon. Lieutenant Dana reported several soldier's reactions:

> Many women used to go bathing in the river before and among the men, and many went down especially to look at them. Among others that beast [Nevil] Hopson used to spend half the day at the river bank .... Those sights of naked women have not been seen, I believe, since we left Camargo.... Poor Terrett, he was a man of a troublesome degree of modesty, and at Reynosa whilst he was in bathing once a couple of women came down and sat on the bank close to him, looking at him with perfect innocence. He was in a great quandry how to get out, and they kept the poor fellow in a long time. At last they stripped right off and went in alongside of him. Terrett left the place in perfect disgust and towering indignation, swearing that Mexican women were no better than beasts nor half so modest and that he would never go near the river again by daylight whilst he was in Mexico .... Captain [Electus] Backus tells a story: whilst he was riding near the river at Reynosa one day, a woman came up to him out of the water, perfectly stark naked, stood and talked with him and had not even the decency to put her hand before it ....

4: THE BATTLE OF MONTEREY

1. Henry, *Campaign Sketches*, p. 185. Mexican General Anastacio Torrejon ordered a Mexican citizen shot in the cemetery at Marin on September 14, 1846, for communicating with General Taylor.

2. The Bishop's Palace (*La Obispada*) is one of the few remaining structures in Monterrey that stands as a reminder of the Mexican War. Parts of the *Obispada* are now crumbling, and the facade is literally dissolving from the effects of acid rain in this highly industrialized and modern city. A fine historical museum now exists nearby on the same hill.

3. J. Smith, *The War with Mexico*, vol. 1, p. 233. The Citadel, which commanded the eastern and nothern entrances to Monterrey, was a strong fortification. The fort was built around an unfinished cathedral located on a slight elevation. Around these thirty-foot walls and columns, a bastioned earthwork was thrown up with ditches twelve feet deep. A garrison of 400 soldiers, artillerists, and lancers manned the walls that were fitted with eight guns. A system of semaphore enabled communication between the fort and Monterrey during daytime and was continued at night by colored rockets.

4. Heitman, *Register*, vol. 1, p. 670; Cullum, *Register*, vol. 1, p. 523. William Whann Mackall graduated from the United States Military Academy in 1837 and was assigned to the 1st Artillery. He served in the Florida War, 1837-1839, and was severely wounded while engaged at New Inlet. Mackall served on the northern frontier, 1839-1845, during the Canadian border disturbances and the Maine boundary dispute. During the Mexican War, Mackall was awarded a brevet for distinguished service at Monterrey. In central Mexico he was engaged at Vera Cruz, Cerro Gordo, the capture of San Antonio and was awarded a second brevet for gallant conduct at Contreras and Churubusco. He was wounded in the capture of Chapultapec Castle. Mackall served in the office of the adjutant general until his resignation on July 3, 1861. He served as a brigadier general in the Confederate Army during the Civil War and died on August 19, 1891.

5. Heitman, *Register*, vol. 1, p. 670; Cullum, *Register*, vol. 1, p. 455. Henry McKavett graduated from the United States Military Academy in 1834 and was assigned to the 7th Infantry. From 1838 to 1840 he served on the northern frontier during the Canadian boundary dispute. He served in the Florida War, 1840-1845, and aided in emigrating Indians to Arkansas. During the Mexican War, McKavett was engaged in the Battles of Palo Alto and Resaca de la Palma and was killed at Monterrey on September 21, 1846, by an enemy cannonball.

6. Heitman, *Register*, vol. 1, p. 844; Cullum, *Register*, vol. 1, pp. 503-04. John Frederick Roland graduated from the United States Military Academy in 1836 and was assigned to the 2nd Artillery. He served in the Florida War, 1836-1838, being engaged in the Battle of Wahoo Swamp and in emigrating Indians to the West. Roland served on the northern frontier, 1838-1840, in the state of New

York. During the Mexican War, he was awarded a brevet for gallant conduct at Palo Alto and Resaca de la Palma and a second brevet for actions at Monterrey. After the war, Roland returned to Florida to participate in hostilities against the Seminoles, 1849-1850. He died on September 28, 1852.

7. J. Smith, *War with Mexico*, vol. 1, p. 230; Ramsey, *The Other Side*, p. 77; Thorpe, *Our Army at Monterrey*, p. 122. There were many reports and rumors of Mexican women leading troops into battle at Monterrey. Smith reported that to innervate Mexican troops, "... Señorita Dosamantes, equipped as a captain, volunteered to fight the invader, and was exhibited on horseback to the entire army, its enthusiasm rose high." In his translation of a Mexican account of the war, Ramsey reported that Senorita Dona Maria Josefa Zozaya passed among the troops on an *azotea* atop a building in the principal square distributing food and ammunition to defenders to "teach them how to despise danger." Thorpe repeated the rumor that a woman commanded a body of lancers at Monterrey and generally gives credence to the bravery of Mexican women in battle by reporting on this inscription found on the tomb of Doña Maria Vicario de Quintana near Mexico City: "she preferred to leave her convent and join the standard of her country, under which she performed many feats of valor."

8. Heitman, *Register*, vol. 1, p. 564; Cullum, *Register*, vol. 2, p. 12. Joseph Findley Irons graduated from the United States Military Academy in 1841 and was assigned to the 1st Artillery. During the Mexican War, Irons was engaged in the northern campaign in the Battles of Palo Alto, Resaca de la Palma, and Monterrey. In central Mexico, he participated in the Siege of Vera Cruz, Cerro Gordo, the skirmish of La Hoya, and Contreras. Irons was mortally wounded by a grape shot through the neck while reconnoitring an enemy battery at Churubusco and died from the wound on August 26, 1847.

9. Heitman, *Register*, vol. 1, p. 468. Lawrence Pike Graham was commissioned a second lieutenant in the 2nd Dragoons in 1837. During the Mexican War, he was awarded a brevet for his services at Palo Alto and Resaca de la Palma. During the Civil War, he was commissioned a brigadier general of volunteers. Graham retired from the service in 1870 at the rank of colonel.

10. Heitman, *Register*, vol. 1, p. 692; Cullum, *Register*, vol. 1, p. 602. James Green Martin graduated from the United States Military Academy in 1840 and was assigned to the 1st Artillery. He served on the Maine frontier during the boundary dispute, 1840-1845. During the Mexican War, Martin participated in the capture of Monterrey in northern Mexico. In central Mexico, he was engaged at Vera Cruz and Cerro Gordo and was awarded a brevet for gallant conduct at the Battles of Contreras and Churubusco. Martin was severely wounded in the latter engagement, losing his right arm. From 1858 to 1861, Martin served on the Kansas-Nebraska frontier, and resigned his commission on June 14, 1861. During the Civil War, he rose to the rank of brigadier general in the Confederate Army and died on October 4, 1878.

11. Heitman, *Register*, vol. 1, p. 237; Cullum, *Register*, vol. 1, p. 530. Edmund Bradford graduated from the United States Military Academy in 1837 and was assigned to the 4th Artillery. Bradford served in the Florida War, 1837-1839, and on the northern frontier during the Canadian border disturbance in 1840. In the Mexican War he served in the capture of Monterrey, the Siege of Vera Cruz, and at Pachaca, Mexico. Bradford resigned his commission in 1849 to take up farming in Virginia and during the Civil War served in the Confederate Army at the rank of major. He died on April 26, 1889.

12. Heitman, *Register*, vol. 1, p. 988; Cullum, *Register*, vol. 1, p. 164. John Rogers Vinton graduated from the United States Military Academy in 1817 and was assigned to the Corps of Artillery. From 1837 to 1842, Vinton was engaged in the Florida Wars, taking part in the defense of Fort Mellon on February 8, 1837. During the Mexican War Vinton was awarded a brevet for gallant conduct at Monterrey in northern Mexico, and was killed on March 22, 1847, at the Siege of Vera Cruz by "the wind of a shell" thrown from Vera Cruz by Mexican defenders.

13. Heitman, *Register*, vol. 1, p. 414; Cullum, *Register*, vol. 2, p. 121. Joseph F. Farry graduated from the United States Military Academy in 1845 and was assigned to the 4th Artillery. During the Mexican War, he fought in the northern campaign in the Battles of Palo Alto, Resaca de la Palma, and the capture of Monterrey. In central Mexico, Farry participated in the Siege of Vera Cruz, the Battle of Cerro Gordo, the capture of San Antonio, and the Battle of Churubusco. Farry was killed leading his men over the enemy's entrenchments at Molino del Rey on September 8, 1847.

14. Monroe, *Papers of Jefferson Davis*, vol. 3, p. 77; Wilcox, *History of the Mexican War*, p. 669. Balie Peyton was born in Tennessee in 1803 and educated in the law. He served as a Whig congressman from 1833 to 1837. Peyton was living in New Orleans and practicing law when the Mexican War began. He joined the 5th Regiment of P. F. Smith's Brigade of Louisiana Volunteers, but the regiment was disbanded in three months. He became a volunteer aide-de-camp to General Worth and participated in the Battle of Monterrey. Peyton, the consummate sportsman and lover of horseflesh, authored *The Making of the American Thoroughbred*. He later served as ambassador to Chile during the Taylor administration. Peyton died in Nashville, Tennessee, on August 19, 1878.

15. Heitman, *Register*, vol. 1, p. 863; Cullum, *Register*, vol. 1, p. 550. Jeremiah Mason Scarritt graduated from the United States Military Academy in 1838 and was assigned to the Corps of Engineers. During the Mexican War he participated in the Battles of Palo Alto and Resaca de la Palma. Scarritt was awarded a brevet for meritorious conduct during the capture of Monterrey. He died on June 22, 1854.

16. Heitman, *Register*, vol. 1, p. 708; Cullum, *Register*, vol. 1, p. 266. Dixon Stansbury Miles graduated from the United States Military Academy in 1824 and was assigned to the 4th Infantry. He served on the frontier, 1825-1836, at

Cantonment Clinch, Florida, and Fort Gibson in Indian Territory. From 1839 to 1845 Miles served in the Florida War and joined Taylor's forces in Texas in 1845. During the Mexican War, he was awarded a brevet for his services in the defense of Fort Brown and was engaged at Monterrey. In central Mexico he participated in the Siege of Vera Cruz. After the war, Miles served on frontier duty in New Mexico, 1851-1859, and was engaged in the combat of June 27, 1857, on the Gila River, north of Mount Turnbull, New Mexico. During the Civil War, Miles commanded Union reserves at First Manassas and later guarded Washington, D.C., and the railroads in that vicinity. He was mortally wounded while defending Harpers Ferry, Virginia, and died on September 16, 1862.

5: THE BATTLE OF BUENA VISTA

1. Heitman, *Register*, vol. 1, p. 434; Cullum, *Register*, vol. 1, p. 444. William Davidson Fraser graduated from the United States Military Academy in 1834 and was assigned to the Corps of Engineers. Fraser participated in construction projects for the improvement of the Hudson River, erection of Fort Monroe, and the improvement of Lake Ontario Harbors, 1834-1837. From 1839 to 1846, he was superintending engineer for repairs to Forts Niagara and Porter in New York. During the Mexican War, Fraser participated in the repair and reorganization of the defenses of Monterrey and as aide-de-camp for General Wool. He was awarded a brevet for meritorious conduct while serving in the enemy's country in 1848. After the war, he was superintending engineer for the repair of Fort Brown and was responsible for numerous construction projects for the improvement of riverways and fortresses and the erection of lighthouses in New York and along the eastern seaboard. Fraser died on July 27, 1856.

2. Heitman, *Register*, vol. 2, p. 60. Andrew Keith McClung was lieutenant colonel of the 1st Mississippi Volunteer Regiment, the Mississippi Rifles. For more information on the life of this colorful writer, duelist, and politican, see F. Smith, *Mexican War Journal*.

3. Heitman, *Register*, vol. 1, p. 813; Cullum, *Register*, vol. 1, pp. 207-08. George Douglas Ramsay graduated from the United States Military Academy in 1820 and was assigned to the light artillery. From 1828 until 1845 he served as ordnance officer at arsenals in Washington, D.C., and in the states of Pennsylvania, New Jersey, North Carolina, and Georgia. During the Mexican War he was awarded a brevet for his services in the capture of Monterrey and served as General Taylor's chief of army ordnance. After the war, Ramsay commanded arsenals at Pennsylvania, Virginia, Missouri, and Washington, D.C., 1848-1861. During the Civil War, he served as chief of ordnance of the United States Army at the rank of brigadier general. Ramsay retired in 1864, "being over the age of 62," and died on May 23, 1882.

4. Heitman, *Register*, vol. 2, p. 61. Thomas Marshall was the brigadier general of the brigade of volunteers from Kentucky.

5. Buchanan, "George Washington Trahern," pp. 78-83; Connor, "Maurice Kavanaugh Simons," pp. 11-12. The "expressmen" who brought the message to Rinconada from Taylor in Saltillo on the evening of February 23, 1847, were "Wash" Trahern and Maurice "Morris" Simons. Taylor had ordered up the heavy artillery, for he expected a renewal of battle the next morning. Wash Trahern remembered that General Taylor summoned him to his marquee on the night of February 23, 1847.

> The old General was a rough old fellow, the wickedest man I ever saw in my life, but a kind man at heart. He says, "Wash, my son, come here." He says "I sent for you, and have got an extra and very dangerous ride for you if you will attempt it." He says, "I want you to go down to Rinconada tonight and carry a dispatch to General Tom Marshall to bring up the heavy artillery... ." He says, "Do you think you can get through?" Says I, "General, I will try... ." "He [Taylor] said to Captain Donelson to give these boys any horses they want in the quartermaster's department." I laughed; says I, "General Taylor, I am riding a horse I wouldn't give for any horse you have got in the army." So we went through and got out of Saltillo, right on the edge of town, and I met a little fellow by the name of Kaegler ... . He says, "Where are you going, Wash?" I says, "to Rinconada." He says, "For God's sake turn back; it is just sacrificing your life for nothing. It is just alive with Mexicans."

Taylor issued identical orders to be carried by Wash and Morris, in case one of the two were captured. After a race through the corn fields, dodging Mexican picquets and bullets they rejoined the main road finally, only to be chased again:

> Them little Mexican horses would run up on us, get pretty close—start and run pretty close—but they are no shots [and for the], long strides of the American horses they had no chance. They run us that way about eight miles, but we just naturally cut them, and got in and delivered the dispatches to Marshall.

General Taylor wrote Simon's father that "he saved the army," and offered a $500 cash reward to young Simons, who turned it down, considering the ride to be the duty of a soldier.

6. Benham, "Recollections of Mexico," vol. 3, no. 6, p. 649; Gregg, *The Diary & Letters of Josiah Gregg*, vol. 1, pp. 270-71. Benham described Don Jacobo Sanchez and his wealth:

> The owner of Agua Nueva, and of the larger portion of these ranches and villages for some two hundred miles or more to the north-west, was one Don Jacobo (or Jacob) Sanchez, a gentleman of education and breeding, though nearly a black Indian in appearance. He was the son, by an Indian woman, of a shrewd and unscrupulous Spanish-Mexican lawyer, who acquired, often unjustly it was thought, these immense properties in the troublous times of the first revolts from Spain. Don Jacobo we sometimes saw in Saltillo, where he had his town mansion; though he generally resided at his hacienda, some thirty

miles southwest, where he lived in princely style, with his own private band of musicians for his own amusement.

Josiah Gregg, in his travels with General Wool's column through the country southwest of Saltillo, noted that:

> The Hacienda de las Hermanas is a large plantation—sugar and corn chiefly cultivated—with some 120 work-hands ... total population, at least 300 souls. The residences are embraced in an extensive building divided into three squares .... This estate is owned by one Don Jacobo Sanchez, who resides in Saltillo.

7. Heitman, *Register*, vol. 1, p. 884; Cullum, *Register*, vol. 1, p. 554. William H. Shover graduated from the United States Military Academy in 1838 and was assigned to the 3rd Artillery. He served in the Cherokee Nation in 1838, emigrating Indians to the West, and in the Florida War, 1838-1842. During the Mexican War Shover participated in the Battles of Palo Alto and Resaca de la Palma and was awarded a brevet for gallant conduct at Monterrey. Shover was awarded a second brevet for his services at the Battle of Buena Vista. After the war, Shover served at the Military Academy as an instructor of artillery and cavalry, 1848-1850. He died on September 7, 1850.

8. Heitman, *Register*, vol. 1, p. 633, vol. 2, pp. 73, 60,47, 54. Archibald Yell was colonel of the Arkansas Mounted Regiment. William R. Mckee and Henry Clay, Jr., were the colonel and lieutenant colonel respectively of the 2nd Kentucky Infantry. John J. Hardin was colonel of the 1st Illinois Infantry. George Lincoln was a brevet captain, serving as General Wool's adjutant.

9. Heitman, *Register*, vol. 1, p. 1007; Cullum, *Register*, vol. 1, p. 170. John Macrae Washington graduated from the United States Military Academy in 1817 and was assigned to the Corps of Artillery. He participated in actions against the Creek Nation, 1833-1834, and again in 1836. Washington opposed the Seminoles in Florida, 1836-1838, participating in the Combat of Locha-Hatchee on January 24, 1838. From 1838 to 1839 he participated in the emigration of Indians to the West. During the Mexican War he served under General Wool and participated in the march from San Antonio, Texas, to Saltillo, Mexico. Washington was awarded a brevet for commanding an artillery battery at Buena Vista and afterward served as military governor of Saltillo. After the war, he served as military and civil governor of New Mexico, 1848-1849. Washington drowned on December 24, 1853, off the Capes of the Delaware when he was washed overboard from the steamer *San Francisco* during a violent storm.

10. Gregg, *The Diary & Letters of Josiah Gregg*, vol. 1, p. 308. Gregg documents the distance from Rinconada Ranch to Saltillo as twenty-one miles, not the longer distance reported by Doubleday.

11. "William Chapman to Helen Chapman," June 10, 1847, Chapman Family Papers; Chamberlain, *My Confession*, pp. 202, 242; Sandwich, *The Great Western*, pp. 14-

20, 62-63. Major William W. Chapman, with the quartermaster's department at Saltillo, records for his wife these impressions of the Great Western:

> The General [Wool] has gone into town and is to dine with the "Great Western." You have no doubt heard of this remarkable personage. She is or was the wife of a soldier whom Capt. Lincoln enlisted many years ago. She was in Fort Brown during the bombardment and made herself highly useful. She is now keeping a boarding house in Saltillo where most of the officers board. She knows every officer in the army whom she has ever seen before, and whenever she meets them either hugs or kisses them. She is really a privileged character and a great favorite. She is large, coarse six feet high woman without a single attraction, except her great kindness of heart. She was very kind to the wounded officers after the battle. During the battle we saw a large woman, ascending a hill between us and the enemy camp, carry water and followed by a black boy with a basket. Poor Lincoln took off his hat and swung it over his head said, Hurrah for the "Great Western." It turned out however to be a large dutch woman. The Great Western (politely called Mrs. Bourgette) has made a great deal of money and keeps the best carriage in Saltillo. A few days ago, she went to Monterey to visit General Taylor, and day before yesterday, she dined in camp with General Wool and remained there an hour or two after. She is a character, and if any novels are ever written on this war, she will figure most conspicuously.

It was rumored that she had been awarded a brevet rank as colonel for services during the war and by order of General Scott received a pension equivalent to that rank. She traveled throughout the West, ending up as the proprietress of an "establishment" at Yuma Crossing in Arizona. Mrs. Bowman-Phillips, as she was known at that time, died in 1866 and was accorded a funeral with full military honors. A watercolor of her likeness, done by Chamberlain, appears in his book.

12. Heitman, *Register*, vol. 1, p. 919. Enoch Steen joined the service in 1832 as a second lieutenant of the Mounted Rangers. During the Mexican War he was awarded a brevet for meritorious conduct during the Battle of Buena Vista where he was wounded. Later, Steen rose to the rank of lieutenant colonel in the Union Army, retiring from the service in 1863. He died on January 22, 1880.

13. Heitman, *Register*, vol. 1, p. 409; Cullum, *Register*, vol. 1, p. 377. William Eustis graduated from the United States Military Academy in 1830 and was assigned to the 3rd Infantry. He served on the western frontier, 1830-1835, and returned, 1837-1839. Eustis attended the cavalry school at Saumur, France, and translated *French Cavalry Tactics* for use by the U.S. Cavalry, 1839-1841. Eustis served in the war with Mexico in northern Mexico, 1846-1847, and on recruiting duty, 1847-1848. He resigned his commission in 1849 and became a farmer near Natchez, Mississippi. Eustis died on July 4, 1889.

14. Pace, "The Diary and Letter of William P. Rogers," p. 275. Captain William P. Rogers walked over the battlefield on February 24, and reported:

Oh it is indeed an awful sight to pass over a battlefield so desperately contested as that at Buena Vista. I first passed over the Mexican slain. There they
lay in heeps [sic], the dead and the dying. The wounded have by their sides
small sacks of parched meal. They have evidently been poorly fed and clothed
as was indicated by their emaciated forms. Some would eagerly beg for "Agua
and Pan ... ." Others also we would see who had passed unhurt through the
fight, but who from exhaustion and emaciation were scarcely able to speak.
Our soldiers were kind to all, giving them water and bread and speaking kindly to them. At length I turned my steps to the ground where the Americans
had fallen—But I could not attempt to describe my feelings—all, all else I
could have seen without feelings of other than sorrow but the bloody evidence
that more than half had been maimed by our cruel foes after being wounded,
very many of whom from their slight gunshot wounds would have recovered,
but not for the bloody monsters who lanced and butchered them on the field.

15. Heitman, *Register*, vol. 1, p. 1013; Cullum, *Register*, vol. 1, p. 242. Lucien
    Bonaparte Webster graduated from the United States Military Academy in 1823
    and was assigned to the 1st Artillery. Webster served as assistant professor of
    mathematics at the Military Academy, 1828-1830. He served in the Florida War,
    1836-1838, and participated in emigrating Indians to the West. During the
    Mexican War, he was active in the defense of Fort Brown and received brevets for
    his actions at Monterrey and Buena Vista. Webster died on November 4, 1853,
    while on duty at Fort Brown, Texas.

6: ROGUERY AND RASCALITY IN MEXICO

1. Heitman, *Register*, vol. 1, p. 252; vol. 2, pp. 61-63; Cullum, *Register*, vol. 2, p. 150;
   Wallace, "The First Regiment of Virginia Volunteers," pp. 61-62. The Lieutenant
   B. mentioned by Doubleday was John A. Brown. Born in Maryland, Brown graduated from the United States Military Academy in 1846 and was assigned to the
   4th Artillery. While the 4th Artillery fought in central Mexico with Scott, Cullum
   lists Brown as "... in the War with Mexico, 1846-1848, in the Northern Mexican
   States." After the war, Brown served against the Seminole Indians, 1856-1857,
   and resigned his commission in 1861 to become a colonel of artillery in the
   Confederate Army. Brown died on October 8, 1877.

   A challenge was a serious matter; many duels were fought in northern Mexico
   after Buena Vista by high spirited officers serving on garrison duty with time on
   their hands. On May 20, 1848, two young lieutenants of the Virginia Regiment,
   Washington L. Mahan and Carlton R. Munford faced off in combat near China,
   Mexico, and both died of the wounds inflicted by the other party. The Lieutenant
   M. referred to by Doubleday could have been one of these men, or Lieutenant
   William J. Minor, also of the Virginia Regiment.

2. Heitman, *Register*, vol. 1, p. 774. "Lieut P." was Francis Engle Patterson from Pennsylvania who joined the 1st Artillery at the rank of 2nd lieutenant. Patterson resigned his commission in 1857, but entered the volunteer service in 1861 as the colonel of the 17th Pennsylvania Infantry. He was promoted to the rank of brigadier general of volunteers on April 11, 1862, and died on November 22, 1862.

3. Heitman, *Register*, vol. 2, p. 44; Wallace, "The First Regiment of Virginia Volunteers," p. 58. Lieutenant Thomas P. August served in the Virginia Regiment in northern Mexico. After the war he was elected major of the 1st Regiment of Virginia Volunteers in 1851, and made colonel in 1853. This may be the reason that Doubleday refers to August by that title. He was appointed colonel of the 15th Virginia Regiment in 1861 and was severely wounded in the Battle of Malvern Hill in 1862. For the remainder of the war, August served as head of the Bureau of Conscription and died in Richmond on July 31, 1869.

4. Heitman, *Register*, vol. 2, p. 61. Gaston Meares served as lieutenant colonel of the Arkansas Mounted Regiment. He stayed on in northern Mexico after the regiment returned home in May, 1847, to serve as captain of an independent company of Arkansas volunteers.

5. The 1850 Census of Cameron County, Texas, lists James Selkirk, a native of Scotland, as the pilot at the mouth of the Rio Grande.

6. Wallace, "The First Regiment of Virginia Volunteers," p. 73; Gregg, *The Diary & Letters of Josiah Gregg*, vol. 2, p. 206. The execution of the five condemned Mexicans occurred on January 19, 1848. A member of the Virginia Regiment described the activities in Saltillo on that day:

> Ten o'clock—witnessed the execution of five men,
>
> eleven o'clock—attended church,
>
> three P.M.—visited the cockpit where the priest who had conducted the morning service was acting as judge,
>
> five P.M.—was at the race course.
>
> So you see we have every kind of entertainment, except bull-fighting, and we expect every day we will have that.

7. Heitman, *Register*, vol. 2, pp. 54, 65; Wallace, "The First Regiment of Virginia Volunteers," p. 70. John F. Hamtramack and Thomas B. Randolph were the colonel and lieutenant colonel respectively of the 1st Virginia Infantry. *The Richmond Enquirer* of December 31, 1847, picked up an account of the attack on Randolph and others at Rinconada Ranch first published in the *Monterey Gazette*: "Colonel Randolph and his party were attacked by a band of about thirty-five *rancheros* on December 2, 1847, who came at them from both sides brandishing lances and pistols."

But Randolph, a veteran of the War of 1812 who was distinguished for leading an advance guard in the attack on Queenstown Heights on October 13, 1812, knew how to defend his party. He quickly formed his men "like a brave and intrepid officer … with the coolness and judgment characteristic of the man." Randolph was on a sick leave to return to the United States at the time of the attack and never rejoined the regiment in Mexico.

8. Wakelyn, *Biographical Dictionary*, pp. 87-88. William E. Barksdale was a captain in the 2nd Mississippi Infantry. During the Civil War he served as a Confederate brigadier general and was killed at Gettsyburg.

9. Heitman, *Register*, vol. 1, p. 409; Cullum, *Register*, vol. 2, p. 164. George F. Evans graduated from the United States Military Academy in 1846 and was assigned to the 1st Dragoons. During the Mexican War, he was awarded a brevet for gallant conduct at Buena Vista. Evans served as an escort for the boundary commission, 1849-1850. He died on March 29, 1859.

10. Gregg, *The Diary & Letters of Josiah Gregg*, vol. 2, p. 193. The young man referred to by Doubleday was probably Lemuel Stephenson from Ohio, who had taken passage with Josiah Gregg to Brazos Santiago, landing there on December 15, 1847.

11. *Ibid.*, vol. 2, p. 204. The famous traveler, Josiah Gregg, was also a botanist, geographer, merchant, translator, and practicing physician. His book, *Commerce of the Prairies*, was a staple item included in nearly every homesteader's wagon that headed west. Gregg set up his medical practice at Saltillo in January, 1848, in the house of Mariano Ramos in the Calle del Guizache, probably a neighbor of Doubleday.

12. Reilly, "American Reporters," pp. 126-28, 218-19; Spurlin, *Texas Veterans*, p. 198. The "eccentric Captain Tobin" referred to by Doubleday was the soldier of fortune George Henry Tobin, who came to south Texas as a Louisiana volunteer and reporter for the *New Orleans Delta*. Tobin was born in Wicklow, Ireland, and attended Trinity College before traveling to the United States. He was considered one of the first American war correspondents and wrote articles and letters for the papers under the title, "Notes from my knapsack. By G. H. Tobin, Late Capt. Louisiana Volunteers." This credit was shortened to "From Tobin's Knapsack," and although he had not attained the rank of captain, he would hereafter be referred to as "Captain Tobin." The editor of the *Delta* summarized Tobin's humorous style of reporting in this statement:

> There is a good deal of George's humor which we would like to soften and modify, but it is a difficult and dangerous task, and we must give him with all his faults, praying that our readers will bear in mind he is a wild rollicking dragoon, who in his multifarious duties hasn't had time to polish and refine style.

Tobin joined the Texas Spy Company of Ben McCulloch in January, 1847, and would rise to the rank of second lieutenant before the company was disbanded in

July, 1847. He participated in the Battle of Buena Vista and was virtually the only newspaper correspondent to report the battle. Other reporters had transferred to central Mexico by this time to report the actions of Scott's army, assuming that no more battles would be fought in northern Mexico. Tobin sent a large packet of correspondence to the *Delta* by messenger to Monterrey, but as the roads from there to the Rio Grande were blocked at that time by guerrilla activity, the messenger left the packet at the Monterrey Post Office for delivery through conventional channels. The *Delta* received Tobin's packet on April 10, 1847, too late to be timely news.

13. Wallace, "The First Regiment of Virginia Volunteers," p. 74. Kenton Harper, editor of the *Staunton Spectator*, joined the Virginia Regiment and was captain of the Light Infantry Company of that regiment. Harper, was appointed as military governor of Parras de la Fuente, a town ninety-eight miles west of Saltillo and famous for its wines. Harper wrote his commanding officer soon after assuming office that, "The people of Parras have thus far indicated to us the most friendly dispositions and it shall be my aim to cultivate and receive them by all proper means in my power." However, on March 18, 1848, the bodies of Moses Hurt and Israel Peck, privates in Harper's company were found outside of town, the victims of foul play. Two Mexicans, believed to be guilty by Harper, were imprisoned on March 19. With the approval of many of the citizens of Parras, the two prisoners were executed, and the tense atmosphere that existed in Parras quickly returned to normal.

14. Gregg, *The Diary & Letters of Josiah Gregg*, vol. 2, p. 91. The stone dam, built around 1777 by the Marquis de Aguayo, was a part of an internal improvement project instigated by the Spanish government. The length of the dam was 170 yards with a height of about fifty feet and a thickness of sixteen feet. The project was designed to furnish irrigation water for the valley but quickly filled with mud, rendering the impoundment useless.

7: WE LEAVE MEXICO

1. Heitman, *Register*, vol. 1, p. 805; Cullum, *Register*, vol. 1, pp. 365-66. James Henry Prentiss graduated from the United States Military Academy in 1830 and was assigned to the 1st Infantry. He served in the Artillery School for Practice at Fort Monroe, Virginia, until 1832. Prentiss held a post in the adjutant general's office in Washington, D.C., until 1835. He served in the Florida War in 1836 as an aide-de-camp to General Eustis and, continuing in this position, followed General Eustis to Europe, 1836-1838. From 1840 to 1841, he served in Maine during the controversy with England over the boundary of that state. During the War with Mexico Prentiss served as assistant adjutant general for General Wool, accompanying his column on the march to Monclova in 1846. He commanded a battery

of heavy artillery stationed at Rinconada Pass and was ordered to join the army at Buena Vista on the evening of February 23 but arrived too late to participate in the battle. He was assigned to Fort Polk, Texas, near Point Isabel, and died there of disease on September 22, 1848.

2. J. Smith, *War With Mexico,* "Pillow to Wife," September 6, 1846, vol. 1, p. 212. Camargo is on the east bank of the Rio San Juan about four miles above the junction of that river with the Rio Grande. Camargo is about 140 miles from Matamoros as the crow flies but is at least twice that far by boat traveling along the Rio Grande. The town consisted of about 2000 inhabitants in early 1846. Because it was considered to be nominally the head of navigation on the Rio Grande, Camargo became a vast American supply depot during the Mexican War, with supplies transported to this site from the coast by steamboat. From this town, the American army assembled for the march overland to Monterrey, about 100 miles southwest. During this time the camps of American soldiers lined both sides of the Rio San Juan for several miles on either side of Camargo. Sickness swept through the camps in Camargo, followed by wholesale death. Regimental bands so often struck up the chords of the death march in funeral services at Camargo that the mockingbirds of that area began to imitate the sounds of that mournful refrain. An American volunteer officer referred to Camargo as "a yawning grave." It is estimated that about 1500 unmarked graves line the banks of the Rio San Juan around Camargo.

3. Heitman, *Register,* vol. 1, p. 446; Cullum, *Register,* vol. 2, p. 15. Julius Peter Garesche, born in Cuba, graduated from the United States Military Academy in 1841 and was assigned to the 4th Artillery. He served as acting assistant adjutant general of the Rio Grande District at Camargo, Mexico, 1846-1848. Garesche served in Texas, 1849-1851, at Forts Polk and Brown. He returned to Texas, 1853-1855, assigned to garrison duty at Fort Brown. During the Civil War, he served as chief of staff of General Rosecran's Army of the Cumberland. Garesche was killed by a cannonball on December 31, 1862, at the Battle of Stones River, where, according to Cullum, "at a critical moment, when the Commanding General, with his Staff, dashed forward to restore the tide of battle, which was turning against our [Union] arms ... ."

4. Heitman, *Register,* vol. 1, p. 1060. Charles F. Wooster graduated from the United States Military Academy in 1833 and was assigned to the 4th Artillery. He was awarded a brevet for actions in the Battle of Sacramento on February 28, 1847, as a member of Doniphan's command. Wooster died on February 14, 1856.

5. *American Flag,* July 22, 1848. Stationed to garrison Fort Brown on this date were Company E, 1st Artillery, and Company B, 4th Artillery.

6. Coffman, *The Old Army,* pp. 64-65; "Correspondence Between Secretary of War and Major General Zachary," "R. Jones to Major General Z. Taylor," October 8, 1846, "Major General Z. Taylor to R. Jones," November 8, 1846, Special Orders

No. 172, November 6, 1846, Special Order No. 62, May 28, 1847, in 30th Congress, 1st Session, House Executive Document 60; F. Smith, *Mexican War Journal*, pp. 24-25; Dillon, *American Artillery*, pp. 19-20, 84-85; Ganoe, *History of the U.S. Army*, p. 219; Chamberlain, *My Confession*, pp. 192-97. Thomas West Sherman, referred to as "Old Tim" by a member of his company, Lieutenant John C. Tidball, was not happily thought of by all. Tidball's opinions on Sherman, as recorded by Coffman, were: "It was his nature to be unsociable and he cultivated it in every possible way." When Tidball was acquiring the first symptoms of malaria at Fort Brown in 1848, he reported his illness to Sherman. "Hem, a soldier should never be sick, sir, I was never sick in all my life, sir," was the reply. When the company was moved north for a chilly winter in Fort Trumbull, Connecticut, Tidball visited Sherman in his quarters and found him seated in his overcoat with no fire. The room was "comfortless" with only a cot, a keg, and a table for furniture. "That is all a soldier needs; he does not require a fire, it is unhealthy...." As for meals, Sherman told the young lieutenant that "all he needed was bread and some acid fruit to prevent scurvy." Sherman was seen by the company, thankfully, at Sunday inspections only, but that was enough. "One thing after another which he saw, or imagined he saw wrong about the company rapidly advanced him from ordinary wrath to a state of raving madness. He then fairly frothed at the mouth and the air around became blue with his lurid imprecations." Sherman's service during the Mexican War had a rather inauspicious beginning. Neither present at the Battles of Palo Alto nor Resaca de la Palma, he was detached from the 3rd Artillery and detailed for temporary duty to the quartermaster's department, August 28, 1846, in Camargo, Mexico. Captain Franklin Smith, a volunteer quartermaster officer stationed in Camargo, reported that, "Capt. Sherman was much dissatisfied with his position across the river [QM Depot] and had applied to him to be relieved...." But Sherman remained at Camargo while Taylor's Army marched to capture of Monterrey. Sherman seethed to be in action and addressed a letter directly to the general-in-chief. Acting on Sherman's letter to Winfield Scott, Roger Jones, adjutant general of the Army, penned this response to Taylor on October 8, 1846, siding with Sherman but leaving the final decision on Sherman's duty assignment to Taylor:

> General: Captain T. W. Sherman, 3rd Artillery, having addressed the general-in-chief on the subject of his assignment to duty in the quartermaster's department, and his claim to succeed to the company to which he has been promoted, I am desired by the general-in-chief to inform you that company D, 3rd artillery, to which Captain N. B. Bragg has just succeeded by his promotion, is now under orders for Point Isabel. This will afford you an opportunity of placing both Captains Sherman and Bragg at the head of their companies, to which they have been respectively promoted. Should you, however, deem it essential to the good of the service in the field to transfer the two captains, you are authorized by the general-in-chief to do so....

> R. Jones, Adjutant General

Taylor, angry at the rebuff from Washington for his handling of the Battle of
Monterrey, did not take kindly to this letter attempting to override his decision.
In this letter of November 8, 1846, to the adjutant general, he wrote:

> Sir: Your communication of October 8th, relative to the positions of Captains
> Sherman and Bragg, 3d artillery, was received yesterday. You will perceive
> from my "special orders," No. 172, dated the 6th instant, that Captain
> Sherman has already been ordered to join his proper company, and that
> Captain Bragg had been assigned to the command of Company C. In regard
> to this latter assignment I beg leave to say, that on the 18th of June, when
> Captain Bragg legally succeeded to his grade, Capt. M. S. Miller, in whose
> place he was promoted, was company C, to which company Captain Bragg
> was therefore naturally carried. It is not seen how this assignment could be
> affected by the transfer announced in "special orders," No. 69, of August 6th;
> for, at the date of said transfer, Captain Miller, it seems to me, was no longer,
> in point of law, an officer of the 3d artillery. However the question of succes-
> sion may be viewed, it is vitally important, for the good of the service, that a
> permanent and efficient captain, experienced in the field service of artillery,
> should be attached to company C, which is greatly in want of administrative
> care and management. I deem Captain Bragg eminently qualified in all
> respects for this command; and the battery which he leaves has by his care
> been brought into such good condition, and is withal so well officered, that it
> may suffer a change of commanders without material injury. I shall therefore
> retain the present assignment until otherwise ordered.

Z. Taylor, Major Gen. U.S. Army, commanding

The event that probably allowed Sherman to be reassigned to his regiment
was the death of Randolph Ridgely on October 27, 1846. Ridgely, one of the new
breed of light artillery officers, who had been instrumental in the American victories at Palo Alto and Resaca de la Palma, was killed on October 27, 1846, by a
fall from a horse in the streets of occupied Monterrey. Ridgeley had inherited the
command of Company C, 3rd Artillery, upon the death of Ringgold at Palo Alto,
and his death had in turn created a great vacancy. Who would lead this famous
company personally trained by Ringgold, the nation's first company of horse
artillery? By law, an artillery regiment could have only one such company, all
other companies were designated simply as mounted artillery. Orders from Taylor
in Monterrey followed on November 6, 1846:

> 1. Capt. T. W. Sherman 3rd Artillery will be relieved without delay in his staff
> duties at Camargo and will then join his proper company (E) at this place.
>
> 2. Capt. B. Bragg, 3rd Artillery, will join Light Company C, 3rd Artillery to
> which it is considered that his promotion properly carries him. This assign-
> ment will be subject to approval at General Headquarters to which the case
> will be specifically reported.

This order must have been quite a blow to someone of Sherman's volatile temperament. Bragg's promotion to captain was dated to June 18, 1846, while Sherman's dated to May 28, 1846, thus in regular ranks, Sherman was senior to Bragg. However, Bragg had received a brevet to the rank of major on September 23, 1846, for his actions in the capture of Monterrey. In terms of their permanent ranks, Sherman should have been given his choice of assignments, but the brevet rank was taken into consideration. The guarded wording of this order though indicated a degree of uncertainty by Taylor. The decision by Taylor in favor of Bragg could have been the basis of Doubleday's comments about Taylor's decision not to allow Sherman to command at Buena Vista. In fact Sherman's battery performed yeoman service at Buena Vista for their country, and Sherman was awarded a brevet for his actions. On March 3, 1847, Congress enacted a law allowing each artillery regiment to have two companies of light artillery; Taylor responded with Order No. 62 on May 28, 1847, "Capt. T. W. Sherman's Company (E) of the 3rd Artillery, is designated as the additional Light Artillery Company of that Regiment ... ." Brevet Major Sherman was not liked by the enlisted men at Monterrey. Known as "Battery" Sherman by the men, Samuel Chamberlain remembered that "Sherman was an eccentric, weak, tyrannical officer, allowing his men no privileges, and resorting to the most severe punishment for the most trivial offense." On one occasion, Sherman ordered a soldier who had been arrested for selling whiskey to the troops to receive fifty lashes, laid on with a mule whip. One-by-one the guard detail refused to administer this punishment, and one-by-one they were bucked and gagged for disobedience. Six of the guard were bound before a terrified seventh soldier agreed to administer the barbaric punishment. Sherman then preferred charges against the six soldiers and they were court-martialed.

7. Heitman, *Register*, vol. 1, p. 296; Cullum, *Register*, vol. 1, p. 523. William Warren Chapman graduated from the United States Military Academy in 1837 and was assigned to the 2nd Artillery. Chapman served in the Florida War, 1837-1838, and assisted in the emigration of Indians to the West in 1838. He served on the northern frontier during the Canadian border disturbance, 1838-1841. During the Mexican War he served on quartermaster duty and marched with Wool's column into Mexico. Chapman was awarded a brevet for gallant conduct at Buena Vista. After the war he was stationed in the Department of Texas, serving at Fort Brown, Brazos Island, and Corpus Christi, 1848-1855. Chapman died on September 27, 1859.

8. Major W. W. Chapman to Major Sherman, September 4, 1848, and September 12, 1848, Chapman Family Papers. The following letter probably caused the arrest of W. W. Chapman by Sherman:

> Major: Your letter of the 8th instant was handed to me yesterday on my return from the Brazos and in reply I have to state that its contents do not in the least degree alter my opinion of a principle as old as armies are and one which has been recognized in all military bodies in every age and country from time

immemorial, viz. that a junior officer cannot command a senior. I know of no instance in the history of our Army where a contrary principle has ever been attempted to be established. It is true, so far as my peculiar duties as quartermaster are concerned and whilst not controlled by the express instructions of a superior officer, but acting solely on my own responsibility, I do claim to interpret the Army Regulations and decide on the custom of service according to my own judgment and not in obedience to the mandate of another whose order would in no wise relieve me from the responsibility of any act done by me and not approved by the government. The exercise of such limited function does not however as you infer, "have the effect of making the Quartermaster the bona fide commanding officer." I should be wanting in self respect and duty to my profession by allowing the closing remarks of your letter to pass without comment, "and cannot for a moment be listened to." This language from a superior to a contumacious inferior might perhaps be justifiable, but its use between officers of the same grade addressed too by a junior officer to a superior in rank is to say the least exceptionable if not positively offensive. As the orders referred to in your letter were not complied with by me, no property or money responsibility was incurred and, therefore, they are of no use to the files of my office. Accordingly, they are respectfully returned.

I am, Major,
Very respectfully
Your obedient servant,
W. W. Chapman

Both Chapman and Sherman received their brevets dated February 23, 1847, for actions at Buena Vista, but in their permanent ranks as captain, Sherman was the senior officer. The argument between the two evidently hinged on whether or not line officers exercised precedence in command over staff officers. Of a more official nature was this message of September 4, 1848, sent by Chapman to Sherman so that business at Fort Brown might at least be expedited:

Major:
I respectfully return your two orders dated August 31 and September 1, 1848: the reasons for so doing will no doubt be obvious to you. Requisitions made on me that do not conflict with previous orders, the regulations of the Army or the custom of the service will be promptly complied with. Special requisitions approved by you will meet with the same attention as if ordered by a commanding officer senior to me in rank.
W. W. Chapman

9. Heitman, *Register*, vol. 1, p. 510; Cullum, *Register*, vol. 1, p. 578. Joseph Abel Haskin graduated from the United States Military Academy in 1839 and was assigned to the 1st Artillery. Haskin served on the northern border during the Canadian boundary dispute, 1840-1845. During the Mexican War he served in central Mexico, participating in the Siege of Vera Cruz and was awarded a brevet

for gallant conduct at Cerro Gordo. Haskin fought at Oka Laka, Contreras, and won a second brevet for meritorious conduct at the capture of Chapultapec Castle where he lost his left arm. After the war, he served in Texas at Fort Brown, 1851-1852. During the Civil War, he commanded the northern defenses of Washington, D.C. Haskin died on August 3, 1874.

10. Fort Brown Monthly Post Returns, July-October, 1848. Abner Doubleday appears on the post returns of Fort Brown for the first time in July, 1848, where he is listed as "arrived post July 22, 1848, Acting A.C.S." The post was commanded at this time by Captain Edward Deas. By August, the post was garrisoned by Company E, 2nd Artillery, Company E, 3rd Artillery, and Companies B and K, 4th Artillery. Captain and Brevet Major T. W. Sherman assumed command of the post on August 9, and Doubleday is listed as "Asst. Commissary of Subsistence." But by September 26, a Lieutenant Brown had relieved Doubleday as A.C.S. The September return lists Doubleday as "in arrest." Neither Sherman's nor Doubleday's name appears on the October returns. Doubleday was sent to Fort Columbus and Sherman to Fort Preble.

11. Chapman, *News From Brownsville*, p. 81; Long, *Memoirs*, pp. 32, 36-37. Prentiss' death is reported by Helen Chapman to have been caused by yellow fever. Prentiss and Robert E. Lee were close friends. Prentiss served as a groomsman in Lee's wedding and was a messmate when stationed in Washington, D.C. Lee was also assigned to Wool's column to Chihuahua as an engineering officer in 1846 and the two were messmates on this march.

12. Heitman, *Register*, vol. 1, p. 335. Ichabod Bennet Crane joined the Marine Corps in 1809 as a 2nd lieutenant. He resigned this commission in 1812 and was subsequently commissioned as a captain in the 3rd Artillery in the same year. Crane was awarded a brevet in 1813 for "meritorious service and general good conduct in the army." He rose to the rank of colonel in the 1st Artillery by 1843. Crane died on October 5, 1857.

13. *DAB*, vol. 20, pp. 380-81; Cullum, *Register*, vol. 1, pp. 201-02; Heitman, *Register*, vol. 1, p. 1049; Wakelyn, *Biographical Dictionary*, p. 442. John Henry Winder graduated from the United States Military Academy in 1820 and was assigned to the artillery. He resigned his commission in 1823 but was reappointed to the artillery in 1827. He was an instructor of military tactics at West Point, 1827-1828, and was stationed in Maine during the Canadian border dispute, 1840-1842. During the Mexican War he was promoted to brevet major for gallant and meritorious conduct in the Battles of Contreras and Churubusco. A second brevet was awarded for his actions in the assault on Mexico City. He was promoted to the rank of major in 1860 but resigned his commission in 1861 and received a commission as brigadier general in the Confederate Army on April 27, 1861. Cullum states that Winder "became the inhuman jailer of the Libby and other Southern prisons." In fact, he was placed in command of Libby and Belle Isle military prisons in Richmond and became the provost marshal of that city.

His reponsibilities included maintaining order in the city, the arrest and return of deserters, and he often was required to fix commodity prices in the city. By 1864 he was also placed in command of the military prisons in Alabama and Georgia. While Winder was widely accused of the inhuman treatment of Union prisoners of war, Malone is careful to present a balanced treatment of Winder's many thankless duties. Winder was no respector of rank and privilege, which must have been the basis of much criticism from the influential persons who dealt with him. His speech and manners were naturally sharp and abrupt and his rigid military bearing was not a characteristic that endeared him to the many persons with whom he came into contact. The naval blockade of the South meant that medicine, clothing, and food were in short supply for both the military and civilian populations of the South. How much shorter must have been the supply of rations to the prisoners? In the earlier stages of the war, a prisoner exchange system shuffled many Union soldiers back to the North and minimized their time of incarceration. Grant refused, however, to continue the prisoner exchange system in 1864, and from that time on the suffering of Union soldiers was great. Winder died in Florence, South Carolina, on February 8, 1865, from disease brought on by the anxieties of his duties.

14. Heitman, *Register*, vol. 1, p. 606. Minor Knowlton graduated from the United States Military Academy in 1825 and was assigned to the 1st Artillery. He rose to the rank of captain in 1846 and retired from the military in 1861. Knowlton died on December 24, 1870.

15. Heitman, *Register*, vol. 1, p. 875. Truman Seymour graduated from the United States Military Academy in 1842 and was assigned to the 1st Artillery. He was awarded two brevets for actions at Cerro Gordo and the Battles of Contreras and Churubusco. During the Civil War Seymour received many promotions in rank for gallantry and meritorious conduct. His recognitions include the defense of Fort Sumter, the Battle of South Mountain, Battle of Antietam, and the capture of Petersburg. Seymour retired from the service in 1876 at the rank of major general and died on October 30, 1891.

16. Cullum, *Register*, vol. 1, p. 25. Fort Hamilton, New York, is located on the southwestern extremity of Long Island at the Narrows on the east side of the entrance to New York Harbor.

17. Heitman, *Register*, vol. 1, p. 946. Francis Taylor graduated from the United States Military Academy in 1821 and was assigned to the 4th Artillery. He received two brevets for actions at Cerro Gordo and Churubusco. Taylor was promoted to the rank of captain of the 1st Artillery in 1855 and died on October 12, 1858.

18. Maury, *Recollections*, p. 71. Dabney Maury remembered Jackson's concern with his health:

> One day while we were at West Point we were surprised by a visit from young Major Stonewall Jackson, who had been serving since the war with an

artillery company on duty in New York harbor. At that time he was convinced that one of his legs was bigger than the other, and that one of his arms was likewise unduly heavy. He had acquired the habit of raising the heavy arm straight up so that, as he said, the blood would run back into his body and lighten it. I believe he never after relinquished this peculiar practice, even upon the battle-field.

19. Heitman, *Register*, vol. 1, p. 337; Swanberg, *First Blood*, pp. 1-3, 172, 178, 183, 291, 328. Samuel Wylie Crawford joined the service in 1851 as an assistant surgeon. Crawford served at Fort Sumter during the bombardment and wrote a book of this experience, *The Genesis of the Civil War*. During the Civil War he was appointed a brigadier general of volunteers and was recognized on several occasions for meritorious conduct. He was cited for his actions at Gettsyburg, Wilderness, Spotsylvania, Jericho Mills, Bethesda Church, Petersburg, Globe Tavern, and Five Forks. Crawford was mustered out of the volunteer service at the rank of major general and retired from the service at the rank of brigadier general. Crawford died on November 3, 1892.

20. Heitman, *Register*, vol. 1, p. 962. Otis Hammond Tillinghast graduated from the United States Military Academy in 1843 and was assigned to the 1st Artillery. He rose to the rank of captain by 1861. He died of wounds received at the Battle of Bull Run on July 23, 1861.

21. Heitman, *Register*, vol. 1, p. 586; Warner, *Generals in Blue*, pp. 258-59. Philip Kearney was born in 1815 in New York City into a wealthy family. In 1836, he inherited a million dollars from his grandfather and began to live his life's dream—to serve in the army. He joined the dragoons in 1837 at the rank of 2nd lieutenant. In 1839, Kearney attended the French Cavalry School at Saumur and fought with the *Chasseurs d'Afrique* in Algiers in 1840. During the Mexican War Kearney was awarded a brevet for his actions at Contreras and Churubusco. At Churubusco he received a severe wound to his left arm, requiring amputation. After the war, he was impatient with the peacetime army and resigned his commission in 1851 to travel the world. In 1859, he served in Napoleon III's Imperial Guard and fought in the Battles of Magenta and Solferino in Italy. He took part in every cavalry action of these battles, "with his reins clenched in his teeth." Kearny returned to the United States with the outbreak of the Civil War and commanded a division of volunteers at Second Manassas. He was killed at Chantilly, Virginia, on September 1, 1862, when he mistakenly rode into Confederate lines and was shot from his horse while attempting to escape capture.

8: THE GARDINER MINE CLAIM

1. Smith, *The Presidencies of Zachary Taylor & Millard Fillmore,* p. 167. Charles Magill Conrad from Louisiana was secretary of war, 1850-1853, in the administration of Millard Fillmore.

2. House Report 1, Memorial of George A. Gardiner; *National Intelligencer*, March 18, 1853; House Report No. 1, declaration of John C. Gardiner; *National Intelligencer*, May 3, 1854. George A. Gardiner was born on March 18, 1818, in the State of New York. Witnesses at his trial reported seeing him in Mexico as early as 1840, at Vera Cruz in 1841, and in Mexico City from 1842 to 1844, where he practiced his profession as a dentist. By 1846 he was found in Guadalajara where a witness remembered seeing his sign in the street, "Jorge Gardiner, *Dentisto Curijano*." Another witness testified that he saw Gardiner in Mexico City in 1847 at the time of the decree for the expulsion of all Americans in Mexico. Gardiner passed as a Cuban, and as he wanted to remain in Mexico asked the witness not to divulge his true nationality. George Gardiner appeared in Washington, D.C., in early 1849, retained influential legal counsel and presented his claims for compensation to the Mexican Claims Board in that year. While the board felt that his claims were questionable, he was awarded the sum of $428,760. An employee of the State Department, who had lived in Mexico, later examined the documents presented in the case and found them to be fraudulent. Based on this evidence, the government obtained an indictment against George Gardiner for "the crime of false swearing in support of the claim" and the first trial began on February 17, 1853. This trial, extensively covered in the papers, resulted in a mistrial on May 30, 1853. A second commission was sent by the government to Mexico and upon their return a second trial was scheduled. The second trial began on December 13, 1853, and resulted in Gardiner's conviction on March 3, 1854. He was sentenced to ten years in prison but committed suicide rather than serve this sentence.

   John Charles Gardiner, younger bother of George A. Gardiner, was born in 1828 on the island of Cuba, where his parents resided at that time for the health of his mother. Witnesses reported seeing the younger Gardiner in Mexico during the 1840s, and would often confuse him with his brother. He was employed during the Mexican War as an interpreter for General Winfield Scott and reported his residence in 1852 as Washington, D.C., where he was employed as an agent before Congress to represent certain French business interests in Mexico. He was indicted by the government for "the crime of false swearing" in 1853 for his part in the false mine claim. His trial was scheduled for May 1, 1854, but he jumped his bond and failed to appear to answer charges. His further whereabouts were unknown.

3. House Report No. 1, 32nd Congress, 2nd Session, p. 2; Heitman, *Register*, vol. 1, p. 357. Charles W. Davis was a clerk in the State Department and had served as the last secretary of the board of commissioners appointed to mediate American claims under the Treaty of Guadalupe Hidalgo. Davis was a veteran of the Mexican War, having entered the army on August 8, 1846, at the rank of captain in the quartermaster's department. He served in northern Mexico and was honorably discharged on February 23, 1849.

4. Letter from John H. Mears, House Report No. 369, 33rd Congress, 1st Session, pp. 23, 27. John H. Mears listed his permanent residence as Charleston, South Carolina, but in 1851 resided in Cadereyta, Nueva Leon, Republic of Mexico. He had received $153,125 from the Mexican Claims Commission for his claim to the destruction of a quicksilver mine in Mexico during the Mexican War. Mears was indicted in 1853 for "the crime of false swearing" but the date and disposition of his trial is unknown. It is possible that his residence in Mexico at that time prevented him from being extradited to face these charges. Witnesses living in the Department of Rio Verde, where the mine was supposed to be located, swore that "no mine of silver or quicksilver has ever been discovered" in this department.

5. A *vara* is a Spanish unit of measurement 33 ⅓ inches long.

6. *DAB*, vol. 4, pp. 546-48; Cullum, *Register*, vol. 2, p. 139. John Jordan Crittenden, a Kentuckian, was attorney general in the administration of Millard Fillmore. Prior to the Fillmore administration, Crittenden opposed the annexation of Texas in the Senate and was skeptical about the justice of a war against Mexico. Once war was declared, however, he supported it by recruiting volunteers in Kentucky and voting for the appropriations bills. He had supported Taylor for the presidency but refused any cabinet position in the Taylor administration. In the years preceeding the Civil War, he advocated compromise and attempted to preserve the Union. With the bombardment of Fort Sumter, he returned to Kentucky and strongly advised his fellow citizens to remain in the Union but to maintain a strong position of neutrality and to supply neither men nor money for the subjugation of the South. But the two positions were incompatible. He subsequently opposed the confiscation acts, the enlistment of black troops, the Emancipation Proclamation, and the military regime that controlled his state. One of his sons, George B. Crittenden, served as a major general in the Confederate Army, while another son, Thomas L. Crittenden, served as a major general in the Union Army. Crittenden's nephew, William Logan Crittenden, led a regiment of Kentucky volunteers in Lopez's Second Expedition against Spanish Cuba. He was captured and executed by the Spanish on August 16, 1851, at Atares Castle in Havana Harbor. John Crittenden died in Frankfort, Kentucky, in 1863 while campaigning for reelection to Congress.

7. *DAB*, vol. 4, pp. 457-58; J. Smith, *The War with Mexico*, vol. 2, p. 278; Bauer, *The Mexican War*, p. 363; Depositions of Waddy Thompson and Robert G. Corwin, House Report No. 1, 32nd Congress, 2nd Session. Thomas "Black Tom" Corwin was governor of Ohio, 1840-1842; United States senator, 1844-1850; secretary of the treasury in the Fillmore administration, 1850-1853; and minister to Mexico, 1861-1864. Corwin died on December 18, 1865. On the floor of the Senate on February 11, 1847, Corwin denounced the Mexican War as a means for the acquisition of new lands. His widely quoted remark, "If I were a Mexican, I would tell you, 'Have you not room in your country to bury your dead men? If you come into mine we will greet you with bloody hands, and welcome you to hospitable

graves.'" The speech, coming just prior to the Battle of Buena Vista and the long casualty lists that appeared in newspapers, struck many Americans as an act of treason. According to Justin Smith, the speech, "sounded the knell of its author's great political hopes." An effigy of Corwin, dressed in a Mexican uniform, reportedly burned by the Ohio volunteer troops near Buena Vista had these few lines of verse posted nearby: "Old Tom Corwin is dead and here he lies; Nobody's sorry and nobody cries; Where he's gone and how he fares, Nobody knows and nobody cares." Corwin's involvement in the Gardiner mine fraud brought cries from the public that resulted in an investigation by a special committee of the House of Representatives of the 32nd Congress. "Whereas a strong suspicion rests upon the public mind that fraudulent claims have been allowed by the late Mexican Claim Commission, with one of which it is suspected that Thomas Corwin, Secretary of the Treasury, has been improperly connected: Therefore, Resolved: That a committee be appointed ... to investigate all the facts touching the connexion of the said Thomas Corwin ... with the said Gardiner claim ... ." General Waddy Thompson related that a Dr. George A. Gardiner met with him about January, 1849, and asked Thompson to represent him in a claim before the Mexican Commission. Thompson required fifteen percent of all money recovered for Dr. Gardiner as a fee and hired Thomas Corwin, then serving in the Senate, as assistant counsel, to be paid five percent of the recovered monies from Thompson's fee. Mr. Corwin was retained in May, 1849, but by July, 1850, was appointed secretary of the treasury. Prior to Corwin's assumption of this post, he divested himself of his interest in the Gardiner case, which amounted to $80,270, paid to Corwin by George Law of the State of New York with the legal representation of the Gardiner claim taken over by Governor Young of that state. This questionable transaction was reported out of committee, but no further actions were taken and these distinguished gentlemen were never indicted for a questionable practice involving the sale of influence and conflict of interest.

8. *National Intelligencer*, March 30, 1853; Chance, telephone interview with staff at the Naval Historical Center, Washington, D.C., March 18, 1995. Captain William W. Hunter was one of the Senate's commissioners sent to Mexico to investigate the Gardiner claims and to testify in the Gardiner trial during March, 1853. He joined the United States Navy at the rank of midshipman on May 1, 1822. Hunter was listed as a passed midshipman on May 24, 1828, and by May 27, 1830, had been promoted to the rank of lieutenant. Hunter was again promoted to the rank of commander on January 6, 1853, but resigned his commission on April 2, 1861, to cast his lot with the South. During 1861 he served with the Provisional Navy of the Confederate States on station in Richmond and in New Orleans aboard the C.S.S. *Jackson*. From 1861 to 1863, Hunter commanded the naval defenses of the coast of Texas, and was in command of the Savannah Squadron, 1863-1864.

9. *National Intelligencer*, April 1, 1853. James A. Partridge, of Baltimore, Maryland, was one of the Senate's commissioners sent to Mexico to investigate the Gardiner mine claims and to testify for the prosecution in the Gardiner trial during April, 1853.

10. *DAB*, vol. 17, pp. 243-44. Buckingham Smith was appointed secretary of legation in Mexico on September 9, 1850, and served until February, 1852. His father, Josiah Smith, had served earlier as United States consul in Mexico. Buckingham Smith, a transplanted Floridian was interested in the history of that territory and while in Mexico began extensive archival work. In 1855, he was appointed secretary of legation in Spain and served in that post until 1858. His stay in Spain enabled him to continue his historical studies in the Spanish archives. His work resulted in several publications, the most famous being *The Narratives of Alvar Nunez Cabeza de Vaca*, translated by Smith and published in 1851. Smith died in 1871 and willed an extensive collection of papers to the New-York Historical Society.

11. *Who Was Who in America*, Historical Volume, p. 340; Maury, *Recollections*, p. 105. Henry May, whose brother was the famous Mexican War hero Charles May, was born in Washington, D.C., in 1816. He was admitted to the bar in 1840 to practice law and was sent by President Franklin Pierce to investigate the Gardiner frauds in Mexico in 1850. May was a member of the House of Representatives from Maryland in the 33rd and 37th Congresses. May died in Baltimore on September 25, 1866. Dabney Maury recorded this rememberance of Henry May and the May family:

> Colonel Charley May, our commandant, was a "Light Dragoon," although, being six feet four inches tall and of tremendous frame, he was fitter for the heavy cavalry. His brother Julian was in my regiment, and was a remarkably handsome man. He, too, was over six feet in stature. Those Mays were extraordinary men in their physical and mental characteristics. Five of the brothers averaged over six feet three inches in height, and all were men of marked character. The Honorable Henry May, a member of Congress from Baltimore, was a man of ability, and of most kind and courtly manners. In the exciting times incident to the disrupting of the government, Mr. May stood up manfully for the rights of the people. I believe he was imprisoned for it.

12. Simpson, *Many Mexicos*, pp. 243-45; Calcott, *Santa Anna*, pp. 155-61; Maissin, *The French in Mexico*, pp. 25-130. The Pastry War (*Guerra de los Pasteles*) began on April 16, 1838, with a French blockade of the Mexican coast from the Yucatan to Matamoros. A total of 600,000 pesos in claims by French citizens against the government of Mexico had not been paid by a bankrupt Mexican government. The smallest claim on this list of demands was by M. Remontel, a French citizen who operated a pastry shop in Tacubaya. Mexican soldiers had entered his shop and eaten 800 pesos worth of pastry and did not pay the owner. Thus the difficulty between these two countries assumed its tragi-comic name.

As the French had recognized the newly formed Republic of Texas, its blockade did not extend above the Rio Grande. Seeing an opportunity to evade the French Navy, Mexican traders began landing goods on the coast of Texas. Texan custom officers, eager to collect duties, patrolled the coast with vigilance and captured a shipload of contraband Mexican flour in 1838 at a site north of Corpus Christi, Texas. This location thus received the name "Flour Bluff" by which it is still known to this day. After six months of haggling between the diplomatic officers of the two countries had produced no results, French Admiral Baudin resorted to force. In the harbor of Vera Cruz, a shelling from the French fleet reduced the fortress of San Juan de Ulloa to rubble. Coordinated with this attack was the landing of a French raiding party led by the Prince de Joinville (incorrectly identified by Doubleday as "Pursee de Fontville"), son of the French king Louis Philippe, to capture Santa Anna at his Vera Cruz headquarters. Santa Anna escaped his captors and organized a force of resistance that counterattacked the French raiders as they were embarking to return to the fleet. A grapeshot struck Santa Anna in the left leg—an injury that required the amputation of the leg below the knee. Santa Anna proclaimed a great victory over the French and his popularity began to grow again as his people made an effort to forgive him for the defeat of San Jacinto. A treaty of peace was agreed to by France and Mexico on March 19, 1839.

13. *DAB*, vol. 4, pp. 345-46. Alfred Conkling was appointed minister to Mexico by the Fillmore administration in 1852 and served until 1853. Prior to this ministerial position, he had served as federal district judge for the northern district of New York for twenty-seven years. Conkling died in 1874.

14. A literal translation is, "Well Sir, there is no shortage of stony ground nor hills."

15. Velazquez, *Historia de San Luis Potosi*, vol. 3, pp. 241-55. The governor of the Mexican state of San Luis Potosi at that time was Julian de los Reyes. Don de los Reyes was assassinated on January 8, 1853.

16. Heitman, *Register*, vol. 2, p. 44; Kenly, *Memoirs of a Volunteer*; Bartlett, *Personal Narrative of Explorations and Incidents*, vol. 1, pp. 19, 149; *National Intelligencer*, March 23, 25, 1853. Captain Edmund Barry served in the famous Baltimore Battallion (Maryland and District of Columbia Battallion) which saw action in both northern and central Mexico. He served after the Mexican War as part of a military escort for the boundary commission survey conducted by Bartlett. Knowing that the surveying party needed to traverse more than 800 miles through hostile Indian country, Bartlett organized "... the mechanics and laborers into a rifle corps, under the command of Captain Edmund Barry, an officer who had served in the army during the Mexican war." Captain Barry testified for the prosecution in the Gardiner trial.

17. *The Papers of Jefferson Davis*, vol. 2, pp. 124, 330-32, 374-76; vol. 3, p. 14; Ford, *Rip Ford's Texas*, pp. 196-205; *New Orleans Picayune*, March 9, 1852, August 6, 1853. The Howell family was well connected. Joseph Davis Howell was born on November 23, 1824, the eldest child of William Burr and Margaret Kempe Howell. He was the namesake of Joseph E. Davis, older brother of Jefferson Davis, who was a business partner of William Howell. Varina Howell Davis, sister of

Joseph Howell, was Jefferson Davis' second wife. Joseph Howell spent a brief time in schools in Princeton, New Jersey, and Edge Hill near Philadephia. In May, 1846, Joseph Howell joined the famous 1st Mississippi Regiment "The Mississippi Rifles" as a private in Company C, the Vicksburg Southrons. Varina, fearing for his safety, stated in a letter, "great was our terror lest his six feet seven inches would make him a mark for the enemy." Young Howell participated in the Battle of Monterey, but was discharged on December 5, 1846, for illness. The discharge certificate described him as "six feet six inches high, fair complexion, black hair, black eyes, and by profession when mustered in, a lawyer." He stayed in Mexico as a clerk in the quartermaster's depot in Camargo until July, 1848. Howell sought a commission in the newly formed 3rd Dragoons in 1847, but received no support from Jefferson Davis for this appointment. In a letter to his father, he wrote that he planned to travel to California from Monterrey in the column of Major John Washington, which consisted of "five companies of Dragoons ... a light Battery, and 100 wagons" but whether he accompanied the army on this journey is unknown. He went on a trading expedition to Oregon in 1850. The census of 1850 for Cameron County, Texas, records a "J. D. Howell, a lawyer of age 27, with property valued at $15,000." Howell was possibly drawn back to the Texas-Mexico border by prospects of a filibustering expedition into Mexico, which was carried out in September, 1851. Under the leadership of General José Maria Jesus Carbajal, acting under *El Plan de la Loba*, an armed force collected near Rancho Davis to invade northeastern Mexico. According to Rip Ford, "Another of General Carbajal's officers was Captain Howell, a brother-in-law of Jefferson Davis." The force swept over Camargo, and advanced on Matamoros. The *pronunciados* captured Fort Paredes on the western edge of the city and moved into the city as far as the customs house on the main plaza before being mysteriously withdrawn by General Carbajal. The *pronunciados* retreated to Camargo and the restless Americans, disappointed by Carbajal's vacillations, disbanded and returned to the United States. For these filibustering activities, Howell and others were indicted by the United States District Court at Brownsville, Texas, on February 17, 1852, and again in 1853. The parties were charged with violations of United States neutrality laws. The case was transferred to Galveston, Texas, under a change of venue. The final disposition of this case is unknown. In 1853, he wrote Jefferson Davis, then secretary of war, requesting a commission in one of the new regiments being formed to protect the overland wagon trains to Oregon but was unsuccessful. Howell returned to California in 1854. The 1857 *New Orleans Directory* lists Howell as a resident, where he continued to live until 1859. Howell mysteriously disappeared from family records past this date and little else is known of his life or whereabouts.

18. *Diccionario Porrua*, p. 1151. The municipality of Lagunillas, is located in southern San Luis Potosi state. The region is crossed by spurs of the Sierra Madre Oriental which form the valleys of Penihuan, Lagunillas, and St. Raphael. The Rio Verde crosses the northern portion of Lagunillas, creating the beautiful waterfall of

Penihuan. The inhabitants of this region are found in ranchos and haciendas, with the principal center of population (about 800 souls) at the village of Lagunillas.

19. *National Intelligencer*, April 25, 1853, May 17, 1853; Heitman, *Register*, vol. 1, p. 892; vol. 2, p. 43; Edgar W. Abbott served as lieutenant colonel of the Massachusetts Regiment. The regiment was stationed initially in northern Mexico at Matamoros and Monterrey, where its members committed many crimes against soldiers and civilians alike. The regiment was ordered to central Mexico and saw action there. Abbott testified for the defense in the Gardiner trial and was forced to admit under cross examination that he had once served in the United States Army. He entered the service from Baltimore as an officer, but had been court-martialed for embezzlement and giving liquor to a soldier. He was reduced to the ranks and later honorably discharged as an invalid.

20. "Secretary of the Treasury on Gardiner Mexican Claim Investigation," House Report No. 1, 32nd Congress, 2nd Session, p. 24. Manuel Verastegui was the prefect of the Rio Verde Region of the state of San Luis Potosi, which encompassed the municipality of Lagunillas. Several of the documents presented by Gardiner to authenticate his mine ownership bore the signature of Don Verastegui.

21. Rippy, *United States and Mexico*, p. 225. John Black was the United States consul to Mexico City.

22. *National Intelligencer*, March 4, 11, 1854. On the date of his conviction, Dr. Gardiner was taken into custody by the deputy marshal and placed in jail. The *Intelligencer* reported that "He had not arrived there but a very little time before he was attacked by severe spasms … at a quarter past three o'clock P.M. he died." A coroner's inquest was ordered. This report, issued on March 10, found that "from the large portions of the contents of the stomach yet completely analyzed, we are convinced that the virulent poisons [commercial strychnine and brucine] are present in quantity more than sufficent to have produced death [*National Intelligencer*, March 11]." The jury of inquest ruled the death of Dr. George A. Gardiner to be suicide.

9: INDIANS IN TEXAS AND FLORIDA

1. Crimmins, "Report on the Eighth Military Department," vol. 51, p. 170; Heitman, *Register*, p. 354. Major Jeremiah Y. Dashiell was a paymaster at the army depot in San Antonio, Texas, in 1853. His pay district included Forts Inge, Duncan, and Clark, a total distance of 430 miles through some extremely remote and dangerous territory. He completed this route every four months to pay troops, even though army orders prescribed payment every two months. Dashiell generally kept the public money for which he was responsible, denominated in gold and silver coin, in a safe in his office. According to Freeman, "His office records and

accounts exhibit commendable system and exactness." Dashiell was dismissed from the service in 1858 and served in the Confederate Army. He died in 1888.

2. Webb, et al., *Handbook of Texas*, vol. 1, p. 627. Fort Inge was located on the east bank of the Leona River in Uvalde County, Texas. The fort was garrisoned in 1849 with two companies of the 1st Infantry. By 1856, the post consisted of about a dozen buildings surrounding a parade ground. These buildings included a stone hospital, with the remainder being mostly jacales. Confederate troops were stationed at Fort Inge during the Civil War, but it was reoccupied by Federal troops in 1866. The fort was abandoned in 1869; the original buildings are now in ruins.

3. Ferris, *Soldier and Brave*, p. 329. The site of Fort Duncan, Texas, is in Maverick County at the Fort Duncan Park in the city of Eagle Pass. The fort was established in 1849 to guard a strategic crossing on the Rio Grande and protect American interests. It was evacuated in 1859 and reoccupied in 1860. Fort Duncan was occupied by the Confederates and used as a center for the export of cotton. The fort was reoccupied by Federal troops in 1868 and finally abandoned in 1927. About a dozen buildings remain including a stone magazine of 1849 vintage. The buildings are now the site of Fort Duncan Park.

4. Weaver, *Castro's Colony*, pp. 1-22. The town of Castroville was founded on September 2, 1844, on a site about thirty miles west of San Antonio, Texas, near the Medina River. The town was the first to be located in Castro's Colony. The colony was granted to Henri Castro, a French citizen, by the Republic of Texas for the purpose of colonization and covered an area of approximately nine million acres. Castroville flourishes to this day with a population of slightly less than 2,000 citizens.

5. Waugh, *Castro-Ville*, pp. 38, 41; Olmsted, *A Journey Through Texas*, p. 277; Weaver, *Castro's Colony*, p. 80. The inn was opened in 1848 by:

> M. Tarde, soldier of Napoleon's own guard ... became famous for the comforts and excellent food it provided in that generally unluxurious era .... Madame Clarisse Tarde, with her carved mahogany, her jewels, her husbands decorations to display, and her charm of manner, seems to have been the grand dame of the village [Castroville]. She entertained the guests of the hotel, while her spouse broiled steaks famous a thousand miles away.

The quality of service had not diminished by 1856, when Olmsted visited:

> The hotel, by M. Tarde, [is] a two-story house, with double galleries, and the best inn we saw in the state. How delightful and astonished many a traveler must have been, on arriving from the plains, at this first village, to find not only his dreams of white bread, sweetmeats and potatoes realized, but napkins, silver forks, and radishes, French servants, French neatness, French furniture, delicious French beds, and the Courrier des Etats Unis; and more, the lively and entertaining bourgeoise.

The inn survives to this day in immaculate condition, the residence of Mr. and Mrs. Bill Tschirhart.

6. Jackson, *1850 Census*, p. 31. The Census of 1850 lists Joseph Finger as the only head of household living in Medina County with that surname. He is listed as living in D'Hanis, which would have been on Doubleday's route from Castroville to Fort Duncan.

7. Heitman, *Register*, vol. 1, p. 368; Cullum, *Register*, vol. 2, p. 95. "Captain D." was quite likely Frederick Tracy Dent who graduated from the United States Military Academy in 1843. During the Mexican War he served with the 5th Infantry in central Mexico. He participated in the Siege of Vera Cruz and the capture of San Antonio. Dent was awarded a brevet for gallant conduct at the Battles of Contreras and Churubusco and a second brevet for his actions at the Battle of Molino del Rey. He served on the Texas frontier, 1851-1854, at Forts Belknap and McIntosh and on the Clear Fork of the Brazos. Dent was transferred to Oregon in 1856 and participated in the battles and combats of Four Lakes, Spokane Plain, and Spokane River. During the Civil War, he was engaged in staff assignments and saw no active duty until March, 1864, when he became an aide to General Grant. Dent participated in the capture of Richmond and was appointed military commander of that city. He retired from duty in 1883 and died on December 23, 1892.

8. Heitman, *Register*, vol. 1, p. 795. Joseph Plympton joined the service in 1812 as a 2nd lieutenant of the 4th Infantry. He was awarded a brevet for his actions at Cerro Gordo and died at the rank of colonel on June 5, 1860.

9. Heitman, *Register*, vol. 1, p. 727. Gouverneur Morris was a cadet at the United States Military Academy from 1818 to 1823. He entered the service in 1824 as a 2nd lieutenant of the 4th Infantry. He was awarded a brevet for his actions in the Battles of Palo Alto and Resaca de la Palma. Morris retired from the service in 1861 at the rank of lieutenant colonel. He died on October 18, 1868.

10. Heitman, *Register*, vol. 1, p. 182. Henry Bainbridge graduated from the United States Military Academy in 1817 and was assigned to the 3rd Infantry. Bainbridge was awarded two brevets, the first for his actions in the capture of Monterrey and the second for meritorious conduct during the Battles of Contreras and Churubusco. Bainbridge died on May 31, 1857, in a fire that destroyed a steamboat in Galveston Bay, Texas.

11. Heitman, *Register*, vol. 1, p. 172. Benjamin H. Arthur joined the service in 1839 as a 2nd lieutenant of the 1st Infantry. Arthur died on February 11, 1856.

12. Heitman, *Register*, vol. 1, p. 996. John George Walker joined the new Regiment of Mounted Rifles formed on June, 1846, at the rank of second lieutenant. He was awarded a brevet for gallantry in the affair at San Juan de los Llanos, Mexico. Walker resigned his commission in 1861 and rose to the rank of major general in the Confederate States Army. He died on July 20, 1893.

13. Heitman, *Register*, vol. 1, p. 289. Lewis Cass, Jr., son of the Democratic candidate for president in 1848, served in the dragoons.

14. McReynolds, *The Seminoles*, pp. 167, 169, 175, 194, 225, 251, 281; Mahone, *History of the Second Seminole War*; Porter, "The Seminole in Mexico, 1850-1861," *Chronicles of Oklahoma* (hereafter cited as CO), vol. 19, pp. 153-68, "The Hawkins Negroes Go To Mexico," CO, vol. 14, pp. 55-58, "Wild Cat's Death and Burial," CO, vol. 21, pp. 41-43; Olmstead, *A Journey Through Texas*, pp. 314-55. Wild Cat or Coacoochee was a noted leader of the Seminole Indians in Florida. He was one of the organizers of resistance to the Anglo settlement of Florida that resulted in the Seminole Wars. On February 8, 1837, he led an attack on Fort Mellon in central Florida that resulted in the deaths of Captain Charles Mellon and seventeen defenders. However, Wild Cat's strategy for resistance did not usually consist of open battles; rather a hit-and-run guerrilla warfare was conducted with brief ambushes after which the Seminoles would melt into the dense jungles and disappear. Wild Cat preferred negotiation with American officers and on several occasions, to obtain concessions, he would promise to assemble his people for emigration to Arkansas. The emigration process never went smoothly, however. General Jessup reported to Washington on March 8, 1837, that, "The emigration will be tedious and expensive ... . The Seminoles, however, have less regard for their promises than any other Indians I have ever known." Diplomatic meetings wore thin, and on October, 1837, American soldiers surrounded the Seminole negotiators and imprisoned 137 for forced emigration. In a daring exploit, Wild Cat and eighteen other Seminoles escaped capture and vanished into the jungles to continue resistance. Wild Cat consolidated the remaining Indian resistance and vowed revenge: "I was in hopes I should be killed in battle, but a bullet never touched me. I would rather be killed by a white man in Florida than die in Arkansas." Direction of the war in Florida was then handed to Colonel Zachary Taylor, who landed at Tampa Bay on July 31, 1837. Taylor's forces marched inland and met the Seminole warriors in the Battle of Okeechobee at that lake on Christmas day. Wild Cat and his band of eighty manned the Indian left wing that deployed to receive a direct frontal assault by Taylor's forces, consisting of regulars and volunteers. One colonel of the Missouri volunteers suggested instead an encirclement of the Seminole defenses, but Taylor silenced him by asking "if he was afraid." The total force of less than 400 Indians stood and received Taylor's force of more than twice as many troopers. The battle was short-lived and the Indian defensive lines were breached. The Seminole defenders escaped into the tall grass, leaving twenty-five casualties, while Taylor's forces were victorious with 138 casualties. Direct battles with American soldiers ceased, but the Seminoles continued hit-and-run operations against small parties of travelers and isolated posts. But time was working against the Seminoles. Americans now wisely offered a bonus payment for resettlement and allowed the Indians to retain ownership of their black slaves. Seminole forces were depleted by the resettlement of discouraged warriors; finally by November, 1841, Wild Cat and his followers surrendered

and were transported from their homes in Florida to a reservation near Fort Gibson, Arkansas. Lands assigned to Wild Cat and his people were of poor quality and prone to flooding. Wild Cat demanded lands assigned to the Cherokees tribes and was sent to Washington, D.C., in 1844, as a delegate to voice these concerns, but without succor. On December, 1845, Wild Cat accompanied Indian agent Pierce M. Butler to Texas on a diplomatic mission to forge a peace pact with the Comanches. This trip acquainted him with the vast lands of the Southwest suitable for colonization, and he returned to Arkansas to advocate a plan for an Indian and Negro colony in Mexico, where the Indians could live in freedom. The Mexican government, eager to keep Comanche raiding parties out of their country, granted lands in Coahuila to the Seminoles, Kickapoos, and free blacks in 1852. The lands were located south of Eagle Pass, Texas, at Musquiz, and Nacimiento, near the headwaters of the Rio Sabinas on lands that straddled the traditional route of Comanche raiding parties into Mexico. Olmsted visited this portion of Mexico, and offered an interesting description of the lands and peoples. The resettlement began by 1852, with migrating bands of Indians and Negros crossing the State of Texas. Wild Cat served the Mexican authorities as a scout, being commissioned as a colonel in the Mexican Army, and while on a mission scouting against the Comanches in 1857 contracted small pox and died near Musquiz. Without the leadership of Wild Cat, many of his people abandoned Mexico and returned to their reservation in Arkansas.

15. Hughes, *Memoir*, pp. 32-33; Olmsted, *A Journey Through Texas*, pp. 343-53. San Fernando de Rosas was visited by the columns of General Wool on October 16, 1846, on an aborted expedition against Chihuahua. A description of the town is offered by Hughes:

> The town contains about 2,000 inhabitants, and two plazas, around which are built the better class of houses, which are large, neat, and comfortable. On the main plaza is the parochial church, a building of some architectural pretension. The whole town, surrounded as it is with a belt of large trees, wears a pleasing aspect....

> Olmsted, who visited San Fernando in 1856, reported the streets crowded with unruly and drunk Indians over which the local gentry seemed to have no power. These Indians were probably the result of Wild Cat's resettlement of Seminoles in that area of Mexico. Olmsted offered several interesting descriptions of the local citizens and their life styles.

16. Bliss, "Reminiscences," vol. 1, pp. 60-61. Zenas Bliss remembered the death of this old soldier at the hands of the Indians. He wrote that:

> The man who had been killed was a discharged soldier and had been a musician in one of the companies at the Post. He was out riding about a mile and a half from the Post, with a Mexican, when they saw the Indians approaching. The Mexican wanted to run but the other said no, that they would go in the

chaparal and the Indian could not, or would not bother them. He gave the Mexican, who was unarmed, his rifle and they went into the thicket. It was supposed that the Mexican ran and left him with nothing but his six-shooter, but he made good use of that. He killed one Indian, who was left dead on the field; another died from wounds after crossing the river; and a third was disabled from a bullet which lodged in or near his spine and he was never able to get about after he had received the wound. The soldier was killed and when the Company, which started out as soon as possible found him, he had eleven arrows sticking in his body and five in his head. The Mexican went back to the place, where they had been attacked, as soon as he had reported to the commanding officer and found the man lying there, but not scalped. He put the dead man in front of him on his horse and brought him into the Post; as the troops were going out they met him with a citizen, who had accompanied the troops, rode forward to speak to him. He did not know that there was more than one man on the horse and when he saw the dead man with the arrows still sticking in his head, he fainted and did not go any farther on the scout.

17. Bliss, "Reminiscences," vol. 1, p. 41. Bliss, in a discourse on the variations that occur in the construction of jacales, reported that:

> Some of the officers had their houses built entirely of thatch, the sides as well as the roof. They were quite as comfortable as the others, but a little more liable to take fire, as Lieutenant (now General) Doubleday, found to his cost. He had a house of this kind and it took fire near to the ground and in a few minutes, it had entirely disappeared, barring the ashes.

18. Heitman, *Register*, vol. 1, p. 1062. George Wright graduated from the United States Military Academy in 1818 and was assigned to the 3rd Infantry. Wright was awarded a brevet in 1842 for actions against the Florida Indians. In the Mexican War, Wright was awarded two brevets, the first for actions in the battles of Contreras and Churubusco and the second for meritorious conduct in the Battle of Molino del Rey. Wright had risen to the rank of brigadier general of volunteers when he drowned on July 30, 1865.

19. Heitman, *Register*, vol. 1, p. 285. Eugene Asa Carr graduated from the United States Military Academy in 1846 and was assigned to the new Regiment of Mounted Rifles. Carr rose to the rank of brigadier general at the time of his retirement in 1893. During the Civil War Carr was cited for his actions at Wilson's Creek, Black River Bridge, and the capture of Little Rock. Carr was awarded a Congressional Medal of Honor on January 16, 1894, for his actions at the Battle of Pea Ridge on March 7, 1862. Specifically, Carr was cited for "directing the deployment of his command and holding his ground under a brisk fire of shot and shell in which he was several times wounded while serving as colonel of the 3rd Illinois Cavalry."

20. Heitman, *Register*, vol. 1, p. 299. Frederick Lynn Childs graduated from the United States Military Academy in 1851 and was assigned to the 2nd Artillery.

He resigned his commission in 1861 and rose to the rank of lieutenant colonel in the Confederate Army. Childs died on June 10, 1894.

21. Heitman, *Register*, vol. 1, p. 241. John Milton Brannan graduated from the United States Military Academy in 1837 and was assigned to 1st Artillery. He received a brevet for his actions at the Battles of Contreras and Churubusco. Brannan rose to the rank of major general of volunteers during the Civil War, being cited for actions at the Battles of Jacksonville, Florida, Chickamauga, and the campaign against Atlanta. Brannan retired from the service on 1882 and died on December 16, 1892.

22. Heitman, *Register*, vol. 1, p. 374. Justin Dimick graduated from the United States Military Academy in 1814 and was assigned to the light artillery. He was awarded a brevet in 1836 for actions against the Florida Indians. During the Mexican War Dimick was awarded brevets for actions in the Battles of Contreras and Churubusco and for meritorious conduct in the capture of Chapultapec Castle. Dimick retired from the service in 1863 and died on October 13, 1871.

23. Cullum, *Register*, vol. 1, p. 22. Fort Dallas was located on Key Biscayne Bay on the left bank of the Miami River near the mouth.

24. Heitman, *Register*, vol. 1, p. 781. John Clifford Pemberton graduated from the United States Military Academy in 1833 and was assigned to the 4th Artillery. He was awarded brevets for his actions at the capture of Monterrey and for meritorious conduct in the Battle of Molino del Rey. Pemberton resigned his commission in 1861 and rose to the rank of lieutenant general in the Confederate Army.

25. Cullum, *Register*, vol 2, p. 366. George Washington Custis Lee, son of General Robert E. Lee, graduated from the United States Military Academy in 1854 at the head of his class and was assigned to the the Corps of Engineers. In 1856 and 1857, Lieutenant Lee assisted in the construction of Fort Clinch, Florida. It was in this location that he made his ride for supplies. Lee resigned his commission on May 2, 1861, and joined his father in the defense of his Virginia homeland.

26. Porter, "Billy Bowlegs," *CO*, vol. 15, pp. 227-39. Billy Bowlegs or Holata Micco was a Seminole Indian chief noted for his wise and humane leadership, who came to power after the deportation of Micanopy in 1837. By leading his people deep into south Florida to avoid contact with whites, Billy Bowlegs hoped to live in peace and retain his hereditary home. In 1842, Colonel W. J. Worth announced a plan to terminate the war. The more than 300 Seminoles remaining in south Floria would not be pursued and harassed further by the army if they would remain in peace. But by 1849 white settlements had pushed further south and conflict was inevitable. In July, 1849, a man on the Pease Rivers and two others on the Indian River were reported murdered by Indians. Billy Bowlegs, striving to keep the peace, delivered three of the guilty Indians and the hand of a fourth brave in November, 1849, to General Twiggs. The three braves were subsequently hung. From Washington, the politicians urged a reluctant General

Twiggs to offer compensation totalling $215,000 to the remaining Indians if they would leave Florida. Twiggs communicated this offer to Billy Bowlegs on January 22, 1850, but the Indians broke off further negotiations and returned to their villages in a mute rejection of the offer. The Swamp Act of 1850, that turned over swamp lands to investors for reclamation, created more pressure on the Indians. In August, 1850, a white boy was murdered near Fort Brooke, supposedly by Indians, and again Billy Bowlegs sent in three Indians who confessed to the crime to white authorities. Chief Bowlegs and a party of elders was transported to Washington in 1851 and met with the "Great White Father," Millard Fillmore, and were presented with gifts. Under considerable pressure from Fillmore and his agents, Billy Bowlegs agreed to remove his tribe from Florida. The Indians did not honor this agreement and remained in their homes in southern Florida. In 1855, a surveying party deliberately destroyed an unusually fine grove of bananas in Billy Bowlegs garden, because they wanted to see "how old Billy would cut up." The surveyors did not have long to wait. An enraged Billy Bowlegs led a party of Seminoles against the surveying camp on December 20, 1855, in an action which resulted in several deaths. This incident triggered the so-called Third Seminole War. The small remaining force of Indians fought a hit-and-run guerrilla war against invading forces of American soldiers. By 1858, Secretary of War Jefferson Davis admitted that this type of warfare, "had baffled the energetic efforts of our army to effect their subjugation and removal." But the remaining Indians had been worn down by 1858, and Billy Bowlegs agreed to be relocated for a price of $6,500 for himself, $1,000 to each sub-chief, $500 for each warrior, and $100 for each woman and child. The last large party of the remaining Seminoles, under Billy Bowlegs, departed Florida on May 4, 1858. The Indians were settled near Fort Smith, Arkansas. In 1859 Billy Bowlegs, probably named for his uncle, King Bowlegs, was described as:

> A fine looking warrior, about forty years old ... above the ordinary height, and well proportioned, and evidencing much self possession. His dress included ... a decorated hunting shirt with a broad showy bead belt passing over his breast, and suspended under his arm a beautifully beaded rifle pouch. He wore red leggins, with brass buttons...which was thickly embroidered with beads. Finally, there was a turban wound from a red shawl surmounted with white feathers, encircled with a silver band. Suspended from his neck were silver crescents, to which was appended a large silver medal with a likeness of President Van Buren.... His throat was thickly covered with strands of large blue beads, and he also wore bracelets of silver over the sleeves of his decorated hunting shirt.

27. Peters, *The Florida Wars*, p. 281. Polly was a niece of Billy Bowlegs. In January, 1858, Polly led her uncle from the Everglades to a meeting with the Indian agent that resulted in his emigration from Florida.

28. Cullum, *Register*, vol. 2, p. 257; Heitman, *Register*, vol. 1, p. 1064. The young officer referred to by Doubleday as the "seducer" was Powell T. Wyman. Wyman

graduated from the United States Military Academy in 1850 and was assigned to the 3rd Artillery. Wyman served in the Florida hostilities in 1850, and later in 1856-1857. He resigned his commission on July 13, 1860, but with the advent of Southern secession tendered his services to the state of Massachusetts. He was appointed colonel of the 16th Massachusetts on August 5, 1861, and was killed, at the age of thirty-four, while leading his regiment in a charge at the Battle of Glendale, Virginia, on June 30, 1862.

29. Heitman, *Register*, vol. 1, p. 641. Gustavus Loomis graduated from the United States Military Academy in 1808 and was assigned to the artillery. He resigned his commission in 1863 and died on March 5, 1879.

30. Cullum, *Register*, vol. 1, p. 27. Fort Jupiter was located on the right bank of the Lochahatchee River, about three miles from the mouth at Jupiter Inlet.

31. Sherman, *Memoirs*, pp. 21-23. William T. Sherman was stationed at Fort Pierce at the mouth of the Indian River Inlet and recorded the event which occurred around December, 1840. A steamer anchored off the treacherous bar at the inlet was unloading soldiers of Bragg's Company E, 3rd Artillery, for duty at the fort. A launch had braved the roaring surf once and returned for another load of passengers. The second load of soldiers was upset on the bar of the inlet and swept out to sea. The steamer approached as near as possible to the bar to pick up survivors but none were found. The steamer then launched another boat for rescue, but that boat in turn was upset in the inlet and two more persons perished. The next day Sherman sent out search parties along the beach but found only one or two bodies which had been literally torn apart by the sharks that swarmed the inlet. Sherman ordered that any other boats coming ashore must be beached below the inlet, a policy that "insured us a good ducking, but was attended with less risk to life."

32. *DAB*, pp. 435-36. Owen Lovejoy, brother of the martyred abolitionist Elijah Lovejoy, was an Illinois abolitionist and influential member of Congress. He was an ardent supporter of Abraham Lincoln in the early days of the Republican Party. Lincoln became connected with the cause of the abolitionists by Lovejoy's endorsements. Only when Lincoln publicly repudiated abolitionism was he able to free himself of that label, which his political enemies were hoping would "choke Lincoln to death." Lovejoy was a vigorous enemy of slavery in Congress and continued his support for Lincoln and his policies. He was given the honor of proposing the bill in Congress to abolish slavery, and died March 25, 1864, one year after the Emancipation Proclamation.

10: SOME EXPERIENCES OF WIT, HUMOR, AND REPARTEE IN ARMY AND NAVY LIFE

1. This chapter was prepared from undated notes for a paper prepared by Doubleday to be read at a social meeting of the Lafayette Post of the Grand Army of the Republic.

2. Heitman, *Register*, vol. 1, p. 641; Cullum, *Register*, vol. 1, p. 118. Gustavus Loomis graduated from the United States Military Academy in 1811 and was assigned to the Regiment of Artillerists. Loomis was stationed on the Niagara Frontier in 1813, where he was engaged in the capture of Fort George and was captured by the British at the Surprise of Fort Niagara on December 19, 1813. He served in the Florida War, 1837-1840, being engaged in the Battle of Okeechobee on December 25, 1837. As colonel of the 5th Infantry, he served in Texas at Forts Belknap, McIntosh, and Ringgold, 1852-1855. Loomis retired from active service on June 1, 1863, for "having been borne on the Army Register more than 45 years." He died on March 5, 1872.

3. Fleming, *West Point*, p. 114; Heitman, *Register*, vol. 1, p. 1026. Fleming identifies the sixty-five-year-old Colonel William W. Whistler as the instigator of this order. Whistler was known to be a frequent loser to battles with demon rum and had been brought up on charges of drunkenness. Evidently he was never convicted. Whistler was retained in the service until his death on December 4, 1863. The incident occurred at Corpus Christi in 1845 as reported by Fleming:

> Colonel Whistler found Lieutenant Richard H. Graham of the class of 1838 bringing a small case of books along in the wagon train. "That will never do, Mr. Graham. We can't encumber our train with such rubbish as books," wheezed the old war-horse. Another officer asked if it was all right to bring a small keg of whiskey. He explained that he was not feeling very well and required a "stimulant." "Oh," grunted Colonel Whistler, "that's all right, Mr. Hoskings, anything in reason. But Graham wanted to carry a case of books."

4. Heitman, *Register*, vol. 1, p. 936. Edwin Vose Sumner joined the 2nd Infantry at the rank of second lieutenant in 1819. By 1846, Sumner was serving as a major in the 2nd Dragoons. He was awarded a brevet for his gallantry at the Battle of Cerro Gordo. Sumner received a second brevet for meritorious conduct at the Battle of Molino del Rey. During the Civil War, Sumner was promoted to the rank of brigadier general for his actions at the Battle of Fair Oaks, Virginia. He died on March 21, 1863.

5. Heitman, *Register*, vol. 1, p. 424; Cullum, *Register*, vol. 2, p. 322. Hugh Brady Fleming graduated from the United States Military Academy in 1852 and was assigned to the 6th Infantry. He served on frontier duty at Fort Laramie, Dakota, 1853-1854, where he was engaged in a skirmish near the post on June 17, 1853, and was wounded by the Sioux on August 28, 1854, while defending the post. He served in the Washington Territory at Forts Steilacoom, Bellingham, Walla Walla,

and Fort Dalles, Oregon. He participated in the Combats at To-hots-nim-me, Four Lakes, Spokane Plains, and on the Spokane River in 1858. During the Civil War, he served in California and Nevada as recruiting and disbursing officer. Fleming retired in 1870 and died on April 9, 1895.

6. Heitman, *Register*, vol. 1, p. 248; Cullum, *Register*, vol. 1, p. 460; Marcy, *Thirty Years of Army Life on the Border*, pp. 439-40. Forbes Britton graduated from the United States Military Academy in 1834 and was assigned to the 7th Infantry. His army career was spent almost entirely on the frontier, with tours of duty at Forts Gibson, Coffee, and Smith dealing with the emigration and relocation of Indians. From 1839 to 1843, Britton served in the Seminole Wars, either on commissary duty or dealing with the emigration of Indians from Florida. He was in Corpus Christi, Texas, with Taylor's Army of Occupation in 1845 and was engaged in the defense of Fort Brown, May 3-9, 1846. Britton served in the quartermaster's depot at Camargo, Mexico, and later was reassigned to central Mexico with Scott's army. After the Mexican War, 1849-1850, he was returned to Florida and engaged with the Seminole Indians. Britton resigned on July 16, 1850, and returned to Corpus Christi to become a farmer and merchant. He was a member of the Texas Senate, 1857-1861, and served as a brigadier general in the Texas Militia, 1859-1861. Forbes Britton died on February 14, 1861. He was remembered as a blithe spirit, ever eager to turn a serious scene into a joke. However, such matters could result in serious consequences, as Doubleday related this warning to all potential practical jokers— "Officers were not to be trifled with."

Captain Martin Scott was the most noted marksman and hunter in the entire army; his prowess legendary. The story is told by Marcy of an earlier hunting trip, in which several of his fellow officers spotted a coon in the highest limb of a large tree. Each officer took a turn firing at the coon and each missed. When it became Scott's turn to fire, he pointed his rifle at the coon, who said, "Who are you?" "Why I am Captain Martin Scott," was the answer. The coon replied, "You need not shoot; I'll come down."

Scott, who had killed a man in a duel, was known for his many eccentricities, which were generally overlooked by his cautious comrades. Marcy relates a second anecdote on Martin Scott.

When the Army was encamped in 1846 at Corpus Christi, Scott organized a hunt, in fact a drive through a wooded region near the camp with his hunting hounds to flush out "large jackass rabbits" who were a novelty to the officers of the camp. Scott kept more than "twenty full-blooded dogs of various breeds" in the camp for sporting purposes. The drive was a deadly serious proposition to Scott, who placed each participating officer at a specified station on the edge of the thicket with the instructions to shout "Tally ho," when the pack of rabbits was spotted. In this band of hunters was Forbes Britton, intent on turning this stiff scene into a farce. He did not have long to wait, as the yelping pack of dogs struck a trail and drove some game Britton's way.

Suddenly a loudly braying and kicking mule emerged from the brush with twenty dogs fast on her heels. Forbes Britton destroyed the solemnity and ceremony of the occasion by shouting to the mule, "Sally whoa! Sally whoa! Sally whoa!" The hunting party dissolved into peals of laughter from the officers, and Martin Scott appeared from the brush, "staring daggers at Captain Britton." Scott canceled the hunt, and returned to camp fuming. Back at camp, Scott angrily dashed off a challenge to Britton. It was only with difficulty that their mutual friends were able to adjust the matter without an exchange of shots.

7. Cullum, *Register*, vol. 2, p. 145; Heitman, *Register*, vol. 1, p. 368; Stewart, *John Phoenix, Esq.; A Life of Captain George H. Derby*, pp. 3-4, 30, 50-53, 78, 99, 106, 118-30, 168; Fleming, *West Point*, p. 128; Maury, *Recollections*, p. 39. George Horatio Derby, one of the foremost humorists of his time, was a graduate of the United States Military Academy, class of 1846. In 1844, probably in an angered response to one of Derby's practical jokes, Cadet William L. Crittenden of Kentucky drew his sword on the unarmed Derby and wounded him with three strokes delivered to the head. The politically influential Crittenden family was able to circumvent his expulsion, but William finished as the "goat" of his graduating class. The family, however, could not save young William from a Cuban firing squad in 1851 when he and other Kentuckian fillibusters were captured in an abortive invasion of Cuba led by Narcisso Lopez. Derby graduated seventh in his class and was assigned to the topographical engineers. During the Mexican War he participated in the capture of Vera Cruz and was wounded in the Battle of Cerro Gordo. The story of Derby's encounter with General Winfield Scott on the battlefield at Cerro Gordo is probably part of the folklore associated with Derby but bears repeating. As Derby's wound was being dressed, General Scott spied him, and expressing his condolences said, "My God, Daaarby, you are wounded!" Scott unwittingly had verbally wounded the young lieutenant a second time, as Derby was adamant that his name be pronounced "Durby." Derby retorted quickly to the commanding general of American forces in central Mexico with, "Yes, General Scaaat." "My name is Scott, not Scat" replied the indignant general. "And mine is Derby, not Darby" whispered the young lieutenant in a pained voice. Dabney H. Maury and Joseph E. Johnston, also wounded at Cerro Gordo, were placed together in a small hut with George Derby to recover from their wounds. Maury remembered that, "John Phoenix Derby was an incessant talker, and uttered a stream of coarse wit, to the great disgust of Joe Johnston ... ." The prim and proper Joseph E. Johnston reached his breaking point the next day, and responded angrily to one of Derby's fanciful orders, "If you dare to do that, I'll have you court-martialed and cashiered or shot!" Derby's style of humor flowered in California, during his several tours of duty in that territory during the 1850s. He authored a column of humorous prose and poetry for the *Alta California*, of San Francisco, which he signed with the pseudonym, "Squibob." His columns included many astute observations on the

life and times of early day Anglo California, such as his discovery that the the phrase "Yreka Bakery," listed on a sign board in the little town of Yreka was a palindrome. Derby's columns, appearing now in the *San Francisco Herald*, were widely read by a public starved for humor and wit and widely copied. A column, appearing in the rival *Evening Journal* of that city, was now appearing under the name "Squibob." Derby retaliated by penning a column on the "Death and Spirit Resurrection of Squibob." His subsequent columns were penned under the name "John Phoenix," to signify its having arisen from the ashes. Derby was reassigned to duty in San Diego, California, and at that location perpetrated his greatest hoax. The official voice of the Democratic Party in Southern California was the *San Diego Herald*, edited by the democratic party boss of that region, John Judson "Boston" Ames. Derby and Ames quickly became close friends, and Derby published several humorous columns in Ames' paper. The gubernatorial election of 1853, which pitted the incumbent John Bigler against William Waldo, a Whig opponent, required Ames' presence at party meetings in San Francisco. In an act that Ames would later have cause to regret, he announced his departure in the *Herald* on August 13 and that his replacement, "a friend of acknowledged ability and literary acquirements" would replace him during his absence. In a letter sent to the *Alta California*, John Phoenix urged the California public not to miss the *Herald* publications in the next few weeks as he was the new editor of that journal, and he boasted that, "if you don't allow that there's been no such publication ... since the days of the 'Bunkum Flagstaff,' I'll craw fish and take to reading Johnson's Dictionary." Derby did not disappoint his readers. The *Herald* of August 24, 1853, published with the "slight assistance of Phoenix," endorsed the "Phoenix Independent Ticket" headed by William Waldo, the Whig Candidate. This issue, when received in San Francisco, was the talk of the town, and recoiled first with anger, then humor upon the head of the unsuspecting Ames. Derby's treachery was first pointed out to Ames by Governor Bigler himself while Boston was in the act of pleading for political plums for himself. Ten days later a second edition of the *Herald* was published, with a strong continued Whig endorsement. However, substitute editor Phoenix was beginning to voice second thoughts in regard to his own personal safety. "I have a horrible misgiving that the editor de facto will return ... coming down on me from San Francisco 'like a young giant refreshed with new wine ...' and perhaps in the extremity of his wrath, inflict some grievous bodily injury on me ... ."

Derby's concern for his safety was not misplaced. Boston Ames was a six foot six and a half inch former sailor who had once been convicted of killing a man with his fists in a brawl. Bigler was returned to office, and so also was Ames to San Diego. In the *Herald* of October 1, Derby wrote, in anticipation of their reunion, "Interview Between 'Boston' and 'Phoenix.'"

The *Thomas Hunt* had arrived, she lay at the wharf at New Town, and a rumor had reached our ears that "Boston" was on board. Public anxiety had been excited to the highest pitch to witness the result of the meeting between us. It had been stated publicly that "Boston" would whip us the moment he arrived; but though we thought a conflict probable, we had never been very sanguine as to its terminating in this manner. Cooly we gazed from the window of the Office upon the New Town road, we descried a cloud of dust in the distance, high above it waved a whip lash, and we said, "'Boston' cometh, and his driving is like that of Jehu the son of Nimshi, for he driveth furiously." Anon, a step, a heavy step, was heard upon the stairs, and "Boston" stood before us. "in shape and gesture proudly eminent, stood like a tower ... but his face deep scars of thunder had intrenched, and care sat on his faded cheeks; but under his brows of dauntless courage and considerate pride, waiting revenge." We rose, and with an unfaultering voice said, "well Judge, how do you do." He made no reply, but commenced taking off his coat. We removed ours, also our cravat. * * *

The sixth and last round is described by the pressman and compositors as having been fearfully scientific.

We held "Boston" down over the Press by our nose, (which we had inserted between his teeth for that purpose) and while our hair was employed in holding one of his hands, we held the other in our left, and with the "sheep's foot" brandished above our head, shouted to him, "say Waldo," Never! he gasped— Oh my Big-ler, he would have muttered, But that he dried up, 'ere the word was uttered. At that moment, we discovered that we had been laboring under a "misunderstanding," and through the amicable intervention of the pressman, who thrust a roller between our faces, (which gave the whole affair a very different complexion;) the matter was settled on the most friendly terms—"and without prejudice to the honor of either party." We write this while sitting without any clothing, except our left stocking, and the rim of our hat encircling our neck like a ruff of the Elizabethan era;—that article of dress having been knocked over our head at an early stage of the proceedings, and the crown subsequently torn off, while the Judge is sopping his eye with cold water, in the next room, a small boy standing beside the sufferer with a basin, and glancing with interest over the advertisements in the second page of the San Diego Herald, a fair copy of which was struck upon the back of his shirt, at the time we held him over the Press.

This fanciful account was not even close to the reality; Ames acknowledged publicly in a column that "Phoenix had played the 'devil' during our absence" but that the joke was on him, and that "we may as well 'dry up' and 'let it slide.'" The first publication of Derby, *Phoenixiana; or Sketches and Burlesques*, was published in 1856. His imaginary battle with Boston Ames appears in this text, and, along with his many other keen observations, became known and quoted throughout the country. General Grant, commenting on the precarious position of the Union Army in Virginia in 1864, wrote, "If the troops cannot get through, they can keep the enemy off General Sherman a little, as Derby held the editor of the *San Diego Herald.*" George Derby died on May 15, 1861, probably unaware that his fame and name had become a household word in mid-nineteenth century America. His wife put together a second volume of his collected works and drawings, *The Squibob Papers. By John Phoenix,* in 1865.

8. Cullum, *Register,* vol. 1, pp. 286, 356. The "eccentric Lieut D." was probably either Gustavus Dorr or John P. Davis. Dorr was dropped from the service on November 22, 1843, for neglect of duty caused by "insanity," and Davis was dismissed on April 18, 1845, under section 3 of the Law of January 31, 1823. Dorr died in an insane asylum, and Davis died "in the Cherokee Nation."

9. Heitman, *Register,* vol. 1, p. 892; Cullum, *Register,* vol. 2, p. 307. Henry Warner Slocum graduated from the United States Military Academy in 1852 and was assigned to the 1st Artillery. He served in Florida against the Seminole Indians from 1852 to 1853 and resigned his commission in 1856. Slocum practiced law in New York and was a member of the House of Representatives of that state in 1859. During the Civil War he rose to the rank of major general of volunteers in the Union Army, participating in numerous battles in northern Virginia, Gettysburg, and the march through Georgia. Slocum resigned his commission in the volunteer service in 1865 and returned to his law practice. He died on April 14, 1894.

10. Brackett, *History of the United States Cavalry,* pp. 149-50. Two captains of the 2nd Cavalry, then serving in Texas under the command of General Twiggs, were Captains Edmund Kirby Smith and George Stoneman. As Smith was wounded by the Indians in Texas, he was probably the officer disliked by Twiggs.

11. Heitman, *Register,* vol. 1, p. 382; Cullum, *Register,* vol. p. 1, 262; *Picayune,* July 7, 1846. Anthony Drane was probably not a veteran of the War of 1812, as suggested by Doubleday. He graduated from the United States Military Academy in 1824 and was assigned to the 5th Infantry in that year. He served as an assistant quartermaster from 1829 to 1835 and resigned his commission late that year. He was reinstated in the army in 1842 as a captain of the 5th Infantry and served in garrison at Detroit from 1842 to 1843. Drane was in arrest and suspended from service from 1843 to 1845. He came to Texas in 1845 as a part of Zachary Taylor's Army of Occupation but was cashiered from the service on July 10, 1846, for "drunkenness on duty." The *Picayune* reports that Captain Drane was in the battles of May 8-9, 1846, but was "struck with paralysis of the right side" and had been removed to Louisville Marine Hospital, Kentucky. Perhaps he was cashiered at this location. Drane was employed as a counseler of law in New Orleans in 1847 and died in the Louisville Insane Hospital in 1852.

12. *The New York Herald,* November 16, 1849. The event celebrated in New York City on this date was touted by the reporter as "One of the grandest funeral pageants ever exhibited on the stage of this world." Laying in state in the Governor's Room of the City Hall the previous evening were the remains of

General William Jenkins Worth, Colonel James Duncan, and Brevet Major Collinson R. Gates. The three officer's bodies had been placed in identical coffins covered in black silk and bordered with silver edging and silver plates attached to the sides. The silver plates on each coffin were engraved with the names of the principal battles in which they participated. On General Worth's coffin lay four magnificent swords with jewel-incrusted scabbards and handles. The most impressively ornate sword had been presented to Worth by the president of the United States on a resolution of Congress for "his gallantry and good conduct in storming Monterey." The other swords had been presented to Worth variously by the state of Louisiana, the citizens of Hudson and Kinderhook, New York, and the governor of New York. On Duncan's coffin were two swords: the first, his service sword which was plain and rusted; the second a gold-sheathed blade presented to him by the citizens of Newburgh, New York. At noon on November 16, in response to the boom of cannon from the Battery, three hearses were loaded and the procession began up Broadway. The streets were choked with citizens; men and boys had climbed trees for a better view and the windows, balconies, and roofs of the buildings that lined the procession were packed with spectators. Escorting the hearses were the men and officers of the New York militia. The First Brigade was led by General Storms, the Second by Brigadier General Morris, the Third by Brigadier General Hall, and the Fourth by Brigadier General Ewen. Each hearse was followed by official mourners, relatives of the deceased, and pall bearers. In the rear of the procession, in barouches, were the clergy, poet of the day, band, and then the officers of the army and navy, followed by a crowd of lesser officials and potentates. A small barouche bearing Lieutenants Doubleday and Ricketts, Captain French, and a small Jewish tailor from the Bowery apparently escaped the notice of the reporter. The procession required an hour and a quarter; along the route buildings were draped in black as a sign of respect. The head of the parade reached a platform erected in front of City Hall at 3 P.M. By 4 P.M. the program had been turned over to John Van Buren, Esq., son of the former president, who delivered a significant funeral oration. The remains of General Worth were interred in Greenwood Cemetery, Duncan's remains were sent for burial in the family cemetery at Cornwall, and Gates remains were interred at Governor's Island.

13. Heitman, *Register*, vol. 1, p. 437. William Henry French graduated from the United States Military Academy in 1833 and was assigned to the 1st Artillery. French was awarded two brevets, the first for actions at the Battle of Cerro Gordo and the second for meritorious service at the Battles of Contreras and Churubusco. During the Civil War he rose to the rank of major general of volunteers in the Union Army and was cited for his actions at Fair Oaks, Antietam, and Chancellorsville. French retired from the service in 1880 and died on May 20, 1881.

14. *National Cyclopedia*, vol. 3, pp. 278-79. Henry Eagle was born in New York, New York, on April 7, 1801. He entered the navy in 1818 and shipped aboard the

Macedonian on a cruise of the Pacific coast of South America. His second cruise, aboard the *Enterprise*, was to the West Indies in search of pirates. The ship struck an uncharted reef on the Little Curaçoa. In 1827, he was commissioned lieutenant and sent to the West Indies again aboard the sloop-of-war *Natchez*. On subsequent cruises he patrolled the Pacific Coast and the coast of Brazil. During the Mexican War, he commanded the bomb vessel *Etna* which participated in the capture of Tabasco in southern Mexico. After the war, he commanded the *Princeton*, which was sent to search for the sloop-of-war *Albany*, that had been lost at sea. During the Civil War, Captain Eagle commanded the *Monticello*, which participated in the blockade of the James and Elizabeth Rivers in Virginia, and next commanded the *Santee* which passed a year blockading Pensacola, Florida, and Galveston, Texas. He was commissioned commodore on July 16, 1862, but retired shortly thereafter. He died on November 26, 1882.

15. Hamilton Fish was the Whig governor of New York from 1849 to 1850.

16. Jackson, *Texas 1860 Census Index*; *Flakes Daily Bulletin*, August 3, 1866; *Rio Grande Courier*, February 24, 1867; Records of the City of Brownsville; Kearney, *Boom and Bust*, pp. 150-51. Edward Downey was listed in the 1860 census as a resident of Brownsville, Texas, and was postmaster of Brownsville during the days of the Confederacy. Postal records indicate his appointment to that position in March, 1864, with the consent of both the president and the Senate. Since possession of Brownsville at that time was contested by Union and Confederate forces, it is not clear who approved Downey's appointment. A Galveston newspaper, in an article reporting the reopening of post offices in Texas, listed Edward Downey as having been appointed Brownsville postmaster on March 1, 1866. By February 24, 1867, a Brownsville newspaper listed Downey as "an agent of the New York Board of Underwriters and steamboat agent," with a business at the corner of 13th and Levee. Taking a turn at local politics, he served as mayor of the city from March 25, 1869, until November 25 of the same year. Downey was reappointed postmaster of the city in April 28, 1870, and served in that capacity until April 20, 1874. Downey even served a stint as county judge of Cameron County during these troubled times. On December 10, 1867, Israel Bigelow was removed from the post by order of the military commander of occupied Texas and replaced by Edward Downey. Downey served in that capacity apparently until July 13, 1870, when he was replaced by the order of radical Republican Governor E. J. Davis who suspected Downey of being soft on reconstruction.

17. Heitman, *Register*, vol. 1, p. 998. George Weed Wallace entered the service in 1839 at the rank of lieutenant in the 1st Infantry. He was promoted to the rank of major in the 6th Infantry in 1862 and to lieutenant colonel of the 12th Infantry in 1866. Wallace retired in 1870 and died on October 12, 1888.

18. Bliss, "Reminiscences," vol. 3, pp. 51-53; Webb, *Handbook of Texas*, vol. 1, p. 381; Winkler, "The Bexar and Dawson Prisoners," p. 319. The two chained prisoners were identified by Bliss:

Mr. [John] Twohig was captured by the Mexicans in the Mexican or Texan War, at San Antonio, and was a long time a prisoner in Mexico, and worked on the streets in a chain gang chained to old Major [Ludovic] Colquhoun, a man twice his size, and of a very irrascible temper. Both men were taken prisoner by Gen. Adrian Woll on Sept. 11, 1842, and marched overland on a grueling walk to Perote Castle in central Mexico. Texians of the Santa Fe and Mier Expeditions were also inmates at this infamous prison. According to Bliss, Twohig was very mysterious as to how he escaped from Perote Prison, but his statements seemed to suggest that he had been rescued by a band of robbers and had been required by them to take an oath of secrecy.

Neil's Diary states that "John Twohig escaped from Perote 2 July 1843; reached home." Twohig was a wealthy banker and, according to Bliss, a great favorite with the officers stationed in Texas, "... he never allowed any of them to pass through San Antonio without at least taking one meal with him." Bliss offers this description of Twohig: "He is short and thick set, and an Irishman by birth, and was as fond of fun and frolic as a man could be." Twohig died in San Antonio in 1891. Ludovic Colquhoun, while a prisoner in Perote Prison, made several copies of a map of the area between Vera Cruz and Mexico City that were later used by other prisoners to escape the country. Colquhoun was released on March 24, 1844, and returned to San Antonio. His died between 1882 and 1883.

19. Heitman, *Register*, vol. 1, p. 928; Cullum, *Register*, vol. 2, p. 117-18. Charles Pomroy Stone graduated from the United States Military Academy in 1845 and was assigned to the Ordnance Department. During the Mexican War he was engaged at Vera Cruz, the Battle of Contreras, and was awarded a brevet for his actions in the Battle of Molino del Rey. He was awarded another brevet for gallant conduct at the capture of Chapultepec Castle and participated in the capture of Mexico City. He continued to serve in the Ordnance Department until his resignation in 1856. Stone served the Mexican government as chief of the scientific commission for the exploration and survey of the public lands in the states of Sonora and Lower California from 1858 to 1860. During the Civil War he was appointed brigadier general of volunteers in May, 1861, and in command of the Special Corps of Observation on the Upper Potomac until August, 1861. On August 10, 1861, he was arrested and held as a prisoner at Forts Lafayette and Hamilton without charges being preferred against him until August 16, 1862, when he was released. Stone was engaged in the Siege of Port Hudson, and participated in Banks' Louisiana Campaign. He resigned his commission in 1864 and died on January 24, 1887.

20. Heitman, *Register*, vol. 1, p. 345; Cullum, *Register*, vol. 2, p. 104. Thomas Jefferson Curd graduated from the United States Military Academy in 1844 and was assigned to the 1st Artillery. He was stationed in Corpus Christi with Taylor's Army in 1845 and fought in the Battles of Palo Alto and Resaca de la Palma in 1846. He transferred to the 4th Artillery and participated in the capture of

Monterrey. Curd resigned his commission on December 4, 1847. From 1847 to 1849 he served as a professor of mathematics at the College of the Holy Cross in Worcester, Massachusetts. He died on February 12, 1850.

21. Heitman, *Register*, vol. 1, p. 515; Cullum, *Register*, vol. 2, pp. 146-47. Edmund Hayes graduated from the United States Military Academy in 1846 and was assigned to the 1st Artillery. During the Mexican War he served in garrison at Tampico and Puebla. After the war he served in the Florida hostilities, 1849-1850, and on frontier duty in Texas at Fort Brown, Ringgold Barracks, and the Indianola Department, 1850-1853. Hayes died on November 25, 1853.

22. Heitman, *Register*, vol. 1, p. 467; Cullum, *Register*, vol. 1, p. 579. Henry Dearborn Grafton graduated from the United States Military Academy in 1839 and was assigned to the 1st Artillery. Grafton served on the northern frontier during the Canadian border disputes from 1841 to 1845. During the Mexican War, he participated in the Skirmishes of La Hoya and Oka Lake and was awarded a brevet for gallantry at the Battles of Contreras and Churubusco. After the war Grafton took part in the Seminole Wars from 1849 to 1853. He resigned in 1854 and died on April 13, 1855. Grafton was the author of *The Camp and March*, published in 1854.

23. Ferris, *Soldier and Brave*, p. 331. The site of Fort McKavett, Texas, is in Menard County at the town of Fort McKavett. The fort was established in 1852 as part of a chain extending across northwestern Texas to protect Texas and Mexico from Indian incursions. McKavett was evacuated in 1859 and reoccupied by Federal forces in 1868. In 1869, the post was repaired and expanded to garrison army troops that participated in the Red River War (1874-1875) and the Victorio Campaign (1879-1880). Many of the remaining stone buildings form the Fort McKavett State Historic Park, with some being used for residences and businesses.

24. Heitman, *Register*, vol. 1, pp. 659, 669, 721. Heitman lists three officers whose last names start with the letter "M" and had previous service records as midshipmen in the United States Navy. These are Edwin Stanton McCook, John Baillie McIntosh, and Benjamin D. Moore.

25. Heitman, *Register*, vol. 1, pp. 933, 996; Cullum, *Register*, vol. 2, p. 166; Maury, *Recollections*, pp. 57-59. James Stuart graduated from the United States Military Academy in 1846 and was assigned to the Regiment of Mounted Rifles. During the Mexican War Stuart served at Vera Cruz, Cerro Gordo, and was awarded a brevet for gallant conduct at the Battles of Contreras and Churubusco. He was awarded a second brevet for his actions in the capture of Chapultapec Castle and participated in the capture of Mexico City. After the war Stuart served on frontier duty at Fort Vancouver, Washington, and was mortally wounded in a skirmish with Indians, dying on June 18, 1851. John George Walker joined the Regiment of Mounted Rifles in 1846 and was awarded a brevet for gallantry at San Juan de los Llanos, Mexico, in 1847. Walker resigned his commission in 1861 and rose to

the rank of major general in the Confederate Army. He died on July 20, 1893.

Maury remembered his friend James Stuart in later years.

Among my friends of those far-away days was Captain Stuart, who was the son of an able editor of the Charleston Mercury, and was a great-nephew of Sir John Stuart, who won the Battle of Maida and who at his death was the nearest survivor of the royal family of Stuart. He served with me in the Mounted Rifles, and was one of the most interesting characters I have ever known. Handsome, and gentle as a woman, no soldier of our army surpassed him in courage and daring, and after two years of active service the commanding general said in his report of the last battle of the Mexican War, "Lieutenant Stuart of the Rifles, leaping the ditch, was the first American to enter the city of Mexico."

The Rifles were sent overland to Oregon at the termination of the Mexican War, and spent four years of active service in that wild region of the country. At the end of this tour of duty, the Rifles were to march to California to meet ships that would return them to the U.S. The march was pleasant but one night Captain John G. Walker, who shared a tent with Stuart was awakened by the anxious man:

Stuart said he had not been able to sleep at all because of a conviction that his death was at hand. He could not rid himself of the feeling, and he wished Walker to see to it that the wishes he now desired to impart would be carried out. In vain Walker tried first to laugh away all this as a sort of nightmare. Stuart agreed that it might be so, but he urged his friend to listen and promise him to be the executor of his last request, to which Walker at last assented ... . The next day's march justified Stuart's anxieties; for they found that the Rogue River Indians had begun hostilities, and came upon the trail of a large Indian war party. At their breakfast next morning, Stuart told of a vivid dream which had troubled him,—how an Indian warrior appeared at the door of his tent, drew his bow upon Walker first, and then changing his aim to Stuart, shot him through the body. The Rifles forces went in search of the hostiles in two bodies of men; the party with Stuart was sent down by the river where they encountered a war party, and charging through their midst scattered them. The chief seemed to surrender to Stuart, who ordered him to drop his bow, and to emphasize the order tapped him upon the head. Instantly the chief drove an arrow through Stuart's body. He lived a few hours in great agony; his grave was made under a tree at the forks of the road, and carefully marked.

26. Doubleday had later marked this anecdote with the directions, "not to be printed."

27. *DAB*, vol. 11, pp. 39-40. George Law was a famous New York contractor and transportation promoter. He began his construction business with an inclined plane construction for the Lehigh Canal. Shortly thereafter, he was involved in the building of several canals and railroad construction in Pennsylvania. Law eventually

became a millionaire by the construction and management of railroad and steamship lines. He lived in New York City, dying there on November 18, 1881.

28. Heitman, *Register*, vol. 1, p. 202; Chamberlain, *My Confession*, 44-45. Benjamin Lloyd Beall was a cadet at the United States Military Academy from 1814 to 1818. Beall became a captain in the 2nd Regiment of Dragoons in 1836, and participated in the Florida Wars. For his gallant conduct in this campaign, Beall was awarded a brevet in 1837. During the Mexican War he served in both northern and central Mexico, being awarded another brevet in the latter location for actions in the Battle of Santa Cruz de Rosales, Mexico, in 1848. By May 1861, he was serving as colonel of the 1st Cavalry. He retired in 1862 and died on August 16, 1863. A trooper of the 2nd Dragoons shared these recollections of Beall during their stay in San Antonio in 1846:

> One evening there was to be a Mexican "Fandango" at San Jose. Several of us obtained a pass until reville from our company commander, and I took it to Major Benjamin L. Beall, 2nd Dragoons Officer of the Day, to be countersigned. He was a short red-faced-and-nosed man, and looked the Major all over; it was evident that nature intended him for that position and nothing else. He was known in the army as "Old Brilliant," and from his unusual brilliant appearance at this time I judged that the influence of old Rye had something to do with it. The jolly Major signed the pass and remarked, "Report to me at the Guard Tent at Tattoo." Accordingly at that time half a dozen of Uncle Sam's Bold Dragoons drew up in line in front of the guard quarters, when the Major soon joined us with the 2nd Dragoons Band. Old Brilliant was a little more so and carried with him a number One Camp Kelly, for a drum. We started down the bank of the San Antonio, a jolly party enough. The Major went down several times before we reached the ford, but he still held on to the camp kettle. The water was a good three feet deep at the ford and running like a mill race. We stripped but the fat Major would wade through without undressing, got swept away and it was with difficulty we saved him. But alas, the Camp Kettle was lost! The arrival at the ballroom of so distinguished a party, rather surprised ... But ... we were cordially invited to participate in the festivity. The Major dashed into a Waltz with a dark skinned white robed Senorita, on whom he certainly produced an impression. For hours the Fandango was all fun and frolic, the Major's voice could be heard, "brilliant! by G_d brilliant," ... as we approached Camp, we saw to our dismay Colonel Harney. We expected to be roughed ... . To all that was said by Harney, our Major had only one reply: "Brilliant Fandango, brilliant! By G_d, brilliant girls, Colonel! Brilliant night!" Harney placed him under arrest....

29. Crimmins, "Report on the Eighth Military Department," p. 167; Heitman, *Register*, vol. 1, p. 206. James Belger joined the ranks of the 2nd Infantry and by 1838 had risen to the highest non-commissioned rank: sergeant major. He was commissioned as a second lieutenant of the 6th Infantry in 1838. By 1840 he was

promoted to the rank of captain, and for "meritorious conduct in the performance of his duty in the prosecution of the war with Mexico," was awarded the rank of brevet major in 1848. W. G. Freeman reported on his inspection of the 8th Military Department in 1853, that the quartermaster's department of the San Antonio Depot, "...is now and for some time past under the charge of Bvt. Maj. James Belger." Freeman found that, "... too much praise cannot be awarded to Bvt. Maj. Belger for the order and judicious economy introduced into every department." Belger retired from the service in 1879 and died in 1891.

30. Heitman, *Register*, vol. 1, p. 493; Brackett, *History of the United States Cavalry*, pp. 38, 46; Sandweiss, *Eyewitness to War*, p. 22. That "wild young dragoon officer" was Lieutenant Fowler Hamilton of the 2nd Dragoons. The 2nd Dragoons were organized in 1836 at Jefferson Barracks and Brackett noted with pride that "there was more dash about it than other regiments." Samuel Chamberlain, a young dragoon, noted that "In our squadron were broken down Lawyers, Actors and men of the world, Soldiers who had served under Napoleon, Polish Lancers, French Cuirassiers, Hungarian Hussars, Irishmen who had left the Queen's service to swear allegiance to Uncle Sam and wear the blue." Dragoon regiments, by custom, were allowed the freedom to wear their hair long and to grow beards and mustaches. Mexican war era sketches and lithographs, such as the fanciful "Capture of Genl La Vega by the Gallant Capt. May," depicts Charles May leading a charge in flowing beard and shoulder length hair. The favorite dragoon song, "The Dragoon Bold," generally sung by a voice moistened with "old Bourbon" had this stanza: "Oh! the Dragoon bold he knows no care, As he rides along with his incropp'd hair; Himself in the saddle he lightly throws, And on the weekly scout he goes."

31. Heitman, *Register*, vol. 1, p. 874; Cullum, *Register*, vol. 2, p. 204. *DAB*, vol. 3, pp. 435-36. James Donald Cameron, son of Simon Cameron, graduated from Princeton in 1852 and returned to Pennsylvania to work in the Bank of Middletown and the Northern Central Railroad, interests owned by his father. He quickly rose to prominence in both businesses and during the Civil War was active in forwarding Union troops to the scenes of battle on the "Cameron Road." With his father paving the way, the two Camerons took control of the Pennsylvania politics. In 1876, his father's political influence landed James Cameron the position of secretary of war in the Grant administration (1876-1877). The elder Cameron surrendered his seat in the United States Senate to James Cameron, beginning his twenty-year term in the Senate, marked by his support of high tariffs and business interests. He was an ante-room politican and preferred making political deals there over the use of public debate and statesmanship to settle the issues of the country. James Cameron resigned from the Senate in 1897 and died on August 30, 1918. Augustus H. Seward, son of William H. Seward, graduated from the United States Military Academy in 1847 and was assigned to the 8th Infantry. Seward served on frontier duty at Fort Towson and in Texas at Fort Phantom Hill from 1848 to 1851. He was on the Utah Expedition

from 1859 to 1860 in the 5th Infantry at the rank of captain. He was promoted to major of the 19th Infantry in 1861 but declined the promotion. During the Civil War, he served at Washington, D.C., paying troops and was awarded a brevet in 1865 for faithful and meritorious services in the pay department during the rebellion. Seward died on September 11, 1876.

32. Heitman, *Register*, vol. 1, p. 335. The commanding officer at Fort Preble during Doubleday's tour of duty in 1845 was Ichabod Bennet Crane. One wonders if Crane had ever met Washington Irving?

33. *American Flag*, August 29, 1846. A typical advertisement for a deserter reads:

> $5 Reward.——Absconded from Fort Polk, Texas, on the 25th instant, John Kendall, acting commissary sergeant, and formerly a sergeant in the U.S. Infantry. He is about five feet six inches high, gray eyes, dark sandy hair, slender form, and sallow complexion; had on when he left a small red silk sash, and wore a white felt hat with crape. He is probably walking about Matamoros, and the above award will be given for his apprehension and delivery at the guard-house on the Plaza in the city, or at Point Isabel.

> G. W. Rains,
> A. a. q. m. U.S. Army
> Fort Polk, Texas, Aug. 26, 1846.

34. Muller, *The Twenty Fourth Infantry*, not paginated; Heitman, *Register*, vol. 1, p. 749. The quartermaster at Fort McKavett at that time was Captain John B. Nixon.

35. Coffman, *The Old Army*, pp. 225-29; Harris, *Black Frontiersman: The Memoirs of Henry O. Flipper*, pp. 4-7. African Americans were brought into the regular army in 1866 when Congress created six black regiments. The regimental and company commanders were most always whites (only eight blacks received commissions in the army from 1866 to 1898) The three line officers from this group were all West Point graduates: Henry O. Flipper, John H. Alexander, and Charles Young. Flipper graduated in 1877 and was assigned to the 10th Cavalry, then on duty in Oklahoma. Flipper was dismissed from the service by a controversial court-martial at Fort Davis, Texas, in 1882. He was a commissary officer and reportedly careless with his accounts. An investigation resulted in the court-martial and a harsh sentence that other officers convicted of the same offense seldom received. In 1976, however, the Army Board of Corrections for Military Records "converted his separation to a certificate of honorable discharge." Between 1870 and 1889 twelve blacks attended West Point, but only half remained after their first semester. Young graduated in 1889, thanks in part to the special tutoring of George W. Goethals; not another black graduated from West Point until 1936.

36. Bliss, *Reminiscences*, vol. 3, pp. 72-155; Bowden, *The Exodus of Federal Forces*, pp. 106-18. Captain Zenas Bliss was stationed in Texas at Fort Quitman on March 1, 1861, when General David Twiggs surrendered all Federal forces in that state. In

obedience to orders, Bliss marched his company to San Antonio. While camped at San Lucas Spring, Federal forces were surrounded by a much larger force of Confederates, commanded by Earl Van Dorn, and compelled to surrender. Van Dorn interned the enlisted men as prisoners of war and paroled the officers. The last of the enlisted men were not exchanged until February 1863. Bliss spent the remainder of 1861 as a paroled prisoner in San Antonio and recounts the turbulent times in Confederate San Antonio during 1861. By February, 1862, Bliss was ordered to Richmond, Virginia, to be exchanged. Someone, however, had evidently reported Bliss for spying on southern military installations, and he was imprisoned. Bliss was incarcerated at Castle Godwin, a three story brick building with barred windows that had been used as a prison for blacks before the war. The jail principally housed Union sympathizers. Bliss was finally released on April 4, 1862, and sent north.

37. Grant, *Memoirs*, p. 343. This oft-repeated anecdote on Braxton Bragg was related by Grant in this manner:

> On one occasion, when stationed at a post of several companies commanded by a field officer, he [Bragg] was himself commanding one of the companies and at the same time acting as post quartermaster and commissary. He was first lieutenant at the time, but his captain was detached on other duty. As commander of the company he made a requisition upon the quartermaster— himself—for something he wanted. As quartermaster he declined to fill the requisition, and endorsed on the back of it his reasons for so doing. As company commander he responded to this, urging that his requisition called for nothing but what he was entitled to, and that it was the duty of the quartermaster to fill it. As quartermaster he still persisted that he was right. In this condition of affairs Bragg referred the whole matter to the commanding officer of the post. The latter, when he saw the nature of the matter referred, exclaimed: "My God, Mr. Bragg, you have quarrelled with every officer in the army, and now you are quarrelling with yourself!"

38. Heitman, *Register*, vol. 1, p. 952. George Thom graduated from the United States Military Academy in 1835 and was assigned to the topographical engineers. He rose to the rank of colonel, retiring in 1883. Thom died on June 29, 1891.

39. Heitman, *Register*, vol. 1, p. 903. Sidney Smith joined the service in 1839 as a second lieutenant of the 4th Infantry. Smith died on Sept. 16, 1847, of wounds received in the capture of Mexico City.

40. *DAB*, vol. 8, pp. 426-27. James Findlay Schenck, a naval officer, was born in Franklin, Ohio, on June 11, 1807. He was appointed midshipman in the navy in 1825, to passed midshipman in 1831, to lieutenant in 1835, and commander in 1855. During the Mexican War, Schenck served on the frigate *Congress* and participated with Commodore Robert Stockton in the conquest of California. He participated in the bombardment and capture of Guaymas and Mazatlan. In

1860, he commanded the *Saginaw*, which came under fire in the harbor of Cochin, China. The *Saginaw* returned the fire, silencing the battery. In 1864, at the rank of commodore, Schenck commanded the *Powhatan* and later the third division of the North Atlantic Blockading Squadron. He participated in two attacks on Fort Fisher and was commended for his actions by Admiral David Dixon Porter. Schenck was then transferred to the brown water navy and commanded the naval station at Mound City, Illinois, for two years. He was commissioned rear admiral in 1868 and was retired by law in 1869. Admiral Schenck died on December 21, 1882.

41. *DAB*, vol. 20, pp. 488-89. Levi Woodbury was a senator from New Hampshire (1825-1831, 1841-1845), secretary of the navy and later the treasury in the administration of Andrew Jackson and an associate justice of the Supreme Court of the United States (1845-1851). Woodbury died on September 4, 1851.

42. Heitman, *Register*, vol. 1, p. 664; Cullum, *Register*, vol. 1, p. 559; Chamberlain, *My Confession*, pp. 80, 86. Irvin McDowell graduated from the United States Military Academy in 1838 and was assigned to the 1st Artillery. McDowell served on the Northern Frontier from 1838 to 1840 during the Canadian border disturbances. During the Mexican War, he served as assistant adjutant general for General Wool's column on the march to Chihuahua and continued in this position for the duration of the war. McDowell was breveted for his actions at the Battle of Buena Vista. During the Civil War, he commanded the Army of the Potomac during First Manassas and was awarded a brevet for his actions at the Battle of Cedar Mountain. McDowell died on May 4, 1885. During the Mexican War, McDowell's actions as an officer in Wool's column caused one exasperated enlisted man, trooper Samuel Chamberlain, to declare that he was "the most obtuse intellect in the army...." This same dragoon was amused, while on a scout near Saltillo, to respond to "a fearful yell of anguish" and find McDowell

> ... lying on the ground groaning most fearfully, with a "Turk's Head" (a species of the Cactus) fast to the most prominent part of his person! In spite of the discipline the escort greeted this exhibition of the stern realities of a soldier's life in Mexico, with shouts of laughter. Poor thick headed McDowell, his horse had thrown him and he had found a landing on a cactus that had thorns an inch long! His orderly came back with his horse but "Mac" declined to ride and walked to camp. A story circulated later that a Surgeon and a pair of tweezers was required to rid the gentleman of his tormentors.

43. *Who Was Who*, p. 351; Powell, *North Carolina Biography*, vol. 4, pp. 189-90. Duncan Kirkland McRae was born in Fayetteville, North Carolina, on August 16, 1820. He was admitted to the North Carolina Bar in 1841 and, after a term in the legislature, practiced law in Raleigh from 1844 to 1851. He quickly gained a reputation as an attorney and orator, and it is rumored that as a youth of five years of age, he delivered an eloquent welcoming address to the Marquis de Lafayette, who was touring North Carolina in 1825. He was renowned for a case in which

he defended his childhood sweetheart, Ann Simpson, who was charged with murdering her husband. Her obtained her acquittal, but later admitted that he had known that she was guilty of the crime. McRae served as U.S. consul to Paris, France, 1853-1857, and was an unsuccessful candidate for the governorship of North Carolina in 1858. During the Civil War, he served as colonel of the 5th North Carolina Regiment and saw action with the Army of Northern Virginia. He led his regiment on a charge against a strong Union position at Williamsburg, Virginia, on May 5, 1862. General Winfield S. Hancock, defending the position would later state in admiration that the 5th North Carolina "should have 'immortality' inscribed on their banner." Leading a brigade at the Battle of Sharpsburg, McRae was severely wounded as his men fought in Miller's Cornfield. He was sent as an envoy to southern Europe to secure a market for southern cotton in 1862 and returned to become editor of the *Confederate*, published in Raleigh. After the war, he practiced law in Memphis, Tennessee, and returned to Wilmington, North Carolina in 1880. McRae died on February 12, 1888.

44. Heitman, *Register*, vol. 1, p. 604. The "Lieut. K" described by Doubleday in this anecdote was probably Joel T. Kirkman, who joined the 21st Illinois Volunteers in 1861 at the rank of second lieutenant. He was mustered out of the volunteer service on April 9, 1866, at the rank of captain and joined the 17th Infantry on February 23, 1866, at the rank of second lieutenant. He remained with the 17th Infantry until September 21, 1866, and was promoted during that time to the rank of first lieutenant.

45. McReynolds, *The Seminoles*, pp. 156-61; Heitman, *Register*, vol. 1, p. 943; Cullum, *Register*, vol. 1, p. 383. The battle occurred at a crossing of the Withlacoochee River in central Florida on December 31, 1835. General Duncan L. Clinch of the regulars had joined the Florida volunteer forces, commanded by General Robert Keith Call, on a mission to bring the elusive Seminoles under Wild Cat to battle. The Seminoles hid at the crossing until about 200 regular troops had been transported across the river and attacked the smaller party. The volunteer forces on the other side were only spectators of the battle that ensued. From the high grass that surrounded the crossing the Seminoles poured death and destruction into the ranks of the regulars. General Clinch ordered a bayonet attack that dislodged the Seminoles to another defensive position where more fire was aimed at the soldiers. After a third bayonet charge, the Indian force melted into the thickets and disappeared. Fifty-seven of the 200 regulars with Clinch were killed or wounded, while only three officers and twenty-seven men of the Florida Volunteers took any part in the battle. Call defended the volunteers by taking credit for the orderly retreat and for discovering better means for re-crossing the river than Clinch had employed in the crossing.

The "Capt. T. of the Artillery" referred to by Doubleday was probably George Henry Talcott, a graduate of the United States Military Academy in 1831. He participated in the Florida Wars, 1835-1836, and was engaged in the Combat of

Withlacoochee on December 31, 1835. Talcott was awarded a brevet for "good conduct" for his actions on this day. He fought in the Mexican War at Cerro Gordo in command of the Howitzer and Rocket Battery, at Contreras and Churubusco, and at Molino del Rey where he was severely wounded. For "gallant and meritorius conduct" at Molino del Rey, Talcott was awarded a brevet. He died on June 8, 1854.

46. Cullum, *Register*, vol. 1, pp. 518-20; Benham, "Recollections," *Old and New*, vol. 3, pp. 644-56, vol. 4, pp. 45-48. Henry Washington Benham graduated from the United States Military Academy in 1837 and was assigned to the Corps of Engineers. He was awarded brevet for his actions at Buena Vista, where he was wounded. In the early battles of the Civil War, Benham served as a brigadier general of volunteers in command of a brigade in West Virginia, from August to November, 1861. Doubleday's amusing account of Benham must have occurred at this time. During the remainder of the war he commanded an Engineering Brigade and was engaged in bridging rivers. On July, 15 1864, his brigade completed a 2,000-foot pontoon bridge across the James River at Fort Powhatan. By the end of the war he was mustered out of volunteer service and returned to the regular service at the rank of colonel. Benham died on June 1, 1884. His experiences during the Mexican War contain an accurate and honest account of the Wagon Train Massacre at Marin that seems to have been overlooked by many historians.

47. Doubleday penciled in this comment, "It wont do to publish this. It will hurt the feelings of one of my friends."

48. Powell, *Dictionary of North Carolina Biography*, vol. 3, p. 319. Hamilton Chamberlain Jones was a North Carolina humorist, journalist, and lawyer, born on August 23, 1798. Ham Jones was a well-known storyteller who could draw large crowds on occasion to hear him recount his most famous story, "Cousin Sally Dilliard." The tale concerned an intractable witness in a legal case, probably drawn from his personal experiences. The story was a favorite of Abraham Lincoln and was first printed in *Atkinson's Saturday Evening Post* in 1831 and from there widely copied. Jones became the editor in 1832 of the *Carolina Watchman*, an anti-Andrew Jackson journal. The paper published other stories of Jones, such as "The Lost Breeches," and "A Buncombe Story." Jones continued his low-key farcical and outrageous brand of humor in stories such as "McAlpine's Trip to Charleston," and "Going to Muster in North Carolina" that appeared in *The Spirit of the Times*. He simply signed these pieces "By the author of Cousin Sally Dilliard," which was enough to guarantee a readership. Jones was a delegate to the convention of 1861 and a signatory to the North Carolina Ordinance of Secession. He died on September 10, 1868.

49. *National Cyclopedia*, vol. 5, p. 421. Donald MacLeod, the writer and poet, was born in New York City in 1821 and educated at Columbia College for the Presbyterian ministry. He instead took orders in the Protestant Episcopal Church,

and was the rector of a small church. In 1852, after returning from a two-year trip to Europe, he announced his conversion to the Roman Catholic faith. He entered the priesthood and was subsequently appointed to a faculty position at Mount St. Mary's College, Ohio. MacLeod authored a history of Mary, Queen of Scots, a volume of poetry, and several other works. He died on July 20, 1865.

50. *The Papers of Jefferson Davis* vol. 2, pp. 25, 155; Nance, *Attack and Counterattack,* pp. 152, 173, 277, 606; *The American Flag,* January 18, February 19, April 12, May 31, July 22, 1848. The Mexican invasion of the Republic of Texas in February, 1842, led by General Rafael Vasquez, brought a quick response from volunteers in the United States. Among those volunteers was Captain Walter Hickey, leading the "Natchez Mustangs," a company of fifty-seven men mustered for six months service. When the Mexican invasion turned out to be nothing more than a brief raid on San Antonio, the Mississippi volunteers remained inactive in camp near old Texana, Texas, bivouacked with the remainder of the Republic of Texas Army. The Texas army was ordered disbanded in July, 1842, because the government could not afford to supply the needed food and equipment. Bitterness pervaded the volunteers, and Hickey exchanged "hot words" with Captain Stephenson of the St. Louis Volunteers over the use of a boat. A duel followed and four shots were exchanged from a distance of ten paces. The last shot wounded Hickey dangerously, the bullet passing through one thigh and lodging in the other, fracturing both thighs. However, by August, 1842, he was reported to be rapidly recovering. By 1844, Walter Hickey was a vitriolic editor of the *Vicksburg Sentinel,* where his published attack on Judge George Coalter, demanding Coalter's impeachment, "... as a criminal abettor of murder ..." earned him a $500 fine and a sentence to six months in jail. Two days later, Hickey was pardoned by the governor. As editor, he became embroiled in a dispute between Thomas E. Robins and James M. Downs. On May 6, 1844, Hickey was attacked by Vicksburg dentist, Dr. James F. Maclin, and in the struggle dispatched Dr. Maclin with a stab wound. Hickey was indicted for manslaughter but acquitted by reason of self-defense. Pleading his case before the jury, he described Maclin as "a man who had a wide-spread reputation for daring and energy, of herculean strength and scientific training in the arts of assault and defense." *The American Flag* of January 15, 1848, contains this card:

> The friends of Walter Hickey, announce him as a candidate for the Senate of the State of Texas, from Nueces District, to fill a vacancy caused by the resignation of Col. H. L. Kinney. The candidate we propose, resides at the mouth of the Rio Grande, and is identified in interest with all persons in this vicinity. The object of bringing about a division of the county, thereby having nearer home those offices at which application in all cases of land or other litigation, is too important to be entrusted to one who is not positively known to favor the measure, or who may be lukewarm in its support. In Capt. Walter Hickey the measure will have an able advocate—one who will give it his whole attention.

The *Flag* of April 12, 1848, reported the results of this election:

MANY VOTERS

Capt. Hickey received heavy voter support from the Rio Grande precincts, viz.

	Walter Hickey	Edward Fitzgerald
Santa Rita	70	27
Freeport	47	12
Mouth of Rio Grande	313	2
Brazos Island	81	2

However, the election was nullified, the vote from the Mouth of Rio Grande being declared illegal, as this site had not been designated as a polling place.

By March 16, 1848, Jesse Carr and Walter Hickey placed an advertisement that they would "close the business heretofore transacted at the Mouth Rio Grande, under the name and firm of "CARR ANDERSON & CO." The issue of May 31, reports that the newspaper *Free Trader* of Natchez, Mississippi, records the departure of Captain Hickey from that city to return to the Rio Grande accompanied by his aged father. By July 22, 1848, Walter Hickey appears to have settled in the Camargo-Rio Grande City area, employed as a merchant. *The American Flag* of that date reports this card of thanks to Lieutenant R. P. Campbell of the 2nd Dragoons for his actions against bandits on the Monterrey road:

Camargo, Mexico, July 17, 1848 On behalf of the merchants on the Rio Grande line we present you the accompanying watch, as a slight token of the high personal regard in which they held you, and in admiration of the skill and gallantry displayed by you in destroying the bloody Martinez and clearing the roads of the bands of robbers by which they were infested. For your success and prosperity accept our best wishes.

Walter Hickey
Ben. S. Grayson
John R. Baker
Wm. Greene

Hickey served on a committee to organize a July 4th celebration to commemorate the signing of a peace agreement between Mexico and the United States. An invitation, addressed to Major General J. E. Wool, Commanding Army of Occupation, Mexico, which was "omitted in a previous number" is found in *The American Flag* of July 22, 1848:

Rio Grande City, June 30, 1848
Sir: We the undersigned, appointed by the citizens of Rio Grande city, beg leave to tender to you an invitation to partake of a public dinner at this place. To the Texan, whether in the crowded village or lonely hut, there is

no opportunity more acceptable than that of offering to the distinguished patriot a sincere and heartfelt welcome. The high moral and intellectual endowments evinced by you in vindicating your country's honor on the memorable field of Buena Vista have won for you the lasting admiration and esteem of this community. And when in looking back upon your past life we find united in the accomplished soldier those qualities of heart which constitute alike the true dignity of our national character and our common nature the duty of tendering to you a merited tribute of respect to us is the more pleasant and agreeable. With sentiments of respectful regard and esteem we have the honor to be

Your obedient servants,

H. Clay Davis	A. G. Stakes
O. C. Phelps	B. S. Grayson
J. R. Baker	Walter Hickey
G. A. Phelps	D. F. Douglass
Wm. Green	E. Doughtery

The American Flag of November 22, 1848, announced the dissolution of the co-partnership between Walter Hickey, E. M. Anderson, Aug. Williams, and J. D. Carr, who operated a business at the mouth of the Rio Grande. The same notice, dated September 2, 1848, describes the new business, Hickey & Anderson, which hopes to "solicit a share of patronage." The 1850 Census for Starr County does not list Walter Hickey as a resident, so we might assume that the death of Hickey occurred between the dates of September, 1848, and November, 1850, the date of the collection of census data for Starr County. However, the serial microfilm copies of *The American Flag* end by December 6, 1848, and another source of data was needed. *The New Orleans Picayune* often picked up newsworthy items from *The American Flag* and reprinted them in a special column. After a scan of the microfilms of this New Orleans paper, the following item from the issue of May 24, 1849, sealed the fate of Walter Hickey:

A duel was fought opposite Clay Davis's, (Rio Grande City,) on the 7th inst., between Joseph Moses and Walter Hickey, which terminated in the death of Col. Hickey. Col. Hickey was the former editor of the *Vicksburg Sentinel*.

BIBLIOGRAPHY

Alexander, Edwin P. *Civil War Railroads and Models*. New York: Clarkson N. Potter, Inc., 1977.

Arvin, Newton. *Longfellow: His Life and Works*. Boston: Little, Brown and Company, 1962.

Bartlett, John Russell. *Personal Narrative of Explorations and Incidents....* Chicago: The Rio Grande Press, Inc., 1965.

Bauer, K. Jack. *The Mexican War 1846-1848*. New York: Macmillan Publishing Co., Inc., 1974.

Bell, Thomas W. *A Narrative of the Capture and Subsequent Sufferings of the Mier Prisoners of Mexico....* James M. Day, ed. Waco, Texas: Texian Press, 1964.

Bemrose, John. *Reminiscences of the Second Seminole War by John Bemrose*. John K. Mahone, ed. Gainesville: University of Florida Press, 1966.

Bill, Alfred Hoyt. *Rehearsal for Conflict: The War with Mexico, 1846-1848*. New York: Alfred A. Knopf, 1947.

Boston, Talmage. *1939: Baseball's Pivotal Year*. Fort Worth: The Summit Group, 1994.

Bowden, J. J. *The Exodus of Federal Forces From Texas 1861*. Austin, Texas: Eakin Press, 1986.

Brackett, Albert G. *History of the United States Cavalry, From the Formation of the Federal Government to the 1st of June, 1863*. New York: Argonaut Press, Ltd., 1965.

Breton, Arthur J. *A Guide to the Manuscript Collections of the New-York Historical Society*. Westport, Connecticut: Greenwood Press, 1972.

Briscoe, Eugenia Reynolds. *City By the Sea: A History of Corpus Christi, Texas, 1519-1875*. New York: Vantage Press, 1985.

Brown, Charles H. *Agents of Manifest Destiny*. Chapel Hill: The University of North Carolina Press, 1980.

Callcott, Wilfrid H. *Santa Anna*. Hamden, Connecticut: Archon Books, 1964.

Cazneau, Mrs. William L. *Eagle Pass or Life on the Border*. Robert C. Cotner, ed. Austin: Pemberton Press, 1966.

Chabot, Frederick C. *Corpus Christi*. San Antonio: privately published, 1942.

Chamberlain, Samuel E. *My Confession*. New York: Harper & Brothers, 1956.

Chance, Joseph E. *Jefferson Davis's Mexican War Regiment*. Jackson: University Press of Mississippi, 1991.

Clayton, Lawrence and Chance, Joseph E., eds. *The March to Monterrey: The Diary of Lt. Rankin Dilworth*. El Paso: Texas Western Press, 1996.

Cleaves, Freeman. *Rock of Chickamauga: The Life of General George H. Thomas*. Norman: University of Oklahoma Press, 1949.

Coffman, Edward M. *The Old Army: A Portrait of the American Army in Peacetime, 1784-1898*. New York: Oxford University Press, 1986.

Coker, Caleb, ed. *The News From Brownsville: Helen Chapman's Letters From the Texas Military Frontier, 1848-1852*. Austin: Texas State Historical Association, 1992.

Cullum, George W. *Biographical Register of the Officers and Graduates of the U. S. Military Academy at West Point, N. Y.* 7 vols. Boston and New York: Houghton, Mifflin, 1891-1930.

Curtis, Samuel Ryan, *Mexico Under Fire: Being the Diary of Samuel Ryan Curtis 3rd Ohio Volunteer Regiment During the American Military Occupation of Northern Mexico, 1846-1847*. Joseph E. Chance, ed. Fort Worth: Texas Christian University Press, 1994.

Dana, Napoleon Jackson Tecumseh. *Monterrey is Ours!: The Mexican War Letters of Lieutenant Dana, 1845-1847*. Robert H. Ferrell, ed. Lexington: The University Press of Kentucky, 1990.

Diccionario Porrua: Historia, Biografia, y Geografia de Mexico. 2d ed. Mexico City: Editorial Porrua, 1965.

Dillon, Lester R. *American Artillery in the Mexican War 1846-1847*. Austin, Texas: Presidial Press, 1975.

Doubleday, Abner. *Reminiscences of Forts Sumter and Moultrie in 1860-61*. New York: Harper & Brothers, 1876.

Elderkin, James D. *Biographical Sketches and Anecdotes of a Soldier of Three Wars, as Written by Himself.* Detroit: n.p., 1899.

Ewell, R. S. *The Making of a Soldier: Letters of General R. S. Ewell.* Percy Gatling Hamlin, ed. Richmond, Virginia: Whittet & Shepperson, 1935.

Ferris, Robert G., ed. *Soldier and Brave: Historic Places Associated with Indian Affairs and the Indian Wars in the Trans-Mississippi West.* Washington, D.C.: United States Department of the Interior, National Park Service, 1971.

Fleming, Thomas J. *West Point: The Men and Times of the United States Military Academy.* New York: William Morrow and Company, Inc., 1969.

Flipper, Henry O. *Black Frontiersman: The Memoirs of Henry O. Flipper, First Black Graduate of West Point.* Theodore D. Harris, ed. Fort Worth: Texas Christian University Press, 1997.

Ford, John Salmon. *Rip Ford's Texas.* Stephen B. Oates, ed. Austin: University of Texas Press, 1987.

Freeman, Douglas S. *Lee's Lieutenants: A Study in Command.* 3 vols. New York: Charles Scribner's Sons, 1944.

Freemantle, Arthur J. L. *Three Months in the Southern States.* Lincoln: University of Nebraska Press, 1991.

French, Samuel G. *Two Wars: an Autobiography of Gen. Samuel G. French.* Nashville: Confederate Press, 1901.

Fuess, Claude M. *The Life of Caleb Cushing.* 2 vols. Hamden, Connecticut: Archon Books, 1965.

Galloway, B. P., ed. *Texas: The Dark Corner of the Confederacy.* 3rd ed. Lincoln: University of Nebraska Press, 1994.

Ganoe, William A. *The History of the United States Army.* Ashton, Maryland: Eric Lundberg, 1964.

Giddings, Joshua R. *The Exiles of Florida.* Gainesville: University of Florida Press, 1964.

Grant, Ulysses S. *Personal Memoirs of U. S. Grant.* E. B. Long, ed. Cleveland: The World Publishing Company, 1885.

Greer, James K. *Colonel Jack Hays: Texas Frontier Leader and California Builder.* New York: E. P. Dutton and Company, Inc., 1952.

Gregg, Josiah. *Diary & Letters of Josiah Gregg.* Maurice Garland Fulton, ed. 2 vols. Norman: University of Oklahoma Press, 1944.

Hammond, John H. *The Camera Obscura: A Chronicle.* Bristol: Adam Hilger Ltd., 1981.

Hawkins, Walace. *The Case of John C. Watrous United States Judge for Texas.* Dallas: University Press in Dallas, 1950.

Heitman, Frances B. *Historical Register and Dictionary of the United States Army, September 29, 1789 to March 2, 1903.* 2 vols. Washington, D. C.: Government Printing Office, 1903.

Henry, W. S. *Campaign Sketches of The War with Mexico.* New York: Harper & Brothers, Publishers, 1847.

Henry, William Selph. *The Story of the Mexican War.* Indianapolis: The Bobbs-Merrill Company, 1950.

Herring, Ethel and Williams, Carolee. *Fort Caswell: In War and Peace.* Wendell, North Carolina: Broadfoot's Bookmark, 1983.

Hitchcock, Ethan Allen. *Fifty Years in Camp and Field: Diary of Major-General Ethan Allen Hitchcock, U. S. A.* W. A. Croffut, ed. New York & London: G. P. Putnam's Sons, 1909.

Huson, Hobart. *Refugio: A Comprehensive History of Refugio County from Aboriginal Times to 1953.* 2 vols. Woodsboro, Texas: The Rooke Foundation, Inc., 1953.

Jackson, Ronald Vern, Teeples, Gary Ronald and Schaefermeyer, David, eds. *Texas 1850 Census Index.* Bountiful, Utah: Accelerated Indexing Systems, Inc., 1976.

_____. *Texas 1860 Census Index.* Bountiful, Utah: Accelerated Indexing Systems, Inc., 1976.

Jefferson, Joseph. *The Autobiography of Joseph Jefferson.* Alan S. Downer, ed. Cambridge: The Belknap Press of Harvard University Press, 1964.

Johnson, F. Roy. *The Nat Turner Story.* Murfreesboro, N.C.: Johnson Publishing Company, 1970.

Kearney, Milo and Knopp, Anthony. *Boom and Bust: The Historical Cycles of Matamoros and Brownsville.* Austin: Eakin Press, 1991.

Kenley, John R. *Memoirs of a Maryland Volunteer.* Philadelphia: J. B. Lippincott and Co., 1873.

Kerby, Robert L. *Kirby Smith's Confederacy: The Trans-Mississippi South, 1863-1865.* New York: Columbia University Press, 1972.

Kirk, Russell. *John Randolph of Roanoke: A Study in American Politics.* Indianapolis: Liberty Press, 1978.

Long, A. L., ed. *Memoirs of Robert E. Lee: His Military and Personal History.* Secaucus, N. J.: The Blue and Grey Press, 1983.

Longstreet, General James. *From Manassas to Appomattox: Memoirs of the Civil War in America.* James I. Robertson, Jr., ed. Bloomington: Indiana University Press, 1960.

Lossing, Benson J. *The Pictorial Field-Book of the War of 1812.* New York: Harper & Brothers, Publishers, 1868.

Magoffin, Susan Shelby. *Down the Santa Fe Trail and Into Mexico.* Stella M. Drumm, ed. New Haven & London: Yale University Press, 1962.

Mahone, John K. *History of the Second Seminole War: 1835-1842.* Gainesville: University of Florida Press, 1967.

Malone, Dumas. *Dictionary of American Biography.* New York: Charles Scribner's Sons, 1933.

Maissin, Eugene. *The French in Mexico and Texas (1838-1839).* Salado, Texas: The Anson Jones Press, 1961.

Major-General Abner Doubleday and Brevet Major-General John C. Robinson in the Civil War. Albany, New York: J. B. Lyon Company, Printers, 1918.

Mansfield, Joseph K. F. *Mansfield on the Condition of the Western Forts, 1853-54.* Robert W. Frazer, ed. Norman: University of Oklahoma Press, 1963.

Marcy, R. B. *Thirty Years of Army Life on the Border.* New York: Harper & Brothers, Publishers, 1866.

Maury, Dabney Herndon. *Recollections of a Virginian in the Mexican, Indian, and Civil Wars.* New York: Charles Scribner's Sons, 1894.

Meade, George Gordon. *The Life and Letters of George Gordon Meade.* vol. 1. New York: Charles Scribner's Sons, 1913.

McCaffrey, James M. *Army of Manifest Destiny.* New York: New York University Press, 1992.

McCall, Major General George A. *Letters From the Frontiers: Written During a Period of Thirty Year's Service in the Army of the United States.* Philadelphia: J. B. Lippincott & Co., 1868.

McEniry, Sister Blanche Marie. *American Catholics in the War with Mexico.* Washington, D.C.: Catholic University, 1937.

McIntosh, James T., ed. *The Papers of Jefferson Davis*. vol. 2. Baton Rouge: Louisiana State University Press, 1974.

McIntosh, James T., Crist, Lynda L. and Dix, Mary S., eds. *The Papers of Jefferson Davis*. vol. 3. Baton Rouge: Louisiana State University Press, 1981.

McKee, Christopher. *Edward Preble: A Naval Biography 1761-1807*. Annapolis, Maryland: Naval Institute Press, 1972.

McReynolds, Edwin C. *The Seminoles*. Norman: University of Oklahoma Press, 1957.

McWhiney, Grady. *Braxton Bragg and Confederate Defeat: Volume I, Field Command*. New York: Columbia University Press, 1969.

Muller, William G. *The Twenty Fourth Infantry Past and Present*. Fort Collins, Colorado: The Old Army Press, 1972.

Nance, Joseph Milton. *Attack and Counterattack: The Texas-Mexican Frontier, 1842*. Austin: University of Texas Press, 1964.

Nason, Jerry, et al. *Famous American Athletes of Today*. Boston: L. C. Page & Company, 1940.

National Cyclopedia of American Biography. New York: James T. White and Co., 1906.

Neale, William. *Century of Conflict*. Waco: Texian Press, 1966.

Newcomb, W. W., Jr. *The Indians of Texas From Prehistoric to Modern Times*. Austin: University of Texas Press, 1961.

Nichols, Edward J. *Zach Taylor's Little Army*. Garden City, New York: Doubleday & Company, Inc., 1963.

Nichols, Edward J. *Toward Gettysburg: A Biography of General John F. Reynolds*. State College: Pennsylvania State University Press, 1958.

Oates, Stephen B. *The Fires of Jubilee: Nat Turner's Fierce Rebellion*. New York: Harper & Row, Publishers, 1975.

Olmsted, Frederick Law. *A Journey Through Texas*. Austin: University of Texas Press, 1978.

Owen, Tom [Thomas Bangs Thorpe]. *Anecdotes of General Taylor and the Mexican War*. New York: D. Appleton and Company, 1848.

Parker, William Harwar. *Recollections of a Naval Officer, 1841-1865*. New York: Charles Scribner's Sons, 1885.

Perry, Oran, ed. *Indiana in the Mexican War*. Indianapolis: Wm. B. Burford, Contractor for State Printing and Binding, 1908.

Peters, Virginia Bergman. *The Florida Wars*. Hamden, Connecticut: The Shoe String Press, Inc., 1979.

Powell, William S. *Dictionary of North Carolina Biography*. Chapel Hill: The University of North Carolina Press, 1979.

A Prisoner. *Two Months in Fort Lafayette*. New York: Printed for the Author, 1862.

Ramsey, Albert C. (translation of work by Ramon Alcarez). *The Other Side: or Notes for the History of the War between Mexico and the United States*. New York: John Wiley, 1850.

Richardson, Rupert Norval. *The Comanche Barrier to South Plains Settlement*. Glendale, California: Arthur H. Clark, 1933.

Rippy, J. Fred. *The United States and Mexico*. New York: Alfred A. Knopf, 1926.

Ross, Malcolm. *The Cape Fear*. New York: Holt, Rinehart and Winston, 1965.

Salinas, Martin. *Indians of the Rio Grande Delta*. Austin: University of Texas Press, 1990.

Sandburg, Carl. *Abraham Lincoln*. 6 vols. New York: Charles Scribner's Sons, 1949.

Sandweiss, Martha A., Stewart, Rick, and Huseman, Ben W. *Eyewitness to War: Prints and Daguerrotypes of the Mexican War, 1846-1848*. Washington: Smithsonian Institution Press, 1989.

Sandwich, Brian. *The Great Western: Legendary Lady of the Southwest*. El Paso: Texas Western Press, 1991.

Scott, Winfield. *Memoirs of Lieut.-General Scott, LL.D., Written by Himself*. New York: Sheldon and Co., 1864.

Scribner, Benjamin F. *Camp Life of a Volunteer*. Philadelphia: Grigg, Elliot and Co., 1847.

Sherman, William T. *The Memoirs of General William T. Sherman*. 2 vols. New York: D. Appleton and Company, 1904.

Simpson, Harold B. *Cry Comanche: The 2nd Cavalry in Texas, 1855-1861*. Hillsboro, Texas: Hill Junior College Press, 1979.

Simpson, Lesley B. *Many Mexicos*. Berkeley: University of California Press, 1967.

Smith, Charles W. and Judah, Charles. *Chronicles of the Gringos*. Albuquerque: The University of New Mexico Press, 1968.

Smith, Compton. *Chile Con Carne, or The Camp and The Field*. New York: Miller and Curtis, 1857.

Smith, Elbert B. *The Presidencies of Zachary Taylor & Millard Fillmore*. Lawrence: University Press of Kansas, 1988.

Smith, Ephraim Kirby. *To Mexico With Scott: Letters of Captain E. Kirby Smith to his Wife*. Emma Jerome Blackwood, ed. Cambridge: Harvard University Press, 1917.

Smith, Franklin. *The Mexican War Journal of Captain Franklin Smith*. Joseph E. Chance, ed. Jackson: University Press of Mississippi, 1991.

Smith, Isaac I. *Reminiscences of a Campaign in Mexico....* Indianapolis: Chapmans & Spann, 1848.

Smith, Justin H. *The War With Mexico*. 2 vols. New York: The Macmillan Company, 1973.

Spaulding, Albert G. *America's National Game: Historic Facts Concerning the Beginning Evolution, Development and Popularity of Baseball*. New York: American Sports Publishing Company, 1911.

Spurlin, Charles D., ed. *Texas Veterans in the Mexican War: Muster Rolls of Texas Military Units*. n.p., 1984.

Starker, Leopold A. *Wildlife of Mexico: The Game Birds and Mammals*. Berkeley: University of California Press, 1959.

Stewart, George R. *John Phoenix, Esq., The Veritable Squibob: A Life of Captain George H. Derby, U. S. A.* New York: Henry Holt and Company, 1937.

Swanberg, W. A. *First Blood: The Story of Fort Sumter*. New York: Charles Scribner's Sons, 1957.

Thorpe, Thomas B. *Our Army at Monterey*. Philadelphia: Carey and Hart, 1848.

Thorpe, Thomas B. *Our Army on the Rio Grande*. Philadelphia: Carey and Hart, 1846.

Townsend, E. D. *Anecdotes of the Civil War in the United States*. New York: D. Appleton and Company, 1884.

Velazquez, Primo Feliciano. *Historia de San Luis Potosi*. 3 vols. San Luis Potosi: Archivo Historico del Estado de San Luis Potosi, 1982.

Viele, Teresa Griffin. *Following the Drum: A Glimpse of Frontier Life*. Sandra L. Myres, ed. Lincoln & London: University of Nebraska Press, 1984.

Wakelyn, Jon L. *Biographical Dictionary of the Confederacy*. Westport, Connecticut: Greenwood Press, 1977.

Wallace, Edward S. *General William Jenkins Worth: Monterey's Forgotten Hero*. Dallas: Southern Methodist University Press, 1953.

Wallace, Lew. *An Autobiography*. 2 vols. New York: Harper and Brothers, 1906.

Warner, Ezra J. *Generals in Blue*. Baton Rouge: Louisiana State University Press, 1964.

Warnock, Roland A. *Texas Cowboy: The Oral Memoirs of Roland A. Warnock and His Life on the Texas Frontier*. Kirby F. Warnock, ed. Dallas: Trans Pecos Productions, 1992.

Watkins, Sam R. *"Co. Aytch": A Confederate Soldier's Memoirs*. New York: Collier Books, 1962.

Waugh, Julia Nott. *Castro-Ville and Henry Castro Empresario*. San Antonio: Standard Printing Company, 1934.

Weaver, Bobby D. *Castro's Colony: Empresario Development in Texas, 1842-1865*. College Station: Texas A&M University Press, 1985.

Webb, Walter Prescott, Carroll, H. Bailey, and Branda, Eldon Stephen, eds. *The Handbook of Texas*. 3 vols. Austin: Texas State Historical Association, 1952, 1976.

Who Was Who in America: Historical Volume, 1607-1896. Chicago: The A. N. Marquis Company, 1963.

Wilcox, Cadmus. *History of the Mexican War*. Washington D.C.: Church News Publishing Company, 1892.

Wislizenus, A. *Memoir of a Tour to Northern Mexico*. rpt. Glorieta, New Mexico: The Rio Grande Press, Inc., 1969.

NEWSPAPERS

Corpus Christi Gazette, Corpus Christi, Texas, 1846.

The American Flag, Matamoros, Mexico, 1846-1848.

The Daily National Intelligencer, Washington, D. C., 1852-1854.

The New Orleans Picayune, 1848-1850.

The New Orleans Tropic, 1845-1847.

The New York Herald, 1849.

Rio Grande Courier, Brownsville, Texas, 1867.

Flake's Daily Bulletin, Galveston, Texas, 1866.

Richmond Enquirer, Richmond, Virginia, December 31, 1847.

GOVERNMENT DOCUMENTS

"Case of Gardiner and Mears, claims on Mexico under treaty of Guadalupe Hidalgo." 33rd Congress, 1st Session. House Report No. 369.

"Correspondence Between The Secretary of War and Major General Zachary Taylor." 30th Congress, 1st Session, House Executive Document No. 60.

Hughes, George W. "Memoir of the March of a Division of the United States Army, Under the Command of Brigadier General John E. Wool, fron San Antonio de Bexar, in Texas, to Saltillo, in Mexico." 31st Congress, 1st Session, Senate Document No. 32.

"Orders of Gen. Zachary Taylor to the Army of Occupation in the Mexican War, 1845-1847." Office of the Adjutant General, Record Group 94, U.S. National Archives and Records Service, Washington, D.C. 32nd Congress, 1st Session, Senate Executive Document No. 83. (Microcopies in National Archives: No. 29, Rolls 1, 2, 3, 1942.)

"Returns from Military Posts, 1800-1916: Fort Brown, Texas, May, 1846-February, 1861." Microfilm, Record Group 617, National Archives and Records Service, Washington, D.C.

"Secretary of Treasury on Gardiner Mexican Claim Investigation." 32nd Congress, 2nd Session. House Report No. 1.

MANUSCRIPTS AND LETTERS

"Abner Doubleday Collection," Manuscript Department, The New-York Historical Society, New York, New York. The papers consist of a volume of accounts of the battles of Monterrey and Buena Vista, a trip to Parras, Mexico (1848), and the Gardiner Mine Claim, a volume titled "Chapters II and III of My Military Biography, Including the Fall of Montery," a volume titled "From Mexican War to the Rebellion, First Rough Draft," and a volume called "Some Experiences of Wit, Humor, and Repartee in Army and Navy Life." The collection includes a small selection of miscellaneous newspaper clippings and letters.

Bliss, Zenas R. "Reminiscences." Center for American History, University of Texas at Austin.

Chapman Family Papers, Collection of Caleb Coker, Jacksonville, Florida.

Connor, John E. "Maurice Kavanaugh Simons." Texas A&M University—Kingsville, undated, unpublished (editor's collection).

Letters and Papers of George Horatio Derby, microfilm copy, Bancroft Library, University of California at Berkeley.

Diary of Lieutenant Rankin Dilworth, United States Army, in the collection of Charles Passel, Abilene, Texas.

Henry Edwards Journal, Indiana Historical Society Library, Indianapolis.

Diary of Sgt. James Mullen, Jr., Justin Smith Transcripts, Latin American Collection, University of Texas at Austin.

DISSERTATION

Reilly, Thomas W. "American Reporters and the Mexican War, 1846-1848." University of Minnesota, Minneapolis, 1984.

ARTICLES

Bragg, Braxton [A Subaltern]. "Notes on Our Army." *Southern Literary Messenger*, vol. 10, 1844.

———. "Our Army Again." *Southern Literary Messenger*, vol. 11, 1845.

Benham, Henry W. "Recollections of Mexico and Buena Vista." *Old and New*, vol. 3, no. 6, 1871, vol. 4, no. 1, 1872.

Boyd, Mark F. "Asi-Yaholo, or Osceola." *Florida Historical Quarterly*, vol. 33, 1955, 249-305.

Buchanan, Russel A., ed. "George Washington Trahern: Texan Cowboy from Mier to Buena Vista." *Southwestern Historical Quarterly*, vol. 58, July, 1954, 60-90.

Carroll, John M. "The Doubleday Myth and Texas Baseball." *Southwestern Historical Quarterly*, vol. 92, April, 1989, 596-612.

Covington, James W. "Cuban Bloodhounds and the Seminoles." *Florida Historical Quarterly*, vol. 33, 1954, 111-19.

Crimmins, M. L., ed. "W. G. Freeman's Report on the Eighth Military Department." *Southwestern Historical Quarterly*, vols. 51, 52, 53, 1948-1950.

Dobie, J. Frank. "Mustang Gray: Fact, Tradition, and Song." *Tone the Bell Easy*, Publications of the Texas Folk-lore Society, no. 10, 1932.

Nance, Joseph Milton. "Brigadier General Adrian Woll's Report of his Expedition into Texas in 1842." *Southwestern Historical Quarterly*, vol. 58, no. 4, 1955, 523-52.

Pace, Eleanor D. "The Diary and Letters of William P. Rogers, 1846-1862," *Southwestern Historical Quarterly*, vol. 32, 1929.

Porter, Kenneth W. "Billy Bowlegs in the Seminole Wars." *Florida Historical Quarterly*, vol. 15, 1937.

_____. "The Episode of Osceola's Wife, Fact or Fiction?" *Florida Historical Quarterly*, vol. 26, 1947.

_____. "The Hawkins Negroes go to Mexico." *Chronicles of Oklahoma*, vol. 24, 1946.

_____. "The Seminole in Mexico, 1850-61." *Chronicles of Oklahoma*, vol. 19, 1951.

_____. "Wild Cat's Death and Burial." *Chronicles of Oklahoma*, vol. 21, 1943.

Roland, Charles P. and Robbins, Richard C., eds. "The Diary of Eliza (Mrs. Albert Sidney) Johnston." *Southwestern Historical Quarterly*, vol. 60, no. 4, 1957.

A Subaltern [Bragg, Braxton]. "Notes on Our Army." *Southern Literary Messenger*, vol. 10, 1844.

Tyler, Ronnie C. "Exploring the Rio Grande: Lt. Duff C. Green's Report of 1852." *Arizona and the West*, vol. 10, Spring, 1968.

Wallace, Lee A., Jr. "The First Regiment of Virginia Volunteers, 1846-1848." *Virginia Magazine of History and Biography*, vol. 77, January, 1969.

_____. "Raising a Volunteer Regiment for Mexico, 1846-1847." *North Carolina Historical Review*, vol. 35, January, 1958.

Ward, May McNeer. "The Disappearance of the Head of Osceola." *Florida Historical Quarterly*, vol. 33, 1955.

Winkler, E. W. "The Bexar and Dawson Prisoners." *Quarterly of the Texas State Historical Association*, vol. 13, no. 4, 1910.

INTERVIEWS AND LETTERS

DeAnne Blanton to Joseph E. Chance, August 29, 1995. Communication from National Archives, Washington, D.C.

Telephone interview. Joseph E. Chance with staff of the Naval Historical Center, Washington, D.C., regarding unpublished records.

INDEX